Tom Symons
A Canadian Life

Tom Symons on the Faryon Bridge at Trent University, with the Bata Library in the background.

Photo Credit: C. William Phillips Photography

Tom Symons

A Canadian Life

Edited by
RALPH HEINTZMAN

Raul,

A book about a great Canadian, for another great Canadian!

Ralph

24 September 2011.

University of Ottawa Press
Ottawa

uOttawa

The University of Ottawa Press acknowledges with gratitude the support extended to its publishing list by Heritage Canada through its Book Publishing Industry Development Program, by the Canada Council for the Arts, by the Canadian Federation for the Humanities and Social Sciences through its Aid to Scholarly Publications Program, by the Social Sciences and Humanities Research Council, and by the University of Ottawa.

We also gratefully acknowledge The Symons Trust at Trent University whose financial support has contributed to the publication of this book.

www.press.uottawa.ca

LIBRARY AND ARCHIVES CANADA CATALOGUING IN PUBLICATION

Tom Symons : a Canadian life / edited by Ralph Heintzman.

Includes bibliographical references.
ISBN 978-0-7766-3043-4

1. Symons, T. H. B. (Thomas Henry Bull), 1929-.
2. Trent University–Presidents–Biography.
3. Educators–Canada–Biography.
I. Heintzman, Ralph Ripley

LA2325.S96T64 2011 378.713'67 C2011-902334-2

For Tom Symons
with admiration, gratitude, and affection

Table of Contents

Preface

This book might be called a *festschrift.* But, if so, it is a rather unusual one. A festschrift, in academic terminology, is a collection of essays presented to a distinguished academic figure by a group of colleagues as a way of honouring his or her achievement and influence. Traditionally the chapters in a festschrift might have little or even nothing to do with the person being honoured. Contributors might sometimes make a nod toward the honoree, or might choose a topic that reflected in some distant way that person's interests or preoccupations. But otherwise the papers were often a heterogeneous collection reflecting the current research interests of the contributors more than anything else.

Recently the editors of academic festschrifts have begun to plan more coherent collections of essays with greater organic unity and a more consistent link to the honoured figure. This book takes that trend even further. All of its chapters are explicitly about Tom Symons himself. Each one deals with some period of his professional life, or some theme or aspect of his work. And they are also arranged more or less chronologically. So, taken as whole, they add up to a professional biography of Tom Symons.

Taken as a whole seems to be the right way to view him. Because the sum is even more impressive than the parts. Even for readers who think they already know all about Symons, or who think they have him pegged somehow, this book should come as a revelation. Some people may think of him, primarily, as the founder of Trent University. Others think of him as the guru of Canadian studies. Some others may know something of his work in the field of human rights. But very few are likely to have a handle on the astonishing variety of areas of Canadian and international life in which Symons was engaged over the course of his career, or the deep ways in which he usually influenced them. Putting it all together is almost overwhelming. One cannot help being left with feelings not just of admiration but even of wonder, about how one man could have had the time or the energy to do so much. Especially when you reflect that—as Charles Beer, for one, reminds us—many of the activities described in individual chapters were going on at the same time.

Credit for getting this book started should go to Jon Grant. It was he who proposed to me almost seven years ago that I should edit a book of essays about the life and work of Tom Symons. Jon has taken a supportive interest in the progress of the book ever since, for which I am grateful. And he showed admirable patience when the project was slowed down by some roadblock or other, for which I am even more grateful.

I am also indebted to Jamie Benidickson, chair of the Symons Trust for Canadian Studies at Trent University, and to the other trustees. Jamie himself kindly agreed to contribute one of the important chapters to the book, and the trust, under his leadership, provided support for research assistance and for publication.

The editor and many of the contributors are grateful to Kathryn McLeod for the helpful way in which she carried out her role as research assistant for the project. Her great familiarity with the Symons Papers in the Trent University Archives, her responsiveness to research queries, her judgment and discernment, and her thoughtful suggestions made an enormous contribution to the success of the project.

Winnie Janzen, administrative assistant and research centre coordinator of the Frost Centre for Canadian Studies and Indigenous Studies at Trent University, provided invaluable support for the administration of the project. The staff of the Trent University Archives was generous in their time and efforts in locating and copying documents and photos for the book, and in providing access for contributors and researchers. I should particularly like to thank Bernardine Dodge, University Archivist Emeritus; Janice Millard, Curator, Archives, Special Collections, Rare Books and Gifts; and Jodi Aoki, Archives, Special Collections and Art Collection Co-ordinator. Mariella Choo Fon, Information Officer with the Historic Sites and Monuments Board of Canada, was helpful in providing photos from the board's collection. Michael O'Hearn and Eric Nelson of the University of Ottawa Press welcomed this book project from the start and provided helpful support throughout the publication process. It is a happy thing that the press is the publisher of this book, because both Tom Symons and his grandfather, William Perkins Bull, were honoured to receive honorary doctorates from the University of Ottawa.

Finally, I should like to say a word of warm thanks to my fellow authors who responded to the invitation to contribute to this book with enthusiasm and commitment. That does not mean they set aside critical judgment. One of the premises of the book was that authors were encouraged, where appropriate, to introduce critical perspectives or to raise issues or debates. Far from detracting from a book in Tom Symons's honour, we believed such perspectives would help to make the book's implicit tribute to its subject more persuasive. But the fact that the contributors were so willing to recount a crucial chapter or analyze an important theme of Tom Symons's professional life shows how they feel not just about the work but about the man.

Although this book has twenty chapters, it does not tell the whole story about Tom Symons. There are many dimensions even of his professional life that could not be included or are touched on here only in passing. And of his personal life the book says comparatively little. This is perhaps appropriate in a festschrift, which naturally focuses on professional achievements. In Tom Symons's case, however, it is unusually difficult to distinguish between the professional and the personal. So many of his professional accomplishments are directly related to his personal character and style, especially the unusual human warmth, the kindly courtesy and gracious friendliness on which almost all the contributors agree. As their chapters make clear, the authors are motivated in their contributions to this book by respect and affection for the man himself at least as much as by admiration for his uncommon professional distinction.

In the first chapter I have tried to suggest where some of this human character may have come from. But I have also recently had the opportunity to re-read *Ojibway Melody*, his father's charming collection of stories about life at Pointe-au-Baril on the Georgian Bay. And I did so in a location designed to enhance the appeal of these stories. Even in that place, I was struck again by the fact that the spell they weave has as much to do with a certain moral insight as with their drollness and local colour. Harry Symons's stories are filled with appreciation for certain human qualities of kindliness, gentleness, integrity, and courage. Here, for example, is one passage in which Tom Symons's father expresses his admiration for a certain kind of human character, a character some of you may recognize:

> Even though the years roll by more swiftly, the wonder of them and the wisdom, and the gentle firmness are too apparent to be missed. Like rocky crags in a rugged promontory, they stand out for us to see, and respect and admire. Timeless, and beloved, and revered. . . . There is a bravery, and a kindly gentleness, and a saintly sort of wisdom about them that is extremely beautiful and touching to behold. Their love for life and for mankind is so transparent. The sunsets still stir them with deep joy and wonder. They are never jaded, and they come to anger more slowly. With a deft touch, and a vast knowledge they still quietly direct, and urge, and condole, and applaud. The world is so much better a place because of them, and they, in that mysterious way, will never really die, but rather become a legend that grows immortal.

Perhaps a passage like this one from his father's writing may serve as an appropriate epigraph for this book, which is presented to Tom Symons by his friends and colleagues with admiration, gratitude, and affection.

Ralph Heintzman
Chenodin, Sans Souci
The Georgian Bay, Ontario
August 2010

CHAPTER 1

Becoming Tom Symons

RALPH HEINTZMAN

Tom Symons is a man of roots. The roots have a surprising result, the opposite of what you might expect. But if you want to understand the man, you have first to understand the roots.

Tom Symons's roots go deep not just in Canadian history but, quite literally, in Canadian soil. Many of Tom Symons's family were and remained—until his own generation—farmers. And proud of it. With good reason, as we shall see. This fact may help explain why Tom has such a strong sense not just of history and culture but also of place. For Tom, there has never been any difficulty in answering Northrop Frye's rhetorical question: Where is here? He is at home.

In Canada, of course, and in all parts of it. But that's just the beginning. Because being truly at home in your own skin seems to open you up, paradoxically, to the whole world.

The most recent arrival in Canada was on his father's side. Tom's paternal grandfather, William Limbery Symons, was born in Devon in 1860.[1] He immigrated to Canada with his parents, where he eventually married Georgina Ester Lutz, from a farming family of "Pennsylvania Dutch" (i.e., German) origin, long settled near Jordan village in the Twenty Valley of the Niagara peninsula, now known for its splendid vineyards and restaurants. The Lutzes were proud descendants of United Empire Loyalists, with roots, therefore, extending back to the founding of English-speaking Canada. Tom's Grandmother Symons always emphasized that she came from Jordan "of the Twenty," because that signified it was twenty miles distant from the American border![2] William Symons eventually became a prominent Toronto architect, a member of the new Royal Canadian Academy of Arts.[3] And, by a happy accident of fortune, Tom's eldest son and his family now live in a Toronto house designed by Tom's grandfather. (Talk about feeling at home.)

Tom's father, Harry Lutz Symons, was twenty-one years old, a student at the University of Toronto, and—though not a big man and slight of build—playing "rugby" football with the Toronto Argonauts, when the First World War broke out.[4] He initially joined the Canadian Expeditionary Force and served in France until August 1916, when he was seconded to the new Royal Flying Corps. With his athletic ability, he became one of the war's celebrated flying "aces," credited with six official victories in flying combat.[5] However, from the point of view of Tom's life—indeed whether there was even to be one—the important event in his father's war years was the time he spent at a London convalescent hospital for Canadian officers, established and maintained by an expatriate Canadian, William Perkins Bull. There Harry met, fell in love with, and later married, Bull's daughter, Dorothy.

Tom's maternal forebears had roots equally deep in Canadian soil. His mother was the great-great-granddaughter of Bartholomew Bull, of Tipperary, Ireland, who arrived in York (later Toronto), Upper Canada, in 1818, at the age of twenty-seven, and established a prosperous farm near the junction of what are now Dufferin Street and Davenport Road. Springmount, the house he built there in 1830, was reputedly the first brick house in York township.[6] In 1842, Bartholomew's eldest son, John Perkins Bull—"J. P."—established his own large farm in the fertile area further north from the town of York: west of Yonge Street and north of what is now Wilson Avenue. A year or two later, when J. P. brought home his new bride, Caroline Amelia Carpenter—also a descendant of United Empire Loyalists, so Tom is descended from Loyalists on both sides of his family—she called her new house "Downs View." Some years later the two words were joined, and Downsview became the name not just of the Bull farm but of the whole surrounding community.[7] (By another happy accident of fortune, almost exactly 160 years later Tom became a member of the Board of Downsview Park, a federal government initiative to turn the de Havilland airport and aircraft plant—which later occupied much of the Downsview area—into a large urban park like New York's Central Park.)

J. P.'s son, Bartholomew Hill Bull, also farmed for a time at Downsview. But, with his wife, Sarah Duncan (whose own family roots went back to Henry Mulholland, who settled in York County in 1806, twelve years earlier even than Bartholomew's grandfather, the first Bartholomew[8]), he later moved further west, to Hawthorne Lodge in Chinguacousy Township of Peel County, near the county town of Brampton.[9] Here he developed what eventually became a renowned dairy farm and a world-famous Jersey cattle breeding business, B. H. Bull & Son. The second of Bartholomew Hill Bull's four children, William Perkins Bull, born at Downsview in 1870, was Tom's grandfather.

Perkins Bull was an extraordinary person and a great influence on Tom's life. A tall, lean, darkly bearded young man, with large appetites and ambitions and an intense, romantic, Faustian look about him, Perkins began his career as a successful Toronto lawyer, personal solicitor to Timothy Eaton, and, at the age of thirty-eight, apparently the youngest King's Counsel in the British Empire.[10] But the law was not enough for a man like Perkins Bull. When his father died in 1904, Perkins took over the family breeding business at Brampton and soon branched out into other businesses as well. He had already invested in a Cuban sugar plantation, and now became involved in land development, especially in western Canada, as well as oil and timber companies. In 1906, he and his wife, Maria Brennen, daughter of a prominent Hamilton businessman, moved into Lorne Hall, a large Second Empire house on a three-acre lot at 3 Meredith Crescent in the Rosedale neighbourhood of Toronto.[11] However, marketing western Canadian lands to British investors led Perkins to move to England in 1911, where he was soon joined by his wife and children. That was how he happened to be resident in London when war broke out. But it was his own energy, social ambition, patriotism, and expansive, gregarious personality that prompted him to finance the convalescent hospital for Canadian officers, where his daughter Dorothy met Tom's father, Harry Symons.

After the war Perkins Bull's four sons all remained in England. But after Dorothy Bull and Harry Symons were married at St. Mary's Church in Wimbledon on 27 October 1920, they eventually returned to Toronto and began to raise their family. Tom, the fifth child, was born on 30 May 1929, and in 1934 was formally baptised in Downsview United Church, founded by his great-great-grandfather, J. P. Bull, in 1870.[12] Harry and Dorothy Symons had eight children in all, but the eldest—called William Perkins, after his grandfather—died at the age of two. So Tom grew up right in the middle of a large family, the fourth of seven children, with a sister, two older brothers, and three younger brothers. This was in many ways a perfect family position to shape the man Tom was to become. With his parents focusing whatever attention they had to give on the three oldest and the three youngest, Tom was left free to observe, to learn, to reflect, to grow, and, gradually, to lead.

The Symons family lived first at 39 Rosedale Road and then, after Tom was in elementary school, just up the street, at 45 Rosedale Road. Finally, after Tom was in university, the Symons moved again to a slightly smaller but strikingly handsome brick house around the corner, at 45 South Drive, a property contiguous to Lorne Hall, built in a portion of its original garden.[13] A large family made for a lively household. At 45 Rosedale Road, where Tom really grew up, most of the boys were lodged on the third floor, which sometimes had the boisterous atmosphere of a locker room or boys' camp.[14] Tom found the family atmosphere accommodating, encouraging, and caring—but not too caring. Mealtimes were always interesting, not just because of the crowd around the table but because his father was a marvellous raconteur—a quality Tom admired and obviously absorbed.[15]

After returning from the war, Harry Symons entered the real estate and property management business, finally becoming a vice-president of Confederation Life, responsible for its many properties. But his real interests were probably elsewhere. He was a sociable man with a large group of friends, including in the militia, of which he remained an officer after the war. From his father, he inherited an interest in architecture and took an active interest in preserving buildings of architectural or historical importance (including the home of William Lyon Mackenzie, the first mayor of Toronto), an interest he clearly passed on to his son, Tom.[16] He also enjoyed the out-of-doors. Before the First War he had worked as a young survey assistant at Pointe-au-Baril, north of Parry Sound, on the east coast of Georgian Bay. He had fallen in love with the special beauty of this part of the Thirty Thousand Islands—one of the world's greatest archipelagos, now designated as a UNESCO Biosphere Reserve.[17] After coming back to Canada one of his dreams was to return to Georgian Bay, and he soon purchased a Pointe-au-Baril island. The cottage was the second oldest in the Pointe-au-Baril district, built in 1903 by an American family from Ohio, who named it "Yoctangee"—Shawnee for "Painted Waters."[18] So Tom's family spent much of their summers at Pointe-au-Baril, where his father evidently felt so much at home. In the other seasons they spent many of their weekends at another property outside the city, a farm his father purchased north of Pickering and named "Friendship."

Yoctangee and Friendship also played important roles in Harry's other life, his growing passion for writing. From the mid-1920s, he began to write short stories and articles, many of them published under a pseudonym in the *Toronto Daily Star*.[19] From the mid-1930s he turned his attention to books, beginning with books about life and adventures at the Symons family's vacation homes. *Friendship* was published in 1944, and *Ojibway Melody*, about Yoctangee and Pointe-au-Baril, in 1946. Harry's talent as a witty raconteur carried over into the stories and books. He wrote as he talked. And, as a result, *Ojibway Melody* earned him a kind of lasting fame, winning the first Stephen Leacock Medal for Humour in 1947. Since about 1935 he had also been working on a historical novel about Christopher Columbus, which was eventually published in 1949 under the title *Three Ships West*. By coincidence, 1949 was also the year of a big-budget, Technicolor movie, *Christopher Columbus*, starring Fredric March as Columbus and his wife, Florence Eldridge, as Queen Isabella.[20] Publicity for the movie sparked interest in Harry Symons's book, and some people even assumed that the movie had been based on the book.[21] Tom accompanied his father to the premiere of *Christopher Columbus* at the Odeon Carlton theatre on College Street, one of Toronto's largest movie theatres, where Harry was introduced and three copies of his book were awarded to members of the audience.[22]

If young Tom Symons was influenced by his father's gift for witty story-telling and his love of history, he was perhaps shaped even more by the near presence of his remarkable maternal grandfather. His Grandfather Symons had died when Tom was not yet two years old. But his Grandfather Bull was living just around the corner from the Symons house, at Lorne Hall. After the First War, Perkins Bull had returned his base of operations to North America. Perhaps reflecting Canada's drift into a new empire, he now split his time largely between Toronto and Chicago, where he was associated with Colonel William Horlick of the Horlick Malted Milk Company. It was at this stage that he began to develop a kind of notoriety. Rumours of the most extravagant nature about his relations with the Horlick family circulated around Toronto, and when he suffered a serious car accident on the drive back from Chicago in February 1931, Toronto police were actually obliged to issue a public statement that Chicago mobsters were not involved in the affair.[23]

Perkins Bull's lean, dark features of the pre-war years had gone, replaced by a large bald skull and great white beard. Though the eyes were still deep set, his girth was now vast, and, with his height, he was a massive, imposing presence. There had always been something theatrical about Perkins Bull, and he now seemed almost to enjoy his sulfurous reputation, playing the role to the hilt for the local children. Timothy Findley, the Canadian novelist, who grew up around the corner from Lorne Hall, remembered, "He was a gigantic man who wore flowing cloaks and was bearded, rather like God. I swear he deliberately played the role of neighbourhood terror, grimacing and growling if any of us approached him."[24]

To Tom, of course, his grandfather was a very different sort of person. As a boy, Tom spent much time at Lorne Hall, including one long convalescence in quarantine there.[25] He enjoyed his grandfather's company greatly. From a young age he was allowed to open the morning mail and was shown how to unfold the envelopes very carefully so Perkins could use them again as writing paper. He would then watch closely as Perkins wrote out his replies or other correspondence and business, always in a graceful longhand, sitting at a writing table in the morning room.[26] From time to time, he might be summoned to the dining room to meet one of his grandfather's famous friends, such as Alfie Byrne, the great Lord Mayor of Dublin, known as the "shaking hand of Dublin." Or even Sir Harry Lauder himself, the greatest British entertainer of them all, and at one time the highest paid performer in the world, a superstar before the age of superstars.[27]

Perkins Bull's motor accident had another result that greatly influenced Tom's life, and does so to this day. With time on his hands due to his convalescence, Perkins was now able to embark on a project that may already have been stirring in his mind. Prompted by the idea of collecting a Canadian library as a wedding present for his youngest son, Michael (a London barrister), he decided to continue collecting Canadiana and to record not only his family history but the whole social history of Peel County, his boyhood home and still the site of the family dairy farm and breeding business. With his characteristic expansiveness and energy, he soon assembled a large team of research assistants who scoured the countryside and archives to find the documents, records, papers, oral recollections, and other raw materials for these projects. Over the next decade he produced some thirteen publications devoted to the history of the Davenport, Downsview, and Peel communities, covering everything from sport, medicine, and military affairs to religion, botany, and zoology. But he also assembled a large collection of historical artefacts, tools, photographs, drawings, and paintings, some of them specially commissioned. Perkins Bull was amassing a large and varied collection of historical Canadiana decades before it became fashionable to do so. And, in the process, he was widening the definition of Canadian culture and heritage to include all the elements of the human and natural environments, a broad definition that would have a profound influence on the life and work of his grandson, Tom.[28] After his grandfather's death in 1948, Tom and a friend rescued much of the collection from a barn in Peel where it had been stored.[29] And ever since, one of Tom's pleasures and filial duties has been to preside over the care and disposition of the Perkins Bull Collection, much of which is preserved at the Peel Heritage Complex in Brampton, including, now, a Digital Collection and a William Perkins Bull Reading Room.

Tom's primary education began at Rosedale Public School for kindergarten and grade one, and then continued at Crescent School and the Upper Canada College (UCC) Preparatory School for three years each, before he entered the University of Toronto Schools (UTS) in grade nine. Although Tom enjoyed the UCC Prep and met one of his lifelong friends, Jeffrey Norman, there, it seems to have been Crescent School that made the biggest difference in this stage of Tom's early life. As a newer school, with less emphasis on competitive sports—something at which Tom never excelled—Crescent seemed to make room for other things. It left Tom with a profound sense of the importance of reading and books, for example, and gave him the opportunity to explore them, something he continued to do during his years at the Prep.[30] By the time he got to UTS, he seemed—to his new friends—to have read more and to know more than most of them did.[31] It was the beginning of his rise to leadership.

At UTS Tom made many new friendships that were to last a lifetime, including with Dick Sadleir and John Leishman, both of whom were later to join him at Trent University. He also encountered teachers who made a lasting impression. For several years in high school he was taught history—especially Canadian history—by Andy Lockhart, a teacher passionately interested in his subject but with a rich sense of humour too. Lockhart seems to have enjoyed Tom.[32] And the feeling was mutual. For Tom, Lockhart was one of the most inspiring teachers he ever had, better than any university teacher. For two years he was taught English by Joe Gill, a profoundly erudite man with a special interest in the Enlightenment, who introduced Tom to Locke, Rousseau, Adam Smith, and the rights of man. Tom remembers the relish with which Gill spat out Voltaire's slogan: "Écrasez l'infâme!" "Symons," he cried, "that must be your leitmotif for life!"[33]

Although Tom's intelligence, genial nature, and self-possession were already giving him a wide subterranean influence, UTS was a boys' school, heavily dominated by sports. From grade ten on Tom began to make his mark in school activities like debating, but social prestige in the school was still awarded largely by athletic ability.[34] It wasn't until Tom reached Trinity College at the University of Toronto that his full gifts began to be revealed. With its intimate size and rich—some would say too rich—sense of tradition, Trinity was the perfect setting for Tom to flourish. He was soon recognized as a natural leader, who seemed to know everything and everybody, and how everything was supposed to work, and who carried all this with an easy grace, wit, and good humour that made him liked as well as respected.[35] He continued his involvement in debating and was soon elected Trinity's representative to the Student's Administrative Council (SAC), the university-wide student governance body. As an active member of SAC he also came into contact with the university administration, especially the university's affable and distinguished president, Sidney Smith. An honours history student, Tom also got to know Smith through the Historical Society on the occasions when it met at the president's house.[36] Smith and Symons had much in common, and they instinctively liked and trusted each other, as events were soon to show.

Enrolling as a history student in the late 1940s brought Tom into a rich intellectual atmosphere that stimulated and marked him for life. Then still lodged in the intimate setting of Baldwin House, on the east side of St. George Street north of College Street, the U of T Department of History was one of the strongest at the university and one of the liveliest centres of scholarship and debate in Canada, especially for a student of Canadian history. It included older scholars such as Chester Martin—still to publish his magisterial volume on the Canadian parliamentary tradition, *Foundations of Canadian Nationhood*—as well as mature scholars like Frank Underhill and Donald Creighton—already the famous author of *The Commercial Empire of the St. Lawrence* and *Dominion of the North*, and well advanced on his great biography of John A. Macdonald, the first volume of which would appear the year after Tom's graduation—and young scholars not much older than Tom himself, such as Maurice Careless, whose own landmark history of Canada would appear only a year later. The strident disagreements between Underhill, the continentalist Liberal gadfly, and Creighton, the Britannic Conservative curmudgeon, were legendary. Coming on top of the influence of his father and grandfather, and of Andy Lockhart, studying history at U of T during these exciting post-war years cemented Tom's lifelong interest in the shape of the Canadian experience and Canadian culture, and in the future of the Canadian community, in their broadest senses.

During his undergraduate years Tom was much more than a history student, however. In his first year, following his father's example, he joined the Canadian Officers' Training Corps (COTC) and spent one summer at the army base in Shiloh, Manitoba. A driving mishap at the wheel of a tank that summer became the subject of many friendly jokes thereafter and apparently cured him of any wish to drive for the rest of his life. He also joined his father's fraternity, Zeta Psi, of which he was elected president in his final year. Tom's immense social gifts were becoming more evident and polished, already exhibiting that curious blend of formality and warmth that was to become his trademark. Several times a year he hosted large formal dinner parties at his parents' home, often in honour of somebody or some achievement. He already had a sense of occasion and ceremony. And on weekends he and several friends would often drive out to the aptly-named Friendship for long walks, tree pruning, and other conservation activities. These were times when old friendships grew even deeper.[37]

About this time Tom also began to exercise another kind of leadership, within his family. Perhaps somewhat fatigued by the burdens of raising seven children, Harry and Dorothy Symons withdrew from some of the responsibilities of parenthood, passing them on to their middle son. So, barely out of his own childhood, Tom started to replace his father and mother at parent/teacher interviews for his three younger brothers.[38] Given that one of them was Scott—soon to become an *enfant terrible* of Canadian cultural life, and already showing signs of his later erratic behaviour—this must have been an early testing ground for Tom's maturity and judgment.

At Trinity Tom became acquainted with Allan Ashley, a distinguished Commerce professor who lived in the college and who invited him for tea one day in his rooms. They soon formed a lasting friendship, and Ashley had a deep influence on Tom and on his ideas, especially about college life. Tom was also greatly impressed and influenced by Dr. R. S. K. Seeley, a classicist who was Provost of Trinity College—"Joe Prov," as he was known to Trinity students. Their conversations about university education clearly impressed Seeley as well because, in Tom's fourth year, Seeley and Sidney Smith invited him to the annual meeting of the National Conference of Canadian

Universities (NCCU) in Montreal to speak at a special symposium on extra-curricular activities.[39]

Tom's talk to the assembled university heads showed that, even as an undergraduate, he had already formed a clear idea of what a university should be, based on "the fundamental concept of the university as a single *community*." He emphasized the importance of student community—the "fundamental value" of opportunities, outside the classroom, for "an exchange of ideas, and an opportunity for some synthesis of their interests and studies"—but, even more, the importance of community between students and faculty. He deplored the development of "an unfortunate dichotomy" between students and faculty, observing perceptively that the modern university's growing emphasis on research was being achieved at the expense of higher education itself. Professors now felt increasingly obliged to devote themselves exclusively to their research interests, "to the exclusion of their participation in the undergraduate life." "While no one would minimize the absolute importance of research, it is difficult," he warned, "for the university to be a community upon this basis. The values of research may not always be well purchased at the cost of a segregated university community and of an undergraduate life devoid of faculty guidance and stimulation."[40]

It was a remarkable performance. Remarkable for its insight and candour—and also for the way it already anticipated one of the main themes of Tom's whole life, and his professional focus for the next two decades. Remarkable also for the fact that it took place at all. The invitation itself—the only one to an undergraduate student—was very significant. It was a striking gesture of respect from Seeley and Smith, and a sign of things to come.

From Trinity, it was probably inevitable that Perkins Bull's talented grandson would go to Oxford, like all of his sons. But Tom had first to earn his way there. He was awarded a Massey Scholarship by the Massey Foundation. But to go beyond the bare necessities, he also applied for the Edward Kylie Fellowship, a competitive scholarship administered by the Ontario Department of Education. Having heard nothing for three months after the exam, Tom assumed he had been unsuccessful. So when he met Professor Alexander Brady in the political science department one day, he enquired who had won. "Dear Boy," said Brady, "Why, *you* did. Did I not tell you? How remiss!"[41] Tom went off to Oxford in the fall of 1951 not just with his two scholarships but also with a letter of introduction in his pocket from General Georges Vanier, then Canada's ambassador to France and a future Governor General of Canada. Vanier had been a frequent patient and guest at the Perkins Bull Convalescent Hospital during the First World War, especially after his leg amputation, and had retained a grateful affection for the Bull family ever since.[42]

At Oxford Tom entered neither Magdalen nor Christ Church, his uncles' colleges, but another college located just behind Christ Church, the venerable college of Oriel, whose charter went back to 1300 and whose Visitor was the King. The Provost of Oriel was Sir George Clark, a distinguished professor of English and European history, who set a strong academic tone for the college. Tom's own academic advisor was J. W. Gough, a specialist in the history of thought, another expert on Locke. Tom got an early idea of how the time horizon changed once you were in England, when he told Billy Pantin, an Oriel history don, that he was interested in the history of the Commonwealth. Quite right, said Pantin, "we need a fresh look at Cromwell!"[43]

In the breaks between Oxford terms, the Kylie scholarship allowed Tom to take advantage of his proximity to the continent by spending time in Paris, Leiden, Heidelberg, and Rome. In Rome he stayed at the British School and met up with Christopher Seton-Watson, an Oxford specialist in Italian history, who gave Tom a guided tour of the sites related to the history of modern Italy. He also had a private audience with Pope Pius XII, arranged by James Cardinal McGuigan, a good friend of his grandfather.[44]

In Oxford Tom became involved in activities outside his college, such as the Raleigh Club, devoted to the affairs of the modern Commonwealth. It met about a half dozen times a year, often with a prime minister or other leader from some part of the Commonwealth. But the focus of his Oxford years was on Oriel itself. He lived in the college for both years, in the third quad—St. Mary's Quad—which had once been an independent hall before being absorbed by Oriel. He had different rooms, but always on staircase seventeen, where Thomas More had once lodged. He was a member of the College

Dining Society and was elected president of the College History Society.[45]

The experience of Oxford and Oriel did not form Tom's ideas about university education. They confirmed ideas he had already begun to develop from his experience of Trinity and U of T. His time at Oxford strengthened the views he had already expressed at the NCCU meeting in Montreal about the importance of human relations in higher education: between students themselves, and between students and faculty. He could see, again, how a small college within a larger university could help to make this possible. It could create community. It could also help furnish an academic advisor for every student and promote mentoring between the experienced and the less experienced. It could bring students and professors together, across disciplinary lines, in a single community of scholars. Oxford also strengthened his conviction about the importance of small-group teaching. He could see the value of large, formal lectures, especially if they were good. But he thought they worked best if they were balanced by smaller forums where real dialogue was possible between students and their teachers.[46]

Tom brought these ideas and convictions back to Canada in the summer of 1953. He had been awarded the Cumming Fellowship at Trinity College to allow him to continue his graduate studies in history that fall, and would live in Trinity as a residence don. It never seems to have occurred to Tom to pursue anything but a university career. His friends never heard him mention anything but an academic life.[47] That was in the cards from the start.

But then something happened that not only changed Tom's life but hurled him onto a swiftly moving escalator that did not let him off until ten years had passed.

One week before the autumn term was to begin, Tom received a call from Provost Seeley to inform him that Trinity's Dean of Men had suffered a heart attack and would be unable to carry out his duties. There was no time to find a replacement. Would Tom agree to fill in for the year? Tom accepted, and so, at the age of twenty-four—younger than many of the College's Divinity students—he was appointed with the title of Assistant Dean. But in practice he was now Trinity's Dean of Men in all but name. With the ideas he had been developing for six years and had strengthened in Oxford, Tom was the right man in the right place at the right time. He was keen, for example, to bring more non-Arts students into the Trinity residence to realize the interdisciplinary ideal he now associated with college life. He threw himself into this new challenge with enthusiasm and was relieved to discover that the Trinity students, even those older than himself, were understanding and supportive.[48]

It must have gone well, because, at the end of the first year, when it was apparent that the former dean could not return to his post, Tom was asked to continue in the role, now with the upgraded title of Acting Dean. Tom was in his element and was glad to continue this work. He had been delighted to be reunited at Trinity with Allan Ashley, and the two were now good friends, who had much fun in each other's company and similar ideas about the college. Tom had also begun to be active in wider university affairs. It was then the custom to invite a graduate student or younger faculty member to chair the Students Administrative Council, and Tom was asked by the Council to assume this role. As chair of SAC, Tom again came into frequent contact with President Smith. Perhaps as a result, Tom found himself asked to join a number of other university-wide committees.

Obviously Smith had his eye on this young Trinity dean, because at the end of Tom's second year at Trinity, the president made him an astonishing proposal. He invited Tom to become the permanent dean of the university's own Halls of Residence, three red stone buildings around an open quadrangle at the corner of Hoskin Avenue and Devonshire Place, right beside Trinity College. This was an extraordinary proposal to make to such a young man. But, in fact, Tom was the answer to the president's prayer, and Smith was smart enough—or concerned enough—to see it. Because he had a big problem.

The U of T Halls of Residence were the oldest university residence buildings in Ontario still serving their original purpose. They had been established in 1905 as a result of a fund-raising effort, spurred by an offer—made by the wealthy brother of the premier of Ontario—to pay for the construction of one residence hall, if funds could be raised to build the other three sides of a quadrangle. In the end, only enough money was raised to build three of the four sides. But that was apparently enough, and the residences were built anyway.[49] As the university's only residences for members of non-Arts faculties, they had a worthy history over the intervening decades but had recently suffered from neglect, both financial and otherwise, and had become, in truth, something of an academic slum, physically run down, and the site of much rowdy and irresponsible behaviour. They were in danger of becoming an embarrassment to the university, and the president obviously knew he had to do something about it. He was imaginative and brave enough to see that this young Acting Dean at Trinity had exactly the leadership qualities and instincts he needed.

For Tom the president's invitation was a great honour and opportunity. But it also represented a turning in the road, though Tom only recognized this slowly over the coming years. Assuming a leadership role in the university at such a young age meant he was unlikely to complete his graduate studies or obtain a PhD. He would become a university leader, a thinker, and a teacher, but not a conventional scholar and researcher. He would create and lead and support. But he would not spend his own life at the scholarly coal face, toiling in archives like other historians. He sometimes remembered a conversation he had at Oxford with the Regius Professor of Modern History. Vivian Galbraith had told him to beware "the cloven hoof of the card index."[50] Maybe there was more than one meaning in that warning.

The truth was this new road appealed to him more deeply than the other. It engaged him more profoundly and spontaneously than his own graduate studies were now doing.[51] It responded more closely to what the preceding years had already revealed as his true genius. His real gift was to create community. He had started by creating communities of friends, then fellow students. Now he had begun to build and lead university communities. He would go on to do the same thing on larger national and even world stages. But he would always remain rooted in the university world, and in university values. Tom Symons had found his calling.

Tom also liked and admired Sidney Smith deeply, and was honoured by the suggestion he could be of help to such a considerable man.[52] So, barely twenty-six years old, he accepted the president's offer. Then he set about the simple task of accomplishing what later seemed a miracle.

The miracle was achieved largely through the force of Tom's own personality: his vision and force of conviction. But also the kind of man he now was. The experience of his family, his schooling and education, and his rapid rise to university leadership—as well as his own tastes—had fashioned what might be called the distinctive Symons style. As his undergraduate years had already shown, it was a kind of self-contradiction. A curious blend of formal, deliberately old-fashioned—almost courtly—manners and dress, on the one hand, and, on the other, an unusually genial, outgoing warmth of personality.

The courtly formality and courtesy probably had several sources. No doubt the example of his father and grandfather—who had, after all, come of age in Victorian and Edwardian times—played a part. The extraordinary speed of his rise to institutional leadership may also have had something to do with it. Being thrust prematurely into the role of dean for students not much younger—or even older—than himself may have encouraged Tom to adopt the dress and mannerisms of an earlier generation, in order to give himself the authority of someone twenty years older—just as his grandfather Bull, as a young lawyer, had grown a beard to appear older in the company of men like CPR President William Van Horne.[53] But there was a deeper reason. For Tom, formal courtesy and graciousness were—and are—a way of showing respect, a way of building community by showing everyone the deference and attention due to them, a way to ensure that all feel included and appreciated for the unique persons they are, a way to make them feel noticed and at home, able and welcome to play their part.

The warmth and genial humour may have been encouraged by family role models too. But they were also pure Tom, one of his most consistent characteristics since high school days. He had a gusto for life and for people, and a ready, even mischievous, mirth and wit. Tom simply enjoyed people, and he enjoyed life. He had fun, and the fun was infectious.

The paradox that was Tom Symons didn't work for everyone. But for a great many it did. And for his new role it was perfect. The formality of dress and manner served to lift his new institution up by its bootstraps, giving it almost immediately a new sense of dignity and decorum with which its former rowdiness soon seemed somehow incompatible. But the friendly warmth saved Tom from seeming stuffy. He took what was obviously a genuine interest in the members of the residence. His mischievous sense of humour meant that, when it came to practical jokes, he was capable of giving as good as he got. And he was as keen on a good party as anyone else. In fact, as soon as he could, he expanded the dean's quarters on the third floor of East House—overlooking the walkway between Trinity College and what is now the John Graham Library—so that he could host large receptions there.[54]

The miracle was not accomplished simply by force of personality, however. It was also the result of vision, imagination, determination, and skilful leadership. First of all, vision. Great leadership usually starts with an insight about the deficiencies of the present condition and a vision of some better future state. This was always to be one of the characteristics of Tom's leadership, and it was immediately evident in his new role as dean of the University of Toronto Halls of Residence. Tom was deeply concerned about what he perceived to be the deteriorating quality of student life in the modern university. He could see the extent of this problem all around him at U of T. Under the impact of the post-war demand for university education, the university was now growing rapidly, but without any breakdown into smaller, liveable, human-sized units, or any concern for the quality of the university experience that was being offered to this new generation of students. That was, it seemed to him, one of the arguments for fraternities at U of T. He was grateful to his own fraternity for the opportunity to form friendships with non-Arts students, and with students from arts colleges other than Trinity. The fraternity filled a gap resulting from the absence of other university units designed to create community. In his new role he was determined to help fill that gap and to remedy the declining quality of university life.[55]

His first priorities were not overly ambitious. He aimed, first, at a reasonable treatment of the buildings by the residents, and a reasonable treatment of each other. As far as the buildings themselves were concerned, he soon began writing memos to the senior administration arguing for better maintenance and new investment.[56] But he didn't wait for new funding. He took simple steps such as adding curtains to the residence windows, a basic amenity they had previously lacked. He found rugs and furniture in the basement and used them to refurbish the common rooms. He found donors to provide some painting for the walls and rented others from Douglas Duncan's Picture Loan Society.[57] Before long the university took notice and decided to make its own investments to upgrade the facilities.

In the meantime, Tom had tackled the challenge of the residents themselves. He started by talking to them. He met each new student individually and gradually built up a personal relationship with the whole student body.[58] As he did so, he developed the concept of membership in one community, an innovation, because previously the identity of residents, if any, had been to their own house, not to the Halls of Residence as a whole. He pushed this wider locus of identity further by establishing a single student governance council spanning the three houses. Making the residents responsible for their own governance and discipline was an important step to establishing a higher standard of behaviour and decorum.[59]

As a result of these small leadership gestures, and the combination of dignity and friendliness Tom brought to his own role, a perceptible change soon came over the Residence. The students began to treat it, and each other, differently—with more respect, the respect befitting a genuine university community.

Tom was now able to go further toward his ultimate goal. He appointed academic dons in each house, ultimately two per house. The dons were young faculty members, many of them of considerable distinction or promise, some of whom would eventually follow Tom to Trent, including Denis Smith and John Pettigrew. The presence of dons of this calibre soon gave the Residence the feeling not just of a dormitory but of a genuine community of learning and scholarship. Tom also began to link the residence outward to the university and to the wider community. He established advisory committees—a de facto governance structure—involving some of the leading faculty deans, thereby giving the academic leaders of the university a sense of ownership, a stake in the residence and in its success. Beyond the university, Tom invited prominent citizens like the Director of the Art Gallery of Toronto to give talks at the residence, thus establishing a community presence while, at the same time, giving residence life a whole new cultural and intellectual dimension.[60]

Little by little the university's shabby, rowdy, embarrassing student barracks were being transformed into a college. One thing needed to complete the transformation was a new name. But Tom had thought of that too. He liked the name of the street that ran down in front of the open quadrangle to meet Hoskin Avenue, and so he approached the Duke of Devonshire to ask whether the Duke would consent to the use of his coat of arms for the residence. The Duke agreed. And the University of Toronto Halls of Residence were reborn as Devonshire House, a college in all but name.[61] It was a miracle. A miracle that did not go unnoticed.

But, in the meantime, Tom had many other things on his plate. Throughout his time as Dean of Devonshire House he continued to teach history in three different ways. For Trinity he was an instructor in Greek and Roman history. For the Faculty of Arts he taught the Renaissance and Reformation periods. And for the professional faculties of medicine and engineering he taught world history. His students in this decade included a future prime minister (Paul Martin), a future minister of foreign affairs (Bill Graham), a future Chief Justice of Ontario (Roy McMurtry), future leading members of the bar (such as Ian Scott), and a future Master of Champlain College at Trent University (Brian Heeney), with many of whom he maintained friendly relations throughout their professional lives.[62] For some time he also kept up his historical research on the Pacific Scandal for a future thesis. But gradually other priorities and responsibilities began to crowd out the time for research, and he had to let it go. From time to time he was in contact again with Vivian Galbraith, and the Regius Professor would always ask him, "Are you keeping true to your path?" Tom hoped he was.[63]

He also assumed wider roles and responsibilities in the university. A year after Tom had left Trinity, Provost Seeley asked him to undertake a fact-finding visit to Harvard to study the Harvard "House" system and what could be learned from it for the U of T colleges, and for Trinity in particular. A grant from the Rockefeller Foundation allowed him to spend the summer of 1956 at Harvard. His report was entitled *Each Tub on Its Own Bottom*, reflecting President Lowell's conviction that each college or house needed sufficient independence and funding to develop its own character and life.[64] Tom returned to Harvard for another summer term a year or two later for a second look at the Harvard Houses.

As a result of his growing friendship with Sidney Smith, Tom began to play a role as a sort of informal assistant to the president. He had many chats with Smith on such things as student life and young faculty members. The president asked him to take on a number of tasks, including a joint project with Queen's University to study what US universities were thinking and doing about student housing and residences. Together with a young Queen's colleague, Ron Watts—also destined to make a mark on Canadian university life—whom Tom had known both at Trinity and at Oriel, Tom undertook a study tour of ten American universities.[65] Tom and Ron's report—combined with a paper Tom presented to a symposium on the academic significance of residence halls at the NCCU's annual meeting in 1957[66]—became the basis of a joint article published a year later in the *Queen's Quarterly*.[67]

In September 1957, two years after he had appointed Tom as dean, Sidney Smith left U of T to become minister of external affairs in the new Diefenbaker government. (He did not leave, however, without a plan Tom had drafted, at his request, for a new Commonwealth scholarship scheme, a plan Smith was soon able to put into effect.[68]) Tom thought he might have put a foot wrong with Smith's interim successor, Moffat Woodside, the Dean of Arts. Doggedly pressing his case with the acting president for additional investments in Devonshire House, Tom was firmly told by Woodside to back off. He assumed he had blotted his copybook.[69] But far from it, as events would show. Woodside was just as impressed as Smith by this young Dean of Devonshire House.

One indication of the esteem in which he was now held by the senior leaders of the university was an invitation from the new president, Claude Bissell, to join Woodside and a number of other university luminaries—including Northrop Frye, Marshall McLuhan, Vincent Bladen, Ernest Sirluck, and Robin Harris—on a new Presidential Committee on Policy and Planning. The committee met every two or three weeks for the whole afternoon and evening.[70] Membership on this committee brought Tom into the inner circles of the university. He got to know the university's most prestigious academic leaders, and they had a chance to assess him, his abilities, and his judgment. The assessment was obviously favourable, because the committee soon asked Tom to take on some major tasks. The first was a study of how the university was and should be functioning during the summer months. By April of 1960, Tom was able to submit a substantial report reviewing the extent to which the university was now active in the summer—he found that U of T already had "as large or larger an academic attendance upon her campus during the summer months than has any other University in Canada during the regular year"[71]—and surveying not only the core offerings in graduate and undergraduate studies in the arts and sciences but also summer activities in the areas of education, nursing, social work, medicine, music, athletics, residences, and so on. The report offered one general recommendation—an office to coordinate and plan all this summer activity—and many specific recommendations. From the point of view of Tom's future life, some of the specific recommendations were premonitory. They included recommendations for a Summer Seminar in Canadian studies—embracing "Canadian history, politics, institutions, law, literature, music, and art"—and expanded teaching of French and other languages.[72]

Tom's second assignment from the Policy and Planning Committee was even more pregnant with implications for the future. He was asked to look into the potential need for some new residential colleges at U of T, to respond to the educational and housing needs of a rapidly growing student population. This was obviously right up Tom's alley, and the report he submitted in March 1961 was a manifesto, restating all the convictions about university education he had been developing for over a decade, and that had already been foreshadowed in his *Queen's Quarterly* article (with Ron Watts) three years earlier. His argument was based on the educational need to create community. New U of T colleges "could play an invaluable role, as social and cultural communities, in bridging gaps which exist between the various faculties and divisions of the university."[73] Smaller academic "communities" within an expanding university could also make a fundamental educational contribution to the "climate of scholarship" by cultivating "a relationship between students and staff which could not otherwise be possible in a very large university. The existence of such a relationship is important both for the teacher and the student. It enables the one to inform and direct his teaching to best effect, and the other to enquire further and to find encouragement for giving of his best."[74] Beyond scholarship, the "more intimate relationship" between students and faculty in a residential college could assist the broader development of students by acquainting them with "good individual standards" in thought, speech, and conduct. "Any community in which there is confidence, sympathy, and a helpful relationship between students and staff, and student and student," Tom argued, "will be making an important contribution to the temper and character of the life of the whole University." New residential colleges would help "to re-create a sense of community within the university." They would refurbish "the notion of the university as a community of scholars."[75]

Tom's report went on to recommend the creation of seven new colleges on both sides of St. George Street, and also explored the potential for the redevelopment of existing facilities on the main campus, including, of course, Devonshire House, but also Knox College, Wycliffe College, Hart House—and also "Old Knox College," then the Connaught Laboratories, on Spadina Crescent. In remarkable detail, it described the facilities, design, administration, and staff required for these new colleges. It also referred in passing to what might prove the Achilles heel of this conception: the challenge of funding, and the need to obtain "strong support from individuals and from corporate donors."[76]

It was a remarkable, holistic educational vision. It was to have a significant impact on the University of Toronto in the 1960s, especially in the creation of New and Innis Colleges on the West Campus. But it was also a detailed blueprint for a new university—a new *kind* of university.

Busy though he was during his years as Dean of Devonshire House, Tom was not wholly taken up by university matters. He carried on his grandfather Bull's legacy by becoming Historical Advisor to the Peel County Historical Society, and by presiding over the Perkins Bull Foundation and the Perkins Bull Collection. He was also beginning to exhibit the broad concern for public issues and causes that would become a hallmark of his later life. He became a founding member of the Society for the Abolition of the Death Penalty, for example, and was soon its secretary. He accompanied its gruff, cigar-chomping chair, Wallace McCutcheon, to many public meetings, amazed at how this quintessential Bay Street tycoon could talk persuasively even to groups of farmers.[77] McCutcheon later went on, like Sidney Smith, to become a member of the Diefenbaker cabinet, and a candidate for the leadership of the federal Progressive Conservative Party. He showed it was possible—maybe even essential—to combine Conservative convictions and loyalties with a strong social conscience.

Tom also had time for his friends. Friendship was always one of Tom's great gifts, and his professional life was often just an expression or extension of this gift for friendship. His vision of college and university life might almost be said to be that of a community of friends. He sought to make working relationships a kind of friendship. And he liked to involve his friends in his own professional activities. He invited many of them to social events at Devonshire House, helping at the same time to broaden residents' awareness of wider professional horizons. But he also made time for his friends outside of Devonshire. His study tour to Harvard, for example, concluded with a long motor trip with three friends through the Maritime provinces. On many weekends he would leave Devonshire House to spend time at a friend's farm or house in Toronto, enjoying long walks and meals, much talk, and maybe a trip to the movies.[78]

One friendship was becoming particularly important. In the early 1960s Tom hired a new assistant with the astonishing name of Christine Ryerson. Astonishing, because Christine was a direct descendant of William Ryerson, the Methodist preacher who, with his brother Egerton, was one of the regular visitors at Bartholomew Bull's homestead on the Davenport Road back in the 1820s. In 1826, at the age of twenty-eight, William had preached in the living room of Bartholomew's first log house and enrolled twenty-nine adherents to Methodism.[79] Talk about roots! There seemed to be something fated about this encounter. Christine was a lovely, intelligent young woman with sparkling eyes, a well-stocked mind, and a ready quip, very much the equal of Tom. His habit of turning colleagues into friends went even further this time. The first his other friends knew something was up was when one of them spotted Tom and Christine walking hand in hand down Avenue Road past the Royal Ontario Museum.[80] On 17 August 1963, they were married, and Christine became Tom's friend and indispensable companion for life.

By this time, however, both their lives had been turned upside down once again. The escalator Tom had stepped onto ten years earlier just kept on moving up. One day in 1961, shortly after he had submitted his report on new residential colleges, he received a phone call from a Dr. Donaldson Whyte in Peterborough. Whyte was a vice-chairman of the board of directors of something called Trent College Limited, a group in Peterborough who were trying to start a university there. Could their executive committee come and see Tom at Devonshire House? Well, yes, Tom thought they could!

As it turned out, the Peterborough group had been working with a panel of three advisors from the big Ontario universities—Toronto, Queen's, and Western—a panel that included Moffat Woodside. The advisors had developed a short list of possible candidates for a president to lead the planning and development of the proposed new university, and Woodside had strongly recommended Tom as the best on the list.[81] Tom did not realize the meeting was to be a job interview, but after talking to him in his office at Devonshire House, the Trent executive agreed with Woodside. In April the whole board endorsed their decision. And after Tom's first visit to Peterborough in May, the offer was put formally in writing. It was not until more than a year later, however, in October 1962, that the official announcement was made. Tom was appointed president-designate of Trent University and would take office on 1 July 1963, only one month after his thirty-fourth birthday. He would be the youngest university president in Canada.[82]

The long preparation was over. He had become Tom Symons. And he was ready for the many future adventures of his professional life, beginning with the great adventure of Trent University.

Notes

1 Headstone inscription, St. James Cemetery, Toronto. http://freepages.genealogy.rootsweb.ancestry.com/~hutchfield/ontario11.html.

2 Interview with T. H. B. Symons, 26 July 2009.

3 http://www.rca-arc.ca/en/about_members/since1880.asp; Eric Arthur, *Toronto: No Mean City*, rev. by Stephen A. Otto, with new essays by Christopher Hume, Catherine Nasmith, Susan Crean, and Mark Kingwell (Toronto: University of Toronto Press, 2003), 260–1; Symons, William Limbery, in *Biographical Dictionary of Architects in Canada, 1800–1950*, http://dictionaryofarchitectsincanada. org/architects/view/1345.

4 *The Toronto World*, 10 October 1914, 9. http://news.google.com/newspapers?nid=22&dat= 19141010&id=KyQBAAAAIBAJ&sjid=WSgDAAAAIBAJ&pg=2355,5353495.

5 Harry Creagen, "H. L. Symons—Ace and Author," *The CAHS* [Canadian Aviation Historical Association] *Journal* 2, no. 4 (1964): 113. See also: http://www.theaerodrome.com/aces/canada/symons.php. "An ace is a military aviator or airman credited with shooting down five or more enemy aircraft. The term ace originated in World War I when French newspapers described Adolphe Pègoud as l'as (French for ace) after he shot down five German aircraft." http://www.theaerodrome.com/aces/. The top three "aces" of World War I were Manfred von Richthofen (the "Red Baron"), René Fonck, and Canada's Billy Bishop.

6 William Perkins Bull, *Spadunk, or From Paganism to Davenport United* (Toronto: The Perkins Bull Foundation, 1935), 124.

7 William Perkins Bull, *Downsview, or From Oxford to Ontario: A History of the Downsview Community* (Toronto: The Perkins Bull Foundation, 1941), 87–90, 196.

8 Ibid., 94–96.

9 Ibid., 235–36.

10 Scott Symons, "The Duke of Rosedale," *Toronto Life* (March 1984): 109.

11 On Lorne Hall, see Tom Cruickshank and John De Visser, *Old Toronto Houses*, 2nd ed., rev. ed. (Richmond Hill: Firefly Books, 2008), 76.

12 William Perkins Bull, *Downsview, or From Oxford to Ontario: A History of the Downsview Community* (Toronto: The Perkins Bull Foundation, 1941), 306, 209–19.

13 On 45 South Drive, see Tom Cruickshank and John De Visser, *Old Toronto Houses*, 2nd ed., rev. ed. (Richmond Hill: Firefly Books, 2008), 220–1.

14 Interview with R. H. Sadleir, 3 November 2009.

15 Interview with T. H. B. Symons, 26 July 2009.

16 Biographical notes for Harry Symons, Symons Papers, Trent University Archives.

17 http://www.gbbr.ca/.

18 Harry L. Symons, "Yoctangee," in *Ojibway Melody* (Toronto: Ambassador Books, 1946), 24–28. Interviews with T. H. B. Symons, 26 July 2009 and 26 January 2010.

19 Biographical notes for Harry Symons, Symons Papers, Trent University Archives.

20 http://www.answers.com/topic/christopher-columbus-film-2.

21 *Sarnia Canadian Observer*, 5 November 1949.

22 Interview with T. H. B. Symons, 26 July 2009.

23 "Chicago Gangsters are Not in Toronto, Detectives Assert," Toronto *Globe and Mail*, 20 February 1931, 11, cited in Robert J. Burns, "William Perkins Bull, K.C., LL.D., 1870–1948: Historical Background," in Ontario Heritage Trust, *Featured Plaque of the Month, November 2007*, 4. http://www.heritagefdn.on.ca/userfiles/page_attachments/Library/1/149277_William_Perkins_Bull_ENG.pdf.

24 Fran Bennett, "No Bull about Bull: Short Stories under Tall Trees," *The Women's Post*, April 2005, 11.

25 Interview with T. H. B. Symons, 26 July 2009.

26 Interview with T. H. B. Symons, 24 January 2010.

27 Interview with T. H. B. Symons, 26 July 2009.

28 Robert J. Burns, "William Perkins Bull, K.C., LL.D., 1870–1948: Historical Background," in Ontario Heritage Trust, *Featured Plaque of the Month, November 2007*, note 22, 7.

29 Interview with R. H. Sadleir, 3 November 2009.

30 Interview with T. H. B. Symons, 26 July 2009.

31 Interview with R. H. Sadleir, 3 November 2009.

32 Ibid.

33 Interview with T. H. B. Symons, 26 July 2009.

34 Interview with R. H. Sadleir, 3 November 2009.

35 Ibid. Interview with John Stevenson, 2 November 2009. See also Michael Tait's reminiscence in Walter Pitman's chapter in this book.

36 Interview with T. H. B. Symons, 26 July 2009.

37 Interviews with R. H. Sadleir, 3 November 2009, 8 March 2010.

38 Ibid.

39 Interview with T. H. B. Symons, 26 July 2009.

40 T. H. B. Symons, "The Proper Place of Extra-Curricular Activities in the Students' Programme," *National Conference of Canadian Universities,*

Twenty-seventh Meeting, Held at McGill University, 30 May–1 June 1951, 24–26. Emphasis added.

41 Interview with T. H. B. Symons, 2 October 2009.

42 Interview with T. H. B. Symons, 27 January 2010. Much of Vanier's wartime correspondence was written from or about the Perkins Bull Hospital, which he called "my old English home." Of Perkins Bull himself Vanier wrote warmly, "He is a charming man and outside the battalion has seen more of me than anyone else during the last two years." *Georges Vanier: Soldier—The Wartime Letters and Diaries, 1915–1919*, ed. Deborah Cowley (Toronto: Dundurn Press, 2000), 288, 199. Vanier's beautiful tribute to Tom's grandmother, Maria Bull, on her death in 1934, can be found in William Perkins Bull, *Spadunk, or From Paganism to Davenport United* (Toronto: The Perkins Bull Foundation, 1935), 11–12. Almost forty-five years after the war, Vanier told Tom's brother Scott that their "Grandmother Bull was the loveliest person, the finest lady I ever knew." Scott Symons, "The Duke of Rosedale," *Toronto Life* (March 1984): 113.

43 Interview with T. H. B. Symons, 2 October 2009.

44 Ibid.

45 Ibid.

46 Ibid.

47 Interview with R. H. Sadleir, 3 November 2009.

48 Interviews with T. H. B. Symons, 1 October 2009 and 28 January 2010.

49 T. H. B. Symons, "Devonshire House: Fiftieth Anniversary of the University Residences on Devonshire Place," *University of Toronto Graduate* (January 1957): 18–20.

50 Interview with T. H. B. Symons, 29 January 2010.

51 Ibid.

52 Ibid.

53 Scott Symons, "The Duke of Rosedale," *Toronto Life* (March 1984): 109.

54 Interview with R. H. Sadleir, 3 November 2009.

55 Interview with T. H. B. Symons, 1 October 2009.

56 T. H. B. Symons, *A Report on Residence Requirements at the University of Toronto*, Submitted to the Statistical and Fact Finding Sub-Committee of the Advisory Planning Committee of the Board of Governors, 5 December 1956.

57 Communication from S. G. D. Smith, 22 February 2010.

58 Interview with T. H. B. Symons, 1 October 2009.

59 T. H. B. Symons and R. L. Watts, "The Residence Hall and The University: An Aspect of Liberal Education," *Queen's Quarterly* 64, no. 4 (1958): 567.

60 Interview with T. H. B. Symons, 1 October 2009.

61 Ibid.

62 Ibid.

63 Interview with T. H. B. Symons, 29 January 2010.

64 Interviews with T. H. B. Symons, 1 October 2009, 22 February 2010. Unfortunately Provost Seeley never received Tom's report as he was killed in an automobile accident that same summer.

65 Interviews with T. H. B. Symons, 1 October 2009, 22 February 2010.

66 T. H. B. Symons, "Are University Residences Beneficial Academically?" Paper presented to the Thirty-Third Annual Meeting of the National Conference of Canadian Universities, University of Ottawa, June, 1957.

67 T. H. B. Symons and R. L. Watts, "The Residence Hall and The University: An Aspect of Liberal Education," *Queen's Quarterly* 64, no. 4 (1958): 552–68.

68 Mike Johnson and Adriano Ferreri, *Professor T. H. B. Symons and the Founding of the Commonwealth Scholarship Plan: An Interview in Celebration of the Plan's 50th Anniversary in 2009* (Ottawa: Foreign Affairs and International Trade Canada and Canadian Bureau for International Education, 2008). [Video].

69 Interview with T. H. B. Symons, 1 October 2009.

70 Ibid.

71 T. H. B. Symons, *The University in Summer,* A Report prepared for the Presidential Committee on Policy and Planning of the University of Toronto, April 1960, 53. Symons Papers, Trent University Archives, Box 31, Files 12–17.

72 Ibid., 16–18.

73 T. H. B. Symons, *The Planning and Operation of Some New Residential Colleges at the University of Toronto,* A Report prepared for the Committee on Policy and Planning of the University of Toronto, March 1961, 4. Symons Papers, Trent University Archives, Box 31, Files 12–17.

74 Ibid., 7.

75 Ibid., 9–10.

76 Ibid., 34.

77 Interview with T. H. B. Symons, 1 October 2009.

78 Interviews with John Stevenson, 2 November 2009 and with R. H. Sadleir, 8 March 2010.

79 William Perkins Bull, *Spadunk, or From Paganism to Davenport United* (Toronto: The Perkins Bull Foundation, 1935), 98; Thomas H. B. Symons, "William Ryerson," in *Dictionary of Canadian Biography* X, ed. Marc La Terreur (Toronto: University of Toronto Press, 1972), 640–41.

80 Interview with John Stevenson, 2 November 2009.

81 A. O. C. Cole, *Trent: The Making of a University 1957–1987* (Peterborough: Trent University, 1992), 11.

82 Ibid., 12.

CHAPTER 2

Tom Symons and the Founding of Trent University

DENIS SMITH

On a balmy autumn day in September 2009, Tom Symons sat in the front row for the joint installation of Trent University's eighth president and tenth chancellor. From his place of honour on the University Court, he could look past the platform party during the ceremony to the shaded windows of the Bata Library, outwards across the Otonabee River to the science buildings and colleges on the east bank, and upwards as flights of geese and gulls streamed north along the river. Behind him were rows of gowned faculty and guests—and scores of students pausing between classes to sit on the steps above and listen to the promises of fresh dedication to their university. Almost fifty years earlier, Tom Symons stood on empty grasslands at the same site, inviting members of the provincial Advisory Committee on University Affairs to share his vision of a new national university. Long before 2009 that vision was realized.

When Tom Symons became dean of Devonshire House at the University of Toronto in 1955, Devonshire was a neglected and run-down residence for engineering, medical, and dental students. When he left it in 1963 to become founding president of Trent University, it was a proud place, restored in fabric and confident in spirit. The transformation of Devonshire House, achieved with quiet firmness by its young dean, became the model and inspiration for a larger dream that became reality on the banks of the Otonabee

River. There, Tom Symons conjured Trent University into precocious life. Tom Symons was the magician of Trent and, fifty years on, the University bears the indelible marks of his founding inspiration.

John Pettigrew and I were two of Tom Symons's dons in residence at Devonshire House during the late 1950s; both of us were fortunate to observe Tom's skill in converting a formless dormitory for two hundred students into a collegiate residence of civility.[1] At the same time, he was the author (along with Ronald Watts of Queen's University) of a creative study of the benefits of small university halls of residence—a subject little considered in Canadian universities during the early postwar years.[2] In 1957, when the University of Toronto planned to dispose of Devonshire House as a residence for professional students by selling it to the adjacent Trinity College, the dean of Devonshire (who had not been consulted) mounted a quiet but intense lobbying campaign within the university to reverse the board's decision. The University of Toronto in the 1950s was a complacently hierarchical place,[3] and this kind of rebellion from the grass-roots was unprecedented. Tom Symons, both courtly and Conservative, seemed—at a superficial glance—an unlikely rebel. But the cause made sense: why destroy a community that had just been revived with so much care and imagination? His campaign impressed some deans and members of the university's board, and the decision to close Devonshire was indefinitely postponed.[4] Tom Symons was beginning to make his mark as a university administrator.

During those months of anxious lobbying, Tom, John Pettigrew, and I spent evenings in the dean's rooms at Devonshire House tossing around ideas about liberal education, university bureaucracy, the growth of academic specialization, the forthcoming expansion of Canadian universities, and all their accompanying perils and opportunities. We indulged our fantasies, and talked about what we would do if we had the unlikely chance to found a university. We read Cardinal Newman on *The Idea of a University*. We plumbed our own experiences at Toronto, McGill, Oxford, and Cambridge. We agreed with Stephen Leacock that, "If somebody would give me about two dozen very old elm trees and about fifty acres of wooded ground and lawn—not too near anywhere and not too far from anywhere—I think I could set up a college that would put all the big universities of today in the shade."[5]

We didn't expect it to happen. We dreamed, and then we put the dreams aside as we went our separate ways.[6]

In the early 1950s, after a temporary postwar bulge in enrolment to accommodate the returning armed forces, Canadian universities had reduced their enrolments to pre-war levels and receded for a few years into placidity. They lived quietly on the fringes of Canadian society, unexciting and unthreatened in their traditional ways. In Ontario, four universities—Queen's, Toronto, McMaster, and Western—monopolized the field and took for granted their perpetual ascendancy.

But by the end of that decade of population growth, economic boom, and Cold War, governments began to sense the advantages of university expansion. More and more citizens sought higher education. Suddenly there was talk of an explosion in university enrolments. Provincial governments would have to provide the operating and capital grants, Ottawa would provide the funds for advanced research, and the existing universities (they assumed) would reap the benefits of growth and increased public recognition.

When the pressures for university growth were finally recognized in the late 1950s, the old institutions made their plans for expansion and discouraged the thought that any new universities should be created. In Toronto, a committee proposing a new urban university was reined in by the University of Toronto and a cautious provincial cabinet. The result was that York University was hobbled as a temporary ward of the U of T, chartered but unable to grant independent degrees for up to eight years.[7] After all, such upstarts couldn't really be trusted: they might drain off enrolments, faculty, and government dollars and challenge the older universities with strange and unsound new curricula.

But the pressure for growth was inexorable. Even in Britain (which still offered the preferred model for most Canadian universities) a Tory government audaciously chartered and financed six new universities in 1960, to be built on green pastures on the edges of six provincial towns. Across Canada's border in the United States, universities and colleges already accommodated three times the proportion of university-age students than Canadian institutions did.

Those infections were catching and, within a few years, the pressures for new student places changed the political atmosphere in Ontario as well. All the old universities except Queen's acceded to the huge demand for student places and opted for massive expansion. Small, church-affiliated arts colleges in Ottawa, Toronto, Waterloo, Windsor, and Sudbury transformed themselves into secular bodies to qualify for provincial funding to finance their growth. And ambitious local boosters across Ontario talked of the prospect of new universities in their neighbourhoods.

In December 1957, the president of Quaker Oats of Canada in Peterborough, Reginald Faryon, wrote to the *Peterborough Examiner* to suggest that funds from the sale of the city's gas utility should be reserved to support the founding of a new two-year college in the city.[8] "If we had a Junior College in Peterborough," he wrote, "hundreds of Peterborough young men and women would be able to obtain part of their college or university education while living at home. . . . I think this is the greatest opportunity Peterborough has probably had in its history; and I also believe that to a great extent, the future progress of the City depends on it."[9] Robertson Davies, the editor of the *Examiner*, took up the cause on his editorial page in the first of many commentaries, insisting on a university in Peterborough, not "a glorified vocational school."[10]

The local response was enthusiastic, and early in 1958 the Mayor of Peterborough created a widely representative committee of fifteen citizens to examine the proposal. Reg Faryon joined it as an "interested citizen," alongside members from council, industry, schools, churches, and trade unions. At its first meeting in April 1958, the committee chose its chairman—a gruff, genial, and determined divisional manager at Canadian General Electric by the name of Charles K. Fraser.

For three years the local committee made its case for a two-year junior college to the provincial ministry and to the existing universities—with repeatedly dismal results. Peterborough received nothing but discouragement from Queen's Park until, in May 1960, the committee brought three advisors from Queen's, Toronto, and Western into its counsels.[11] (They became known informally as The Midwives.) Their first advice was to find a leading academic as a potential president-designate, and to turn over all academic planning to him. By the spring of 1961, the Peterborough committee (which had now become the board of an incorporated company, Trent College Limited) had generated a list of several dozen names for consideration by the three advisors. They examined it and responded with a short list of ten, headed—at the strong urging of Moffatt Woodside of Toronto—by Tom Symons. Both advisors and executive committee members conducted interviews—or perhaps more accurately, informal soundings—with some of the candidates. (When he was interviewed at his Devonshire House rooms, Tom Symons was uncertain about the nature of the encounter.) One member of the Peterborough executive later remarked that they were looking for someone who had academic weight, who was also "a Conservative, an Anglican, and a man with potentially good connections at Queen's Park."[12] (This was still, after all, old Ontario of the early 1960s.) They found him; on 12 April 1961, the Board of Trent College voted unanimously to offer the presidency to Tom Symons.

Tom was thirty-one years old, bright, amiable, wry, slightly at odds with modern technology, bulky, and canny beyond his years. He already had a certain ageless gravitas, accompanying his droll good humour and discreet irreverence. And he had a calculating prudence, a rare capacity to measure opportunities, to judge limits, to choose the moments for boldness and action—or for patience and inaction. He visited Peterborough, toured a one-hundred acre property owned by Canadian General Electric at Nassau Mills, which the company was ready to offer as a university site, and inspected the former South Central School on Rubidge Street, which might be available as a temporary campus. He established immediate rapport with the Trent College Board—and especially with its chairman, Chuck Fraser. But the "university" he was asked to lead was still a mirage. It had no charter and no promise of provincial funding. Tom asked for time: to seek a group of personal academic advisors, and to measure support for the project in the community, in his own university, and in the provincial government. For an initial year, starting 1 July 1961, Tom Symons accepted an appointment—not as president but, more modestly, as academic consultant and chairman of an academic planning committee of his own choice—while he continued as the dean of Devonshire House and as a lecturer in Toronto's Department of History.

He faced simultaneous efforts on many fronts: to orchestrate planning for a university that would satisfy his own high vision; to educate and carry with him the Peterborough board that had appointed him; to win favour from a local community with little experience of a university in its midst; to persuade the provincial government of the benefits of a college in Peterborough rather than, say, in Oshawa or Lindsay (where there were also local advocates); and to create wider public sympathy for a new and expensive public institution on the edge of the Ontario backwoods. It was still possible that all this would come to nothing.

Tom's involvement coincided happily with a change of generations at Queen's Park. In October 1961, John Robarts, an imaginative and energetic former minister of education, became premier of the province, and soon afterwards Leslie Frost, the retiring premier, was appointed to a new, six-member Advisory Committee on University Affairs charged with bringing order to policy-making on Ontario's universities.[13] Less than a year later, William Davis, a classmate of Tom Symons at the University of Toronto a decade before, became minister of education and university affairs. These were good omens.

Meanwhile, the new president-designate convened an academic planning committee chosen from friends and academic colleagues. Its first formal recommendation was to call for a full degree-granting university charter, rather than the limited powers of a junior or affiliated college.[14] This was what all of us on the planning committee wished for—and it was also an uncompromising statement of position. We knew that the provincial government and the established universities remained doubtful. The proposal surprised Chuck Fraser and his executive by its boldness: these would be no milquetoast advisors. When Fraser, Symons, and the local executive made a pitch soon afterwards to the new provincial advisory committee, they firmly asserted the degree-granting proposal. The committee was impressed but hesitant. It made no commitments and called for information about fundraising and enrolments, which the Peterborough group could not provide without further study. That meant a delay of at least one year in gaining a charter from the Ontario legislature, which was a disappointment for the local board but a boon for all of us on the academic planning committee. We would now aim for an opening date in September 1964 rather than 1963, which gave us time for thorough planning and recruitment—something that was unique in the rush (already becoming a stampede) to Canadian university expansion of the early 1960s.[15]

Over the next six months, the president-designate guided his board as it prepared for a public fundraising campaign, while he plunged into an intense round of lobbying to win government support for a new university in Peterborough. This was his own individual and unrelenting task—and he chose his targets shrewdly. In his efforts of persuasion, Tom found key strategic supporters in Floyd Chalmers and Leslie Frost on the provincial advisory committee, Jack McCarthy (who was secretary of the committee and later deputy minister of university affairs), and J. Bascom St. John (the *Globe and Mail*'s education columnist). They were all won over by Tom's persistence and by the refreshing ideas he put forward with such quiet conviction.

The academic planning committee was busy as well, ranging far beyond curricular planning. With Tom's encouragement, the committee began to sketch the outlines of its broad vision for the university, its desirable rate of growth, teaching methods, collegiate organization, and architectural planning. From the beginning, the committee made the point that detailed planning for the university would be in the hands of faculty members. Any doubts that members of the local board expressed about this tilting of the balance away from the powers of the board were soothed by the president-elect's reassurances that this was the way that universities were (or should be) run. (This gentle veiling of the truth about Canadian university governance reflected an emerging sense among young faculty members that scholarly quality and independence demanded a shift in the internal balance of power in their favour. That sense was becoming widespread in the universities of the early 1960s: we were just fortunate to be handed a clean slate on which to design a new institution, without the entrenched habits of older places. Through Tom's insight and diplomatic talent, the opportunity to create a fresh balance was recognized and exploited.)

All these preliminaries occurred in an atmosphere of political uncertainty, which the president-elect managed with fine strategic discretion. Tom's negotiations with the provincial advisory committee continued through the winter of 1961–62. The provincial government had committed itself to university growth in general; but there were hesitations about its scale and nature. Early in 1962, when planners for another new university in St. Catherine's, Ontario, had reason to doubt that the province would grant them a full university charter, they sought Tom's advice. On his urging, Trent's academic planning committee quietly threatened collective resignation unless both Trent and Brock University were granted full charters. (By this time the province had been convinced that the Trent proposal was a serious one that it could not afford to lose.) The province conceded and, on 31 May 1962, Premier Robarts announced the approval for both new universities. They would get their independent charters and would open in the autumn of 1964.

Meanwhile the Trent College Board had undertaken a massive fundraising campaign, staffed by local and national volunteers, to demonstrate to the province the community's commitment to its new institution. Tom inspired the fundraisers with his constant attention and enthusiasm, and the Founding Fund surpassed its target by more than thirty percent, raising more than two million dollars for the university's initial capital projects. This was an astonishing success. Over one-third of that total was raised by payroll deductions from Peterborough's factory workers, setting a new model for university fundraising across the country.

In early 1963, the Ontario legislature passed the Trent University Act, and appropriated modest funding for the university's planning year. A small core of staff and faculty arrived in Peterborough in July—a month or two before the president-elect arrived, newly married to Christine, to occupy Marchbanks, the grand nineteenth-century house on Park Street formerly owned by Robertson Davies.[16] The Symons's hospitality at Marchbanks quickly set the tone for the new institution in town. It would be friendly, outgoing, generous, and mindful of the city's history, literary heritage, and historic architectural highlights. Tom's own sensitivity to his new community was absorbed by all of us who joined him in those early months of Trent's life. His serious yet always light-hearted chuckling and joshing spirit inspired all those who worked with him as the university took shape.

All of Trent's original faculty members, and many of its early students, carry memories of Tom Symons's inimitable personal touch. My own most startling recollection of his impish spirit is of an autumn day in 1967 when a group of new students, supervised by Bob Johnstone and me, was placing stones in a shore-edge breakwater beside Champlain College. It was heavy, hot, and unrelieved labour. Late in the day Tom came by to offer encouragement. As he greeted the work crew at riverside, he offered me an unexpected challenge: "If I jump into the river, I'll bet you won't do it too!" And he leapt instantly (and fully clothed) into deep midstream, disappearing ominously before resurfacing. I thought quickly, stripped my watch from my wrist, and took the dare by following him into the freezing Otonabee waters. We scrambled soddenly ashore, to the delight of the exhausted volunteers, and adjourned the day's work for a round of cold beers.

In 1963, the university's first offices were opened in the old South Central School, now re-named Rubidge Hall. Tom furnished his office (a spacious former classroom) with Canadian antique furniture, including a grandfather clock, a handsome pine harvest table and captain's chairs from St. Augustine's Seminary in Toronto, and a giant Renaissance oil painting from his family collection (if I recall) of voluptuous nudes and prancing cherubs. In those congenial surroundings the new president orchestrated Trent's planning year with a light touch and consummate attention to every detail, despatching streams of notes to colleagues written with his fat, broad-nibbed fountain pen, consulting everyone as he leaned into his desk, clutching his giant (and always brimming) teacup.

The university's new master planning architect, Ron Thom, who had been selected after a national competition in the spring of 1963, began his work with renovations at Rubidge Hall, and later at the two historic houses purchased as residential colleges in the centre of the city. Before the arrival of the first class in September 1964, they had become Peter Robinson College and Catharine Parr Traill College. Meanwhile, for twelve months, he was engaged in a continuing seminar with Tom and the planning group on the nature of a residential university.[17]

On what would become the permanent campus at Nassau Mills, the university board approved the purchase and expropriation of lands beyond the original CGE gift of one hundred acres. This involved a substantial risk, since the provincial government had not yet agreed to finance any expansion. Tom viewed the landscape with his new campus planning committee, and recommended a campus of 1,100 acres reaching to the horizons on both sides of the Otonabee River. The lands were acquired, and the province provided the funds in retrospect. With close support from the campus planning committee, Ron Thom produced the university's architectural master plan, calling for twelve colleges and a science complex in a walking campus that would straddle the river. Within two years Champlain College was under construction. Its cornerstone was laid jointly by Premier John Robarts of Ontario and Premier Jean Lesage of Quebec in October of 1965, three hundred and fifty years after Samuel de Champlain and his Huron guides had passed down the Otonabee River where the college would stand. It was soon followed by the delicately arched Faryon Bridge, the Bata Library, the first science buildings, and Lady Eaton College, all of them in regional grey stone colouring, crouching low beneath the drumlins framing the campus on both sides of the river out of respect for the university's striking natural surroundings. National and international architectural awards flooded in.

Tom's guidance during the planning year and beyond touched every feature of what was to come. New faculty members were sought out in the core arts and science disciplines, all of them appointed only after exhausting personal interviews in Peterborough. The first faculty members were mostly young, but leavened by a sprinkling of distinguished senior academics, drawn to Trent by their admiration for Tom's remarkable vision and integrity. Under his leadership this group formed an unusually cohesive team. The university's original board was broadened, on the president's recommendation, by the addition of distinguished national members who enthusiastically shared Tom's beliefs about university teaching and government.[18] The vision that Tom conveyed, with all his quiet passion, was of a small, residential national university taking public service and critical study of the national interest (in all its subtleties) as its *raison d'etre.* For him—without any boastful trumpeting of the cause—engagement in the creation of a new university was a higher calling. He invested the place with that enlarging spirit.

Beyond his absorbing activities at Trent, Tom was also cultivating a parallel career as a political advisor and diplomat. In the 1950s, he was the key consultant to Sidney Smith at the University of Toronto in the creation of the vast Commonwealth Scholarship program. In the 1960s, he maintained close relations with André Laurendeau, editor of *Le Devoir* and co-chairman of the Royal Commission on Bilingualism and Biculturalism. He participated in the Progressive Conservative party's 1964 conference on national policy at Fredericton and became a trusted, confidential advisor to Robert Stanfield after his selection as party leader in 1967. (Trent's faculty members and students simultaneously pursued their own lively—and heterodox—political lives.)

An early decision was made by Trent's academic planning committee to grow slowly, adding no more than one hundred students a year for the university's first few classes. Trent would remain relatively small, at a time when most other Ontario universities aimed to become instant 'multiversities' on the model of Clark Kerr's giant University of California. Maximum enrolment was set at four thousand students, and two elements above all guided the university's early planning. First, attention would be focused on good undergraduate education designed, wherever appropriate, around a system of tutorials and seminars—education, in the president's mind, through disciplined and informed conversation. (This required, ideally, a high proportion of about one faculty member to every ten students.) Second, the university would create a series of small residential colleges, intended to encourage mixing among the academic disciplines, and a sense of social attachment to these face-to-face communities among both students and faculty. In the direct tradition of Oxford, Cambridge, and the Inns of Court, the colleges would, at best, be centres of close friendships and celebration—as well as of learning.

Tom's convictions about small group teaching and the college system were the products of his own education at Trinity College in the University of Toronto and at Oriel College in Oxford, and of his experience and long reflection as dean of Devonshire House. In the face of that education and experience, he saw North American universities moving relentlessly, by the early 1960s, into their future as large-scale manufacturing plants and research institutions with slight interest in the direct and patient nurturing of individual young persons to live in a humane society. At Trent he hoped to establish a small alternative community, just as others were attempting it at York University in the UK and at Santa Cruz in California. He knew that the model was costly; he hoped that an enlightened provincial government (and a few generous philanthropists) might meet the bills. He understood that the dream might be unachievable—but the early sixties were, briefly, a time when the effort seemed possible and worthwhile.

While Trent's curriculum emphasized traditional degree programs, interdisciplinarity was encouraged by designating many courses for credit in more than one discipline. And the curriculum would increasingly be marked by new departures that broke through disciplinary boundaries: in Canadian studies, aboriginal studies, freshwater ecology, environmental and resource studies, development studies, and northern studies. The university launched a quarterly *Journal of Canadian Studies* in a field that the Canada Council refused for years to recognize as legitimate. Three language departments undertook pioneering "year abroad" programs. The annual academic timetable departed from the Canadian pattern with "reading weeks" in autumn and midwinter. An academic advisory system assigned a personal faculty advisor to every student. The university's athletic program would emphasize intramural rather than intercollegiate competition. For the first few years, Trent students proudly wore green gowns to classes—although this practice faded as formalities relaxed in the late sixties.

The college system, small group teaching, and the advisory system placed unusual responsibilities on Trent's faculty. In the early years, faculty members devoted themselves exhaustingly to these duties because most of them had come to Trent wholeheartedly sharing the president's instincts and convictions about higher education.

From the beginning, faculty members were at the centre of all planning. Every idea, in those early days, spawned a new committee reporting to the president. For more than three years before the creation of the Senate in 1965, two key committees—the academic planning committee and the campus planning committee—reviewed and recommended policy in all areas (including finance, land purchases, internal organization, and architecture) before it was considered by the Board of Governors. On the formal creation of the Senate, both board and Senate acknowledged that this practice would continue—as it did for the next thirty-five years. University budgets were drafted and considered first by the Senate, before their adoption by the Board of Governors, and all campus planning decisions were initiated and elaborated in detail at the academic level (through the site development committee of the Senate) before their ratification by the board. By common understanding, no major university policy could be adopted without due consideration and approval by the academic Senate. The university, under Tom Symons's leadership, was determined to create a system of internal self-government by consensus.

While the Senate was the centre point of university government, another layer of decision-making and administration was added beneath it: the colleges each had academic councils that discussed all Senate business and made their recommendations to the Senate before it took its decisions. These councils were key democratic elements in Trent's system of government, involving every member of the academic staff in cross-disciplinary discussions of university policy. And the colleges, of course, were both the points of informal contact between faculty and students, as well as the centres of social life in the university.

In the heady 1960s atmosphere of unlimited university expansion, which swept all the prudent cautions of the previous decade out the window in Ontario, Trent's principles were an unusual (indeed, radical) mixture. Its academic principles were thoughtfully backward-looking, conservative in the sense of seeking to preserve good things like small classes and personal teaching that were being thoughtlessly abandoned elsewhere. Its interdisciplinary programs were a novelty in Canada. Its principles of governance were radically forward-looking.

Tom's traditionalism meant that, in one area, the university was slow to move. There would be separate residential colleges for men and women; and women faculty members at first faced unevenness in their terms of appointment, salary levels, and leave arrangements (as they did at other Canadian universities in the 1960s). The unacknowledged barriers at Trent—as it turned out—were swinging doors which would gradually open when pushed. But for an initial decade or more, the doors had to be leaned upon—despite the university's self-image as a place offering a general challenge to the status quo.[19]

There was widespread doubt that Trent could hold to its principles and live up to its claims. The large universities scoffed. Provincial funding agencies needed constant persuasion and reassurance—but responded to Trent's plans with supplements to their formulaic operating grants in recognition of the benefits of the university's small size and special character. Trent proved attractive to faculty members, who came to it understanding what it intended to do, and sharing in its determination to succeed. The first classes of students quickly absorbed the sense of novelty and commitment that imbued the place and became vigorous partners in the adventure. And in those early years, Tom Symons took infinite and unassuming care to know Trent's students one by one.

Trent's system of governance by consensus-building was time consuming, sometimes repetitive, and confusing to observers. A vast pattern of internal committees developed.[20] But by isolating itself at least partially from the demands of the North American educational marketplace and the habits of older institutions, Trent found itself at the forefront of experiments in undergraduate education and in governance. The sixties brought a more general movement of reform in Canadian university government, but Trent moved ahead of the tide.

Within a decade the university had proven its academic quality, and it was difficult to avoid seeing this success as an overwhelming mark of Tom Symons's educational and diplomatic genius. His ten years as president were inspired by his imagination, his patience, his unfailing warmth and generosity of spirit, and his attachment to the communities of both Trent and Peterborough.

Tom retired from the presidency in 1972 but remained on the faculty as Vanier Professor. In a moving tribute to him on his retirement as president and chairman of the University Senate, the historian Stuart Robson reminded the Senate that Trent was a place of grace and civility because Tom Symons had made it so.

> Whatever else the university may be, it must first be a place where care is taken, care for words, care for implications, care for others. If this Senate has been competent, if it has been at all effective as a parliament of academic change, credit must go above all to its chairman, who has shown us that we must take care. . . . The tolerance which has guided the Senate has shaped the university. . . . You have given us ten years of your life, you have given us an idea, and you have given us the civil spirit to pursue the idea. We thank you, for those are gifts indeed.[21]

Tom's talent as a creator and conciliator left unusually high expectations among the faculty that his successors—in changing financial circumstances and with differing personal qualities—would always be hard pressed to match. (His wide-ranging and distinguished career is elaborated in the chapters that follow.) His irreplaceable qualities in creating the university community included a fine sense of historic continuity, a matchless instinct for ceremony and symbolism, and a capacity for genuine friendship and trust that reached out to every level of faculty, staff, and students—and beyond that into the Peterborough community. Later, various enquiries conducted at times of financial crisis in the university could not work out how the whole machine worked in those early days—or could not quite explain that it had worked through Tom Symons's deceivingly diffident and captivating charm.

In many respects, Trent University in the twenty-first century is not the place that Tom Symons set out to create. Perhaps, above all, the residential college system, small group teaching, and the advisory system became the victims of the university's growth and financial stringency. Dilution of the ideal had already begun before his retirement as president, but habits and strong convictions about Tom's ideals remained among many faculty members, who continued working to fulfil his inspiration. If we had been calculating realists at the beginning, we might have said that the dream was impossible. Tom refused that kind of pessimism and inspired a generation of teachers and planners to sustain Trent's idealist spirit.

The system of government Tom Symons had created at Trent worked remarkably well as long as provincial funding to universities continued to grow through the 1960s. During the 1970s and 1980s, as government funding shrank, budget limitations and cutbacks strained the university's ambitions and provoked a series of crises. The university grew larger and more centralized than Tom Symons had hoped. Class sizes increased. The colleges were overshadowed by discipline-based departments. Competing visions of the university gained greater prominence as the faculty expanded. The Board of Governors grew more conventional. But still the system of consensus worked (most of the time), and faculty and student commitment to it deepened.

This was clearly a place of decency, where deeply felt policy discussion was tolerated, where academic differences were respected, where time was taken to find areas of agreement, where compromises could be made with dignity, and where decisions on the way forward could still be achieved. This was the first president's legacy. Only in late 2001 was the constitutional system altered, when the Ontario Court of Appeal sustained a decision of the Board of Governors to override a Senate recommendation on a major matter of policy for the first time in the university's history.[22]

Despite that break in continuity, Trent still lives—in its civility, in its physical distinction, in its high academic quality, in its care for students—as the embodiment of Tom Symons's dream of a new university on the banks of the Otonabee River, not too near to anywhere and not too far from anywhere. Trent University would never have existed without the wisdom and determination of this inspired and quietly rebellious conservative visionary, this teacher and scholar, this Dickensian gentleman, this man of profoundly humane conviction and sensibility. As the university approaches its fiftieth anniversary in 2014, nothing would honour Tom Symons more than a campaign to endow the revival and growth of Trent's residential college system, which lies at the heart of his vision of Trent.[23]

Notes

1 Two other dons in this period were Alan Davenport, who subsequently made a notable career as the founder of the University of Western Ontario's Boundary Layer Wind Tunnel and the leading expert on the wind engineering of high buildings and bridges throughout the world; and the biologist Charles Lennox, who succeeded Tom Symons as dean of Devonshire House.

2 See T. H. B. Symons and R. L. Watts, "The Residence Hall and the University: An Aspect of a Liberal Education," *Queen's Quarterly* 64, no. 4 (1958).

3 The historian John Saywell described the University of Toronto in this period as "in bondage to a history from which ghosts could be summoned to defeat any argument for more than incremental change. At every level it was top-down." *Someone to Teach Them: York and the Great University Explosion, 1960–1973* (Toronto: University of Toronto Press, 2008), 6.

4 Devonshire House was eventually acquired by Trinity College in 1998; after its restoration, it was reopened as the Munk Centre for International Studies.

5 From "On the Need for a Quiet College," in *Model Memoirs and Other Sketches from Simple to Serious*, quoted in John Robert Colombo, *Colombo's Canadian Quotations* (Edmonton: Hurtig Publishers, 1974), 340. We subscribed also to Leacock's advice (written long before the US Surgeon General's report) that "If I were founding a university. . . I would found first a smoking room; then when I had a little more money in hand I would found a dormitory; then after that, or more probably with it, a decent reading room and a library. After that, if I still had money over that I couldn't use, I would hire a professor and get some text books." (From "Oxford as I See It," in *My Discovery of England*, quoted in Colombo, 338.)

6 John Pettigrew left Devonshire and continued his teaching at the University of Toronto as a scholar of Tennyson and Shakespeare in the Department of English; I returned to Oxford to complete a thesis in politics and then joined the initial staff of York University in January 1960.

7 For the history of York University, see Michiel Horn's *York University: The Way Must be Tried* (York University, Toronto, 2009), especially chapter one, "Founding a University," 3–19. For a more detailed and astringent

reflection on York's painful early trials, see John T. Saywell's *Someone to Teach Them: York and the Great University Explosion, 1960–1973.*

8 For this and other specifics of Trent's founding years, see A. O. C. Cole, *Trent: The Making of a University 1957–1987* (Trent University, 1992).

9 Quoted in Cole, 2.

10 Ibid., 3.

11 The members of this academic advisory committee, recommended by their university presidents, were Julian Blackburn, chairman of the Department of Psychology at Queen's; Moffatt Woodside, Principal of University College in the University of Toronto; and Frank Stiling, dean of Arts and Science at the University of Western Ontario. Julian Blackburn later became Trent's first professor of psychology.

12 Norman Crook, quoted in Cole, 11.

13 The other members of the Committee were Chief Justice Dana Porter (chairman), George Gathercole, Floyd Chalmers, Senator D'Arcy Leonard, and R. W. Mitchell. Gathercole, a former provincial economist for Ontario, was a close advisor of Frost; Chalmers was the publisher at Maclean-Hunter; and Mitchell was president of Supertest Petroleum. The hardest head to crack in that company was George Gathercole's—but Tom Symons did it.

14 The committee consisted of Tom Symons as chairman, Denis Smith as secretary, and Allan Ashley, George Connell, Dr. J. A. MacFarlane, John Pettigrew, and Dick Sadleir. Ashley was a professor emeritus in economics at Trinity College, Connell was an assistant professor of chemistry at the U of T, MacFarlane was a former dean of medicine, and Dick Sadleir—a school and university colleague of Symons—was a housemaster and English teacher at Upper Canada College. The committee's minutes, covering over three years of life and twenty-six meetings, can be found in the Trent University Archives. Connell convened a notable subcommittee that made proposals for the creation of the university's science programs. He was later president of the University of Western Ontario and the University of Toronto.

15 As a current faculty member of York University in 1961–62 (which was then in its second teaching year), I was especially anxious to assure that Trent had time for fundamental planning that York had lacked. York had received its first students almost coincidentally with the arrival of its first faculty members, who played no role in initial decision-making about the size, the pace of growth, the curriculum, the site, or the architectural planning. The result at York in its early years was a distracting conflict among faculty, president, and board, which more

time for initial planning might have prevented. My experience simply supported Tom's own instincts and preferences.

16 Those who arrived for the planning year, with their families, were Tom Symons (president/history), Denis Smith (assistant to the president/politics), Dick Sadleir (dean of men/English), Marion Fry (dean of women/philosophy), John Pettigrew (registrar/English), Jack Martin (librarian), Jack Brook (bursar), and Jack Anderson (superintendent). Jack Brook and Jack Anderson departed during the planning year, to be replaced by John Leishman as chief financial officer, and Art Parker and Bob Johnstone as chief engineer and supervisor of buildings and grounds.

17 This seminar included two trips for Ron Thom: the first to Oxford, Cambridge, and the six new English universities; and the second to Harvard, Yale, and Amherst, accompanied by John Pettigrew, Dick Sadleir, Jack Anderson, Jack Brook, and Denis Smith. The trip to Yale resulted in the architect's choice of rough stone set in concrete as the building form for Champlain College and the University Library, inspired by Eero Saarinen's new Yale colleges.

18 Among the early members of faculty were Fernande Bassan (French), Julian Blackburn (psychology), Bernard Blishen (sociology), Maurice Boote (economics), Stewart Brown (biochemistry), Ian Chapman (chemistry), Roy Edwards (biology), Christopher Greene (history), Andy Guinand (mathematics), Kenneth Kidd (anthropology), Jack Lodge (physics), Stuart Robson (history), John Schonleber (philosophy), Michael Sidnell (English), Dawn Smith (Spanish), Robert Stairs (chemistry), and soon afterwards Peter Adams (geography), Gerald Aspinall (chemistry), Gilbert Bagnani (classics), Janet Bews (classics), David Cameron (politics), Robert Chambers (English), Margaret Doxey (politics), William Dray (philosophy), Geoffrey Eathorne (English), Rosa Garrido de Gonzalez (Spanish), Jeronimo Gonzalez-Martin (Spanish), Freddy Hagar (history), Bruce Hodgins (history), Jim MacAdam (philosophy), Ray March (chemistry), David Morrison (politics), W. L. Morton (history), Bill Neville (politics), Tom Nind (mathematics), Robert Page (history), Gordon Roper (English), Lionel Rubinoff (philosophy), Ian Sandeman (biology), Margery Seeley (sociology), Kenneth Tracey (anthropology), José María Valverde (Spanish), Joe Wearing (politics), and Alan Wilson (history). Nan Belfry, Alf Cole, Arlene Davis, Ralph Heintzman (history), Elizabeth McLeod (politics), Walter Pitman, Nancy Sherouse, John Stubbs (politics), Michael Treadwell (English), and Paul Wilson were early

staff members. The board's national members included Thomas Bata, Dr. G. D. W. Cameron, H. A. Dyde, J. Alec Edmison, Eugene Forsey, Gilbert Monture, J. J. Robinette, and Barney Sandwell.

19 On this subject, I declare a conflict of interest: my wife, Dawn, was the founding faculty member in Spanish. The residential colleges were integrated in 1973. Aside from differential salary levels between men and women, there was a particular issue at Trent over the appointment of wives of faculty to regular, tenure-stream positions. This dispute took several years, and real tension, before it was resolved. Salaries were only equalized after comparative analysis in the 1980s.

20 In 1968, when other universities were disrupted by student protests, this included the creation of a Senate Committee on Rape and Pillage, designed to offer friendly and consensual advice on avoiding such disturbances. The response seemed to work, as students were progressively (and peacefully) included in the university's governing bodies. (Student protests at Trent only came later). The committee's report is available in the Trent Archives.

21 Stuart Robson, "Remarks at the Seventy-fourth meeting of the Trent University Senate, 24 May 1972." The full text appears in this book as an appendix.

22 The challenge by three faculty members attempted to reverse a unilateral Board of Governors decision (opposed by the Senate) to close the two downtown colleges and resulted in a split two-to-one judgment in the Ontario Court of Appeal in favour of the board's decision. Trent's small, decentralized administration and its faculty-dominated constitution were novelties in an era of bigness. In effect, the appeal court deprived the university Senate of its traditional and accepted role in general policy-making, and thus extinguished the most participatory system of university government in Canada—unless customary practice can somehow restore it. (Kulchyski, McLachlan, and Wernick, Appellants, and Trent University, Respondent in appeal, and Attorney General of Ontario, Intervenor, 18 September 2000, cited as Kulchyski v. Trent University, 2001 CanLII 11691 (On C. A.), 148 O. A. C. 165.)

23 For an emphatic report on the widespread renaissance of residential colleges in the United States, Australia, Singapore, and China, see the annual Ashley Lecture, "The value of university residential colleges," delivered at Trent in February 2010 by Dr. Donald Markwell, Warden of Rhodes House, Oxford.

CHAPTER 3

Classrooms, Conversations, and Communities: Tom Symons's Perspectives on Learning

JAMIE BENIDICKSON

The arrival of a Chinese researcher who visited my office to pursue his interests in Canadian environmental law and to share his expertise in corresponding Chinese arrangements, took me back to the early 1970s, when, along with Tom McMillan, Michael Jenkin, and a number of others—including the editor of this volume of essays—I worked for Tom Symons on the preparation of a report to the Association of Universities and Colleges of Canada on Canadian Studies. A chapter of that document, "Canadian Studies Abroad," encouraged the creation of the funding program that brought my Chinese counterpart to the University of Ottawa about forty years later. My colleagues learned from him, as, I understand, he may have learned from us—everyone was enriched with a somewhat better understanding of ourselves and of each other.

Although I was never Tom Symons's student in the classroom, I learned a great deal from working with him at the Canadian Studies Commission, and I now welcome the opportunity to reflect in the context of these essays and reminiscences on the subject of Tom Symons's contribution to teaching and learning.[1]

Much of the formal working interaction between Commissioner Symons and his research staff was triggered by a four-letter message: "MWDP," an abbreviation for "May We Discuss Please." MWDP was often attached to a newspaper clipping, a piece of correspondence, or a scholarly essay. The origin of these documents was, in itself, a lesson in international intellectual geography, for the clippings came regularly from a number of continents. On occasion, and more alarmingly, MWDP might appear on a piece of one's own drafting. Uh, oh! But the underlying invitation to participate in an exchange of views was always cordial and conveyed two simple elements: this might be worth thinking about and perhaps we can learn from each other in conversation. More broadly understood, MWDP crystallized larger messages: almost everything is worth thinking about and perspectives other than one's own are always illuminating. Perhaps MWDP—rumoured to have found its way onto an Ontario license plate—continues to encourage reflection and inquiry on the province's busy highways.

The familiar combination of tea cups and pipe smoke that characterized the offices of the Canadian Studies Commission, as it did Tom Symons's more formal teaching sessions in classroom settings around Trent and elsewhere, clearly signalled an atmosphere of contemplation rather than intellectual confrontation. Neither a cup of tea nor a pipeful of tobacco offers its attractions to anyone in a hurry. Thus, ideas, new and old, and points of view, conflicting or converging, were to be enjoyed, vigorously explored, and then savoured or digested—carefully. There might always be something else to consider, or what we know might appear less certain in the light of a new day. Purposeful indecision was an important contributor to understanding, for if you were irrevocably certain of "the final answer" before the conversation got underway, not much learning was likely to occur.

Learning and understanding, the beneficial consequences of inquiry, reflection, and exchange, have been central elements of Tom Symons's educational mission in a vast range of settings. His encouragement of scholarship is certainly the most obvious. But thoughtful and deliberate efforts to promote discussion were equally characteristic of the several policy-making enterprises in which he so actively engaged.[2] Indeed, there are indications that Professor Symons's approach to teaching was very apparent in the manner in which he tackled the policy assignments that increasingly came his way. It is also noteworthy that those deeper experiences of public life derived from advising governments on the state of the federation, on human rights and minorities, and on cultural matters were eventually reflected back in the classroom.

"I was tremendously lucky in my teachers throughout my life," Tom recalled a few years after his retirement from the classroom. The category of teacher he defined broadly, encompassing formal instructors, of course, but also "mentors, wise and thoughtful people who might or might not be in the guise of a formal teacher."[3] As he put it in another context, "some of the best and most effective teaching by professors is done outside the classroom in their informal discussions and shared activities with students." To anchor that assertion, he remarked that "the professor who taught me most, taught me nothing. By which I mean that I did not have him as a teacher in any class, but simply as a mentor and, eventually, as a friend." The mentor in question, Alan Ashley, was a professor of accounting and, Tom added, "lucky not to have me as a student."[4]

Tom credits both his father and his grandfather with early influence on his educational orientation. With professional backgrounds in real estate and architecture, these family mentors placed research and inquiry "in a broad frame," a contribution that he also recognized in wonderful classroom teachers whose gift was to place things into context when, as a schoolboy, Tom found himself "wrestling with situations." Andrew D. Lockhart at the University of Toronto Schools was among the first of a series of educational guides who helped to ingrain a disposition, an attitude, or an approach to learning that eventually became characteristic of Tom himself.

Then, as Tom put it with reference to his studies in Modern History at the University of Toronto from 1947 to 1951, "I had luck." That perhaps underestimates the significance of encounters at Victoria College with Northrop Frye, eventually a lifetime friend, who in Tom's undergraduate years was someone available around the campus that could be dropped in on from time to time, "to have a chat." Describing himself quite improbably as a "rambunctious undergraduate," Tom also recalled an exchange with the renowned Canadian historian Donald Creighton. The conversation was initiated when the young student ventured an observation in relation to some episode in the life of John A. Macdonald, whose biography was the keystone of Creighton's work.[5] "Sir, I wasn't sure that that was the right conclusion." The distinguished scholar and prize-winning biographer "reacted splendidly. He was kind and patient and talked it through with me. That was itself a learning experience."[6]

Maurice Careless, George Brown's biographer, was another instructor from Tom's days at the University of Toronto whose influence endured.[7] Careless contributed to Tom's formal education in Canadian history and was also his predecessor as chairman of the Historic Sites and Monuments Board of Canada, where Tom served from 1986 to 1996.

A number of Oxford dons, whom Tom got to know both as a student at Oriel College (1951–53), and during subsequent visits, also helped to shape his outlook and understanding of university education. J. R. R. Tolkein, for example, "conveyed to me what a gift it was to have the imaginative power to create a whole universe."[8] And another was Max Beloff, a prominent twentieth-century historian.[9] Jeremy Catto, a mediaevalist at Oriel, though younger than Tom, also served as "a teacher and a mentor by example" for the considerate manner in which he dealt with students. Tributes accorded Catto on the occasion of his retirement are entirely reminiscent of Tom's own outlook on the importance of university education and the hallmarks of its success. The proposition that no undergraduate would emerge from the tutorial experience "unappreciative of what it means to know how to think," or that "a university education should be the most potent of all civilizing experiences," is entirely consistent with Tom's own commitment to teaching, both in the classroom and in the nurturing of the surrounding institutional environment, the learning community.[10]

Another observation of considerable significance in understanding the intersection between the teaching style and the policy-maker's inquiring attitude emerged in conversation: "The right answer—there isn't always a right answer. There is the best you can do under the circumstances, or what may be and that is so very often the situation, rather than black and white."[11] This disposition to consider circumstances and to measure performance in context is another characteristic of a theory of learning that resonates equally in the policy sphere.

Tom's own classroom career began in the fall of 1953 at the University of Toronto where, despite his own specialization in Canadian and Commonwealth History, he faced the interesting challenge of teaching Medieval and Renaissance History and Greek and Roman History. Notably, he continued to teach throughout his term as president at Trent. This was a First Year Canadian History seminar, proceeding chronologically with an emphasis on the foundational period leading up to Confederation, but continuing through to the middle of the twentieth century. More thematic elements dominating the latter segment of the course included a cluster of seminars on the North in Canada, or the contemporary challenges of bilingualism and multiculturalism. The commercial and economic dimensions of Canadian history, together with their interpreters, were not absent from the curriculum, but the perspectives of former teacher Donald Creighton and of W. L. Morton, who came to Trent from Manitoba, were more enthusiastically embraced.

Despite the curiosity, perhaps even the astonishment, of fellow university presidents, such as Claude Bissell of Toronto, that he was actually teaching an undergraduate course at the First Year level, Tom considered this an essential aspect of his contribution to Trent. To manage the scheduling challenges, at the beginning of the year, "I simply put in the dates of my seminar. And all the other stuff that pushes and shoves around had to push and shove around those dates." Tom considered the Canadian History seminar "far and away" the single most rewarding experience on his agenda.[12]

For students, a class with the president of the university called for something of an adjustment in demeanor and may have notched the anxiety level up just a little. Nevertheless, the president's willingness to engage the class in participatory conversational exploration of the subject at hand is fully corroborated. One student, responding to a course evaluation inquiry to rate the instructor's effectiveness in tutorials and seminars, commented that "Prof. Symons has an excellent way of encouraging those who are shy or apprehensive and a polite way of cutting off the students who might tend to monopolize." In the words of another, Professor Symons's love of Canadian history was "palpable," such that he "infused" the subject into his students, often encouraging an enduring respect and curiosity for the story of Canada.

Veterans of the early years of the Canadian History seminar had absolutely nothing to recall in conversation about the life and times of Samuel Champlain. Instead, they were more likely to remember being encouraged or invited by the president to assume some responsibility for guiding visitors to the new university, or for serving on a planning committee, or being personally introduced to national and community leaders or aboriginal elders who were on campus for a speech or a meeting. They were equally inclined to say they believed Professor Symons was proud of his students, or even that he was "immensely tolerant of the foibles (unspecified) of seventeen- and eighteen-year-olds." *Peterborough Examiner* coverage of a student protest at a Mike Pearson speech in Lindsay against the unfortunate—for students who were not yet residents of their new university communities—timing of the 1965 election included a readily identifiable photograph of one of the participants. The student in question recalls a very respectful discussion with his History professor, informally initiated with a soft-spoken inquiry, "... I suppose you've seen this."

In response to a question about the elements of successful teaching, Tom offered these observations:

> You would always reflect after a class about whether you would have done it more efficaciously if you had done a different approach or sequence. In other classes there would be a magic experience when you could watch your students digesting a point. And you could almost see occasionally a light go on. And it was particularly rewarding when this might happen with a student who was not obviously of a scholarly mind or background. Anybody can take a first class student and turn out a first class student. What is really challenging is to take students who haven't yet been awakened to the challenge of learning. . . . and help them to find those things.[13]

The summing up of successful teaching corresponds directly with Tom's own assessment of the contribution he attributes to his own early teachers and mentors: "Learning feeds the quest for more learning."[14] Trent graduates, at least, will note the congruence between this aspiration and the university's motto, *Nunc cognosco ex parte,* taken from Paul's First Letter to the Corinthians 13:12: "When I was a child, I spoke as a child, I understood as a child, I thought as a child: but when I became a man I put away childish things. For now we see through a glass, darkly; but then face to face: now I know in part, but then shall I know even also as I am known."

Elements of this conception of learning as a lifelong journey oriented around self-understanding appear equally in *To Know Ourselves: The Report of the Commission on Canadian Studies.* The rationale for Canadian Studies embodies this perspective:

> An otherwise intellectually alert person who lacks self-knowledge will be constantly at odds with himself. He will be constantly tripping. . . over his own feet. Lacking self-knowledge, he will inevitably entertain a false conception of himself and must try to act, more or less adequately, in accord with that false assumption. Moreover, his attempt to act in a certain manner to comply with that conception may change his nature just enough to add to the confusion.

The Canadian Studies report asserts that self-knowledge is equally relevant at the scale of society or nation, and does so with direct reference to the theme of communities that figured so prominently in Symons's teaching:

> If. . . the citizens of a country, which in reality is composed of many diverse regions and more than one culture, think of it as a homogenous country that can and should be governed in a uniform manner through centralized institutions, this idea of the country will appear to receive confirmation from the fact that its leaders do attempt to govern in this manner. If the citizens are not alive to the contradictions inherent in this false image of the country, the conflicts within the country may be exacerbated rather than contained or ameliorated.

To complete the cycle of learning, the report underlines the close ties between individual self-knowledge and understanding of the social context. "Hence, if a Canadian is to seek the self-knowledge that is essential for both health and wisdom, he must have access to a wider self-knowledge of his historical community and its contemporary circumstances." That was the ultimate answer to the foundational question: "Why be concerned with Canadian studies?"[15]

What eventually became Tom's trademark course was initially introduced in 1979–80, when, having resigned as university president in 1972, he returned to Trent as Vanier Professor after a period of active engagement in a range of other educational and policy-related activities. Canadian Studies 403 began as a course on the intellectual and cultural life of Canada, later evolving into The Vanier Seminar on Cultural Policy in Canada. This was an interdisciplinary experience drawing heavily upon original documents and reports, frequently supplemented by the classroom participation of the authors.

In its 1993–94 iteration, the prospectus provided the following indication of what might lie ahead:

> An interdisciplinary seminar to examine the inter-relationships between culture, education and public policy, and the formulation and operation of Canadian public policy in the fields of culture and knowledge.
>
> The seminar will explore public policy issues and processes in the areas of culture and knowledge, including: questions about the condition and prospects of the arts and letters in Canada; the state of education and research as the knowledge base of culture and of informed public policy; and the problems and opportunities which arise from the cultural diversity of Canada.
>
> The human rights dimensions of cultural, educational, and public policy questions will be an important aspect of the seminar's work throughout the year.
>
> The seminar will also examine some of the cultural and educational dimensions of Canadian foreign policy.

Contemporary issues of Canadian cultural policy and the institutional arrangements in which they were under examination were specifically selected to form the basis for an enriched classroom experience. And, one imagines, the classroom experience may well have reciprocated through its contribution to Tom's ongoing intellectual odyssey.

Any number of Symons's intellectual forays might serve to illustrate his enduring curiosity in combination with a firm commitment to give a little something in return. Publishing, library science and administration, statistical compilation and census analysis, cultural heritage, human rights, and commonwealth studies all come to mind. But for the sake of illustration, the North will do.

Symons served on the boards of the Arctic Institute of North America (1981–85) as well as the Northern Studies Trust of the Association of Canadian Universities for Northern Studies (1982–90) before assuming the position of chair with the Northern Science Award Selection Committee (1986–90) and the Canadian Polar Research Commission Study (1988–90).[16] He headed up the Science Council of Canada's 1990 Conference on Northern Science and Northern Society, and a few years later played a comparable role in the Meta Incognita Project of the Canadian Museum of Civilization.[17]

Insights and professional acquaintances from the kinds of institutional contact and policy-making inquiries in which Symons participated regularly made their way back to the Vanier Seminar. Student reports flesh out the operational details.

> The weekly seminars, involving students from a myriad of disciplines, usually begin with a group discussion and analysis of various news articles, press releases and government policies on issues ranging from Quebec independence to the Governor General's Book Awards, crime statistics in Canada to diseased bison, and heritage railway stations to education spending. In the process, the members are challenged to be critical and thorough in their analyses of the issues, such that the seminar invariably leads into a heated and insightful debate.

The seminar culminated annually in a trip to Ottawa for meetings and discussions between participating students and some of the policymakers and cultural administrators who had hands-on responsibility for files the students might have been studying. By way of illustration, the 1991 iteration of the cultural studies field trip involved meetings with the Hon. Robert Stanfield; Dr. Christina Cameron, Director General of National Historic Parks and Sites; James Page, Education Support Programme of the Secretary of State; Hugh Winsor, *Globe and Mail*; Dr. Marianne Scott, National Librarian; Dr. Ivan Fellegi, Chief Statistician; Dr. Dan Gallacher, Canadian Museum of Civilization;

Dr. Max Yalden, Canadian Human Rights Commission; and Jean Pigott, chair of the National Capital Commission.[18]

The testimonials are legion, but one will serve. Its author, a mid-career high school teacher of English with the Lambton County Board of Education, spent a sabbatical year at Trent in 1979–80, enrolling in five Canadian Studies courses. His report to the school board refers to Canadian Studies 403 as a seminar on "the current state of Canadian intellectual and cultural life." He concluded, "In retrospect, I think my association with Tom Symons. . . a man who instills love of country, the understanding and objectivity of the scholar along with a passion for the curing of injustices in a reasoned, humanistic manner, could alone justify my year at Trent."[19]

This observation, emphasizing the integration of scholarly objectivity alongside a humanistic concern for society in the context of the Vanier Seminar, might equally refer to another dimension of Tom Symons's contribution to teaching—his openness to interdisciplinary inquiry. Programs in Native Studies, in Environment and Resource Studies, and, of course, in Canadian Studies were initiated while he presided at Trent and reflect a considerable sympathy for the innovative proposals advanced in various quarters of the university in response to broad and emerging educational challenges.

President Symons's sympathy for interdisciplinary teaching and research, and his willingness to encourage interdisciplinary experiments in learning, emerged from a couple of sources. First, given his own educational formation, he found that "history is a comfortable jumping off pad for inter-disciplinarity because every discipline has a history and their histories flow into one and other." Second, given his concern for Canada, he reflects that his interest in its totality was also a contributing factor:

> In the address at the opening of the university I said that I hoped the university would become among other things a centre for the study of Canadian civilization. . . and if you feel that way about an entity you must look at its science, its terrain. . .[20]

Colleagues from Laval—Marc-Adélard Tremblay, an anthropologist, and Louis Hamelin, a geographer who pioneered the concept of 'nordicity' as a comprehensive framework for studies of the North[21]—credited Tom with "the Symons theorem" on Canadianity, a concern for "the totality of the civilization."[22] Their enthusiasm for "the Canadianity thing" may have been a principal stimulus for Tom's willingness to contemplate and promote interdisciplinarity.

The teaching legacy extends well outside the classroom, even taking into account the cosmopolitan atmosphere that participants in the Vanier Seminar might have encountered and the "totality" aspects of interdisciplinarity. Tom's perspective on the conditions necessary for effective university teaching was very wide ranging. It was initially articulated in advisory work carried out for the University of Toronto President Sidney Smith and was subsequently introduced in practice as his own career in academic administration got underway.

As dean of Devonshire House at the University of Toronto during the 1950s, Symons had observed that the crowded and dated facilities of the University's Residence for Men might have reached a state where they were "detrimental to the academic work and well-being of members."[23] He was, more broadly, sympathetic to the proposition that "where and how a student lives is of large educational significance."[24] Beneficial effects of suitable residential arrangements on learning were by no means confined to the individual:

> The nature of undergraduate activities and outlooks, the degree of sympathy between student and Faculty, the notion of the University as a community of scholars, the educational capacity of the University itself, will all be affected by the point of view which members of a successful Residence carry with them about the campus.[25]

After elaborating upon these and related themes to wider audiences over a period of years,[26] Symons spearheaded planning for the development of new residential colleges at the University of Toronto. In concluding an extensive report on the operational and planning implications of an expanded college system at Toronto, he highlighted the educational attractions and potential of the proposed arrangements:

> The new Colleges. . . would. . . also make it possible, for the first time really, for members of the non-Arts Faculties to share extensively in the advantages of a College system.
>
> The new Colleges would. . . be the means of preserving within a large and expanding university many of the special values of a smaller academic community. In these Colleges the student could obtain many of the academic advantages—of tutorials and instruction, of association, and of environment—which must otherwise be lost in a very large university.
>
> The colleges would make a vital contribution to preserving the reality of an academic community within the university as it grows larger. They would provide perhaps the only effective means of bridging the gaps which have developed between the various faculties and departments, and of countering the tendency to isolation between the many divisions of the university.[27]

The formative elements of the institutional design for Trent University explicitly reflected similar ideas a few years later. An intellectual orientation that emphasized collegial conversation was embodied in the vision Symons formulated for Trent University. Colleges, as settings for ongoing interaction in social contexts as well as the intellectual exchange generated through tutorial and seminar instruction, made an important contribution. As the president remarked at the opening ceremonies:

> The philosophy which inspires Trent is based upon the conviction that education is, inescapably, an individual experience—individual to each student, to each teacher, and to every scholar who may come to it. And this philosophy is reflected in the teaching methods of Trent University which seek to encourage each student to find a close and direct contact with his teachers through the tutorial and seminar approach to instruction.[28]

Some years later he re-visited the question of learning priorities in the university setting, stating even more strongly the fundamental place of the search for knowledge in the framework:

> The most important thing about university education is, or should be, its commitment to the ideal of knowledge for its own sake. That is not to say that knowledge is not useful, or that it cannot play a helpful role in promoting many good causes: social justice, health, and the alleviation of pain, economic improvement, enhancement of the quality of life, growth in the arts, scientific and technological break-throughs, and much more. But the bottom line is—and must, I think, always be—the goal of knowledge for its own sake. The other things will follow.[29]

The thrust of "small group learning," as it was often described, tilted strongly towards the participatory end of the participation-pontification spectrum of teaching. From the outset, faculty encouraged students to respond to questions, make presentations, and express their views and opinions—preferably on the basis of some familiarity with the reading list. Discussion initiated with something along the lines of "What do you think about so-and-so's criticism of what's-his-name's explanation of. . ." were clearly intended to encourage a degree of information processing and analysis going well beyond the mere accumulation of facts and data. Thus, in a History class, for example, those who had not moved much past limited familiarity with dates and names might find the discussion a bit awkward at times.

The physical and social configuration of the evolving Trent campus was intended, like the earlier institutional reform proposals at Toronto, to encourage the kind of intellectual contact, interaction, and collegiality that Symons had found so rewarding in his own education and upbringing. "It is, of course, important that there be good teaching in the classroom and in the laboratory," he acknowledged. But he was equally insistent that "perhaps the most important teaching at a good university takes place outside the classroom and outside the hours of formal instruction. Students learn as much, or more, from one another than they do from their professors."[30]

Bus travel figured prominently as an initial contributor to social interaction, as students and faculty alike shuttled around the somewhat disjointed circuit of residential and industrial structures that had been reconstituted as Trent's initial halls of learning. One former student, the proud owner of a small Vauxhall, also recalls with some amazement that on occasion the president piled in alongside a few fellow classmates to travel to college dinner following a History tutorial. In time, however, campus construction made its own distinctive contribution to the social experience of learning in the context of a growing community.

In 1963, Ron Thom, a prominent and highly regarded architect then in the midst of construction for Massey College at the University of Toronto, accepted an invitation to oversee Trent's master planning process. Professor Denis Smith, one of the small group of founders who, along with Tom Symons, recruited Thom to his task, later remarked that "the buildings that rose on the banks of the Otonabee River over the next eight years were an embodiment of the University's ideals, an enrichment of a beautiful natural site, as close to perfection as a great work of art can be." Ron Thom made the connection between Tom Symons's ideals for the university and the natural setting in which it was established. As Smith explained, "The University's academic inspiration was collegiate, drawn from medieval European sources; but it is a twentieth century North American institution, whose roots had to be set in its own province and country and time."[31] Distinctive collegial spaces continue to contribute to a sense of clustered but not cloistered communities across the evolving campus.

In a trenchant response to what he perceived to be an unwarranted criticism of some aspects of collegial life in the early years of Trent's existence, Symons set out a more elaborate rationale and justification for the efforts made to promote a sense of belonging and community. "Relationships between students and faculty, and amongst students, amongst faculty, and of both students and faculty with administration, are crucial to the success of a university, as a place of learning and in every other way," he continued to argue. But in looking back on the 1970s, a period of considerable turmoil in university settings across North America, Symons asserted that the comparative level of civility maintained at Trent was not simply a matter of good fortune. Trent, he insisted, was—at least in part—"spared most of the appalling, destructive, and costly infighting that occurred. . . at universities almost everywhere in the 1970s because of the good relationships and trust that were built up, as a habit and standard, during its formative years." He underscored how those relationships had been nurtured. "It was not chance. It was hard work. And it helped to avoid the collapse of a sense of community that occurred elsewhere."[32]

The hard work extended well beyond Symons's genuine concern for the quality of the built environment and its natural setting, for "you are not going to have a great place of learning without scholarly values." Faculty recruitment, accordingly, constituted another vital responsibility for Symons as a founding university president. And it is entirely appropriate to include such hiring among his contributions to teaching: "Good education involves good teaching. It depends on good teaching." He has repeatedly emphasized—invoking on occasion the dictum of Henry Adams—"a teacher is for eternity. One can never tell where his or her influence ceases."[33] In the formative period of Trent's development there were some distinctive considerations. "[Y]ou had to look for people who were prepared to engage in an adventure and share in an initiating experience, be open to innovation and be creative." There was equally an effort to fill administrative ranks with those who, as Tom put it, "liked and respected students," and were thus willing to serve as academic advisors to students, to participate in college life, and perhaps to even engage in some teaching.[34]

As a final gesture after stepping down as founding president, and to underscore the significance of the teacher's role, Tom—together with Christine—established the Symons Teaching Award. Its objective, very successfully achieved on the basis of the outstanding recipients over more than thirty years, was to recognize good teaching and, importantly, "exemplary concern for students." Over a number of years, roughly comparable acknowledgements of the accomplishments of teachers and students were established at numerous institutions where Symons had been invited to speak on various aspects of higher education. He typically redirected whatever honorarium had been offered to seed small endowments for these purposes.[35] These contributions are entirely in keeping with Symons's own formulation of a personal rationale for his career in education: "You just bloody have to care about students. That's what matters. That's why I started the university."[36]

Notwithstanding the emphasis on the individual student experience of learning that is so often underscored in Symons's remarks on education, it is worthwhile in closing to recall the social and community-based context in which learning takes place, and to note the integration, linkages, and consistency between his career in education and the wider array of policy fields to which he contributed. A 2009 speech at an Ontario Heritage gathering, while seemingly quite unrelated to Tom's career in university education, is illustrative of his views on the relationship between learning and context:

> Today, we recognize that our communities are unique, that each has been shaped by geography, and by the beliefs and values of its founders and their desire to build something they could leave to their children and grandchildren. Communities evolve, slowly. And the best communities have one foot firmly planted in the past as they move into the future. Over the years, the shape and colour of that future has changed. Just as our definition of the term 'heritage' has expanded to include the natural environment, landscapes and myriad cultural components, we now recognize that 'heritage,' 'arts,' and 'culture,' are not three separate and distinct entities, but integral parts of each other. Creativity and recognition of the importance of 'creative workers' are key to each of the three components. There is growing recognition that, at the nexus of these creative forces, there is an opportunity to stimulate the economy, foster innovation, and enhance the quality of life.[37]

Here familiar themes intertwine. The acquisition of knowledge, including self-knowledge, is an ongoing and dynamic process intimately connected with the diverse historic experience of communities. Subjects that might appear to be separate and unrelated may eventually be more fully understood in their "totality" as "integral parts of each other." The knowledge gained from patient reflection and inquiry is valuable, not only for itself but for its potential practical and applied contributions to a collective well-being that extends throughout interrelated cultural, economic, and environmental dimensions—and across generations. So, there is always something to talk about: MWDP?

Notes

1 I am grateful to Paul Delaney, Richard Johnston, Harvey McCue, Norman Moyer, and Andrew Robinson for providing insights and personal reminiscences.

2 Federal Cultural Policy Review Committee (Applebaum-Hébert Commission), member, 1979–82; Ministerial Commission on French Language Secondary Education in Ontario, chair, 1971–72; Ontario Advisory Committee on Confederation, member, 1965–72; Task Force on the Native Peoples and Employment Opportunities in the Public Service of Canada, member, 1975–76; Ontario Human Rights Commission task force to review the state of human rights in Ontario, chair, 1976–78.

3 Interview with T. H. B. Symons, 16 February 2007.

4 *The Idea of the University: Community, Scholarship, and Learning, Notes for Remarks*, 24 March 1994.

5 *John A. Macdonald*, 2 vols., (Toronto: Macmillan, 1952–55).

6 Interview with T. H. B. Symons, 16 February 2007.

7 *Brown of the Globe*, 2 vols. (Toronto: Macmillan, 1959–63).

8 Interview with T. H. B. Symons, 16 February 2007.

9 *Imperial Sunset* (London: Methuen, 1969).

10 Alan Duncan, "A Don Who Embodies the Idea of a University," *The Spectator*, 10 June 2006, 16.

11 Interview with T. H. B. Symons, 16 February 2007.

12 Ibid.

13 Ibid.

14 Ibid.

15 *To Know Ourselves*, 14–15.

16 *The Shield of Achilles: The Report of the Canadian Polar Research Commission Study*, T. H. B. Symons, Chair, Ottawa: DIAND, 1988.

17 T. H. B. Symons, ed., *Meta Incognita: A Discourse of Discovery: Martin Frobisher's Arctic Expeditions, 1576–1578*, 2 vols. (Ottawa: Canadian Museum of Civilization, 1999).

18 Rod Cumming and Shirley Hunt, "From the Classrooms of Trent to the Boardrooms of Ottawa: Vanier Seminar in Canadian Cultural Policy," *Trent Alumnus* (1991): 6.

19 John F. Burke, "Report on the 1979–80 Sabbatical Leave of John F. Burke," Trent Archives, Symons Papers, 31 December 1980, 2.

20 Interview with T. H. B. Symons, 16 February 2007.

21 *Canadian Nordicity* (Montreal: Harvest House, 1979).

22 Interview with T. H. B. Symons, 16 February 2007.

23 T. H. B. Symons, "A Report on Residence Requirements at the University of Toronto" December 1956, 1.

24 Ibid., 6.

25 Ibid., 12.

26 T. H. B. Symons, "Are University Residences Beneficial Academically?" (A paper presented to the Thirty-Third Annual Meeting of the National Conference of Canadian Universities, Ottawa, June 1957); T. H. B. Symons and R. L. Watts, "The Residence Hall and the University: An aspect of a liberal education," *Queen's Quarterly* 64, no. 4 (1958).

27 T. H. B. Symons, "The Planning and Operation of Some New Residential Colleges at the University of Toronto: A report prepared for the committee on policy and planning of the University of Toronto," March 1961.

28 Opening address, 16.

29 *The Idea of the University: Community, Scholarship and Learning, Notes for Remarks*, 24 March 1994.

30 Ibid.

31 Denis Smith, Trent Archives, Symons Papers, Accession Number 97-019, Box No: 34, file 4, 1923–86, 5 November 1986.

32 T. H. B. Symons to David McRobert, 11 May 1987.

33 *The Idea of the University: Community, Scholarship and Learning, Notes for Remarks*, 24 March 1994.

34 Interview with T. H. B. Symons, 16 February 2007.

35 Symons Scholarship in Canadian Studies, McMaster University; Symons Fund for Canadian Studies, College-Universitaire de Saint Boniface, University of Manitoba; Symons Prize in Canadian Studies, Lakefield College School; Symons Award in Canadian Studies, Crescent School; Symons Prize for Canadian Studies, Upper Canada College; Dorothy Symons Scholarship in Canadian Studies, Havergal College; Symons Library Endowment Fund, Lethbridge University.

36 Interview with T. H. B. Symons, 16 February 2007.

37 Notes for Remarks to the Opening Session of the 2009 Ontario Heritage Conference: Heritage in Creative Communities, 29 May 2009.

CHAPTER 4

He Walked in Our Moccasins and Mukluks: Tom Symons and Native and Northern Studies and Policy

HARVEY McCUE

In the fall of 1967, following a successful political campaign the previous spring to become the third president of the Champlain College Student Council at Trent University, I began my third year of undergraduate studies (and my second year at Trent) eager to immerse myself in campus politics. I was also mindful that, as a status Indian undergraduate, I had membership in a small, very small, group of university students. In 1964, my high school graduation year, there were fewer than ninety status Indian undergraduates throughout Canada—eighty-eight to be exact. Although the enrolment had increased by 1967, nationally the group was still very modest, numbering only one hundred and forty-two!

Sometime before the end of the autumn term, I received a note from the president's office informing me that the president of the university, T. H. B. Symons, wished to meet. Because of the unique college system that Tom and his colleagues implemented at Trent, my principal political relationship as a student politician revolved around the faculty head of the college, the master, leaving little or no reason for me or the other two student college presidents at Trent to interact with the university president other than on a social basis. Consequently, I had some apprehension over the invitation—I neither knew him nor had we developed any kind of meaningful connection during my previous year. Although, early in my tenure as student president, some tension had emerged among Champlain students over the college master's edict concerning the wearing of ties to dinner, there didn't seem to be any campus political issue to warrant a face-to-face meeting with the president, particularly since the grief over the wearing of ties was essentially a tempest in a teapot.

Nevertheless, I soon found myself in what amounted to a private meeting with Tom Symons on what would prove to be a topic of immense importance to us both. After the introductory pleasantries and the pouring of tea, Tom informed me that he had nurtured a long-standing interest in Aboriginal people (since this was 1967, I believe the term he used was "Native people") and that he now desired to use his position as president of a university to turn that interest into something tangible. He asked what might he do, and more specifically, what might the university do, to assist Aboriginal people?

During a long silence punctuated by numerous sips of tea, it occurred to me that here was an opportunity to address the appallingly small numbers of Aboriginal university students. It wasn't clear to me at the time how that might be done, but in the face of Tom's request I suggested that any effort he might make to increase the tiny population of Aboriginal students on university campuses, particularly First Nations students at Trent, would be welcomed. Learning just how small the national First Nations university cohort was for the current academic year, Tom thought that this was, indeed, an issue worth pursuing. After exchanging some preliminary ideas on how Trent might address it, we agreed to a further meeting in two weeks to review any possibilities.

Two weeks later, Tom and I began to examine the ins and outs of how Trent might increase the presence of First Nations and other Aboriginal students. We eventually agreed that if Trent could offer courses that spoke directly to the many issues that affected First Nations people and their communities, such as health, federal legislation, the justice system, urbanization, education, community development, and cultural revitalization, not only might they encourage First Nations students to graduate from high school so they could study subject matter of special interest to them at a university, but they might also benefit non-Aboriginal students at Trent, for whom the provincial elementary and secondary school curricula have been typically bereft of anything more than a passing glance on Aboriginal topics. Furthermore, we agreed, if the courses could address Métis and Inuit topics, students from these cultures might be similarly influenced. At the conclusion of our discussion, Tom spoke sincerely about his commitment to our shared objective and he indicated that he was keen to take on the challenge to make Trent more accessible to Aboriginal students sooner rather than later.

To a certain extent, Tom had anticipated these critical initial meetings and discussions by guiding the appointment of Dr. Gilbert (Slim) Monture, a distinguished public servant and a member of the Iroquois nation, to the Trent Board of Governors in 1966. Dr. Monture's position on the board not only reflected Tom's desire to facilitate Aboriginal people taking their rightful place in Canadian society, it also emphasized his commitment to make it a reality.

Tom continued to refine his interest in Native Studies by meeting with faculty in Aboriginal Studies in several universities in Australia during his visit there in the summer of 1968. These meetings included the head and faculty of the Australian Institute of Aboriginal Studies at Canberra, and the feedback gained from these discussions served to confirm his decision on a Native Studies initiative at Trent.

Two short years later, in September 1969, Trent became the first—and for several years the only—university in Canada and the second in North America (quite independent of Trent's action, the University of Minnesota established the Department of American Indian Studies simultaneously) to offer undergraduates courses in a program of studies that focused exclusively on First Nations and Aboriginal academic content. The first course in the soon-to-be developed program, Canadian Indian Studies 10, appeared in the Trent calendar in the academic year 1969–70. It had an enrolment of twenty-eight, five of whom were First Nations students, and Charles Torok, a member of the anthropology faculty, served as the inaugural instructor. The Trent summer school calendar from 1970 included the same course jointly instructed by Torok and me with a substantially increased student enrolment of eighty-two.

In January of 1969, the university senate struck a committee—the Working Committee on Indian Studies—to investigate further the creation of a program of studies at Trent that would, in 1972, become the Department of Native Studies. Faculty members included Professors Ken Kidd (anthropology), who served as chair of the Working Committee; Jack Stanford (psychology); Charles Torok; and Dean Tom Nind, in an *ex officio* capacity. Non-faculty members were Dr. Walter Currie, and me, as the full-time committee secretary. Mrs. W. H. Clark from Toronto also participated in the capacity of a corresponding member.

While some of us were deliberating earnestly the potential width and breadth of the new program, many others in and outside the university were mildly skeptical, at best, and surly, at worst, about the efforts to define the new program and establish it as an academic program of university-level studies. Significant impediments lay ahead.

Since the 1920s, academic research and study of Aboriginal people rested almost exclusively with anthropologists, principally ethnologists, throughout Canadian universities. This approach continued well into the 1970s. Consequently, university courses on Indians and Inuit and their cultures were fairly common in many anthropology departments and were taught either by ethnologists, archeologists, or linguists. Without exception, these courses rarely, if ever, went beyond the theoretical foundations and categories within anthropology; as a result, the content that could have informed students about the political, economic, and social history of Aboriginal people simply didn't exist.

It was a challenging task to convince a community of scholars, which had minimal, if any, scholarly contact with Aboriginal people, of the importance of a program of studies that focused entirely on this largely ignored tile of the Canadian mosaic. What made it even tougher was the realization, by other faculty members, that any new academic program would be taking money out of the budgets of the existing departments to get it off the ground.

As challenging as the academic environment might be towards Tom's vision, the times in general did not offer a positive or fertile foundation for its realization either. "Out of sight, out of mind" summarized Canadians' attitudes towards the Aboriginal population in Canada throughout the first half of the twentieth century, notwithstanding the enormous contributions Native men and women made during the two World Wars as volunteer servicemen and servicewomen. Canada's centenary in 1967 and the celebratory jewel, Expo '67, had been a huge success domestically as well as internationally. It signaled a virtual coming of age for Canada as a whole, yet Aboriginal people steadfastly remained in the country's political and social background, featured only when a politician or an event like Expo '67 required some Native colour, usually feathered-festooned dancers, to add an exotic note to the proceedings. Few Canadians remembered or cared that it was only a scant seven years before Expo that status Indians were able to vote in federal elections for the first time since Confederation. It took another eight years, in 1968, before the first status Indian, Len Marchand, sat in the House of Commons.

Throughout the excitement and optimism produced by Expo, few Canadians knew or cared that more than fifty Indian residential schools still operated throughout Canada and that Indian Agents maintained their iron-fisted dominance over the affairs of the majority of Indian reserves. Despite the general negligence shown by the country towards its Aboriginal population up to and including Expo '67, times were about to change, making Tom's willingness to invest the resources of Trent in the stock of Native Studies not just prescient but visionary. As Dr. Joe Couture, a former chair of Native Studies, remarked in his 1982 memoir,

> Throughout virtually all of Indian North America, 1969–70 marks the moment of the emergence of the Indian movement toward self-determination. That period witnessed the beginning of wide-spread organizational development. Both politically-oriented and service-directed units proliferated across the country.[1]

National and regional First Nations and Métis political organizations sprang up and enabled Aboriginal leaders to unify to express their concerns and visions to policy makers and politicians at all levels throughout Canada. Building on the early efforts of urban First Nations in 1964 to create the Thunderbird Club in Toronto as a venue for cultural and social exchanges, the first Indian Friendship Centre emerged in Toronto in 1972. In Alberta, the Nechi Institute, an Aboriginal addiction counselor training program, emerged in 1974 as a result of the formative work of the Indian Association of Alberta, the Métis Association of Alberta, and the Native Communications Society to create the Native Training Institute in 1969.[2] Tom's vision for a university program that, by its presence, would stimulate the expansion of the university population of Aboriginal students was part and parcel of the Aboriginal self-determination movement.

Symons's objective of providing an academic environment where Aboriginal and non-Aboriginal students could research, analyze, and discuss issues and topics particular to Aboriginal people proved to be a critical stimulus for many others elsewhere. From the outset, Native Studies at Trent blazed an innovative and remarkable trail in Canadian academia, setting standards for others that soon followed. In 1975, Brandon University and the University of Manitoba were the first institutions to emulate Trent's inaugural program with their own Native Studies programs. The following year, the Saskatchewan Indian Federated College emerged as a First Nations' governed and administered college within the academic structure of the University of Regina.

Universities in other provinces soon followed suit and, by the end of the 1980s, colleges and universities in most provinces featured either a Native Studies program or department. Today, they are firmly situated in universities and colleges in every province; in some provinces, like British Columbia, Alberta, and Ontario, a majority of post-secondary institutions offer either Aboriginal, Native, or Indigenous studies.

From its academic inception in 1969, several thousand Aboriginal (Inuit, Métis, and First Nations) post-secondary students have enrolled at Trent to study and research issues and topics that are germane to the future of their communities and cultures; countless thousands of other Trent students have taken undergraduate or graduate courses that enabled them to understand the rightful place of Aboriginal people and cultures in Canada's history and contemporary society.

From day one, Native Studies at Trent took its rightful place in the university academic budget as a fixed line item. This was different from other Canadian universities, where similar programs that quickly followed Trent's lead had to survive on a precarious and unpredictable diet of soft money derived from one-time external grants or special, temporary internal funds for vital expenses such as instructors' salaries and administrative costs.

Tom's commitment to our initial discussions in 1967 never wavered throughout his tenure as Trent's founding president. Its addition to the university budget as a regular academic program of study provided the financial stability that enabled faculty and administrators to engage in the long-term planning and development essential to the growth of a new discipline and signaled unequivocally the university's commitment to its newest academic addition. Equally important, the university's senior officers and Senate recognized the fundamental importance of staffing Aboriginal faculty for the department and, in so doing, approved the academic appointments of Aboriginal scholars as department chairs and as a majority of departmental faculty from its second year of operation in 1970 to the present.

In July of 1971, Trent appointed Walter Currie, an original member of the Working Committee and a recognized Potawatomi-Ojibway educator, as chair of Native Studies, a position he held until 1975. Walter's appointment as chair followed my own brief appointment as acting chair in 1971. Dr. Joe Couture, a prominent Alberta Cree-Métis activist and cultural scholar, served as Native Studies' second full-time Aboriginal chair from 1975 until 1979. Trent also became the first Canadian university to appoint Aboriginal scholars on an ongoing basis, as full-time and tenured faculty whose scholarship was achieved in the field of Aboriginal cultures and languages.

Trent reinforced Tom's seminal and early commitment to Native Studies by approving a Native Studies MA program in 1986. It emerged as a result of the department joining the Frost Centre for Canadian Heritage and Development Studies in 1985, which subsequently led to the creation of the first doctoral program in Native Studies (now Indigenous Studies) in Canada in 1997. It admitted its first doctoral candidates in 1999.

Tom's interest in Aboriginal people extended well beyond his responsibilities at Trent. An active member of the Indian-Eskimo Association (IEA) since 1966, a few years after its formation, he became a member of its national board in 1967.

The IEA emerged from the National Commission on the Canadian Indian, a citizen's organization created in 1957 and chaired by Mrs. W. H. Clark, to examine the difficulties Indians experienced when they relocated to more urban areas. Three years later, the commission concluded that the issues and difficulties of Canada's first peoples required the participation of not just interested citizens but also of the Aboriginal people themselves. To meet this requirement, and to continue the efforts by interested Canadians that led to the creation of the National Commission in the first place, the IEA was formed and incorporated in 1960 with Mrs. Clark as its first president.

As a national organization committed to Aboriginal issues and topics, the IEA became a leading voice in Canada on a range of political, economic, and social concerns affecting First Nations and Inuit communities. Its goal was to ensure that all Aboriginal people had opportunities for progress and fulfillment equal to those of other Canadians. Among its many functions, it encouraged and facilitated the formation of several First Nations and Inuit political organizations; organized workshops on Aboriginal housing, community, and economic development; published and distributed a range of relevant publications; and provided advice and support to Aboriginal communities, leaders, and organizations on different legal matters. By 1968, about one third of its fifty-four directors were Aboriginal.

Tom played an active role as a member of the IEA board. In 1969, as a member of the Association's Legal and Research Committee for the project "Treaty and Aboriginal Rights of Canadian Indians and Eskimos," he participated in the work that led to the publication in 1970 of the seminal *Native Rights in Canada*,[3] an IEA publication that highlighted for the first time in Canada the legal and historical foundation of Aboriginal rights. In 1972, in conjunction with General Publishing, the Association published a revised and expanded version, *Native Rights in Canada: Second Edition*.[4] Tom's advice and comments as the second edition progressed, along with revisions to the original text and additional subject matter, enabled the editors to claim, correctly, that it was substantially a new book.

Both books appeared at a remarkable time in the history of Aboriginal-Canadian relations. One year before the publication of the first edition, the federal government, under the leadership of Prime

Minister Pierre Trudeau and the Minister of Indian Affairs and Northern Development, Jean Chrétien, presented the "Statement of the Government of Canada on Indian Policy, 1969"[5] to the First Session of the twenty-eighth Parliament. Its many recommendations included an end to the special relationship between First Nations and the federal government, removal of the legislative and constitutional basis of discrimination and, in particular, the termination of the historic treaties between the Crown and treaty Indians across the nation.

The 1969 White Paper, as the federal statement came to be known, drew sharp and immediate critical responses from First Nations leaders, who, in concert with concerned non-First Nations supporters, campaigned strenuously for its revocation. Confronted by widespread opposition, the federal government withdrew it in 1971. *Native Rights in Canada* could not have been a stronger and more timely ally for the White Paper opponents, with its sound legal and historical research on the Proclamation of 1763, for example, and the legal bases for Aboriginal and treaty rights in Canada.

Tom's presence at the IEA marked the growing strength throughout Canada of Aboriginal political organizations. Although federal legislation explicitly banned the formation of organized Aboriginal assemblies during the first half of the twentieth century, national issues like the White Paper, and an effort in the mid-sixties by the federal government to create a national Aboriginal political body, the National Indian Advisory Council, and numerous related regional concerns, led Aboriginal leaders in the south to pursue the creation of their own regional assemblies; thus, in 1968, a national organization, the National Indian Brotherhood (NIB) emerged. Its membership included all the chiefs of the more than six hundred First Nations, and its mandate embraced the protection of treaty rights and the pressing need to convince the federal government for increased and improved social and economic programs for status Indians. Walter Dieter, the first national chief of the NIB met with Tom and other members of the IEA leading up to the formation of the national body as well as with members of the Trent Working Committee on Indian Studies.

Fuelled partly by the rising groundswell among southern Aboriginal leaders and their organizations in opposition to the federal White Paper, and ably assisted by the fieldwork of IEA northern staff, two vital northern Aboriginal political organizations appeared and took shape within the span of two years: the Indian Brotherhood of the Northwest Territories in 1970 and the Inuit Tapirisat of Canada (ITC) in 1971. Nowhere was the IEA more instrumental than in the formation of the ITC, and Tom's role as a director could not have been more timely.

From 18 February to 22 February 1971, several Inuit leaders and elders met in the IEA office in Toronto and in the Senate Room of Trent University in Peterborough for inaugural discussions on the creation of a political organization to represent the Inuit and their interests on a national scale. Several months later, in July of 1971, the ITC's founding conference convened at a special meeting of the IEA hosted by Tom at Trent.

Less than a year later, in June of 1972, he was elected president of the IEA, an office he held for one two-year term. As IEA president, Tom consolidated the concerns among members and numerous Aboriginal leaders, particularly those from the recently minted ITC, over the use of the terms "Indian" and "Eskimo" in the Association's official and legal name. With the emergence and general acceptance in Canada of Inuit as the official term designating all people formerly known as Eskimos, and in keeping with the Association's role in the formation of the ITC, it was evident that the IEA required an official name change. Throughout Canada the term "Indian" was gradually being supplanted by "Native People" as Canadians and Aboriginal people sought a more politically-correct term for First Nations than the one that many regarded as a misnomer. In his first year in office, Tom worked with staff, IEA members, and Aboriginal leaders to identify and adopt officially a new name for the association—the Canadian Association in Support of Native Peoples (CASNP)—in 1972.

During his tenure as president, Tom worked to ensure that the reach of CASNP extended far and wide in the Aboriginal community. He met with members of the Métis political community and offered assistance to the Native Council of Canada, the embryonic national Métis organization established in 1971. He convened meetings with Aboriginal prisoners in Stoney Mountain in Manitoba and held discussions with numerous First Nations political and community leaders and, within the limited CASNP budget, chaired board meetings in Winnipeg and Whitehorse.

As the chair of the Historic Sites and Monuments Board of Canada (HSMBC), from 1986 to 1996, Tom also oversaw an important and critical shift in the board's approach and response to the identification of Aboriginal historic sites. In 1990–91 the HSMBC unveiled a Commemoration of Northern Native History initiative that accepted the designation of sites of spiritual and/or cultural importance to Aboriginal people as historic sites without the "industry standards" criteria for verification and approval. This shift in board policy signaled the validity of Aboriginal oral history as evidence in support of a potential historic site and acknowledged that the First Peoples' history and sense of place were not necessarily similar to Canadian interpretations and, furthermore, that Aboriginal-defined historic sites were equally vital to Canada's history as those that were defined and interpreted by historians and other professionals.

National workshops sponsored by the HSMBC from 1992 to 1994 on the history of Aboriginal people in Canada reinforced the 1990 initiative and established several principles to guide the board in the identification of Aboriginal historic sites: the fundamental importance of Aboriginal traditional knowledge to the understanding of the culture and history of all indigenous peoples; meaningful participatory consultations with Aboriginal groups; and Aboriginal people taking a leading role in presenting their history and culture.[6]

These important developments not only elevated the role of Aboriginal people in helping to identify and define sites of historic importance, but they also contributed to "an approach to commemorating the history of Aboriginal people that is based both in Aboriginal values and in the significance of Aboriginal places to all Canadians."[7]

Tom's keen interest in Aboriginal issues also extended to the land, specifically the northern landscape and its culture. Historically, Canada's interests in the North initially rested primarily on resources—gold in particular—and then later on its strategic location in the defence of North America. Unlike the widespread European pre-colonial incursions throughout the North where either furs or blubber, or both, motivated equally their sponsors and harvesters, Canada's early northern political interests were confined to ensuring a measure of peace during the Yukon gold rush and participating with the American government in the construction of the Distant Early Warning radar stations immediately following the end of the Second World War.

This somewhat myopic view of the value of the North all but disappeared with the 1958 federal election of John Diefenbaker as prime minister. Diefenbaker's popular vision of the North challenged astonished Canadians to recognize, perhaps for the first time in the country's modern history, that our cultural legacies and political responsibilities extended beyond provincial northern borders to include two territories of immense geographic, historic, and cultural content, not to mention untold economic potential and two distinctive Aboriginal people, the Inuit and the Dene. Yet as controversial and appealing as Diefenbaker's northern vision was, it proved too ephemeral and elusive for the majority of southern Canadians to sustain, and its fate as a national stimulant withered and all but disappeared from sight.

Tom's interest in the North may have had its roots in Diefenbaker's quixotic vision, but it assuredly represented an organic extension of his visionary commitment to Native Studies at Trent, his vital role with the Indian-Eskimo Association a decade earlier, and his work as the chair of the Commission on Canadian Studies that came hard on the heels of his IEA involvement in 1972. His initial concerns about the North were raised in the 1975 Commission Report, *To Know Ourselves*:

> Increased attention should be given to Northern Studies in all relevant disciplines, as well as by future development of research institutes and transdisciplinary studies. The northern reaches of Canada are of such vast proportions, and their importance in the life of our country is correspondingly great, that the universities and colleges of Canada should make every provision to ensure that they are suitably treated in the curriculum and that knowledge about the region is steadily enlarged through strong programmes of research and publication.[8]

Several years later, in a presentation at the third Annual Conference of the Association of Canadian Universities for Northern Studies in 1980, entitled "Some Thoughts on the Current State of Teaching and Research about Northern Canada," Tom revisited the topic of the North. He reiterated his earlier concerns about the lack of research and, as a consequence, the lack of knowledge in Canadian research and academic institutions about the North, the land, and its people:

> The Canadian north is often depicted as a wasteland of ice and snow because we have not yet given to it the attention in teaching and research which would correct that image. The data I have given to you may suggest that, rather than a wasteland of ice and snow, the Canadian north might more aptly be described as an academic desert! In both applied and basic research, a great deal of attention needs to be devoted to northern studies.[9]

In that same year, Tom reemphasized the degree to which the North remained hidden from Canadians' sightlines, despite its immense geographic presence, in a paper entitled "The Arctic and Canadian Culture."[10] Again, Tom turned his focus on the disturbing data that revealed how little academic and scientific resources, including research dollars, were being allocated to the North, and to the Arctic, in particular. His pleas were not simply based on a heartfelt need to mobilize resources, but rather on a strategic acknowledgement that Canada would remain somewhat truncated without a sound and well-researched effort to understand the North, its people, its ecology, and its special needs in all areas: "Increasing numbers of highly qualified people will be required—in fact are required now—to advance knowledge about the Arctic and to serve its needs."[11]

Fortunately, people were listening. In 1988, the federal government invited Tom to chair the Canadian Polar Research Commission Study, a position he held for two years. Soon after his appointment, the Commission produced *The Shield of Achilles: The Report of the Canadian Polar Research Commission Study.*[12] Tom's report built upon the work by a Study Group commissioned earlier, in 1985, by the Department of Indian Affairs and Northern Development, which recommended in its report two years later the creation of a national body to connect the federal government and researchers in polar science and research.[13] *The Shield of Achilles* succinctly endorsed this recommendation and outlined the mandate, structure, composition, and accountability for a Canadian Polar Research Commission. In 1991, three years after Tom's report, Parliament established the Canadian Polar Commission as Canada's national advisory agency on polar affairs, research, and related activities.

That same year, Tom co-chaired a bilateral conference on Canada-Soviet Cooperation in the Arctic. The work of the conference extended the efforts that led to earlier agreements: the Arctic Science Exchange Program in 1984 and in 1987, which identified scientific cooperation on Arctic and northern issues and an agreement in 1989 between Canada and the Union of Soviet Socialist Republics on Cooperation in the Arctic and the North. A few months after the conference, in February 1992, Prime Minister Brian Mulroney and President Boris Yeltsin signed the Canada-Russia Agreement on Cooperation in the Arctic and the North. Noteworthy among the various clauses of the agreement was the promotion of contact between Aboriginal people as an essential element in the work of local and regional governments.[14]

Tom's contributions to the North continued in 1994 in Yellowknife when he chaired the Conference on Canada and Polar Science. That same year, Mary Simon, an Inuuk from Nunivik, became Canada's first Ambassador for Circumpolar Affairs, a post she held until 2003. It should come as no surprise that Trent University appointed Ms. Simon its seventh chancellor, a position she held from 1995 to 1999 and for one year, 2002, following the untimely death of Peter Gzowski, who took up the office in 2000. As an Aboriginal officer of Trent, she followed Dr. Gilbert Monture, who served as the first Aboriginal member of Trent's Board of Governors from 1966 to 1973, and possibly the first Aboriginal member of any university board of governors in Canada.

Summing up Tom Symons's work in Native and northern studies and policy is fairly easy. Intellectually, and possibly at a visceral and intuitive level, Tom understood and accepted that Canada's greatness as a northern nation depended in no small measure on the absolute necessity of giving Aboriginal people not only a voice in the affairs that affected them but also the power to influence their outcomes, whether they lived in Inuvik, Pangnirtung, Haida-Gwaii, High Level, or Chapel Island. In so doing, he drew Canadians' attention to the rightful place of Aboriginal people in the history of Canada and facilitated their participation as equal and vital partners in its future.

Tom's willingness to commit himself, and the resources of the various offices he held throughout his career, including the presidency of Trent University, to the resolution of several fundamental Aboriginal issues reflected a genuine and deeply held concern for a vital yet ignored segment of the Canadian population. His commitment distinguishes him from numerous peers and colleagues. His recognition of the need to embrace Aboriginal people and to ensure their participation—not just in the issues that mattered most to them but also in the entire range of issues that mattered to all Canadians—occurred during a time when few people, either in academia or in the public and private sectors, shared his view.

Above all, Tom trusted and respected Aboriginal people, their views, their authority, and their leadership. He displayed this trust and respect throughout his professional career, ensuring that Aboriginal people were never excluded from any of his venues. And where and when it mattered the most, he facilitated their presence in strategic and authoritative roles. It can be said that Tom walked the talk and, most importantly, he walked it in our moccasins and mukluks.

Notes

1 Joseph E. Couture, "Native Training and Political Change: A Personal Reflection," *Canadian Journal of Native Studies* 1, no. 2 (1982): 12.

2 Ibid.

3 *Native Rights in Canada* (Toronto: Indian-Eskimo Association, 1970).

4 Peter A. Cumming and Neil H. Mickenberg, eds., *Native Rights in Canada: Second Edition* (Toronto: The Indian-Eskimo Association of Canada and General Publishing, 1972).

5 *Statement of the Government of Canada on Indian Policy*, 1969 (Ottawa: Queen's Printer, 1969).

6 Susan Buggey, "An Approach to Aboriginal Cultural Landscapes," *Parks Canada, Historic Sites and Monuments Board of Canada, Agenda Paper* (1999): 18.

7 Ibid., 17.

8 T. H. B. Symons, *To Know Ourselves: The Report of the Commission on Canadian Studies*, 2 vols. (Ottawa: Association of Universities and Colleges of Canada, 1975), 92.

9 *ACUNS-AUCEN Third Annual Conference: Report* (1980): 40.

10 Tom Symons, "The Arctic and Canadian Culture," in *A Century of Canada's Arctic Islands: 1880–1980*, ed. Morris Zaslow, 319–37 (Ottawa: The Royal Society of Canada, 1981).

11 Ibid., 334.

12 T. H. B. Symons, chairman, and P. Burnet, study coordinator, *The Shield of Achilles: The Report of the Canadian Polar Research Commission Study* (Ottawa: Indian and Northern Development Canada, 1988).

13 W. P. Adams, P. F. Burnet, M. R. Gordon, and E. F. Roots, *Canada and Polar Science* (Ottawa: Indian Affairs and Northern Development, 1987).

14 John B. Hannigan, "Canada's Northern Cooperation with the Soviet Union and Russia: A Natural Partnership?" *International Journal of Canadian Studies* 9 (1994): 12.

CHAPTER 5

Quiet Revolutionary: Tom Symons, National Unity, and Linguistic Rights

CHARLES BEER

Introduction

From an early age, Tom Symons demonstrated a strong interest in public affairs and public policy. He had a fascination with the history of his own family, and a continuing and consuming interest in local history and heritage, and in the affairs of his province, his country, and the broader world around him. He was blessed to grow up in a family that provided him with a very strong supportive environment. He understood that he had a responsibility to give back to his community and to his country in whatever way he could. The old adage that to whom much is given much is expected would have been accepted and understood by him in a very unassuming and uncomplicated way. He chose to be involved in many of the key public policy issues of the latter part of the twentieth century, but he did it in a way that was unique to him. He always maintained that one could play a vital role in the life of one's country and in the development of important public policy initiatives through other means than getting elected. His life has been a testament to this fact.

Symons's Canadian identity is rooted solidly in his deep understanding of Canada's Aboriginal, British, and French past, but it has never been buried there. He has continued to be open to the influence of Canada's evolving multicultural and multiracial identity. It is this centered belief to both learn from the past and be open to the future that has continually allowed him to contribute so much to Canadian life.

For approximately a decade—beginning in 1965—Tom Symons was heavily involved in shaping Ontario's position on the role of Quebec in Canada, on the place of the French language in Ontario, and on constitutional reform. It must be recognized that his activities on these issues took place at the same time as he was in the process of establishing a new post-secondary institution, Trent University in Peterborough on the banks of the Otonabee River, and serving as its first president.

He was also busy with a myriad of other interests and voluntary activity. This is demonstrated by his seminal work on Canadian Studies, *To Know Ourselves*; his many activities in support of Canada's Aboriginal peoples; his leadership in the field of human rights in Ontario and Canada; his longstanding commitment to the betterment of relations between Canada's two official language communities; and his equally longstanding involvement with the Commonwealth through a number of important initiatives.

During this same period, Symons was also an active participant in the political process at both the provincial and federal levels. He was a Progressive Conservative when both of these words were important to the party's identity. Symons himself placed a heavy emphasis on the word "progressive." In the 1960s and early 1970s, he had a close relationship with Ontario's Premier John Robarts and was also a key supporter of, and advisor to, Robert Stanfield, the federal Progressive Conservative leader and former premier of Nova Scotia, who had replaced John Diefenbaker in the fall of 1967. Symons was in no way a blind partisan but was extremely thoughtful in his approach to political issues and their solutions. His conservatism was forward looking, values based, and open to new ideas and to the ideas of others, no matter their political affiliation.

This essay seeks to set out the important role Tom Symons played during a time when the issues of Quebec and linguistic rights were at the forefront of the Canadian political agenda.

Those Days from These Days

At this point in the twenty-first century, it is not always easy to remember in a vivid and visceral way the social, economic, cultural, and political climate of the 1960s. That decade remains for many Canadians one of the most transformational of the twentieth century. This in a century that saw the Great Depression, the two World Wars, the rise and fall of communism, the advent of technology in our daily lives, and the emergence of popular culture as a key determinant of who we are. Canada was no exception to the waves of change spreading throughout the globe. The Canada that emerged at the end of the decade was greatly altered from the country that lived through the post-war era. Throughout this period, Quebec and Ontario, and their two leading cities, Montreal and Toronto, saw themselves as the centre of the country in all respects, and not just because of geography. The great hockey battles between the Canadiens and the Maple Leafs in the 1950s and 1960s defined the importance of this relationship in the popular culture. The roles that Alberta and British Columbia, and their principal cities of Edmonton, Calgary, and Vancouver, were to play in the Canadian political landscape were not yet fully developed, although their growing importance on the Canadian political stage would not be long in coming. What needs to be understood today is how prominent, immediate, and controversial the combined issues of Quebec and language were in the national political fabric, particularly in the 1960s and 1970s. They often dominated the agenda in a very different way than they had before these crucial decades. The 1960s and 1970s changed our ideas of Canada and Ontario, for the better.

To understand Tom Symons's role in this important change in the provincial psyche, it is critical that we understand those times and some of the players. Symons was not a solitary participant. He was part of a team of Ontario academic and public servant thought leaders who, through the 1960s and early 1970s, played a somewhat quiet and backroom role, but one that was essential in dealing with the constitutional issues Canada then faced. The story of his role is, in fact, also the story of this broader political, bureaucratic, and academic leadership that existed in Ontario at that time. His own contribution was substantial; Ontario's relationship with Quebec, and the place and the role of the French language in Ontario, owe much to his personal commitment and strong leadership.

Clearly, these issues did not emerge in the early 1960s out of the blue. The post-war period with its social and economic challenges, the growing importance of post-secondary education, manpower training, immigration, labour mobility, and the need for expanded public health and social services all were changing the relationship between the provinces and the federal government. The growing pressures sparked renewed debate regarding the two levels of governments' constitutional responsibilities and their spending powers.

These issues, in disparate ways, began to raise questions about Canada's identity, and about the place and use of Canada's two historical languages, English and French. What role did our British and French heritage still play in defining us as a people? What did our proximity to the greatest economic and military power the world has ever known mean for our identity and our sense of who we were? Was the French language only to be used in Quebec or should it have a place at the national level and in other provinces? What role should Quebec play as the spokesperson for French-speaking Canadians throughout Canada? More broadly, Canadians were asking themselves what it meant to be Canadian and what Canada's linguistic duality meant to our identity. The great flag debate of 1964, when the Parliament of Canada approved the new red maple leaf, produced a heated debate about who we were and where we wanted to go. If this debate was divisive for some, the World Exposition in Montreal in 1967 brought Canadians together as never before. This single event in fundamental, if surprising ways, caused Canadians throughout the country to ask themselves exactly what it meant to be a Canadian.

For many in the 1960s, the concept of linguistic duality would have been both foreign and even, if understood, anathema. Canadian public opinion would have been much more focused on the role the English-speaking peoples (Britain and the Commonwealth and the United States) were playing in the world and on the growth and strength of the English language for future world progress. A review of commentary in Canadian newspapers and magazines would have demonstrated that, for many in English-speaking Canada, it would be best if Quebec and French Canada recognized that the future, their future, lay with assimilation into the broader North American English-speaking reality.

If you compare the Ontario of 1950 to the Ontario that emerged by the end of the 1960s, what is striking is the extent to which public opinion not only began to change but also began to be shaped around the issues of Quebec and language. This shift was caused by a number of factors, but included what was happening worldwide with independence movements among former European colonies in Africa and Asia, the civil rights movement in the United States, and the evolution of Quebec as an increasingly modern state where French was, or would need to be, the principal language of communication. This was coupled with the recognition by political and opinion leaders in many parts of Canada, but certainly in Ontario, that significant change was in order if the country was to resolve the growing issues around Quebec's place in Canada and around the use of the French and English languages. None of this would happen easily: there would always be a strong undercurrent of opposition to Quebec and linguistic rights during this time.

In the late 1950s, on the cusp of the transformational decade to come, Tom Symons was a young professor at the University of Toronto. He was involved with senior members of the university in rethinking what role a modern post-secondary institution should have, and in helping to fashion forward-looking changes to implement this new role. He was also beginning to work on the development of what would become the new university in Peterborough. At the same time, he was unquestionably aware of all these other issues as they began to move more to the centre of Canadian political debate. They saw their political expression in four key elections, which took place in the early 1960s. All four were to have a profound influence on shaping the role and place of Quebec within Canada, and on defining the role of the French and English languages provincially and federally. How much of an effect they would have no one yet knew.

In the spring of 1960, after the deaths of Maurice Duplessis and of his reformist successor, Paul Sauvé, Quebec elected the Liberal government of Jean Lesage on a platform of profound change, what came to be called the "Quiet Revolution." At the same time, after nearly a decade of Conservative rule, New Brunswick elected not only a new Liberal government but one led for the first time by an Acadian, Louis Robichaud. In the fall of 1961, Ontario's Conservative government saw the retirement of longtime Premier Leslie Frost, and his replacement by John Robarts, a compromise candidate from London selected only after several ballots. Finally, in the spring of 1963 after six years of John Diefenbaker and his Conservatives, Lester Pearson returned the Liberals to power in Ottawa with a minority government.

What was significant about these four elections was that each brought forward a government that was to become activist on a broad social, economic, and cultural front. To observers, the emergence of John Robarts as an agent of change might have been initially surprising, but as the decade moved on he demonstrated a particular grasp of the importance of dealing with the concerns of Quebec and the place of the English and French languages in Canada. Most importantly, he recognized the vital role that Ontario, as the largest English-speaking province, would have to play as the historical counterpart to Quebec and as the province with the largest French-speaking population outside of Quebec.

Quebec and the federal government had been engaged in a series of issues that had put them at loggerheads for several years. The federal role in the funding of post-secondary education, the Canada Pension Plan, the Canada Health Act, and Labour Market training were but four key ones. The whole move to expand broad social, educational, and health programs after the Second World War had placed great stress on the federal-provincial relationship. With the election of Pearson, there appeared to be a prime minister and a government prepared to begin the dialogue with Quebec on its role and place in confederation. In October of 1962, Lesage had been reelected with a mandate to be "maitre chez nous," or masters in our own house. While much of the Quebec approach centered on gaining more control over broad social and economic powers, it also raised important questions about the place of the French language in Quebec and in Canada. Ontario, New Brunswick, and to a slightly lesser extent, Manitoba, were seen as the most critical provinces with respect to the place of the French language outside Quebec.

At this stage in the early 1960s, the significant point to make is that the other provinces, while having strong interests on various broad social, economic, and fiscal program initiatives, had not yet focused more specifically on the overall federal-provincial relationship or on constitutional reform in the way that Quebec under Lesage had begun to do. Their approaches tended to be more reactive to federal initiatives, particularly with the interventionist Pearson government. Well before Peter Lougheed and the Alberta Conservatives came to power in 1971, Ontario had begun to move in a more concerted way to develop an overarching approach to federal-provincial relations and constitutional issues. It is important to recognize that these other broad social and economic issues were inextricably intertwined with the ongoing federal-provincial debates and discussions on Quebec and language. None of these debates existed in a vacuum.

The first key move on the language question from the federal government came in the Liberals' first Throne Speech when the government announced the creation of the Royal Commission on Bilingualism and Biculturalism. The commission had been created to respond to the growing concerns in Quebec, and among French Canadians generally, that their language and culture needed protection and that French-speaking Canadians needed greater opportunities to participate more fully in Canada's political and economic decision making. The commission was headed by two prominent Canadians—Andre Laurendeau, the distinguished editor of *Le Devoir*, and Davidson Dunton, former president of Carleton University and former head of the CBC. Laurendeau had himself argued for the creation of such a commission in the pages of *Le Devoir*.

It was the commission's Preliminary Report in February of 1965 that clearly set the stage for the debate that would then emerge in a much more specific way throughout the country. In the introduction to their report, the commissioners stated clearly and emphatically that Canada, without being fully aware of it, was passing through the greatest crisis in its history. How it dealt with the fundamental questions of Quebec's place in Confederation, and the role of Canada's two historic languages, English and French, would determine, they stated, Canada's future course and survival as a country. This report, and its wide dissemination through the media, ensured that Quebec, and the role and place of the French language in Canada, were at the top of the public agenda. In all, the commission produced six reports as part of its findings: *The Official Languages* (1967), *Education* (1968), *The Work World* (1969), *The Cultural Contribution of the Other Ethnic Groups* (1969), *The Federal Capital* (1970), and *Voluntary Associations* (1970). It is a remarkable body of work and it played a critical role in influencing public policy at both the federal and provincial levels for the next several decades.

It cannot be emphasized enough how powerful an impact the report had in Ontario. The political, business, labour, media, and academic thought leaders all recognized that this was a seminal report with profound implications for the country. The federal government understood that Ontario's response and position on the issues raised would be crucial to the country's future. Pearson knew that Robarts's initial comments would be critical if the commission's work was to have a larger impact on the country. Speaking before the Institute of Chartered Accountants of Ontario in March of 1965, Robarts welcomed the Royal Commission's report. He underlined the importance and the seriousness of the developments in Quebec, and he stated how important it was for the people of Ontario both to appreciate their immense responsibility in responding to Quebec in Canada's future development as a country and to understand that Ontario's actions would carry great weight with Quebec and French Canada. These remarks were to underpin the approach he followed throughout his term as premier. Had he responded with either indifference or, indeed, hostility—as former Ontario premiers (such as George Drew or Mitch Hepburn) might have done—the future of the country may have taken a very different direction.

In that same year, and before the publication of the Preliminary Report, Robarts had indicated that Ontario would, in fact, be an involved and positive player in the ensuing debate. In the province's Speech from the Throne in January of 1965, he announced the creation of the Ontario Advisory Committee on Confederation to advise the government and the province on the stance Ontario should take on constitutional and federal-provincial issues. The OACC, over its six-year history, influenced very directly the shaping of the Robarts government's strategy regarding Quebec and linguistic issues. In addition, through its two volumes of *Background Papers and Reports* (published in 1967 and 1970), the OACC also influenced a generation of Ontario opinion leaders and scholars.

Tom Symons, the president of Trent University, at the age of thirty-five, would be the youngest member of the new committee. Here he would be called on to play a pivotal role in the committee's deliberations and in the shaping of its recommendations on Quebec and linguistic rights. He was now entering a much larger stage.

The Ontario Advisory Committee on Confederation

The role of the Ontario Advisory Committee on Confederation was to advise the government on "the present and future Constitutional requirements of Ontario considered both independently of and in relation to the Constitutional changes and amendments which have been established or are being studied by any Province or by the Federal Government." In laymen's terms, they were to look at a wide range of federal-provincial and constitutional issues, as well as to advise the premier (or prime minister as both Robarts and Lesage were known at the time) on issues of the day. The membership of the committee was confirmed in February and it held its first meeting in March of 1965. Thereafter, it met monthly, with the exception of the summer months, until 1971, when, with the retirement of Premier Robarts, the committee was disbanded.

The committee, in addition to Tom Symons, was made up of eighteen eminent Canadians, including Justice Bora Laskin, before his appointment to the Supreme Court of Canada; Professor Donald Creighton, the pre-eminent Canadian historian of his day from the University of Toronto; Dean W. R. Lederman, from the Queen's Faculty of Law; J. Harvey Perry, executive director of the Canadian Bankers Association; Eugene Forsey, an eminent constitutional expert from Carleton University; Professor Edward (Ted) McWhinney, a constitutional expert from McGill University and later a Liberal MP from Vancouver in the 1990s; Professor John Meisel, from Queen's University and an expert in Canadian elections; and Professors Alexander Brady and Paul Fox, both from the University of Toronto's

Department of Political Economy. Interestingly, and perhaps as a sign of those times, there were no women on the committee. While there were two Franco Ontarians, Roger Seguin, an Ottawa lawyer with close ties to Robarts, and Father Lucien Matte from Sudbury, there were no representatives from what today we refer to as visible minorities. The full list of members is provided in the appendix.

The OACC set up three subcommittees: a first dealing with constitutional questions; a second dealing with economic and fiscal issues; and a third dealing with cultural and educational matters. Symons played an important role in all the deliberations of the committee, but it was his leadership on cultural and linguistic issues, particularly through his participation in the Cultural and Educational Subcommittee, that stands out.

The Constitutional Conferences

It is important to recognize the critical role that the OACC played in support of the premier and the Ontario government in the development of Ontario's positions on the various issues discussed at the provincial Confederation of Tomorrow Conference in November of 1967. The committee was also to play a similar role regarding the subsequent federal-provincial constitutional conferences from 1968 through to the Victoria conference in 1971. As an aside, it is important to underline the public's fascination with all the conferences that took place. This was due, in part, to the importance of the issues being discussed, but it was also because of the drama that the televised debates brought to the emergence of Pierre Trudeau—first as Pearson's justice minister and then as prime minister—and his sharp exchanges with Daniel Johnson, the premier of Quebec. The televised conferences in their own way were an earlier version of today's "reality" shows. Many were shown live throughout the day with special programs summarizing the day's events in the evening on both of the two national networks.

The early work of the committee helped to set the stage for the 1967 conference. The issues discussed in the brand new Toronto-Dominion tower that November covered the goals of Canadians: the role of the English and French languages in Canada; the ways in which the federal system could be improved in terms both of institutions and forms of federalism; and the machinery and structure of federal-provincial and interprovincial relationships in Canada. Of these, it was the language issue that would most often catch the broader public's attention, and not always in a positive way. Robarts released a series of background papers shortly before the conference on a variety of issues. The one on linguistic questions raised the most discussion, not all of it positive and some of it from his own caucus at Queen's Park.

It was not at all uncommon for the premier to sit in with the committee through parts of their monthly meetings. He would seek their opinions on many of the fiscal and constitutional issues of the day. The verbatim transcripts of these meetings offer scholars a rare window on the development of public policy at the time. The work of the committee was led in large part by two distinguished public servants. The first was H. Ian Macdonald, who had been brought into the public service from the University of Toronto's Department of Political Economy by Robarts in 1965. He served first as the chief economist of the province and then, when the new Department of Treasury and Economics was created, he became its first deputy minister. He would later serve as president of York University for ten years. The second key public servant was Don Stevenson, who served as the number two to Macdonald. Stevenson, a former Canadian diplomat, had a keen mind for all things constitutional and a deep sensitivity to issues dealing directly with Quebec, particularly around language and the division of powers. Macdonald served as the chair of the OACC. They were supported by a small group of young public servants, some of whom were bilingual, in the newly created Federal Provincial Affairs Secretariat.

Both Macdonald and Stevenson and the secretariat provided significant support to the committee and worked closely with Robarts on all aspects of the committee's agenda and on the development of Robarts's own ideas and actions. The 1967 Confederation of Tomorrow Conference in Toronto, and the premier's groundbreaking speech to the Association canadienne-française de l'Ontario in August of 1967, grew in part out of the work of the OACC but also out of the relationship that developed among Robarts, Macdonald, Stevenson, Randall Dick (the deputy attorney general of the province), and the members of the OACC. Stevenson, who took the lead on linguistic questions and relations with Quebec, worked particularly closely with Symons, Fox, Brady, and Meisel.

It is important at this point to say something about Robarts's approach to Quebec and language. Robarts, on a number of occasions, recalled that, while serving in the Canadian Navy during the Second World War, he was at one time on a destroyer that had a mixed crew from a number of countries. He was always impressed when he entered the officers' wardroom that all the officers would begin to speak in English so he would understand the conversation. That memory stayed with him throughout his life. From 1965 onwards, Robarts set in motion studies and reviews to expand French-language services in Ontario. The expansion of the French-language education system was perhaps the most obvious example of this. He also asked that Macdonald and Stevenson examine how Ontario might increase bilingual services at the municipal level, in the Legislature, in the provincial courts, and in the Ontario public service more generally. As a result, the role of the English and French languages figured prominently in the agenda of the Confederation of Tomorrow Conference. The OACC participated very directly with Macdonald and Stevenson and their staff to develop the analyses and background papers for the conference. The Cultural and Educational Subcommittee was particularly active in the discussions and policy development on language rights.

Robarts had developed a good working relationship with Jean Lesage, the Quebec premier. In 1965, for example, the two men had agreed that they should promote an exchange between their two legislative press galleries, and they did so with two meetings: one at Queen's Park and one in Quebec City. Robarts also ensured that his senior team worked closely with Lesage's key advisors on the major federal-provincial issues of the day.

On a separate front, Symons had invited both premiers to Trent University for the opening of Champlain College in 1965 as a sign of the close historical relationship between Upper and Lower Canada and subsequently between Ontario and Quebec. Both premiers alluded to the close working relationships that Robert Baldwin and Louis-Hippolyte LaFontaine had developed in the 1840s, as well as the historic partnership between Sir John A. Macdonald and George-Étienne Cartier, which led to Confederation. As a follow up to the Trent ceremony, Robarts and Lesage agreed to develop a cooperation agreement between Ontario and Quebec. Subsequently, in 1966, each made a similar commitment in their respective legislatures.

While the Robarts-Lesage relationship was a constructive one, the Ontario premier's association with the Union Nationale's Daniel Johnson, who became premier in the spring of 1966, was even closer, particularly on a personal basis. The two men had known each other since the early 1950s. They had often met when each was involved as a young member of their respective legislatures. In the development of the Confederation of Tomorrow Conference, their relationship was crucial in making it the success it was.

Another initiative that Robarts strongly encouraged was the holding of two key meetings of senior civil servants before the Confederation of Tomorrow Conference. In those days, it was much more common for political leaders to work very closely with their senior bureaucrats and advisors. Premiers and ministers did not have the large political staffs that they have today. The senior bureaucracy was a much more direct player, and this was seen as a necessary, useful, and vital norm.

Both of these meetings took place at Queen's University. The first was held in January of 1967 between delegations representing public servants from Ontario and Quebec. It is interesting to note that Claude Morin, Jacques Parizeau, and Louis Bernard were among the Quebec advisors. All three, of course, went on to play significant roles in the separatist movement. The second meeting with the federal government followed in June. The federal delegation included two senior mandarins, Gordon Robertson and Carl Goldenberg, as well as Marc Lalonde, who went on to become a senior cabinet minister in Trudeau's government. The two sessions were instrumental in developing the agenda for the November conference in Toronto and in the ensuing federal-provincial round of conferences.

A final point to make is why Robarts felt it essential to undertake this initiative. First, he recognized how important it was for Quebec to see Ontario engaged as a full participant and colleague in the ensuing discussions. Again it must be noted that at this time Ontario and Quebec saw themselves as the two key provinces. Robarts understood that, for Canada, Ontario could not sit on the sidelines. Second, he recognized that as long as Ottawa had a minority government, it would be difficult for Pearson to move forward on the constitutional front without having many complex and contentious debates with the former prime minister John Diefenbaker and an increasingly dysfunctional federal Conservative Caucus. In Robarts's view, holding the Confederation of Tomorrow Conference could help the federal government and could clarify some of the key provincial perspectives to the current federal-provincial and constitutional issues of the day. There was no question that his proposal for the conference raised great angst among the political classes throughout the country, but he worked hard to win the confidence of his fellow premiers and of the prime minister. The OACC itself had been divided on the wisdom of a province, Ontario, holding the first such conference and only involving the provinces. Everyone recognized that there was a risk in holding the discussions, but Robarts was convinced it would help ease Quebec's growing sense of isolation. And, indeed, at the conclusion of the conference in November, Pearson phoned Robarts directly to congratulate him on the holding of the conference and the leadership he had demonstrated. The issues raised and the shape of the ensuing discussion owed much to the OACC and, on linguistic issues, to the work of Tom Symons.

The stage was now set for the first federal-provincial conference in 1968 and for the rise of Pierre Elliott Trudeau. Robarts always maintained that, after the election of Trudeau and a Liberal majority government in June of 1968, the province's role would now change. Ontario would need to be more cognizant of its own issues and would not have the same role to play at the national level. Nonetheless, it is clear that Robarts's leadership from 1965 until his retirement was critical in helping Canada find its way through the many stormy constitutional waters that lay ahead.

An Ontario–Quebec Cultural and Educational Exchange Program

It is now time to turn to the particular role Tom Symons played in the deliberations of the OACC. As was noted in the introduction, Symons had a unique understanding of the historical roots of Canada, which was coupled with a strong sense of the importance of the relationship between Quebec and Ontario to Canada.

In the deliberations of the OACC, Symons worked particularly closely with Professors Brady, Meisel, and Fox, who were colleagues on the Cultural and Educational Subcommittee. It needs to be said that, for a large committee of very engaged and committed individuals, the working relationships among them were quite collaborative and professional. That being said, Symons and the three colleagues noted above developed a very close working relationship on a broad range of issues, both linguistic and constitutional. They all made an impact on Robarts in the development of his views.

Symons was involved in all of the OACC's deliberations and discussions, but he played a particularly important role in the Cultural and Educational Subcommittee. One of the first things that the subcommittee addressed was the relationship between Quebecers and Ontarians at all levels of society, particularly focused on cultural and educational exchanges. The Royal Commission had viewed this area as a critical one in ensuring greater and better understanding between the two official language groups. Early in the work of the OACC, Symons agreed, in the spring of 1965, to prepare a paper that set out proposals for *An Ontario Quebec Cultural and Educational Exchange Program.* The purpose of such an exchange program was to foster greater mutual understanding and respect between French- and English-speaking Canadians in Ontario and Quebec as well as between the same groups within Ontario itself.

Today, with the ease of travel for everyone to wander not only around Canada, but throughout the world, this proposal may seem somewhat commonplace. One of the reasons for this was the very leadership Symons gave to ensuring new programs of exchange to help Quebecers and Ontarians know one another better.

Symons made four specific recommendations that were endorsed by the government. The first called for the establishment of an "extensive and sustained" program of cultural and educational exchanges. The second called for a permanent secretariat to be set up within the Department of Education reporting to the deputy minister or to the minister with responsibility to implement the exchange program. The third recommended that Ontario should explore with Quebec, at the highest political level, the possibility of a cultural and educational agreement between the two provinces. It was this proposal that both Lesage and Robarts committed to in 1966. Finally, Ontario was asked to see if other such agreements might also be signed with other provinces or groups of provinces.

The report also led to the negotiation of the Ontario-Quebec Cultural, Educational and Technical Agreement, which was signed in June of 1969 in Quebec City. The agreement itself built upon the OACC report and expanded its reach. For example, each province committed to provide, wherever feasible, public services in the English and French languages, and to provide, wherever feasible, education in their own language to students of the French-speaking and English-speaking minority in each province. These two commitments were historic breakthroughs on their own, especially for a province like Ontario, where French-language instruction had been banned only fifty years earlier. The agreement also provided for a very broad range of exchanges and contacts between the two provinces. The agreement and the exchange programs are still very much alive and prospering. Countless students and citizens from many walks of life have benefitted from these two initiatives. The agreement in its day was seen as a somewhat daring move. France had signed a similar agreement with both the federal government and with Quebec. The Ontario-Quebec Agreement recognized that the English and French languages were the "working" languages of their two provinces and stated that each province would take steps to support its linguistic minority. It also set up a Permanent Commission made up of senior representatives from the two provinces to implement its terms. In an editorial just after the agreement's signing, *Le Devoir* stated that it was not an exaggeration to call the signing an "historic moment."

The Symons Report led directly to the creation of the Ontario-Quebec exchange program in the Department of Education, the development and signing of the Ontario-Quebec Agreement, and the establishment of the Permanent Commission. Each one of these initiatives continues to this day. Indeed, Premiers Dalton McGuinty and Jean Charest in 2009 and 2010 held special sessions of their cabinets at Queen's Park and in Quebec City to underline the ongoing and close relationship between the two provinces.

French-language Public Secondary Schools

The second major area where Symons and the subcommittee played a key role was on French-language secondary education. During the 1960s, this issue had become central to the future existence of the Franco-Ontarian community. Education was seen to be the first place where Canada must ensure protection for its two historical linguistic communities, but since responsibility for education fell under provincial jurisdiction, the federal government needed the support and participation of provincial governments to ensure that this happened.

We must also remember that the OACC deliberations on this issue were set against a backdrop of the deliberations of the Royal Commission on Bilingualism and Biculturalism, whose second report in 1968 focused entirely on the provision of French- and English-language education in Canada. At the same time, the federal government was developing what was to become *The Official Languages Act, 1969*. In addition, New Brunswick was also moving to develop greater opportunities and protections for its English- and French-speaking communities. Language and, more specifically, linguistic rights had finally taken a prominent place in Canadian political discourse and public policy development.

The subcommittee concluded its work by calling for the provision of French-language public secondary schools in which the principal language of instruction should be French. The subcommittee stated that the French-language secondary schools should be provided for by legislation. In concert with the work of the OACC, the provincial government in November of 1967 had created a special committee made up of officials from the Ministry of Education and educators from the Franco-Ontarian community to put forward proposals to expand French-language education within the public system. The legislation, establishing French-language public elementary and secondary schools, was passed and took formal effect on 1 January 1969. The issue regarding the extension of the separate school system would not be resolved for another fifteen years, so the question before the subcommittee related only to the public system.

The Legacy of the OACC

In looking back at the great debates around constitutional reform, Quebec, and linguistic rights, one cannot underestimate the contribution of the Ontario Advisory Committee on Confederation to the approach that Ontario developed. Certainly, political leadership was needed and provided by Premier Robarts, but the work of the OACC ensured significant support and intellectual rigour for the various positions taken by Ontario on these crucial questions. Many of the members were active in other areas of their lives in speaking publically on the various issues under review. The decisions made between 1965 and 1971 were instrumental in placing Ontario as a key and positive player in all matters related to Quebec and its role in Confederation, as well as regarding the place of the French language in Ontario. At all times during this period, Tom Symons brought a thoughtful, principled, and passionate perspective to the committee's deliberations. With Robarts's retirement and the end of the OACC, it was not long before Symons would be called upon to provide further leadership on the provision of French-language education for Ontario's Francophone population. Now he would have to take the various principles developed around linguistic rights and put them into action.

French-Language Education Rights: The Symons Commission

With the passage of the government's French-language schools' legislation in 1969, a new era opened up for the Franco-Ontarian population. It was by no means perfect, but there was now, for the first time, clear legislative underpinning regarding the rights of Ontario's French-speaking community to an education at the elementary and secondary levels in their own language. The implementation of this legislation, however, raised some serious questions. What did it mean for separate schools? If a public school board did not want to do what the local Francophone population thought it should, what recourse would they have? What place would religious education have in the French-language schools? Not a few observers recognized that at some point a schools crisis or two would likely emerge and their resolutions would provide the next steps forward in ensuring clearly that an education in French for Ontario's Francophone population should be a right.

This journey did not end until various attempts by governments under each of Ontario's three political parties, the Liberals, the New Democrats, and finally the Conservatives, brought about the passage of the *Fewer School Boards Act*, which took effect on 1 January 1998, almost a full thirty years since the first legislation for French language schools was passed. Out of this last piece of legislation, four French-language public school boards and seven French-language separate school boards came into existence. The work that Tom Symons carried out as a member of the OACC, as well as his leadership in the early 1970s in resolving two French-language school crises, were part of the reason why today we have fully developed French-language public and separate school systems of education in Ontario.

The experience with the initial legislation on French-language schools demonstrated much success in different parts of the province. However, problems began to arise where the Francophone community was sizable but still in the minority. At issue in a number of instances was a conflict within the French-speaking community itself. Did the Francophone population want a homogeneous fully French-language school, or was it better to be a section within an English-language school where some courses might be given in French? In addition, where the Francophone population was demanding its own school, what would happen to the English-speaking students? How viable would either school be? At the start of the new decade, rumblings began to be heard from several specific communities.

The two crises that are the subject of this review took place in Sturgeon Falls, a short distance from North Bay on the trans Canada highway, and in Cornwall, in southeastern Ontario. In each case, Tom Symons was asked to play the role of mediator and, in the first, to provide the government with suggestions and recommendations to improve on the legislation developed in 1967–68 and brought into law in 1969. His experience with the work of the OACC stood him in very good stead as he took on these responsibilities.

The first crisis in Sturgeon Falls had been brewing for well over a year when, near the beginning of the 1971–72 school year, a number of activist French-speaking students brought it to the attention of Ontario and the nation by going on strike. For Ontario's place in Canada, for its relationship with Quebec, and for its own Francophone population, it was critical that this crisis be resolved as quickly as possible. This was all happening against a continuing backdrop of constitutional conferences and impassioned debates on linguistic rights. It was not long since the October crisis in the fall of 1970 in Quebec and the death of Pierre Laporte, Quebec's minister of labour. Everyone was nervous about language issues and the emotions they brought forward.

As the crisis developed, William Davis replaced John Robarts as Ontario's premier and Robert Welch assumed the education portfolio. On 16 September 1971, the new premier, with the full support of his minister of education and the Conservative cabinet, appointed Tom Symons as a one-man commission and mediator in the Sturgeon Falls dispute. However, Welch was conscious, through his own early involvement in the issue, following his appointment as minister, that simply resolving the current dispute would not be sufficient. He also asked Symons to review the government's 1969 legislation regarding French-language education. He wanted to ensure that the problems that had emerged in Sturgeon Falls did not spread to other board districts.

Both Davis and Welch were well aware of the role Symons had played on the OACC in supporting the aspirations of Ontario's French-speaking population. They knew that he would be sympathetic to the legitimate demands of the Francophone population, but also thoughtful and innovative in determining how the province could move forward. They also recognized that Symons's background and temperament would be a calming influence on those, both in the province and within their own political party, who were often upset at the attention being shown to the "minority" population. Successive Ontario governments from Robarts to this day have had to balance certain internal tensions on this issue as to just how far and how fast a government can go in protecting linguistic rights.

Symons felt that it was important for Ontario to show leadership on the question of language rights. He knew that it was equally important to understand that, for Quebec, Ontario's stand on linguistic matters was critical to Quebec's view of Canada and place in Canada. He also recognized the importance that measuring the mood of Ontario's majority English-speaking community would be in determining what any government would be able to do. Whatever the merits of the particular situation in Sturgeon Falls, if Ontario could further French-language education, this would support the moderate Quebecers who wanted Quebec to remain in Canada. On the issues of Quebec and linguistic rights, Symons's public policy instincts and those of Davis and Welch were very much in harmony.

Symons recognized at the outset that he had first to resolve the simmering Sturgeon Falls dispute before he could turn to the broader part of his mandate, which was to make recommendations on improving the legislative framework and programs for French-language schools. Working with a small team provided by the government, he set out to resolve the immediate problem. In late September and through October, he gathered the necessary information he required regarding the real issues at play. Then, in November, he traveled to North Bay and to Sturgeon Falls to meet with the various players in the dispute.

Symons had a unique approach to the way he carried out his mediation. The first thing to underline is that he worked with everyone in exactly the same way. It did not matter if you were a fellow university president, a political leader, a captain of industry, a labour leader, a high school student, or the local barber. He dealt with everyone on a basis of mutual respect. This was seen and felt by everyone involved, and it helped him to develop early on a sense of trust between himself and the various players. At all times, in every meeting or discussion, he never lost his even-handed and measured approach. He was an excellent listener. As each person spoke, he gave them his undivided attention. At times, tempers and emotions could run high, and his ability to continue to concentrate on the issues at hand in a calm manner served him—and the resolution of those issues—well.

In addition, his appearance, for many, was also somewhat unique, if not even a bit eccentric. Here again style supported substance; what was so different about him played in his favour. The English tailored suits and the homburg hat, together with the many pipes of various sizes and the thermos of tea that he always had in front of him, created a unique picture for the audience. Although he was still in his early forties when he took on this assignment, he came across both as older in years and, equally important, as someone with a thoughtful approach and great experience. Who was this person who has been sent to meet with us and try to resolve our school issues? In the first few meetings in Sturgeon Falls, and later in North Bay, he soon earned everyone's trust, particularly that of the different student groups.

Following his sessions in November, he put together his recommendations and set a meeting with the Nipissing School Board for early December. The essential issue in the dispute centred on whether there should be a new French-language public high school or a French-language section in the existing high school. Symons recognized early on that there needed to be a new secondary school. He reviewed his recommendations with Minister Welch to ensure there would be funds to build it and to renovate the original school in which the English-speaking students would continue to be housed. At a special meeting of the Nipissing School Board on 7 December, Symons made his presentation and convinced the board to support his approach. The details would be followed up by personnel from the Ministry of Education. Symons now moved on to his second task of reviewing the original legislation and setting out some directions.

During the late fall of 1971 and through the winter of 1972, Symons worked on his final report. Before setting out his analysis and recommendations, a word on Symons's writing style and the importance he gave to the printed word is useful. Symons is an excellent writer. He spends a great deal of time on the craft of writing. It is fair to say that one of the reasons that he has had an impact in a number of areas is that his articles, studies, reviews, and books are well thought out and well written. When working with others on different projects, he brings a collaborative approach to the development of the text, but there is no doubt that, in the end, it is his text that is produced. Anyone who has worked with Symons knows that he will often flag issues for further debate and discussion by scribbling the letters "MWDP?" on the margin. This means "May We Discuss Please" and inevitably leads to serious reflection and review on various issues. He always listens to the arguments of others before settling on an approach and on the expression he wants in the text. He is always searching for what the French call "le mot juste."

In the final days of the preparation of his French-language schools report, Symons was also meeting continuously with Robert Stanfield, the federal Progressive Conservative leader. At the time, Symons headed up Stanfield's policy team. Over one particular weekend, Symons moved between floors at Toronto's old Park Plaza Hotel, writing and editing his French-language report and advising the opposition leader on key issues for the upcoming federal election expected later that year. He often tended to have several projects on the go at any one time.

In the development of his report on the Sturgeon Falls French-language school crisis, Symons's scope was fulsome. When one reads it today one can see an underlying unity to his overall approach. He made clear that both English- and French-speaking Canadians have a right to an education in their own language. His recommendations flowed from this fundamental premise. His report dealt with a wide variety of issues to strengthen the overall administration of French-language education. He called for the creation of a council on French-language schools to be chaired by a new senior official within the Ministry of Education with the rank and title of assistant deputy minister. He spoke about the need to provide more Francophone officials in both the ministry in Toronto and in the ministry's regional offices. He called for better teacher education and professional development. He underlined the need for more and better textbooks and curriculum in French. And he called for more programs of special education and continuing education. French-language education, he asserted, had to be properly resourced if Francophone students were to receive the same level of education as their English-speaking compatriots.

Symons also dealt with a number of trickier questions. The role of the French Language Committees (FLCs) established under the 1968 legislation, the place of religious instruction in French-language schools, and, finally, an appeal process when there was an impasse between the Francophone community and the local school board were all addressed. It must be underlined that this was still long before the separate school system was extended to cover all of the secondary years. Indeed, in the 1971 provincial election, the Davis government had said that they would not extend the separate system to the end of secondary school. The political climate was not conducive to raising the issue of separate school expansion solely in the context of the French-speaking population. There was also a review being carried out by the former lieutenant governor, the Hon. Keiller Mackay, regarding religious instruction and courses on religion in the public system, but his report would not make any recommendations that would satisfy the requests of a great number of Franco Ontarians and nor would Symons in his report.

With respect to the existing French-Language Committees, Symons did propose to enhance their role and responsibilities. He recommended that the number of FLC members elected by Francophone ratepayers be increased from four to six; that the chair of the FLC attend and be able to speak at all board and committee meetings; that the FLC receive all board agendas and reports; and that the board provide the FLCs with reasons in writing if they turned down an FLC request. He also set out a lengthy list of the kinds of issues on which the FLCs could advise the boards, including selection of staff, transportation, and school boundaries. It was quite extensive and inclusive. Finally, he proposed changing the committee's name to the French-Language Advisory Committee, or FLAC. Clearly, for many Francophones, this was not seen as going far enough to ensure that the Francophone community would be able to make the final decisions at the board level for their schools and programs. While the mainstream Francophone groups wanted their own trustees and control over French-language education, most recognized that, in the political climate of the day, this could not yet be done.

Symons did go a considerable distance, nonetheless, to meet this concern by also proposing the creation of what he called the Linguistic Rights Commission of Ontario (LRCO). It would have five members appointed by the minister of education. At least two of the members had to be Francophones. Interestingly, this body would be able to hear appeals not only from FLACs but also from French-speaking ratepayers within the separate school system. He also suggested that the commission should have the final say in resolving any appeal, subject only to a further appeal to the minister within thirty days.

On 16 March 1972, Symons presented his report to the minister of education, Tom Wells. Wells moved immediately to set up the council and name an assistant deputy minister. In fact, most of the report's recommendations were accepted and appeared in the new legislation that was proposed in June of 1973.

Finally, a few months before the new legislation was introduced, another crisis emerged—this time in Cornwall. The issues at play were very similar to those that had existed in Sturgeon Falls. One of the differences was that in the city of Cornwall the Francophones were in a small majority. In addition, French-speaking students made up roughly 40% of the Stormont Dundas and Glengarry Public School Board's enrolment. Because of its size, the Francophone population had real political clout. The local federal and provincial elected representatives were French-speaking and very concerned to resolve the dispute. The two provincial Conservative members, one of whom was a cabinet minister and the one federal Liberal MP who also happened to be the Speaker of the House of Commons, pushed strongly for a quick solution and the establishment of a French-language secondary school. Again there was a student strike and, given the proximity of Cornwall to the province of Quebec, a lot of media coverage appeared in the Quebec press.

Symons brought together essentially the same team he had assembled for Sturgeon Falls and quickly went about gathering the facts on all the issues at the heart of the dispute. He went to Cornwall on several occasions in April and began the process, so successful in Sturgeon Falls, of meeting with key individuals and groups. It was clear to him, following his discussions and a review of the information provided by his team, that a French-language secondary school should be provided. Again he won the support of the student leaders for his plan. He also identified early on that the chair of the school board would be a key player. The chair, Fraser Campbell, a widely respected Scot Presbyterian farmer, met with Symons at his farm and there the two of them worked out what would become the basis of the proposal Symons made to the board. Each one believed strongly in the saying that "your word is your bond." When they had completed their discussions and shook hands, Symons knew that their agreement would win the day. Campbell had the necessary standing among his board colleagues that, if he said he thought something was fair and acceptable, he could usually bring the majority to that view. This is what happened, and on 19 April, the board approved the new French-language secondary school.

Symons's Contribution

In trying to assess the contribution made by Tom Symons to the question of Quebec and language rights, it is instructive to read an essay that he prepared in early 1971 before he was called upon to resolve the Sturgeon Falls crisis. His article, "Ontario's Quiet Revolution," appeared in a book entitled, *One Country or Two.* The volume, edited by R. M. Burns of Queen's University, also included contributions from several of Symons's colleagues on the OACC. It provides a clear perspective as to how he viewed the changes set out by Ontario in the 1960s regarding the place of Quebec in Canada and the place of the French language in Ontario. It also provides us with an insight regarding what he felt was important in strengthening the fundamental relationship between English-speaking and French-speaking Canadians.

In his essay, Symons argued that shortly after the arrival of Jean Lesage and the Quebec Liberals in 1960, a comparable "quiet revolution" began in Ontario. The changes in Ontario concerned not just what Symons termed the laws and practices relating to the Franco-Ontarian community but, equally important, the public attitudes towards that community.

Symons's focus was particularly on the provision of French-language education for Ontario's French-speaking population, but he clearly noted that other changes were also going forward that would enhance the role and place of the Franco-Ontarian community in Ontario. The 1960s, as he underlines, witnessed a significant change in the thinking and attitudes of Ontarians towards the advancement of French-language rights. It also witnessed a growing sense of confidence within the French-speaking population to assert its presence and place in Ontario. If, at the beginning of the decade, the prevailing view was that the French-speaking population had little future beyond an increasing assimilation, the end of the decade demonstrated an increasing sense of optimism that there were other more constructive options.

The fact that this was so was the result of many peoples' actions from many sectors of Ontario society. Tom Symons would never say that his role was the only one that mattered in this development. To those who were there and involved in those issues at that time, however, it was clear that he played a critical role in changing how Ontarians broadly thought about Quebec and the place of the French language in their province. They would further say that his leadership and hard work helped to strengthen Ontario's relationships with Quebec, to lay the groundwork for the creation in the late 1990s of French-language public and separate school boards, and to pass the *French Language Services Act, 1986*, which today provides the underpinning for the provision of a broad range of French-language services in the province. To this day, many in the Franco-Ontarian community remember him and his role with great respect and affection.

Symons succinctly set out the heart of his approach on these issues in his essay from *One Country or Two*. He concludes,

> A fair and reasonable recognition of the cultural and educational rights of the French-speaking minorities is the indispensable cornerstone of this distinctive Canadian tradition of cultural pluralism and diversity.

He acted on the principles that have been dear to him throughout his life and, when given the opportunity, provided the leadership to put them into practice. In this field of endeavour, as in so many others, Tom Symons enriched our society and enhanced the rights of both English- and French-speaking Canadians.

CHAPTER 6

Robert L. Stanfield and Tom Symons: A Public Policy Partnership

TOM McMILLAN

In September 1967, when Robert Stanfield became the national leader of the Progressive Conservative Party—at the most exciting leadership convention in Canadian political history—he had been premier of Nova Scotia for eleven years, the most successful politician in the province's history. Stanfield achieved all this electoral success by doing exactly what he was about to do as national PC leader, including—and I would argue *especially*—in policy development. Hard work and tireless attention to detail enabled him to prepare the Progressive Conservative Party of Canada—both for opposition and, it was hoped, for government—more carefully, and to better effect, than any previous Tory leader had ever done before him. On the policy front, as in party organization (almost as badly in disarray), the need for such steady leadership could not have been more dire. His predecessor, John Diefenbaker, a spell-binding orator and unsurpassed stump campaigner, had regarded policy "as a sub-branch of rhetoric and given [it] the very lowest priority."[1] When Stanfield inherited the leadership, consequently, the PC Party was adrift, without a detailed policy on a single issue or even the vaguest idea of where it wanted to take the country. To the surprise of everyone, except those of his admirers who knew him best, Stanfield rose masterfully to the challenge. True to his character, he did what he had always done—exceeded expectations.

To build a policy "cupboard" and lead a team to develop party policy to fill it, Stanfield initially turned to the man who had run third—behind himself and Manitoba premier Duff Roblin—at the September 1967 leadership convention. That man was E. Davie Fulton. Fulton was an excellent choice, for he was a brilliant and scholarly man (indeed, a former Rhodes Scholar). Unfortunately for Stanfield, Fulton was a spent force, both politically and physically, by the time he agreed to undertake this vital policy-development assignment. In fact, he was soon to lose his bid for re-election to the House of Commons, in Kamloops, in the 1968 election. Stanfield was to make a completely different choice for Fulton's successor, reaching far outside caucus. The new policy chair replaced Fulton in April 1968, literally on the eve of the 25 June election campaign, much too late in the game to affect its outcome.

1. Stanfield's Policy Partner

Enter stage right—or, more accurately, left of centre—the new chair of Robert Stanfield's Policy Advisory Committee: Tom Symons, the young president of Trent University. It was he to whom Stanfield turned to play the starring role in a show the director knew urgently required not only a new script but also new players. By amicable agreement, Fulton bowed out as Stanfield's policy committee chair. There really had not been much of a committee to chair. Nor still much policy, either. *Toronto Star* Ottawa editor Anthony Westell had it right: "During the barren Diefenbaker years, the party was shut out of the academic world."[2] Stanfield now wanted a bona fide member of the academic community—somebody likely outside the traditional ranks of the Tory Party—for this pivotal policy role. He sought an individual of unimpeachable stature and with broad contacts who could reach out beyond the PC Party to knowledgeable people in diverse fields. He felt he needed policy experts capable of helping him and the party both devise a new policy direction and develop substantive policies on particular issues. With these policies, he hoped to equip himself and his parliamentary caucus for a wide variety of purposes. That included, following the 1968 election, his own renewed mandate as Leader of

Her Majesty's Official Opposition, to which he intended to devote much time and energy in the immediate period.

What Stanfield sought, as well, was a person with whom he himself would be personally comfortable and who would, in turn, be at ease with him. He contemplated their spending a great deal of time with each other. The new chair needed to be modern enough in his thinking to help lead the party on a new policy course. And yet, he had to be sufficiently sensitive to the party's rich history and heritage and diverse grass-roots makeup to avoid undermining the advancement of Stanfield's other priority: unifying behind him his caucus and rank-and-file members. Who better to fill this dual requirement, Stanfield thought, than the founding president of a university whose very character bespoke the precious value of blending the old with the new?

The chairmanship of the party's *Policy Advisory Committee* and the role of *Chief Policy Advisor* to the leader were to become fused throughout Stanfield's time as leader in the person of Tom Symons, who served in both capacities. The committee was, technically, a creature of the party through its Executive Committee (commonly called "National Executive") mandated by the party's constitution to establish such structures. The advisory role, by contrast, was not a party appointment but a leader appointment and, therefore, not strictly partisan in nature. Indeed, Stanfield was eager that this leader-focused advisory role—and, by extension, the more party-focused Policy Advisory Committee role as well—not be seen unduly partisan. After all, Stanfield expected both roles to focus on outreach to people (experts especially) not necessarily self-identified with the party but open to helping it become, through progressive policies, more welcoming to this very same kind of person. Tom Symons was a progressive Tory in the Macdonald/Cartier Liberal/Conservative coalition tradition. Stanfield believed a man like him would be just what the doctor—or, more accurately, the spirit of the Old Chieftain—ordered.

The policy partnership between Robert Stanfield and Tom Symons was based on two personalities at once very similar and very different. Stanfield was, essentially, a patrician; many of us Maritimers would say "aristocrat." He was the grandson of the founder of the Stanfield underwear industrial empire, Charles Stanfield, to whom

Bob has often been likened by those who know the family well. Charles made his fortune the same way his grandson was to rebuild the shattered Nova Scotia Conservative Party and, later, the national Tory Party: "slow determination and unswerving attention to detail."[3]

Starting his schooling in Truro, Nova Scotia, Stanfield finished his pre-university education at the elite boarding school Ashbury College in the affluent Ottawa suburb of Rockcliffe Park. He then went off to Dalhousie University and, finally, Harvard Law School. At both institutions, he was a stellar student, graduating *magna cum laude* and making the prestigious Law Revue editorial team at the New England ivy-league institution. Scion of such an illustrious family and a wealthy man by most peoples' standards—certainly Maritimers'—Bob Stanfield would be as much at home in the front parlor of a Boston Brahmin as a PEI farmer in a potato field in Idaho. He had the same elite Yankee ethic: hard work; sense of duty; aversion to ostentation; understatement to the point of mute; and, most characteristic of all, a belief embedded in his DNA that, in biblical terms, "to whom much is given, much is expected." In a phrase: *noblesse oblige.*

Tom Symons—fifteen years younger than the Tory leader but, seemingly, much older than his actual years—was cut from a similar cloth to Robert Stanfield's, though blue serge in contrast to Stanfield's Harris tweed. Contrary to myth (which tended to wrap around the Trent president like a boa constrictor), Symons was not born to great wealth. But, influenced by a distinguished Upper Canada family heritage, on both sides, he exuded Old World values and class and style that caused many people to believe that, if his blood were any bluer, he would need to be committed to hospital for hemophilia. Certainly, with or without real wealth, Symons, like Stanfield, was a patrician. In the face of the Trent president's regal bearing and courtly manners, even Colonel Pickering might have been forgiven for taking his leave lest he be thought a philistine by comparison. As significant as anything else, Tom Symons, like Robert Stanfield, carried *noblesse oblige* in his soul as though personally ordered by God to carry out His command that "faith without good works is dead." Both Stanfield and Symons were preternaturally disposed to public service.

In other respects, the two men were very different. Stanfield: reserved, almost shy; awkward and ill-at-ease in social settings and with individuals alike; painfully slow and deliberate speaking—when not surprisingly eloquent if required to rise to the occasion, as he often did. And yet, ironically, Stanfield possessed a seemingly inborn wry sense of humour and rapid-fire wit that, especially in private, left colleagues and staff buckled over in laughter if not too stunned when, as sometimes happened, it entered the profane.

Symons, by marked contrast, oozes charm from every invisible pore; has an uncommon gift of putting at ease the most insecure nervous Nelly; has a silver tongue, in conversation and public forums equally, that would require a Brinks truck for security if ever converted to hard currency; and possesses a sense of humour that, in contrast to Stanfield's drollness, is, counter-intuitively, inclined towards the mischievous and the outlandish (think Benny Hill or Monty Python).

Physically, the men could not have been more different if one had been born a blue heron, the other an Arctic owl: Stanfield, craggy face and gangly height and long neck and arms and legs and boniness; Symons, shorter if only because somewhat stooped like a lord of the manor weighed down by a flowing ermine-trimmed gown; he, stocky and waist-coated and pocket watch-chained, skin slightly swarthy and satin-smooth but firm like a moist petitfour on a mica china saucer. Not birds of a feather, to be sure!

And yet, these two markedly different men—bound more by a shared sense of privilege and attendant commitment to public service than by partisan label—were to form one of the most remarkable partnerships in the history of party politics in Canada. That partnership was consummated at the Priorities for Canada Conference in the city of marital partnerships, Niagara Falls, in October 1969.

2. The Priorities for Canada Conference: 1969

"The Niagara Policy Conference," as the more formally titled "Priorities for Canada Conference" entered the history books being called, was the brainchild of more than one father. But the idea of the conference itself was conceived, primarily, by Stanfield in the embrace of Symons. The latter's sense of moment as an historian made him all too aware of how spectacularly successful the Liberals had been, back in 1960, with their landmark Kingston Policy Conference. Stanfield and Symons saw the Niagara Conference in the manner the Liberals had seen their Kingston Conference, as the first and major step towards reshaping the party's image through progressive policies. PC headquarters' claim—possibly apocryphal—was that it was to be "the largest and most widely representative political gathering to study policies that has ever been held in Canada."[4] The aim was to develop policy in a wide variety of fields—from taxation to poverty to foreign investment to external affairs and foreign aid to federal-provincial relations to parliamentary reform; even to marijuana laws, the liberalization of which the delegates were to come within a puff of supporting. The conference was to showcase the progressive thinkers of the party, expose to the public a more modern and attractive side of Tories, present the party as serious about issues that Canadians cared about, and launch a continuing process to generate the policies that would convince voters this was a party it could trust. The conference was held in the Grand Ballroom of the Sheraton-Brock Hotel, in Niagara, beginning at 7:00 p.m. on Thursday, 9 October, and ending at 2:00 p.m. the following Monday, 13 October.

Stanfield was much more than an honored guest at the conference. He was, in fact, its chairman. Symons was, technically, the "Chairman of the Program Committee." What is more, Stanfield himself chaired one of the major sessions, the panel on fiscal federalism, a subject on which he was as well informed as anyone in the entire country. Stanfield was not primarily interested in making friends with knowledgeable people. He was eager to pick their brains; cultivate a connection with them for future purposes; associate them with the party, however indirectly, both in fact and in public perception; extract from them as many policy ideas as he could, not only at Niagara, but in future as well; and encourage them to stay in contact with one another, so the party would have, in effect, its own self-cultivating internal community of experts as a resource for him and the caucus.

The Niagara Falls Conference—attended by some four hundred delegates, including sixty specialists—succeeded well beyond Stanfield's most optimistic expectations. Stanfield biographer Geoffrey Stevens observed that it "nailed together a party platform that, if not daring, at least brought the Conservative Party into the mainstream of Canadian opinion."[5] It is not quite true that the PC Party got a platform from the conference. But the substantial media attention the party received did do wonders for its image. That was one of the goals Stanfield and Symons had set for it. A party platform, though, was not. Indeed, the two men had never intended that the delegates would vote on individual issues but, instead, would seek a more informal consensus through discussion and reports presented by a "rapporteur" assigned to each session. The process was designed to give the leader and caucus, and party as a whole, a sense of direction on issues, not hard-and-fast policy, let alone dogma.

Apart from any consensus achieved on particular issues—like capital gains (positive), the guaranteed minimum income plan championed by Stanfield, and the "deux nations" concept advanced by some Tories (not so much)—the papers presented by resource people for discussion in the various sessions were consistently of high quality, a few outstanding. David Slater, dean of graduate studies at Queen's University, produced a paper on the "Canadian Economy in the 1970s" that was among the best. In an internal summary and analysis of news media coverage during and after the conference, the PC research office noted the Slater paper "obviously made a strong impression on Mr. Stanfield." Now, when read these many years later, Slater's paper strikes one as eerily prescient. In the *Telegram*, on 20 October 1969, Dalton Camp contrasted Stanfield's constructive expertise-based approach to issues with Diefenbaker's use of "policy" merely to attack political foes: "Mr. Stanfield has introduced his party to the power of positive thinking. In doing so, we have, for the first time in a long time, an opposition party whose policies are more specific than general platitudes and more positive than the customary catalogue of complaint."

Stanfield emerged from Niagara Falls much stronger than before. It was, writes Stevens, "a major move towards modernizing the party's image and overcoming the anti-intellectualism in the party that had long blocked attempts at reform."[6] Stanfield, in partnership with Symons, was beginning to succeed in remaking the party in the new leader's own image, replacing Diefenbaker's prairies populism with something more acceptable to modern voters. Not charismatic, to be sure. But, in that Nixon/Vietnam/Watergate era, with politicians on both sides of the border increasingly seen as corrupt if not fundamentally evil, home-spun Nova Scotian *noblesse oblige* was starting to look darn good to a lot of Canadian voters.

3. The Policy Coordinating Committee

The Niagara Conference also provided the party with something else: a mechanism to formulate party policy after the gathering. In one of the few actual votes taken, the conference, at Stanfield's urging, approved—and the party's Executive Committee later endorsed—a formal motion to establish a Policy Coordinating Committee (PCC) "whereby the policies of the [party] can be given continued study and examination. . ."[7] The membership was to include, notably, "the national leader or his representative." The qualifier "or his representative" was to prove academic; for Stanfield was to attend virtually every meeting, sometimes leaving urgent business elsewhere to do so. In a revealing provision, which Stanfield himself not only approved but also urged, the chairman of the party's new mechanism for establishing policy was to be the leader himself, or, in his absence—equally revealing—the chairman of the Policy Advisory Committee (Symons). If Niagara Falls had been the policy honeymoon, the resolution that established the PCC was, in a reversal of the usual chronology, the marriage license. The hard slogging to make the marriage work was about to begin.

(a) The PCC Structure

At this point, it is necessary to make a distinction between two "structures": the Policy Advisory Committee (PAC) and the Policy Coordinating Committee (PCC). In a letter dated 15 April 1968—sent widely, in effect, "to whom it may concern"—Tom Symons informed recipients that "Mr. Stanfield and the members of the Policy Advisory Committee, at their recent meeting, have asked if I would undertake the chairmanship of the Committee." The PAC was, in essence, not a committee at all, despite the "legal" nomenclature. Rather, it was an elaborate process directed by Tom Symons. That process, with Symons as the continuing wagon-master, was devised to recruit a wide variety of people in a host of different ways to do a host of different things for a host of different purposes at a host of different times but towards one ultimate objective: the formulation of a body of integrated and well-researched policies on a broad range of public issues well before the next election. The policies were intended to help the leader and caucus, both on a continuing basis (in Parliament and elsewhere) and in the election itself, while also helping party candidates and their campaign workers. To the extent the PAC was a "real" committee, this committee consisted of Tom Symons and his assistant acting as a virtual two-man steering committee to achieve the Policy Coordinating Committee's mandate. The Niagara Falls resolution that established the PCC did mandate national headquarters to be the "secretariat" of the PCC, and the "appointment of such a secretariat would be the responsibility of the National Director" (the headquarters' chief officer). Under successive national directors of the party, however, from the beginning of the PCC's work, everyone simply took for granted that, with funding and administrative support from national headquarters, Tom Symons and a full-time assistant (paid by national headquarters but operating under the wing of the leader's operation) would fulfill this role. And they did. I became that assistant.

The Progressive Conservative leader was bound by certain legal and constitutional arrangements. But unless in some egregious way he abused his authority, by whatever provision, his followers typically gave him broad scope to lead them how he wanted. Accordingly, the Policy Coordinating Committee operated under Stanfield's leadership in a fairly informal (almost extra-legal) manner in some respects. As caucus head, the PC leader can pursue almost any channel and can set up almost any structure when he wishes to develop policy for himself and his parliamentary followers. As PC Party head, though, he is subject, at least in theory, to the party's constitution. Under that legal framework, it is the party itself, through its Executive Committee ("National Executive") that has the authority to establish structures to develop policy for the membership and, by implication, for the caucus to the extent that the body feels like part of the institution that gives it its political label. The National Executive authorizes the establishment of a policy committee. But it is, invariably, the leader who appoints its chairman, and the policy committee revolves around him; though it may technically report to the body whose authority it was to establish the committee in the first place. So, Tom Symons's policy work pivoted around Stanfield; it did not focus on, still less emanate from, the party's bureaucracy. The Symons operation did, however, work closely with the PC research office. This research centre, like that of the other parties, was launched by the Trudeau government in the Speech from the Throne in the Twenty-Eighth Parliament, 12 September 1968. The PC research office had ten full-time research professionals and three support staff (at the outset). It worked primarily with the PC caucus, especially the policy committee chairs. The research office was separate from, but complemented, Tom Symons's "volunteer" operation.

(b) The PCC Membership

In addition to the leader, the membership of the Policy Coordinating Committee was defined by the Niagara Conference resolution to consist of the chairman of the Policy Advisory Committee; the national chairman of organization; the PC national president; the national (headquarters) director; the caucus chairman; the House Leader; three caucus members (who, over time, were selected variously); and the president of the PC Women's Association, of the PC Students' Federation, and of the Young PCs Association. In practice, however, that membership was quite fluid. Some people were invited to attend from time to time as the need arose. Others attended "regularly" by virtue of office. Even in this category ("ex officio") attendance was far from static. Some ex-officio members attended regularly for a while but not other times, depending on their personal circumstances. Some attended hardly at all, even though they had the right. (The first time I met Brian Mulroney, my future boss and cabinet colleague, was at a PCC meeting. To my knowledge, he attended that one time only.) The truth is a few people who, technically, had a right to attend only if invited did get invited so often that, after a while, both they and other members took their attendance for granted to the point where no invitation was deemed necessary. They became, *de facto*, the same as *ex officio* members. Indeed, many of the *de facto* members ended up attending more regularly than *ipso facto* ones. (Ain't Latin grand?) All of this must appear byzantine to outsiders. But the process worked because, in practice, it was so simple: if the committee wanted you to attend or *you* wanted to attend, barring Raiders of the Lost Ark, you *did* attend. Stanfield, as chairman of the PCC, almost always attended. He took that role seriously and, following his example, most others did too.

(c) The PCC Dynamics, Modus Operandi

Meetings of the PCC were not a social affair. They were usually held in the boardroom of national headquarters (though the first ones were held at the PC research office). Unless required by the length of the meeting, food was not routinely served—nor, as I recall, was much else, either. Certainly never alcohol! When Stanfield arrived, almost always punctually, the meeting began. Introductions of newcomers were short and perfunctory. Significantly, Stanfield, without a hint of condescension, always noted the presence of French-Canadians with special warmth and extra words of welcome (in French!)—and, it seemed to me, with genuine appreciation. By the same token, Stanfield went out of his way to encourage Francophones to participate and subtly acknowledged, both in French and in English, his keen interest in their remarks when they did. Minutes of a previous meeting, routinely kept, were deemed approved unless corrections were advisable, not usually necessary—because I kept them! Tom Symons sat to the right of the leader at the end of the board table—a little like placing most of the cargo at one extreme of a ship; except, rather than list, the "ship" in this case navigated a lot more smoothly that way as it set a pace and tone both classy and business-like.

There was invariably a formal agenda, about a half-dozen to a dozen items, some of them easily dispatched. If the task at hand was to review draft policy, as it normally was, members rolled up their sleeves, pushed forward chairs, lowered eyes, focused, began detailed line-by-line analysis, and started to share ideas. The party's research office provided a staff member or two as resource people, and the office's director almost always attended, participating actively in the discussions, as did anyone else who wanted to, member and staff alike.

People knew that Stanfield was a man of business. So, the rhythm of the meeting required little discipline or admonition against speech-making or offensive disagreement. Everyone was an equal; but, of course, as is the case in any meeting, respect was gained by quality of contribution, not quantity of words. Stanfield was, clearly, "first among equals," and Symons a close second, no matter who else was in the room. Both Stanfield and Symons exuded that "we're doing something important here" aura that contributed to important things actually getting done. With pipe in hand, whether smoked or not—a different era then—and municipal water tower-size thermos of tea always at the ready, Symons projected an image of gentlemanly informality while telegraphing, consciously or not, the likelihood the meeting was not going to end anytime soon. And it scarcely ever did. A meeting rarely lasted less than an entire afternoon or evening, sometimes the two combined, a few even well into the next day. Again, people were there to work, not enjoy one another's company; though, as people got to know one another better, the atmosphere became steadily more congenial and the process, correspondingly, more productive. To my mind, Symons's greatest skill is team-building. He can create a community out of two people, a nation out of three! Where does such magic come from?

Stanfield's involvement in the PC Party's policy process, steady and active as it was, normally involved matters of fact or technicality, or fairly minor substantive concerns. Stanfield hardly ever dominated the discussion; seldom took sides in a heated debate; never discouraged disagreement, though showed impatience, as many others did, when wheels were spun and progress was stymied, particularly due to any one person's dogmatism. Anything major was generally of a political nature. ("Will this upset caucus member Ima Blowhard?") Draft policy—whether from a conference, the opposition research office, the PCC itself, a study group, or some other outside source—was not likely to recommend either a general direction or a specific turn wildly far from what the leader or caucus or party as a whole would be widely known to find potentially acceptable or, at least, debatable. After all, no one was going to urge the party to publicly support selling Nova Scotia to the Sultan of Brunei to pay off the national debt. When agreement was just not possible (say, because of principle), or practical (say, given time constraints), or desirable (say, in the face of looming political sensitivity), or other reason (say, nobody gave a damn about the subject), the item was held over or simply set aside; sometimes never to be seen again. Stanfield rarely threw the policy train off the rails, just encouraged the conductor to go more slowly or in a slightly different direction. He would—from time to time, but not as a practice—dig in his heels, especially if he thought an idea was dumb politics or just plain dumb, period. In which case, no one in the room—short of somebody still recovering from an earlier Stanfield witty bon mot—would have any doubt how he felt: he made it abundantly clear. He was especially sensitive to proposals that would impact Quebec or French Canada more generally. On one such occasion, at a PCC meeting (24 January 1974), he expressed alarm that policy proposals had, in his judgment, a "centralist bias" and were, therefore "not sufficiently sensitive to the views of French Canada and to other Canadians who favour a more decentralized federation." He was similarly inhospitable to almost anything that seriously grated on provincial sensibilities, as though he were still a provincial premier himself. One particular proposal that leaps to mind (on foreign investment), close to being agreed upon, was taken off the table until further inquiries could be made of the affected province's specific views on the subject. In all cases, one standard was preeminent: could he sell the idea to his parliamentary caucus? The party membership's views appeared less important; because he figured, if he could not get a certain policy through caucus, how the broad membership felt about it was irrelevant: the proposal would not go anywhere, anyway.

Stanfield took notes, though not copiously—less the student in class furiously recording, *figuratively*, every morsel of wisdom from a professor's mouth; more the Duchess of Windsor, known to keep a tiny gold pen and pad discreetly under the rim of her dinner charger to note, *literally*, each morsel served wrong at her elegant dinner parties lest the chef ever again put too much vinegar in the vinaigrette. Stanfield, unlike the duchess, never read the riot act to the culpable "chef" (the draftsman of a shoddy policy paper, say), much less before other committee members; that was left to others, in private. In the many hours I spent in his company in policy discussions, I never once saw him visibly angry—frustrated, yes; tired, to be sure; confused, disappointed, impatient, uneasy, or uncomfortable. . . all those things, certainly. But never expressly angry. Only once did I see even the vaguest hint of tension between Bob Stanfield (a non-smoker) and Tom Symons (then a pipe smoker; though not now, and not for years)—in the countless meetings and conversations to which I was a party or witness over the years. The incident concerned Symons's pipe ("Mind my pipe, sir?"). He had been experimenting with an unusually fragrant pipe tobacco that even I, with a high tolerance, found challenging. Looks may not kill. But, in this instance, Stanfield's stern look—and comment: "What's *that* you're smoking?"—killed any chance of that mean weed ever finding its way into a Symons bong again! Especially in the leader's presence. It never did!

Symons, too, took notes. . . characteristically on a small three-by-four-inch white pad in red or blue ballpoint. These notes—written in Symons's neat and precise and distinct hieroglyphics—when converted to verbal instructions to me, could fill the entire eleven-volume set of Will Durant's history of the world! Or, at least, it struck me that way at the time. All told, the PCC had its own dynamics—Stanfield very much the chairman, Symons not so much the vice-chairman as the *éminence grise.* Even if the man on the throne did not always like his pipe tobacco.

Among the main benefits Stanfield derived from the policy process was this: it helped focus and sharpen his own consideration of issues while the PCC, in particular, served as a valuable sounding board for his personal policy views before he risked expressing them publicly. Ever a cautious man, he often tested his thinking on particular questions with Symons prior to airing them even at the PCC stage.

For his part, Tom Symons applied himself to the policy work with equal measures of commitment and diligence; leaving many a younger participant, myself included, panting and exhausted well before he himself lost first wind, let alone the second and third, which, without fail, he appeared to have in reserve.

A politician, especially one in cabinet, is, more than anything else, a professional meeting attendee. Certainly, he or she spends more time in committee, of whatever size or type, than in any other activity. In all my time in public life, I met no one else with skill close to Symons's in a committee chair—directing discussion, forging a consensus, building team spirit. Making the process work. The skillful manner in which Symons brought together and created a sense of common purpose among individuals and groups from widely diverse backgrounds and of often sharply conflicting views (set aside personalities) never ceased to amaze me. It mattered not whether the forum was a small policy subcommittee or a large regional or even national policy conference: the charm offensive and diplomatic gymnastics always worked their magic. Quite apart from the policy product itself, the policy development process he devised and directed, in partnership with Stanfield, contributed mightily to party cohesion and inclusiveness, another way these men were preparing the PC Party for power. Many of the foot soldiers on the policy front who helped win the 1984 federal election for the party a decade later—not to mention their general, the new prime minister himself, Brian Mulroney—had been conscripted by Symons in the policy work for Stanfield. When I myself was appointed to cabinet by Mulroney, following the 1984 election, what struck me most about the political face of the new government (from cabinet members like me to ministerial staffers to Privy Council appointees, and on and on) was the ubiquity of Symons's "policy alumni." They swarmed the place! I dare say the size of this alumni network rivaled that of the Trent University alumni association Symons had grown in not much more time, employing the same community-building skills.

4. PC Party Resource People

Drawing on the contacts with, and the good will generated among, the policy experts that had been recruited for the Niagara Conference, Symons soon began to put some of these people to work in the service of the party. Former 1965 Diefenbaker campaign manager E. A. Goodman, involved in politics since Methuselah was in diapers, wrote to the Trent University president, on 4 November 1969, soon after the conference. He said, "At no time have we had better liaison and cooperation between members of the academic world and a political party, in my memory."

It was not an easy road for Stanfield and Symons. They often had to haul the former party of Diefenbaker kicking and yelling in the more modern direction they thought necessary if the party was to be both relevant and successful at the ballot box. Former MP and party royal Jean Wadds (a future UK High Commissioner for Canada) was frustrated with her own Niagara Conference policy session compromise on the guaranteed minimum income plan so dear to Stanfield and to her and other Tory reformers. Quoted by journalist W. A. Wilson in *The Toronto Daily Star*, following that session, she lamented, "Mr. Stanfield has been trying to lead his party into a genuinely progressive position. . . but, in the welfare debate [at Niagara], the Conservatives made it inescapably clear. . . there is a hard core that wants the party to be the voice of reaction." Her comment, though made in a specific context, spoke to a broader and continuing truth. Neither Stanfield nor Symons, however, was deterred by setbacks. They were in the process for the long haul.

Before long, not a single expert turned Symons down because of the party's anti-intellectual image, as so many had done in the Niagara Conference planning. The roster of informed people willing to help the process climbed steadily. Soon after the Niagara Conference, the number of volunteers far exceeded that of conscripts. It was beginning to look like a war that could be won.

As valuable as outside specialists were to the process, many PCC members themselves brought a lot of expertise to it—obvious cases in point being Symons and Stanfield. MPs and Senators are too often underrated for the policy experience and expertise they accumulate over the years in the individual areas of special interest to them. Their informed input on the committee—as well as that of the leader's own staff and of many others who participated from within the party—was invaluable.

Stanfield, encouraged by Symons, was not finished shaking up the political home that many of the Diefenbaker loyalists, and others within the party, continued to find quite comfortable just as it was, thanks very much. On 29 June 1970, he announced a round of "policy probes" on a number of specific issues and chaired or co-chaired by well-informed individuals: *Employment and Economic Growth* (Dr. Gillies, Faculty of Administrative Studies, York University, later an MP); *Urban Affairs* (Alvin Hamilton, former agriculture minister, and MP Vince Danser, former president of the Canadian Federation of Mayors and Municipalities); *Consumer Affairs* (Heward Grafftey, a Quebec lawyer and former MP and consumer advocate, and Jill Armstrong, formerly of the Canadian Liberties Association and Oxfam); *Pollution* (Gordon Aiken, an Ontario MP and lawyer, and John Fraser, a Vancouver lawyer and future fisheries minister and House of Commons speaker); and *Housing* (MP Lincoln Alexander, from Hamilton, and the first-ever elected black member of Parliament).

All these policy probe reports—enriched by the party's research office's own work and advised by Symons at a discreet distance—were fed into the fast-developing policy discussion mix. They added to the growing image of the party as serious about public policy. Geoffrey Stevens, speaking of the housing probe, for example, said, "It served to remind the public that there was a party called the Progressive Conservative Party, and that it, too, was concerned about the problems of the cities."[8]

One of the other approaches was study groups that took a particular issue and tackled it in a broader context. This innovative approach gave the party a store of ideas across a range of subjects in a highly-integrated way. Typically, the membership was selected so that a specific facet would have the benefit of knowledge and insights from an individual expert in that area. This approach not only helped the party cover more bases but also gave it fuller perspectives than would have been possible had the relevant issues been studied separately, if at all. A case in point was a wide-ranging study of economic and cultural facets of sovereignty, including foreign investment. Headed by Manitoba's former Attorney General Sterling Lyon—who, in addition to chairing, helped on both legal and political dimensions—the group included international business professor I. A. Litvak and economics professor C. J. Maule, both from McMaster University, handling the purely economic aspects; university law professor Robert Kerr of the University of New Brunswick (legal); and politics professor William Neville of Trent University (cultural). The Lyon group produced one of the best sets of ideas and proposals for the party while Stanfield was leader. Stanfield was to draw heavily from their work, including in a major speech in the House of Commons in response to proposed government legislation on foreign investment.

For the sovereignty working group, as for others in greater or lesser amounts, the party provided funding; in this case, one thousand dollars (equivalent to many times that in today's dollars). I served as secretary of the working group, keeping a record of the content as it progressed. For me, a crash course in economics! I could have had no better teachers. Their report recommended an aggressive approach to the growing concern across the country about American influence on Canada in certain sectors. The group's work, like that of others, was fed into the policy mix to be considered by the PCC. Around this time, syndicated journalist Anthony Westell wrote that "Canadian politics are entering an era of wide-open policy debate and renewed national soul-searching as the major parties seek to identify the great issues of the seventies."[9] The truth of his insight could not have been more applicable to what, under Tom Symons's leadership, the PC Party was doing, and would continue to do, in policy subgroups like the ones described above.

5. Policy Papers: The Sausage Factory

Policy papers are like sausages: they often contain, in addition to new and fresh meat (or one hopes they do), whatever happens to be around. In our own case, the pieces were pulled from many different sources—existing policy, if it existed; the leader and MPs' speeches; the policy content from party gatherings, national general meetings, and regional and local ones alike; study groups; commissioned research; PC research office work; and whatever Symons could sneak in on Native rights (and on a lot of other issues, it can be revealed now, since the relevant Statute of Limitations period has passed). Much of the party's policy after the 1968 election was produced by the elaborate process established, under Tom Symons's direction, through the Policy Coordinating Committee. It was by this process—the experts recruited; the working groups set up; the special studies done and inquiries made; the policy meetings held, all the rest—that much of the raw material was converted into a (more or less) cohesive finished product. The sausage!

On some issues, we had to begin papers from scratch. That was particularly true in the early stages of the overall process, immediately following the 1968 election, when there were very few solid lean pieces of meat in the abattoir to put in the sausage. At this point, Tom Symons was both the abattoir's general manager and the principal sausage maker. His own management ways are, therefore, highly relevant here.

Symons is nothing if not—besides a tea drinker—a reader. But more than books alone, he reads newspapers, from across Canada and also from other countries, especially the United Kingdom. He reads magazines. He reads journals and revues. He reads studies and reports. Not content enough only to read the stuff, he underlines and notates everything that strikes him as particularly salient. Or just interesting. An article would be cut out; photocopied; distributed widely; discussed with staff; acted on, if necessary, and it *always* was. "MWDP?": May We Discuss Please? This is what Symons always wrote, with the broad painterly strokes of his morbidly obese black-and-gold fountain pen, on each manila file folder he stuffed with clippings. The staff would need to study the current file, prepare to discuss it with him, and act on his follow-up instructions. In this context, that staffer was me.

The information and ideas from all such reading frequently constituted the seeds that gave rise to the earliest stages of policy paper drafts. I did the rough initial drafts of most of the policy papers. Symons would then review and substantially rework them, well before they proceeded to anyone else for review. We typically consulted experts at the early stages, about substance and for technical accuracy. By the time we placed the policy papers before the PCC, the papers were invariably advanced enough that they could withstand scrutiny by busy people. Their time, especially Stanfield's, was too valuable to waste with anything less finished. Particularly later in the life of the PCC, people knew the difference between a rough draft and an advanced one. Stanfield *always* did.

Tom Symons is a skilled writer. On a major policy challenge, his talents were especially helpful. He had a good command of the mechanics and musicality and nuances of language. After all, his father, Harry, and a brother Scott were both award-winning writers. It is in the family DNA. Symons, however, had other strong qualities at nuclear war with his writing gifts. My Queen's University graduate thesis advisor, political scientist Tony Lovink (himself the son of an ambassador), described Symons as "the best academic diplomat in the country." As befits a diplomat, Symons had an almost preternatural aversion to controversy. This quality caused him to be, I think, unduly cautious, as an actual diplomat would be, in the revisions he himself did to the drafts before they went to the PCC for its scrutiny. The papers—need I say?—left my own hands Shakespearean in their grandeur, Tennysonian in their poetry, Newtonian in their methodological rigour. Destined for immortality! By the time Symons was finished with them, however, those self-same drafts no more resembled the originals than a deciduous tree in summer's brightest light would mirror itself in the darkest dog days of winter. A lot of greenery added, not many dead leaves pared. To boot, most of the prickly thorns and bitter berries were removed with a ferocity akin to a drug dealer's flushing contraband down the toilet as the drug squad pounds on the door. Or that is how I viewed it all at the time.

No doubt, after these "improvements," the trees were rendered easier to survive the harsh winter: scrutiny by Stanfield and the PCC. But it was, genuinely, at the expense of making the tree a bit too leafy, in some cases. That was the most common criticism by the media, when they were not remarking on, and calling specific attention to, the policy contradictions in the total package. The PCC was well aware of most of the contradictions throughout the drafting process. But, for political reasons largely, they were tolerated—principally, to "reconcile" irreconcilable policy disagreements either within the committee itself or between it and, say, the parliamentary caucus. It was often under this sort of circumstance that Tom Symons's dual skills as a diplomat and wordsmith came into play most helpfully. A case in point concerned the party's call for an industrial strategy for the country. It implied the federal government should identify "winners" and "losers" in allocating tax incentives or direct subventions to help foster specific sectors, presumably at the expense of others. This, in turn, implied that individual industries would not be aided outside the overall strategy. And yet, the PCC recognized the political need to respond to particular cries for government help that would be hard to respond to other than on a case-by-case, ad hoc basis, outside a more strategic approach. For example, the very existence of the Canadian magazine sector was then threatened by foreign "dumping" practices, particularly by *Time* and *Newsweek*. Some PCC members thought the government should lend support, even if publishing itself did not fit into a national industrial strategy. The fig leaf the PCC decided to use to cover its naked effort to have it both ways in this case—a strategic approach, *but*...—was to say we would consider supporting certain industries separately *but* "in the context of the industrial strategy." The compromise (considered a breakthrough by all combatants on the issue) came from Symons, as it so often did. Sometimes, as in this case, the fig leaf was big enough to hide the bare-assed politics (more or less); other times, the leaf may as well have been cellophane for all the transparent duplicity. Diplomacy and word-smithing have their limits, even when practised by a master like Symons.

The contradictions appeared, not only between different papers but also within some of the papers themselves, specific examples of which the media were quick to note. The media criticism had much merit. Still, we were producing political documents, not trying to win a Pulitzer Prize for literature. The amazing thing is that the verbal cocktail had as much kick to it as it did. The papers, in general, were met with both surprise and admiration by most media critics and with appreciation by the party, especially candidates, for their breadth and depth. Re-reading some of the papers now, lo, all these many years later, one marvels, all things considered, at their quality and, in some cases, vision.

6. Symons's Role as Direct Stanfield Advisor

Tom Symons was knowledgeable about a broad range of issues, expert in a number. His expertise was especially notable in education, Canadian studies in particular; Franco-Ontarian matters; cultural property and heritage; Native rights; and human rights. In all those areas, he was widely published and, in some, an authority, especially Canadian studies. There were not many issues Symons did not know well, some better than others. But I would make two major points here. First, the areas where Symons was most knowledgeable—in a word, "social"—tended not to be the ones in which Stanfield was most interested. The areas where Stanfield was expert, and most heavily involved, were primarily economic—monetary and fiscal policies, including taxation, among others. These were not Symons's strongest suit. One could view this asymmetry as an advantage, each man compensating for the other's policy "weakness." To an extent, that was true. Stanfield became more sensitive to, and informed about, certain social policy matters than he would have become had Symons not regularly briefed him on them, whether at policy meetings or in private discussions. It is very revealing that, after leaving politics, Stanfield established The Robert and Mary Stanfield Foundation for Canadian Studies, with Tom Symons as a Trustee. It is inconceivable to me that Stanfield would ever have thought of earmarking his philanthropy in such a way absent Symons's influence over the preceding years. By the same token, in a reversal of roles, Stanfield influenced Symons's own thinking, and deepened his understanding, in economics. He certainly did mine. A case in point was the guaranteed minimum income, never far from the leader's mind, nor lips.

As if to compensate for his lack of expertise in economics, perhaps, Tom Symons made sure that Stanfield had access to some of the best economic brains in the land, notwithstanding the leader's own expertise in this area. Towards that end, for example, Symons set up a series of private off-the-record meetings for me with top economists to pick their brains for Stanfield on the state of the economy and on how best to manage the then-looming dark clouds. Among the economic experts consulted were Arthur Smith (head of the Conference Board of Canada); H. E. English (Carleton University); David MacQueen (Glendon College, York University); John Crispo (University of Toronto, a rising star and media darling); David Wilton (Queen's University); and Stefan Dupré (University of Toronto). These were to be no idle chats: Stanfield discussed with Symons exactly what he felt he needed to know; I had a carefully prepared script (though I asked follow-up questions, as well as others I thought, on the spot, needed to be asked); I took copious and detailed notes, somewhat in the manner of a court stenographer; and, later, I prepared draft reports that were

"Symonized" to the nth degree. Finally, and only then, the product was forwarded to Stanfield. Symons was nothing if not thorough. I was nothing if not bone tired!

Reading the extensive notes decades later, I am struck by how carefully they were prepared; how candid the economists had been; and how prescient most of the predictions turned out on matters like the oil shock's lasting impact, the likelihood of a major recession, and the inevitability (no matter who won power) that the country would have to adopt wage and price controls. Maybe David Slater, of Niagara Conference fame, had lured these economists to his clairvoyance sideline. And Thomas Carlyle said economics is the dismal science. Not when I was there. If I had had any doubts whether all this was worthwhile, they soon proved groundless: my own little private parlour game at PCC meetings involved counting Stanfield's references to the briefing papers.

Symons was every bit the nationalist on culture that a Liberal policy advisor like Tom Axworthy would later be on economic independence; though each would argue, as Symons did, almost as an article of faith, that the two perspectives were only different facets of the same gem and, therefore, required the same high polish. And yet—and this is an important "yet"—Symons was not a propagandist, even in the best sense. It was not in his nature to proselytize or preach to Stanfield. Nor to anyone else, for that matter. But especially not to Stanfield. I say "especially" because it was not in Stanfield's own nature to be proselytized to or preached at. Symons's greatest strength as a communicator is an unerring sense of occasion and of audience. He knew his "audience" in Stanfield; so, on no occasion, by either personal predilection or judgment, would he have lectured Stanfield. Symons raised issues with Stanfield; funneled lots of ideas and proposals to him, in private as at policy meetings; and always made himself available to counsel the leader, either on a particular issue or a range of issues, immediate or longer term (though rarely on technicalities—the job of the PC research office). In the countless conversations to which I was privy between these two men over the years—on the phone or in person, in private or at meetings—not once did I hear Symons try to foist an idea or proposal on a reluctant Stanfield. He would not. If it had happened when I was not present to hear at least one side of, say, a phone conversation, typically Symons's half, the policy chairman would have told me later because he always briefed me on his Stanfield conversations. He did not in this context, so the contretemps just did not ever happen.

With the passage of time, and as Stanfield and Symons developed a higher comfort level with each other—particularly in private and, more particularly, in person (as opposed to by phone)—they talked more often and longer; diversified the subjects discussed; picked more occasions just to chat about nothing or everything; and, increasingly, enjoyed the other's company and the sound of the other's voice. When just shooting the breeze, as it were, the echoes of laughter and merriment sometimes exceeded the thoughtful pauses at both ends. And these were supposed to be reserved patricians! Boys will be boys! They each liked the man at the other end of the line, and the man at the other end of the line liked him.

7. Policy Advisor: Brain Trust Models

"Senior Advisor to the Honourable Robert L. Stanfield" was Tom Symons's official title. But he was not a policy advisor of the sort Charles McMillan would become to Brian Mulroney or Tom Axworthy to Pierre Trudeau. Both Charles McMillan and Tom Axworthy fit a certain model: in-house expert, all-round intellectual guru, and general factotum who has the ear of his boss, eye on the ball, shoulders to the grindstone, and is not farther than a foot from the throne. Such people are strong on body parts, especially the brain. For about the same time (about four years), each served as senior policy advisor to the prime minister of Canada. Each had a unique and august title—"Senior Policy Advisor" (Charley's); "Principal Secretary" (Tom's). But, when all is said and done, each was in the employ of his man. They were government *employees.* Staffers.

Tom Symons's role as Stanfield's Senior Policy Advisor could not have been more different. The Symons Model was as different from the McMillan/Axworthy Models as aged scotch is from draft beer. Tom Symons, unlike Charles McMillan and Tom Axworthy, was *not* a paid government employee. Tom Symons was, in every sense, a Citizen Servant, and *not* a Public Servant (in the bureaucratic sense). Nor was he a political operative, as Charley and Tom certainly were. Still less was Symons a political hack, just as Charley and Tom themselves were not, either—the one major respect in which all three men had something in common, besides brains. Moreover, of the three men, Symons was by far the least partisan. And yet, it was he alone—not either McMillan or Axworthy—whose mandate it was to help blaze a new policy trail, not just for his leader but also for that leader's *party*. Partisan McMillan and Axworthy were recruited to play a public role. Citizen Tory Symons was asked to play a partisan role. If love is just another word for "nothing left to lose," politics is just another word for "nothing left but irony."

Unlike Mulroney and McMillan, Symons and Stanfield had not really known each other; they knew only *of* each other, by national reputation. Stanfield did not seek in Symons a political frat brother; he had a good enough political fraternity of his own already. The new Tory leader had eleven years of experience in government, in Nova Scotia, before becoming PC Leader. Stanfield already had cultivated a tight-knit group of smart and politically savvy people, mostly Maritimers, on whom he could rely for dispassionate and candid political advice. By the same token, Stanfield was not desperate for specialized advice. He himself frequently knew more about the issues than the experts who briefed him on them.

What Stanfield sought in Symons was not a politically astute brain—though Symons, actually, was that. Nor did he seek a policy expert of the McMillan and Axworthy variety—though he was, in certain areas, that as well. Least of all did Stanfield feel the need for a close friend, though, to be sure, the two developed a warm relationship over time. What Stanfield sought, instead, was a mature, academically well-placed, and respected individual of the first rank who, by virtue of that rank and of his own personal standing, could help him with his major priority: to revolutionize the policy content of the Progressive Conservative Party of Canada and, thereby, change, in fundamental ways, both the *reality* and the *public face* of that great national institution. He sought someone who would be every bit as effective on issues as McMillan and Axworthy would subsequently be for their respective leaders. But far different in personal and public standing at the time.

My major point here is that Stanfield's choice of Symons as his chief policy advisor was not based *primarily* on his wish to have Symons advise him directly about issues. As much as he welcomed, and received, specialized knowledge and counsel from Symons, and that was part of Symons's role, it was not at all the main part. The main part was to establish and direct a complex and continuing *process* to develop policy ideas and proposals from others; to process the policy content through the relevant mechanisms (primarily the Policy Coordinating Committee, for which, with me, he served as the secretariat); to recruit and cultivate the many experts required to ensure the policy was innovative (preferably), well researched and fact-based (always), and literate (more or less); and to help deliver policy materials in the right finished format (full papers, pamphlets, resolutions, ballots, fact sheets, media hand-outs—the whole nine yards, and then another bolt of whole cloth for good measure!) to their intended audience (caucus, candidates, targeted public interest groups, the media, the population at large, and, it seemed to me at the time, to creatures on all other planets as well). Could the Invasion of Normandy possibly have been planned with more attention to detail? Surely not. In Symons's hands, nothing was done in half-measure. No wonder my hair started turning seriously grey in the midst of all this!

There are, to my mind, three basic models for a major political leader's senior policy advisor. They can best be thought of as the three "Ps," representing, discretely, "personality," "policy," and "process." Prototypically, Charles McMillan fit the "personality" model; Tom Axworthy fit the "policy" model; and Tom Symons fit a distinctly different one: the "process" model. Not mutually exclusive categories, mind you; for each of the three advisors at hand had many qualities and responsibilities the other two possessed. But these three models are at the heart of the matter. McMillan's relationship to Mulroney was based on *personality* (friendship, personal compatibility and comfort level, loyalty, mutual trust, shared political history and battles, and, especially, guarding the leader's policy flank, including from insider schemers); Axworthy's relationship to Trudeau was based on *policy* (ideology, common policy interests, intellectual stimulation, mutual "academic" respect, and, later, literary collaboration). What Stanfield sought, and found, in Symons was an individual who could help him as much with *process* as with policy per se. It was this "P"—rather than the other two (for "personality" and "policy")—that characterized, quintessentially and uniquely, the Symons Model: *process* rooted in a great cause. . . modernizing, and thereby saving, a great national institution, the Tory Party, in the wake of the previous leader's years of neglect.

8. Political Labels

Few enterprises waste more time and effort than trying to draw boundaries around a politician's ideology. I will, therefore, make no effort here to label definitively the political philosophy or ideological bent of either Robert Stanfield or Tom Symons, except for the following comments. Both were public-spirited men unmotivated by personal gain in any narrow sense. They had already been blessed (in Stanfield's case, at birth) with all the creature comforts and social status either of them felt they needed in life. Neither was absolutist or categorical about most matters, political or otherwise. Each did have a set of principles, not necessarily identical to the other's. Essentially, "what worked" in the real world of the "here and now" was more important to them than "how would this be judged?" in the hereafter. Both men were spiritual, each in his own way, but not particularly religious; Symons less so than Stanfield, for sure. They were practical men doing their respective life's work in the best way they knew how to achieve goals or solve problems, whether chosen or thrust upon them. For neither man was there a Rule Book—sectarian or secular—against which every decision had to be tested. What is the problem? What are the objective facts? What are the options? Would this approach work? Who would be affected, for good or ill, and how? Is there a better solution? No? Then, let's do it! On with the next problem. While oversimplified, no doubt, the dynamic described here is much closer to the truth than the belief that either man would ever ask, "Is this conservative enough?" before choosing a solution.

Other labels, not just ideological ones, can be equally deceptive. Stanfield was much more interested in "economic" questions than "social," Symons the converse; though each had his own hobby-horse in the other's corral. But, anyway, what do "economic" and "social" mean in the real world, as opposed to an academic's tower, ivory or not? Stanfield, for example, saw the guaranteed minimum income as a social issue as much as an economic one. For his part, Symons viewed, say, the Native issue from an economic perspective as much as from a social one. Men like Stanfield and Symons, and women like them, typically duck and bob and weave to thwart the name-stickers as they bolt their way towards them, reams of labels held high in hand.

When it came time to release the first batch of policy papers for the 1971 Annual Meeting, the Policy Coordinating Committee considered packaging them under a catchy title—or bumper sticker, as it were. At one point, "Compassionate Conservatism," of all things, was bandied about as the label of choice—three decades before George W. Bush used the exact phrase as his bumper-sticker slogan against Al Gore in 2000. Stanfield, unlike Bush, vetoed the slogan on the grounds "compassionate" reeked of condescension. The disadvantaged, he argued, deserved more than compassion. In his view, the label implied pity and, therefore, inferiority. He did not see the less fortunate that way, dismissed the recommendation, virtually out of hand, and ordered the policies sent out without a label.

This said, it is difficult to discuss a politician or administration without a hold on one handle or another. Political scientist Gad Horowitz is credited with coining the term "Red Tory" in applying Louis Hartz's "fragment theory" to Canadian political culture and ideological development.[10] Horowitz could well have been thinking of Stanfield and Symons. He advanced the idea that, in both Europe and Canada (but not the United States), ideology is not a straight line, or a linear progression, such that "left" (socialist) and "right" (Tory) are at polar extremes. Rather, ideology is more like a circle, with the "left" and the "right" joined at the ends, around the circle, in how they see (essentially in the same way) the fundamental role of government: acceptance of state enterprises, the welfare state, and other public institutions as instruments to advance the commonweal and to express national character. This is, at its root, how both Stanfield and

Symons viewed the role of the state and the function of public policy that expresses it. By virtue of family heritage, upbringing, advanced elite education, membership in the rarefied world of the moneyed class (in Stanfield's case particularly), and a good nature bestowed by the gods (in both cases), each shared with the other a vision of how the world operated, how it should operate, and how he should comport himself to help it better operate (again, *noblesse oblige*). It was within the framework of this shared world view that the two men forged a partnership to ensure the Progressive Conservative Party—in opposition and, it was hoped, later in government—would be prepared to take the reins of power in order to implement progressive policies.

So for Stanfield, as for Symons, "Red Tory" would do the trick, though the former never applied it to himself within my ear range. "Progressive" would have been more each man's cup of tea. "Reformer" would have done just fine with them, too. Certainly, Stanfield himself demonstrated that fact as premier of Nova Scotia, where his administration was not only reformist but, indeed, pioneering. Geoffrey Stevens quotes Stanfield's agriculture minister (Ed Haliburton) about the premier's overall approach to issues: "Stanfield is not doctrinaire, not dogmatic; his ideas are not rooted in the past."[11] The non-doctrinaire, non-dogmatic Stanfield who ran the province of Nova Scotia was the same Stanfield who, with Symons, reshaped, root and branch, the policies and image of the Diefenbaker party he had inherited virtually without any policy and with an out-of-date image. Stanfield did not apply to the task an inflexible dogmatism, let alone one that could be described as "conservatism" in the contemporary meaning of the word; for he had no ideology that could be labeled as such. Indeed, as Stevens notes, following hours of interviews with him, Stanfield did not know whether he was even a large-"c" Conservative, let alone a small-"c" conservative, despite the rich family tradition in politics—his brother Frank, for example, had been a federal MP—until well into adulthood.[12] He had flirted with socialism while an undergraduate at Dalhousie until finally, over the years, he settled into a "political philosophy" no more complex, and therefore in need of no more complex a label, than "Common Sense": what is the job at hand and what do we need to do to get the job done? Period.

In Symons, Stanfield had found a kindred spirit, a man with passionate views to be sure; but one who, like him, was a prisoner of neither ideology nor dogma. In all the years I worked as a (junior) partner with Symons on policy, we did not once discuss dogma. We frequently did discuss what it meant to be a Tory in the best traditions of the party—the party of Sir John A. Macdonald and George-Etienne Cartier and now, for Symons, every bit the party of Stanfield. In Stanfield, he saw the embodiment of those best traditions. He was eager to ensure it would, indeed, be the party of Macdonald and Cartier and Stanfield—and not of those who would leg-iron it to the heavy ball on its darkest side. Symons's anger, usually kept in a locked box, had special fury for the Diefenbakers and the Jack Horners of the country when they used labels like "true Conservative" or "Red Tory" or "socialist PC" not to inform but as weapons to incite division on tender issues like language and culture. To Symons, their real purpose was often just to consolidate their own standing in the party or the land, not to advance the public interest, even at the risk of destroying the party that Sir John A. had crafted so magnificently with values that were, in this context, exactly the opposite of theirs. For Symons, Stanfield was the gold standard for political integrity and public virtue, values Symons himself embodied. In this sense, Symons was, for the lack of any other way of saying it, a "Stanfield Conservative." Indeed, it was the label he always used to describe himself. That is all the labeling he wanted and all that he felt he needed. It's what he calls himself still: "A Stanfield Tory." It sounds just about right. I can live with *that* label. I know he definitely can.

Some scholars have asked me whether I thought Symons had nudged Stanfield, consciously or subconsciously, farther to the "left"—certainly not to the "right"!—than the leader might have gone of his own inertia, without Symons's continuing progressive influence. I cannot recall either Stanfield or Symons ever discussing policy—or even appearing to think—in any way remotely like that. I guess the words "left" and "right" were not taught in preschools in Truro or in Rosedale. A good thing, too!

It is pointless to characterize as "left" or "right" any particular policy, or range of policies, Symons might have favoured himself, or encouraged Stanfield to consider, in the policy process they devised together. That's because doing so shortchanges the pivotal role Symons played. In all my time with Stanfield and Symons (the summer of 1969 to Stanfield's stepping down in 1976, but most actively before election day of 1974), the two men did not fight once on a substantive issue. Nor argue much even on a lesser one, to my knowledge. In any event, what was most important were not individual policies themselves, as helpful as they emphatically were to Stanfield and his followers in parliamentary and electoral battles. No, the central reality was the process by which those policies were produced under Symons's direction. *Process*—the third of our "Ps." Stanfield and Symons were preparing the Progressive Conservative Party of Canada for power. And just as, in their vision, power was not sought for its own sake, neither was policy. Policy was the by-product of a process by which the party forced itself to think deeply about where it wanted to go, where it wanted to lead the country, and how it was going to get there. Policy was a map. The routes could always be changed, the map replaced with a better one. Policy was not the destination. Nor was the process; it was the journey. The destination was winning power to achieve great things for the country.

9. The 1971 Annual Meeting

The policy mix was to get much richer with the party's 1971 Annual Meeting in the first week of December ("Annual" Meetings were never actually held annually; not even always biennially). Toward the end of 1970, Stanfield released a formal statement in which he described the progress of the policy process to that point. The statement—appended to the minutes of a two-day PCC Annual Meeting "Working Committee" (23 & 24 February 1971)—stated, "We are well along the path towards formulating a comprehensive and integrated policy program to present to the Canadian people when it next chooses a government. That has been our task this year, and *it will continue to be our major challenge in the year to come* [my emphasis]." The Annual Meeting would challenge Symons's operation as never before.

At the 1971 Annual Meeting, Stanfield was not looking for excitement. If, in life, no news is good news, in politics, no excitement is no news. And Stanfield was quite prepared to have "no news" the media's verdict as it covered the meeting. While preparing for the lead-up to the coming federal election, he did not want fireworks, least of all with him in the midst of the flare. He had survived, but barely, a palace revolt on a parliamentary vote concerning Official Languages in which seventeen Diefenbaker caucus rebels, including the embittered former leader himself, perversely voted against not only the legislation but, in effect, Stanfield himself as well. Stanfield had been eager to project a unified and progressive stance on the issue. He was decidedly not eager to have another cabal within the palace throwing china at its principal occupant—himself. What he sought was, essentially, to meet the requirement to hold a general meeting of the party, get the best possible feel for where the membership stood on the issues likely to emerge in the pending election, and put the occasion behind him with minimal damage to party unity and public and media perception.

The 1971 Annual Meeting presented not only Symons but also Stanfield with a heavy challenge, given that it was at the leader's own instigation that the meeting was to be largely about policy. Like china, policy is a cupboard's content a party leader does not want hurled at him as he takes his place among his strongest partisans. In this case, the place was the ballroom of Ottawa's Chateau Laurier Hotel. Symons's job, as *éminence grise*, was partly to ensure that party members did not hurl plates or, at worst, missed Stanfield if they did. There are, after all, limits to *noblesse oblige*!

The three-day Annual Meeting was held from 5 to 7 December 1971. Nathan Nurgitz, president of the party, presided. After Symons outlined for delegates the policy voting procedure, two hundred and sixty policy resolutions were debated in three concurrent sessions. During discussion, delegates were permitted to strike a resolution from the ballot or add to it, but by unanimous agreement only. (Just three of the two hundred and sixty were, in fact, removed; not many more were added.) The individual policy streams were masters of their own discussion, subject to the overall rules. No plenary debate was scheduled. The question of Quebec's place in Confederation was hotly debated, as it had been at the Niagara Conference and would be for a long time to come. The "deux nations" controversy, however, was discreetly avoided. Whether a consensus emerged on such individual issues, in individual sessions, depended on the session and on the issue, not to mention one's interpretation of what constituted consensus.

Debate focused on the individual resolutions prepared by national headquarters, under Symons's eagle eye, based on the PCC's work over many months. All the policy work conducted by or for the party over the preceding months (the policy papers especially) influenced the content of the resolutions. The idea was that the total policy content at the Annual Meeting—resolutions, policy discussion papers (over ninety thousand words in all), background policy materials, fact sheets, question-and-answer summaries, media policy packages—would be drawn from the multitude of sources the party, under Symons's direction, had carefully cultivated over many months. At each stage in the process, the party had consulted experts, and often engaged them in preparing drafts, in a wide range of fields. Typically, the papers were made available in kits (each containing a news release and policy summaries, among other things), not individually but in batches, to maximize both media coverage and general public attention. The delegates, therefore, had an opportunity well before the meeting to study the policy materials.

Critics argued the rules had been deliberately set to stack the kitchen plates against controversy. They were close to the mark. Stanfield was not keen on broken china. Nor was Symons, who oversaw every detail. Extreme positions on sensitive issues would not have made for smooth going for the leader as he headed toward the looming federal election. Delegates, for the most part, knew and accepted this fact; though debate was, nevertheless, vigorous—on some issues, like economic independence, very vigorous—throughout the proceedings. Stephen Clarkson, a well-known academic and Liberal Party activist, attended the meeting as an official observer. In a hotel corridor at the convention, he cornered Symons and tried to nail him—good luck!—on the likelihood the rules would cause the delegates to produce contradictory policy results and, therefore, less danger for Stanfield. "Oh," he quoted Symons as saying—'with a mischievous glint appearing through a puff of [pipe] smoke'—"can you promise?"[13] No such promise needed to be made by Clarkson to Symons because a virtual promise had been kept by Symons to Stanfield: no plate would be thrown, no china broken, no leader hit.

But these limits did not prevent something remarkable and unprecedented from happening: the party members rose as one to cheer the leader's policy advisor—Symons. There had been two years of steady work, often in the face of resistance and skepticism and sometimes hostility. The milestone Niagara Conference had been held. Dozens of position papers had been generated, both for that conference and for others since, including this meeting. Some five hundred and fifteen experts had been recruited and mobilized in the service of the party. And, now, two hundred and sixty issue resolutions had been extracted from seventeen policy papers and presented for delegates to discuss and vote on. The papers had been prepared, and revised repeatedly, with the care of a conservator restoring long-lost renaissance manuscript masterpieces. All this and more had paid off. Not just in policy preparation, but in unsought esteem and affection afforded Symons by party delegates and staff—including, in both categories, some of the very ones who had described him as that crazy egghead up in Peterborough, and a lot worse, not long earlier. As Stephen Clarkson wrote in *The Canadian Forum*, "While it was not surprising that Stanfield received a standing ovation, what impressed this observer was the ovation accorded [Symons] when the policy chairman gave his report to the same meeting." Of Symons's selfless labours for the party in the preceding period, Clarkson wrote that the delegates were "struck" by the sheer magnitude of what he had achieved.[14] Prior to the Niagara Conference, Symons had been the object of abuse and even expletives in some quarters. Now, the party rose in unison in thunderous ovation as he took a discreet bow. The *éminence grise* had done well for the party, and the party paid tribute and homage in kind.

10. The 1972 Election

With the 1972 election looming, the leader embarked on a schedule of work and travel more back-breaking than any previous Tory leader had ever inflicted on himself. A little while earlier, he had become dispirited when Pierre Trudeau invoked the War Measures Act against Quebec terrorists (October 1970)—the first time ever in peacetime. Ironically, this unprecedented show of force by the federal government against its own citizens caused the Liberals' popularity to soar and the PC Party's to plummet (fifty-nine percent versus twenty-two percent at the worst point). It appeared to Stanfield that, no matter how hard he worked to prepare the party—or how committed he was to dragging it from antediluvian to modern—it didn't matter. Sometimes, in life, a strong bloodline and fire in the belly are just not enough. You need luck. And Stanfield's luck was just about to change. Big time. Sometimes life *is* fair.

After a period of deep anxiety and frustration (I thought depression), Stanfield, picking himself up from the mat, accelerated preparations for the 1972 election. As before, policy was central. From the time the Policy Coordinating Committee was established at the Niagara Conference, in October 1969, up to the October 1972 federal general election (thirty-six months), sixteen meetings of the Policy Coordinating Committee were held—one meeting approximately every two months. In that period, up to the holding of the 1971 Annual General Meeting in December 1971, exactly twelve "official" meetings were also held by a special Working Committee of the Policy Coordinating Committee set up to plan the policy sessions and prepare policy papers for discussion and voting at the meeting. Numerous "unofficial" ones were also held. (Minutes of the former were kept, not for the latter—the main difference.) A fast pace.

The Working Committee was, for all practical purposes, just a slightly smaller version of the full PCC. It operated in a more informal manner to allow maximum flexibility concerning membership and modus operandi. The actual membership, though, did not vary markedly between the two. Stanfield did attend Working Committee meetings but, unlike Symons, a slight bit less regularly than he did the PCC per se. When not there himself, however, he closely followed its progress, as a broker would the stock exchange at day's end; he had a lot riding on the "market." The PCC and the Working Committee should be viewed as one and the same thing, except for the above qualifications. All told, twenty-eight policy meetings were held in this thirty-six-month period, about once every month when holidays, parliamentary recesses, and other such occasions are excluded. The Working Committee did meet a number of times, as well, during the Annual Meeting itself. No minutes were recorded then, and these are not included in the totals; but, if they had been, the total of meetings held would be still greater. A rapid pace, indeed.

In the lead-up to the 1972 election, twenty-five policy pamphlets were prepared by the PCC for MPs and candidates and their workers and supporters. These drew heavily on the policy background and discussion papers prepared for the 1971 Annual Meeting, revised and updated as needed; reports of the various regional and local conferences and seminars held across the country; policy work by probes and study groups and pilot projects; research commissioned by the party and carried out by resource specialists on specific questions, sometimes of a technical nature; as well as other sources, not the least the continuing research conducted by the party's research office, very much the PCC's partner.

Throughout the October 1969–October 1972 period, the Policy Advisory Committee (again, Symons and I, acting as the secretariat of the PCC) amassed thirty-five cabinet drawers of files brimming over from floor to ceiling. We also compiled a roster of specialists at the service of the party that numbered five hundred and fifty-five by late-October 1972 before peaking at some six hundred and twenty by 1974. A huge black book! Symons had method to his madness. Not many people—myself included, Stanfield *always* excluded—appreciated it fully back those many years ago.

On 12 September 1972, in the midst of the election campaign, Stanfield released his priorities for a Progressive Conservative government under his leadership. Some of the main issues of the campaign were as follows. *Unemployment*: it would soar to seven percent on the eve of the vote, considered worrisomely high at the time. *Inflation*: it was an emerging problem. Stanfield felt the issue needed to be addressed; and he did address it in the 1972 election, with a qualified wage-and-price controls approach (controls if necessary, but not necessarily controls: shades of Mackenzie King, both economists, at heart, the latter literally). In even more urgent economic circumstances, in the 1974 election, he would sharpen his plan to the great detriment of his party's electoral fortunes, as we will see. *Taxes*:

Stanfield promised to reduce them on personal income to stimulate job growth and abolish them on family-farm capital gains to boost *agriculture.* He would also introduce a constant-dollar approach to taxation to prevent taxpayers from having to pay extra taxes on income increases due to inflation, as opposed to real increases (a revolutionary idea then). And Stanfield stressed a range of other policies, including ones to support *small businesses,* improve *government management* and *planning,* and ameliorate the needs of specific disadvantaged groups. Among those groups were *Native peoples,* to whose plight and heritage Symons was especially sensitive.

A measure of how successful Stanfield and Symons were in modernizing the party, both in policy and in image, came when the passionately Liberal *Toronto Star,* the virtual house-organ of the Liberal Party's left wing and the largest circulation daily in the country, endorsed the Progressive Conservative Party and its platform for the first time in its entire long history.

Despite all the progress in modernizing the PC Party, the question in the air remained: would Stanfield reap any temporal rewards for his labours? Or, would he have to settle for indulgences in Heaven reserved for those who, like himself and Symons, laboured by the divine dictum, and personal *noblesse oblige* ethic, that "faith without good works is dead"? By the night of the federal general election of 30 October 1972, Stanfield, with Symons's help and blessing, had done his good works. Now he would have to await the election results with faith alone. Stanfield *was* rewarded in this temporal world with at least a nod of approbation from above. It was almost enough to make him prime minister of the Dominion of Canada. Life sometimes *is* fair.

On election night, as the returns poured in, the results stunned the nation: it was a dead heat, with Stanfield's Tories taking the lead in parliamentary seats one hundred and nine to one hundred and seven. Although the ratio flipped to the Liberals by the same margin in the end, it had been a near-miraculous achievement. Stanfield whipped the man who, only four years earlier, had given public mania new meaning—and, it seemed, put the old values out of style forever. He had slaughtered the Liberals, both in seats and in popular votes, everywhere across the country. The sole exception was the Liberals' historic bastion Quebec, where their margin of victory was large enough to give them a slim edge in the overall results. Significantly, Stanfield's Tories made dramatic gains across the Prairies—the homeland of Diefenbaker loyalists who had plotted against him at every turn. "The Man with the Winning Way"—six words. Good bumper sticker!

Even more satisfying for Stanfield were his party's huge gains in the cities, among the young and—take a curtain call, Symons!—the educated. . . the very demographic groups the leader's progressive and pro-intellectual policies were designed in large measure to attract. It had been a good night for the PC Party. A good night for Stanfield. And a good night for Symons. At the end of a long day of meetings in Toronto, in his hotel room at the Park Plaza, Symons welcomed the results with a puff of his pipe, a sip of scotch, and phone call of thanks from Stanfield.

Few historic facts are as certain as this one: from the time the Conservative Party was just a twinkle in the eye of founding leader Sir John A. Macdonald to Robert Stanfield's leadership a hundred years later, no Tory leader before had prepared his party for an election and for government with the care and commitment and thoughtfulness that Stanfield applied to the policy task in the period leading up to the 1972 election.

11. Lead-Up to the 1974 Election

Because of the extremely close results of the 1972 election, Robert Stanfield faced a great deal of uncertainty about how to prepare for the run-off election, expected by most political pros and media pundits sooner rather than later. On 2 November 1972, Symons had another phone conversation with Stanfield, this time to discuss strategy for proceeding, including, but not only, on the policy front. Symons always organized his thoughts when initiating a call to Stanfield, or when expecting one (usually by prior arrangement), to avoid wasting the leader's precious time. The preparations typically took the form of cryptic notes, written in red ink in ballpoint on a small white pad, to organize the points he wished to make. The points, during the call itself, would then be ticked off as completed, one by one; if not literally, then in Symons's mind's eye.

This time, soon after the cliff-hanger 1972 election, the call was not of a run-of-the-mill sort (though most were not, anyway). Stanfield wanted to know what strategy his chief policy advisor thought he should follow in light of the closeness of the election results and the uncertainty they caused not just him but also the country. Symons advised caution, saying Prime Minister Trudeau's announcement that he intended to remain in office was not unreasonable. Symons said many people would view as arrogant any suggestion Stanfield might make to the contrary. The emphasis, instead, he advised, should be on a willingness to form a government if asked, but the offer should not be made with "belligerence." "Sabre-rattling" would be self-defeating, he stated. In a telling bit of advice, reflecting how he saw Stanfield himself, Symons said the leader would be "credible only if true to [his] character": "Let Trudeau appear to be clinging to office but do nothing yourself to foster that impression," he told Stanfield. "Use the time to organize for the run-off election and for the responsibilities thereafter and to work with the public in anticipation of the coming election, while [Trudeau] and his government are tied up trying to hold onto office and coping with the duties of office." Most telling of all, Symons urged that "we should offer a clear statement of our policy alternatives. . . what we would do in office should Canadians honor us with the responsibilities of government."

A close examination of Stanfield's remarks to the media soon after he received this advice from his chief policy advisor indicates two possibilities: either Stanfield had not been fundamentally influenced by the cautionary advice from Symons, since he was thinking along the same lines as Symons, anyway; or, alternatively, before speaking with Symons, he had pretty much made up his mind to be aggressive, but modified his tone in light of Symons's cautions. I was in the room with Symons at the time of the call. I am convinced, from my hearing of the Symons's half of the discussion, that the second possibility is much more likely. Certainly, while being aggressive in drawing attention to the fact voters had rejected the government's record at the ballot box, in the 1972 election, Stanfield's overall tone at the relevant news conference—firm but not belligerent; willing to serve but not demanding to be allowed to serve; not resigned to opposition but eager to prepare the party while in opposition to assume the reins of government should the people so wish—could not have been closer to Symons's advice, in content and tone alike, had the senior policy advisor written the script for the leader himself. Which he virtually did.

12. Policy Readiness: 1974

The political calendar was far different following the 1972 election from that of four years earlier. Trudeau's was not just a weak but a perilously weak minority government. When the Trudeau government settled back into office, albeit tenuously, most observers still expected a run-off election before long. The government's fate was held in the balance by the grace and good will and political avarice of the NDP. That party was prepared to exact every concession from a compliant prime minister and cabinet eager to retain power at almost any cost; including, as it turned out, to the Canadian taxpayer. The government gave into one demand after another for new (often expensive) programs on the NDP agenda. In such an uncertain environment, planning by Stanfield for the long term would have been folly, for there seemed no long term. So, instead of setting his sights on a one-year or two-year framework to review existing policies, revise them as needed, and develop new ones on the same basis as he had proceeded before, through the PCC, the goal was more modest and, to him, more manageable, given the political realities he faced. Dazzling the voter with policy fireworks would have to be for another time. Maybe that time had passed. Certainly, the political will for protracted policy formulation had passed for most in Stanfield's inner circle, even if not totally for the leader himself and still less for Symons, already gearing up for the next stage.

In light of the seemingly tight time-frame, the focus ahead would be not on producing new policy materials but, instead, on reworking ones that had already been produced earlier, over many months, with an eye to the 1972 election campaign. At this stage in its policy process (post-1972 and pre-1974 election), with Robert Stanfield now a half-decade into his leadership, the Progressive Conservative Party was not proceeding with a *tabula rasa*, as it had to in the lead-up to Stanfield's first national election in 1968. Indeed, the party had a substantial amount of material in the sausage grinder. It was now a question of reviewing it to determine what needed to be discarded and what was still relevant but needed to be updated or supplemented.

For Stanfield and the party, there was no tomorrow to postpone. Accordingly, Stanfield shifted his policy workshop farther and farther away from the Policy Coordinating Committee and more and more towards the PC parliamentary caucus. Increasingly, he focused on the political implications of policy rather than the policy itself; for, he thought, almost everything that could be done had been done on the substance. This meant, correspondingly, that the entire operation was moved a bit farther from Symons—though, certainly, his role remained important—and closer to individual members of caucus. That was especially the case with those members thought to have both expertise in the areas for which they were given responsibility and, even more important, a political nose for the potential electoral implications of party policy in their respective areas.

What was being worked on now was not so much policy as a partisan platform based on policy. The distinction may seem subtle, but it was real. Policy constituted an officially-approved set of integrated researched-based statements of principles and directions on a broad range of issues that the party committed itself to following should it win power. The platform, by contrast, was to be specific promises drawn from that set of policy materials that the party's candidates and activists could use on the hustings, emphasizing what was inelegantly termed "grabbers." The word meant specific promises and commitments that would "grab" the intention of the voter, especially as it related to his or her particular circumstances or desires as perceived through internal party polling and other sources of political intelligence. The difference between the two categories, however fine, was analogous to that between a provincial road map (policy) and a *MapQuest* print-out (platform). In most cases, the caucus policy chairperson typically assembled several PC parliamentary colleagues to serve with him or her on a committee struck to manage the relevant issue or bundling of related issues. Sometimes, these

MPs accepted, and employed, the provincial map, but used *MapQuest* to choose their own specific route. One such policy chairman, for example, was Dr. James Gillies, MP for Toronto's Don Valley riding, elected in 1972 (and re-elected in 1974, before retiring prior to the 1979 vote). He hailed from York University's Faculty of Administrative Studies, where he had been a colleague of Charles McMillan. Gillies was a world-renowned corporate-governance expert. He drove much of the party's policy on a range of economic and financial issues, both in Parliament and for the 1974 election. That included wage-and-price controls. A force to be reckoned with!

At the first PCC meeting (26 November 1969), on the heels of the Niagara Conference that established it, the Tory leader told committee members their role in crafting a party policy platform could not be played "without full consultation and discussion with all sectors of the Party." For Stanfield, as the 1974 election loomed, "all sectors" effectively meant his parliamentary caucus. Most of his one hundred-plus MPs would be seeking re-election. If he was going to increase their numbers after the election, with an eye to forming a government, he would need them both to help lead on policy development and support enthusiastically the party's platform entering the campaign. The PCC did continue to meet about as regularly as before. Its focus, however, was on managing the body of policy materials the party had already produced over the previous months, as updated by the caucus policy chairs in concert with the PC research office. On 5 February 1974, for example, the PCC worked on the following papers: World of Work, Cultural Opportunities, Regional Development, the Role of Women, Parliamentary and Democratic Reform, and Native Peoples. At this point, most such papers had been processed through more stages than human life itself: from the genesis, in some cases, at the Niagara Conference (e.g., Parliamentary Reform) to the working groups to the PCC's scrutiny to regional or local meetings back to the PCC to the Annual Meeting policy sessions to caucus committees and back to the PCC, and on and on it went. In a small number of cases, if the policy statements had been white bread, and processed any further, a mosquito would have starved on the surviving nutrients. There is such a thing as too many cooks spoiling the broth—and the baking. Certainly, the policy materials had advanced well beyond the point of needing further work other than technical updating and editing. One paper, on Native peoples, did have to be sent back to the drawing board for major work on the grounds it was just not good enough (Symons's insistence!). But it was an exception. All the papers continued to be updated in light of consultations with the broad membership of the party through such devices as questionnaires. At a meeting of the PCC on 10 January 1974, for instance, the party headquarters director, John Laschinger, reported on the results of policy questions that had been mailed to fifteen-thousand party members across Canada. Athenian democracy, indeed!

By the 1974 Annual Meeting (17–19 March), the party had advanced its policy materials in almost every case to the point where the task remaining, in the run-up to the meeting, amounted to little more than improving them editorially; modifying them in light of changing "objective" circumstances (e.g., jobless and inflation rates); or fine-tuning them based on developing political realities (e.g., voter opinion as reflected in internal party polling or caucus angst). Three months before the 1974 Annual Meeting (5 December 1973), Stanfield sent a letter to a massive list of party members (many thousands) in which (saliently, I think) he stressed the role the caucus chairpersons had played in "modifying our basic policy position papers," in concert with the Policy Coordinating Committee. "The Caucus chairmen will have *their* respective papers [my emphasis] updated and ready for discussion at the general meeting." The leader announced he had called on Tom Symons, and he had agreed, "to assume overall planning responsibility for our policy discussions at the meeting." For this meeting, the party sent to delegates, beforehand, yet another thirteen thousand policy questionnaires; all the policy papers completed to that point; and a specific request from the leader himself to party members to forward their policy ideas to either his office or to national headquarters. True to the importance he had always personally attached to policy, Stanfield urged delegates to "do [your] homework on selected subjects." I have no doubt that the leader's message caused many party members to take the entire exercise more seriously than they otherwise would have done. That was what, for Stanfield, policy leadership was all about. A stern school master when it came to preparing himself for class, he was every bit as strict with his students. Each time the leader communicated directly to the membership in such a way, the number of policy ideas the leader's office and headquarters received from that source spiked. Many of the communications reflected a lot of careful thought and were genuinely helpful to the process. They especially helped the leader to take the pulse of the broad PC Party membership on sensitive issues (like proposals for unemployment insurance and other government income-support reforms) on which controversy raged as much within the party as in the population at large.

Just as delegates had felt they needed to be politically careful when debating policy at the 1972 Annual Meeting, on the eve of the election then pending, so also the delegates at the 1974 Annual Meeting approached their policy role keenly aware of the political implications of everything they argued about as the 1974 election loomed ever more ominously. A weak minority government hung in the balance. Most members felt their party had excellent odds to win power this time. They sensed the stakes had never been higher at any other time since Stanfield had become leader seven years earlier. One of those delegates was a future prime minister, Brian Mulroney. As the Annual Meeting approached, he wrote to Symons, on 17 December 1973, to tell him how impressed he was with the policy papers he was then reading and annotating to prepare himself for the meeting. "I have come to recognize," he said, "the indispensable contribution that you, in particular, as the moving force behind the committee, have made." In the middle of the national party gathering (18 March 1974), Douglas Fisher—a former NDP member of Parliament and hard-nosed journalist of distinct progressive persuasion—wrote in his nationally syndicated column: "As a generalization, the Conservatives on coming to power would be rather like the Liberals back in 1963 [following the Kingston Conference]." Fisher added, "Then, Mr. Pearson had a satchel full of legislative initiatives." Fisher could have paid the Progressive Conservative Party no higher compliment. Nor could he have given a greater accolade to the two main architects of the party's policy process that had produced these impressive results. Political party policy-making history had come full circle—from the Liberal 1960 Kingston Conference that was to have such a profound impact on the Pearson government's social policy revolution in the mid-1960s to the point at which the Opposition Progressive Conservative Party was now, in 1974, better prepared for its legislative agenda in government, should it be elected, than any other party in the history of Canada, including, I would argue, the Liberal Party in 1963. That positioning was exactly as Stanfield and Symons—plotting strategy, step by step, in partnership and in shared vision—had all along not only intended but also worked so hard to realize.

13. The 1974 Election: Of Mice and Men

Elections are a game of Monopoly. A political party's policy in an election campaign—no matter how well thought out, researched, or packaged—is a hand-maiden to fate. For all his experience and sound political instincts, Stanfield was to discover in the 1974 election, more than he had in any previous election, federal or provincial, fate can be as fickle and unpredictable as she can be cruel.

Just as Trudeaumania in 1968 swept many candidates in or out with the riptide, no matter their own respective qualities or efforts, a similar kind of contagion did the same in the 1984 election (Mulroney versus Turner), well after Stanfield left the political stage. This also happened in the 1974 federal election. The public's hostility to the PC Party's wage-and-price controls plan advanced in the 1974 election blew out of the water all their other carefully prepared policies, rendering those policies virtually irrelevant to PC candidates' chances for success in the election. That election was one of those in which, if you were a Tory and Moses or a Grit and Jack the Ripper, it would not have made a Mount Sinai or a London back-alley's bit of difference: your fate, for good or ill, was sealed as fast as Trudeau could say, "Zap you're frozen!" The Liberal assault against Stanfield represented by that zinger dominated the media airwaves and smothered the Tory leader in the political tidal waves, as the embattled Tory leader tried his best to explain what he could not explain because the voters, stampeded by the Liberals, would not let him explain: why the country, faced with runaway inflation, needed wage-and-price controls and why, if he became prime minister, he would feel the urgent need to impose them. It was irrelevant that top economists everywhere,

Canada's included, were virtually united in believing that some such approach was necessary throughout the western world. It was irrelevant that the Liberals themselves realized that fact and, indeed, had a similar approach in their back pocket to use if re-elected. Least of all, was it relevant that Stanfield believed fervently in the rightness of his approach, and had given it a great deal of prior thought, including through the Policy Coordinating Committee. The Liberals were able to instill among voters enough fear about the alleged dire impact of Stanfield's anti-inflation plan on them and theirs that the die was cast before any Liberal could say, "Great! Boardwalk!" and any Tory could say, "Darn it! Jail!" That was pretty much how the results shaped up on election night—one hundred and forty-one Liberals and only ninety-five Tories (ironically, two seats fewer than Diefenbaker had won in his last hurrah, in 1965, without any policy). Having won re-election on Stanfield's broken back, Trudeau and the Liberals then kicked him in the face eighteen months later by implementing essentially the Stanfield inflation-controls plan they had so ruthlessly ridiculed and won a federal general election condemning. A just society?

All Stanfield and Symons's careful policy preparation was blown up in one fell swoop. The irony is that, for all the work Symons's operation did for Stanfield and the party across a broad range of issues and over many months, the election pivoted around the very policy—the inflation-controls program—on which the Policy Coordinating Committee had exercised the least influence. As for the anti-inflation plan's real progenitors, after the election, most not only denied parentage, but they also denied the baby had even been conceived, let alone born and raised to adulthood. The only thing faster than the speed of light is rats fleeing a sinking ship in politics. Only Stanfield admitted blame. He took full responsibility for the election debacle, as Richard Clippingdale noted in his *Robert Stanfield's Canada*. "I lost the election of 1974," said Stanfield, "because I made some mistakes after 1972."[15] In Clippingdale's narrative, Stanfield does not elaborate much on what he meant by that statement. Nor does the author himself speculate. I myself am not sure what the former PC leader meant. But, knowing Stanfield as well as I came to, I believe what he meant was as follows.

Stanfield thought he should have—but had not—anticipated the dishonest campaign Trudeau conducted against him. For this failure, he thought he had only himself to blame. Stanfield went to his grave believing *he* should have seen that "monster" coming over the hill. He believed that the fact he did not see it, or did not see it soon enough, cost him the election and his chance to lead the country and do great things for it. Losing "beautiful," however, is nobler than what the US punditocracy sometimes calls "winning ugly." By that it is meant conducting a campaign so negative, so slash-and-burn, so ferociously aimed at winning at any cost, that the perpetrator candidate may end up winning, but at the highest cost of all—that typically borne by the political culture itself. This principled and decent man, the "Man with the Winning Way," was too devoted to his country ever to want to win just *any* way.

Following the election debacle, largely because of the centrality of the wage-and-price-controls plan and its failure in the PC campaign, Robert Stanfield announced plans to exit the Tory stage and the Public Square altogether. I doubt, in light of three election defeats in a row, he would have given a moment's thought to doing otherwise. He was, however, taken aback by the vehemence with which even previously sympathetic editorial writers had called for him to resign. Scolded *The Montreal Star* (on 23 November 1974): "It is clear that the Conservative party will not regain a sense of direction until it finds a new leader. . . [There] is evident need to relieve Mr. Stanfield of a job he no longer has the taste for." Tom Symons, his trusted advisor, followed suit. The truth was, the wage-and-price-controls policy was the child of many parents, including PC caucus economist James Gillies; other caucus members; the PC research office, which had done admirable ground work; the Policy Coordinating Committee (again, to a very limited extent only); and, not least, Stanfield. In all such circumstances in politics, someone has to fall on his sword. This time, it was the leader himself.

14. Symons's Role and Contribution

In his superb biography of John Diefenbaker, *Rogue Tory*, Denis Smith noted that the 1974 election "went badly for Stanfield from the beginning."[16] For sheer understatement, that was like describing the fall of Rome as a failure in urban planning. For Tom Symons, in his policy work for Stanfield, begun the spring of 1968, the end had come. Following the 1974 Annual Meeting—which like the 1971 one he had orchestrated with minimal damage to the leader's policy flank (always a measure of success at such gatherings)—he drafted a letter of resignation to the leader. "I believe that a great deal of value has been accomplished," said he in his draft letter, "and that some very useful service has been rendered to the party and to Canada by this work." His assessment of the value of all the policy work he and others had done for Stanfield and for the party through the elaborate process Symons himself had devised and directed was understated to the point of being wrong. He could not have been more understated had *he* described Rome's fall as a drainage problem. A more objective and accurate assessment, in Symons's favor, was provided by Donald J. Matthew, president of the PC Party, whose Executive Committee bore responsibility under the party's constitution for establishing the Policy Advisory Committee that Symons had chaired, and for the Policy Coordinating Committee for which he had provided the secretariat. Concerning all the work that had been done on policy over the previous half-decade, the party president wrote to Symons, on 11 April 1974, on the eve of the 1974 vote, "While there is no doubt that Mr. Stanfield has played a vital role by his active involvement and support, it is you who must be given credit for pulling all of the pieces together and making it happen."

As it turned out, the moment Trudeau called the election, Tom Symons trashed his draft resignation letter—the first time I ever knew him to discard anything remotely archival. Damn those MWDP files! But I myself saved a copy for the history books. The last thing Symons wanted to do was abandon ship. The *first* thing he wanted to do was make himself available, at a moment's notice, to serve the man he had worked so hard to make prime minister and whom he was eager to help now—his protégé and friend. It was worth one more try. The fact the effort did not make Stanfield prime minister should not be the barometer of whether the effort had been worthwhile. By engaging so many people in a process of thinking both deeply and broadly about how best to advance the public good, Stanfield, in partnership with Symons, elevated the political culture of the land as few other Canadians have ever done, before or since. As Richard Clippingdale put it in his description of "Stanfield's policy mind": "No other political leader [in Canada] in the twentieth century, with the possible exception of Mackenzie King, thought, wrote and spoke about our country, its needs and its troubles with such dedication and creativity for so protracted a period."[17]

With or without a chance to govern, the PC Party had a profound impact on how public policy debate was framed in Canada throughout the decade or so Stanfield led the party (1967–76). Inflation controls, working-poor income support, unemployment insurance reform, deregulation, cost-of-living-indexed pensions and taxation, national unity (Quebec's place in Confederation and federal decentralization, in particular: think "deux nations")—in all such areas, Stanfield either placed the issue on the public agenda or elevated its priority; helped set (or, in some cases, as with the guaranteed minimum income concept, did alone set) the terms of the debate; and, without question in a few major ones, paved the way for action (most notably on wage-and-price controls). One can only speculate how high Stanfield and Symons, together, might have lifted the country had things gone differently electorally. If, as has often been said, including by Clippingdale, as his book's subtitle, Stanfield was the "Best Prime Minister of Canada We Never Had," Symons was, truly, the Best Senior Policy Advisor *that* Prime Minister Never Had.

15. Conclusion: A Cadillac and a Cougar

Tom Symons never drove a car, never knew how, never had a license. His preferred longer-distance transport mode was a sleek black Cadillac operated by Keith Brown's Peterborough limousine service and chauffeured by his trusty driver, Jack. (Symons's critics to the contrary, this was usually a much cheaper mode than air travel, especially for short intercity trips; and it served as a virtual office on the road.) When Jack was not ferrying Symons around from one meeting to the next, and from one destination to the next, I sometimes did so in my own car, not only on party policy business, but also for other reasons. There was a huge difference between Jack's ferryboat-size limousine and my 1970 Mercury Cougar coup. For starters, my Cougar was the color of baby poop and had a hounds tooth-patterned vinyl roof—super cool, I thought at the time! Only much later, in 1977—when, with a tad more maturity, I replaced the Cougar with a sedate blue Chevrolet Caprice Classic sedan—did I appreciate the incongruity between Jack's long Cadillac and my two-door sports car. Not to mention the diplomatic skill Symons must have needed to tame his undoubted embarrassment to be seen riding in such a gaudy vessel; set aside the physical discomfort a man so stocky likely had to endure on all those rides inside a virtual two-seater.

Extended rides in these intimate quarters, however, did afford me opportunities to have long chats with Symons about every manner of subject, some quite personal as we got to know each other better. In one such chat, Symons, in an especially contemplative mood, asked me whether I had ever aspired to greatness. In my mid-twenties at the time, I considered myself fortunate to be able to aspire to making car payments. For me, that was the true measure of greatness! But it was clear to me, even at the time, the question weighed heavily on Symons's own mind, because it was not really about me but rather about himself. I believe Symons did aspire to greatness—shouldn't we all?—not in the least to satisfy ego but to measure whether he had succeeded in his personal mission in life: public service. Symons never became president of Harvard University, "just" Trent University, whose pioneering teaching and research in such areas as Canadian and Native and environmental studies made it one of the best in the country; he never became secretary general of the UN, "just" chairman of the Ontario Human Rights Commission at a time when, under his leadership, it blazed the trail in areas like gay rights; he never wrote world-renowned books or treatises, "just" lesser, though significant, reports, studies, and articles that combined equal measures of lucidity and insight; he never created, in particular, the Great Canadian Novel, "just" a landmark Canadian Studies Commission report that eloquently articulated the value to all Canadians of such a work; he never designed a classic building or streetscape, "just" served as the best-ever chairman of the Historic Sites and Monuments Board, uniquely mandated by Parliament to commemorate the masterpieces of those Canadians who have been our best designers; he was never a towering orator for the ages, "just" an incisive and compelling teacher whose students will reflect his wisdom long after he is gone; he never became a prime minister or leader of the Official Opposition, "just" an *éminence grise* to ones who were. But the sum of Symons's important contribution to public service in each of these and many other domains rivals what most great people could ever achieve in a conventional public career.

Tom Symons brought both this powerful commitment to public service and all this expertise to his policy work for Robert Stanfield, who, in the 1972 election, came within a parliamentary seat of becoming prime minister of Canada. I know, firsthand, how indebted Stanfield felt he was to Symons for all he had done for him and the party and the country. Some other Stanfield staffers might have been older than me, more senior, served him longer, or known him better. But nobody else spent as much time with him as I did on strictly policy development (as opposed to, say, speech preparation, which was outside my field). By the same token, among all the assistants Symons has had over the years, no one else worked with him as long, or in as many different professional capacities, as I did. My other capacities with him, in addition to the one in the PC Party, were with the Ontario Human Rights Commission (executive officer); the Canadian Commission on Canadian Studies (senior research associate); and the Historic Sites and Monuments Board (I was the responsible minister, he was the chairman). I can, therefore, state with authority this inarguable fact: Tom Symons devoted his precious time and labour and talents and expertise to Robert Stanfield and the Progressive Conservative Party of Canada, not for financial reward, for there was none; not for public or party accolades, for there was not much of that, either; not in expectation of future reward, for when it all began, and for long afterwards, the party seemed not destined for the electoral success and government power needed to reward anyone, let alone "some egghead up there in Peterborough." For exactly the same reason Symons labours selflessly in all the other fields to which he has committed his life in public service, he served Stanfield and the PC Party because, for him, it was "just" the right thing to do. So, when the time comes for someone to write the definitive biography of Thomas Henry Bull Symons, I have a suggestion for a title—*Tom Symons: Just a Great Man.*

Notes

1 Peter Newman, "Change in Conservative Style," *Regional Leader Post* (Saskatchewan), 20 June 1968.

2 Anthony Westell, *Brandon Sun* (Manitoba), 16 February 1969.

3 Geoffrey Stevens, *Stanfield* (Toronto: McClelland & Stewart, 1973), 15.

4 John Walker, *Montreal Gazette* (Montreal), 23 June 1969.

5 Geoffrey Stevens, *Stanfield*, 239.

6 Ibid., 240.

7 All official party records, news releases and media statements, PCC minutes, and correspondence cited are housed at the Trent University Archives, Peterborough, Ontario. Unless noted, they, like most newspaper articles quoted, are referenced, for clarity of context, in the chapter narrative rather than individually in these endnotes.

8 Geoffrey Stevens, *Stanfield*, 238.

9 Anthony Westell, *Edmonton Journal* (Edmonton), 5 July 1969.

10 Gad Horowitz, "Conservatism, Liberalism and Socialism: An Interpretation," *Canadian Journal of Economics & Political Science* 32, no. 2 (1966): 143–71.

11 Geoffrey Stevens, *Stanfield*, 126.

12 Ibid., 41.

13 Stephen Clarkson, *Canadian Forum*, (January–February 1972): 4.

14 Ibid., 5.

15 Richard Clippingdale, *Robert Stanfield's Canada: Perspectives of the Best Prime Minister We Never Had* (Montreal and Kingston: McGill-Queen's University Press, 2008), 71.

16 Denis Smith, *Rogue Tory: The Life and Legend of John George Diefenbaker* (Toronto: Macfarlane Walter & Ross, 1995), 568.

17 Richard Clippingdale, *Robert Stanfield's Canada*, 4.

CHAPTER 7

To Know Ourselves: Tom Symons and Canadian Studies

DAVID R. CAMERON

I was completing my PhD at the London School of Economics in 1967 when I first heard of Tom Symons. My mother-in-law, knowing that I would soon be looking for an academic position, and very much wanting her daughter back in Canada, sent me a clipping from *Time Magazine* about this new university being built on the banks of the Otonabee, styled along the lines of the English college and tutorial system. There was a picture of the innovative founder, Tom Symons, smoking his pipe and declaring that a PhD does not represent the hand of God. Much as I wanted at that time to believe that it did, I knew he was right, and I liked the sound of the new place he was creating. That was why I applied for a position in the politics department, and that was how I came to spend eight years of my professional life at Trent.

Modeled on the English university system it may have been, but Trent—owing very much to the leadership and imagination of Symons—was strongly committed to the exploration of the Canadian experience in all its forms. As a young faculty member interested in the life and affairs of his country, I found it exhilarating in the 1960s and 1970s to be part of an exuberantly Canadian enterprise, which is what Trent was in those years: the creation of a vigorous Canadian Studies Program, the founding of the *Journal of Canadian Studies*, the establishment of a Native Studies department, the celebration of Canadian art and architecture, the early concern with the environment, and the powerful interest in Canada's North—Trent, for all that it was the smallest university in the province, was filled with big ideas at that time, and it attracted talented faculty who shared that worldview. It was fun to be part of building something important, and Tom Symons presided over it all with a genial confidence that this was the right thing to do. For Tom, the celebration of Canada was always the right thing to do.

Canadian studies as a field of concern[1] emerged in our universities during the 1960s, as part of Canada's effort to keep its footing during what might be understood as a shift of empires—the head-long post-war retreat of the British Empire, replaced in many parts of the world, including British North America, by a growing American hegemony. For many English-speaking Canadians, concerned with the cultural, economic, and political independence of their country, the massive and growing presence of the US colossus was the chief geopolitical challenge to Canada's national identity and its capacity to form an autonomous society north of the forty-ninth parallel.

The development of Canadian studies and the struggle to limit the number of American faculty flooding into Canadian universities were the yin and yang of this existential matter as it was reflected in the academy. It is hard today to call up just how much heat and passion infused the debate about these issues. In 1972, the Association of Universities and Colleges of Canada, with some reluctance, as I recall, established the Symons Commission on Canadian Studies to look into the "state of teaching and research in various fields relating to Canada at Canadian universities." With the publication of his controversial report, *To Know Ourselves*, Tom became the most prominent and thoughtful exponent of the need to strengthen teaching and research about Canada, as part of a larger national enterprise of "knowing ourselves." The commission aimed to publish four volumes, but in fact completed only three: the first two formed *To Know Ourselves*, published in 1975, and the third appeared in 1984, *Some Questions of Balance: Human Resources, Higher Education and Canadian Studies.*

Despite the absence of the fourth volume, which would have covered libraries, publishing, cultural property, Canadian studies in the schools, and Native studies in postsecondary education, the range of subjects addressed in the other three is sweeping, and justifies the comment that Larkin Kerwin made in 1975, that the commission "is undoubtedly the most significant examination of Canadian studies since the *Massey Report*."[2]

To Know Ourselves was prepared after an extensive process of public consultation. The commission visited every province and held hearings at over forty universities as well as a number of schools and community colleges. More than two thousand five hundred people attended the commission's meetings, about half of whom participated in the discussions. It received more than one thousand briefs and almost thirty thousand letters. The commission held sessions with a wide range of professional, educational, and academic societies and with a large number of government agencies. *To Know Ourselves* reported on Canadian content in the university curriculum; science, technology, and Canadian studies; the Canadian component in education for the professions; Canadian studies abroad; Canadian studies in the community colleges; archives; audio-visual resources; and the private donor and Canadian studies.

It contained nearly one thousand general and two hundred and ninety-five specific recommendations. It was received with widespread interest and some controversy. Reaction, commentary, and the seeking of advice and assistance from the commissioner began with its publication and continued well into the 1990s. James Page in his 1980 *Reflections* assessed the impact of the commission's *Report* in the following way:

> It has encouraged action on a great number of specific problems, and has contributed to a change in the academic climate of this country so as to make advances in Canadian studies possible. The findings reported here [in *Reflections*] document the massive response to the Commission's report and give substance to the view that the Commission has had, and is having, a profound impact on many aspects of teaching, research and publication about Canada. Certainly no other commission on educational matters has elicited such broad public interest.[3]

Some Questions of Balance, based more on data gathering and analysis than on hearings, examined a cluster of issues relating to human resources, higher education, and Canadian studies, some of which were the faculty citizenship question; enrolment projections and forecasts of faculty requirements; the age structure of the professoriate; the status of women in academic life; and foreign students in Canada. It made suggestions and recommendations on a wide variety of matters relating to these subjects. Again, it attracted substantial attention and occasioned some lively debate, particularly with respect to its analysis and proposals regarding faculty citizenship.

All in all, the commission—and the commissioner—had a very powerful influence in fostering greater interest in Canada and things Canadian, especially in English-speaking Canada. For reasons that are buried deeply in our history, its impact in Francophone Quebec was far less.[4]

In some fields, the commission's *Report* had a galvanizing effect; in the area of archives, for example, there is virtually universal acknowledgment of the commission's seminal role in encouraging practitioners, supporting the professionalization of the archival function, and increasing academic and public appreciation of the importance of archives in Canadian life.

The impact of the commission was extended by virtue of the willingness of Symons and some of his colleagues to perform an active advisory role in assisting organizations and institutions that wished to follow up on the *Report*'s proposals. As one academic administrator observed, "For the particular circumstances of this university, the service function of the Commission has been even more helpful than its formal report."[5]

Indeed, so great was the demand on the time of the commissioner after the release of *To Know Ourselves* in 1975 that active preparation of the third and final volume was not resumed until 1981, which explains why it was not published until 1984. The commission functioned in one form or another, then, over a period of twelve years. In subsequent years, Symons continued to provide generous personal support, on an informal basis, as an advisor, proselytizer, and critic, to the advancement of Canadian studies at home and abroad.

More than twenty years after the release of *To Know Ourselves*, I published a study examining what had happened in the field since the publication of *To Know Ourselves.* The report, *Taking Stock: Canadian Studies in the Nineties*,[6] examined the work Symons and a great many others had accomplished in the previous two decades; it sought to assess progress, identify difficulties and challenges, and chart a course for the future. What it found was something of a paradox.

Most people who were interviewed and who chose to comment on the state of the country in general believed that Canada was, if anything, less united, less capable of formulating a coherent national purpose, and less willing to know and celebrate itself than it had been fifteen or twenty years previously—certainly, there was little sense that conditions had materially improved. Yet most people also contended that Canadian studies had made substantial strides during the same period.

Most interviewees did not believe that Canadians—whether students or citizens—knew much more about their country and their fellow Canadians in the 1990s than they had a decade or two before. Indeed, in 1991, the Spicer Commission had declared,

> We do not know enough about ourselves. Without a radically fresh approach to improving what we know about each other, our lack of knowledge of the basic realities of this country will continue to cripple efforts at accommodation.[7]

Yet most of those interviewed argued that, overall, the study of Canada in the humanities and social-science disciplines of our universities was incalculably more advanced than it was in the 1960s or early 1970s.[8] How could this paradox be explained?

Firstly, it is, quite simply, difficult to establish the facts with respect to issues as large and as indeterminate as these. Inevitably, one operates primarily in the realm of observation, impression, and judgment.

Secondly, one should not expect what might be called the "national unity rationale" for Canadian studies to be entirely consistent with the desire for self-knowledge, nor is there any reason that it should be. Symons, for his part, declines to view Canadian Studies as a mission: "It is unhelpful to think of Canadian Studies as a mission. It is simply an area of the human experience which merits thought and examination like any other."[9] To teach about Canada's historical experience and its social and economic life is not necessarily to reinforce each citizen's identification with Canada. To know Canada better is not necessarily to strengthen Canada or to enhance Canadian citizenship, although it is usually assumed that there is a relationship. What is more, a given pattern of affection and loyalty does not predetermine the direction of one's curiosity, although it normally has an impact. Much study of Canada and things Canadian has no evident, direct bearing one way or the other on the large issues of Canadian identity, national unity or patriotism, nor need it have; it is the product simply—and quite properly—of the effort to understand certain phenomena relating to Canada that are of research interest or of educational importance.

Thirdly, in some cases, the deeper and more specialized pursuit of Canadian studies, broadly defined, may produce intellectual results that are less accessible to Canadians in general and may in consequence have less and less bearing on the general education of citizens. Some historians have raised the question whether the evolution of Canadian history away from grand themes and broad-brush accounts of the Canadian story and toward micro-historical enquiries in specialized corners of the discipline has served the cause of humane and civilized Canadian education well.[10]

Fourthly, according to the views of several of the interviewees, the content of Canadian studies in many cases had shifted from issues with a national perspective to topics of more local or regional concern. Canada's character and purpose as a national community, the story of its emergence as a sovereign player on the world stage, the great projects and controversies that have marked its historical development—such themes as these had in many cases given way to an examination of BC's status as a Pacific-rim community, the exploration of Quebec as a "société globale," or an account of the region or urban centre of which the researcher is a member. None of these latter issues is in any sense inappropriate—far from it—but it is possible to reflect, as did a number of the people interviewed, on whether a shift in the pattern of enquiry of this kind would allow as large a contribution to be made to an understanding of the country as a whole.

Fifthly, the situation in the country's community colleges seemed to be by no means as sanguine as that of the universities. If the degree of formal Canadian studies that existed in 1996 was any guide, teaching and learning about Canada appeared to have receded rather than advanced in these institutions; given that they are responsible for more than half of the country's postsecondary enrolment, their capacity to enlighten their students about the Canadian reality is a matter of some moment.

Finally, some modesty is in order. We were, after all, concentrating our attention in the enquiry on teaching and research in higher education. These are activities vitally related to the national interest, but they are by no means alone in enjoying this status, and their impact on the country—and even on those Canadians who are directly involved in postsecondary education—is supplemented or counter-balanced by a range of other powerful forces. The fortunes of a society and its people are determined by a wide array of pressures and opportunities operating within that society and acting upon it from the outside, of which higher education is but one.

At a workshop designed to explore the future of Canadian studies, held at Stoney Lake in Ontario in June of 1992, one participant summed up the situation this way:

> Canadian studies emerged in the 1960s. The part of it that was accepted was that it was legitimate to study Canada. The part of it that was not so easy was the fact that the legitimation of the study of Canada coincided with the de-legitimization of the nation-state and the fragmentation of the academic disciplines—for example, the Creightonian study of Canada disintegrated in history, and women's, local and ethnic history appeared. The edge pieces of the puzzle became very unclear, but in all this the potential for a more democratic and inclusive society, respectful of minorities, emerged.[11]

In a magisterial address, published by the *Journal of Canadian Studies* in 2000, Symons offers up a paradox of his own. Noting that "at best, Canadian Studies as an organized field of study is in a holding mode, and if it is in only a holding mode in this period of fast and great change, then it is in decline,"[12] he points in contrast to "a massive advance, outside the academic institutions and their teaching programs, in the creation and strengthening of the building blocks for Canadian Studies," by which he means: "foundations; archives; libraries; museums; galleries; heritage sites and buildings; publications; organizations; professional, vocational and learned societies; public granting agencies; volunteer bureaux; operational and research aspects of numerous public commissions; and a large array of regional, provincial and local activities bearing upon teaching and research about Canada."[13] Tom notes the paradox but does not seek to explain it, nor does he reconcile the massive advance in Canadian studies infrastructure with his subsequent judgment that "when push comes to shove, neither students, nor governments, nor the public, show any great or sustained wish to learn about Canada or to fund such learning."[14] There are many vexing puzzles in the kingdom of Canadian studies, which make it difficult to draw up a balance sheet and find the bottom line.

It is now thirty-five years since *To Know Ourselves* was released. The Canadian academy has moved well beyond what might be called the "Canadian studies era," although—in a continuation of an earlier preoccupation—universities must still justify to the Government of Canada the hiring of non-Canadian academics. Academic enquiry in the social sciences and the humanities has become more specialized and comparative, and the injunction to know ourselves has assumed a more international flavour. In my own field, a book of reflections was recently published, grounded in the following realization: "Over the past decade, the study of Canadian politics has changed profoundly. The introspective and sometimes insular style that informed Canadian political science for most of its history has given way to a deeper engagement with, and integration into, the theory and practice of comparative politics."[15] *The Comparative Turn in Canadian Political Science* argues that, "increasingly, what unites the study of Canadian politics is the conviction that scholars of *Canadian* politics can both learn from and contribute to the study of *comparative* politics."[16]

This "comparative turn" is in significant degree a manifestation of a striking shift in the context within which Canadian studies exists. The 1960s and 1970s, when Canadian studies emerged as a significant national concern, especially in English-speaking Canada, were pre-Internet; we used to write notes to one another on pieces of paper back then. The United States was approaching its zenith as a world power. The Québécois were in the midst of an intense process of identity transformation, and English-speaking Canada, less demonstratively, was redefining itself as well, with all the insecurities and vulnerabilities that that experience entails; the existential introspection that this experience fostered did not really conclude until the mid-1990s.

What a difference thirty-five years makes. The United States is arguably on the wane as a global power, at least in relative terms, with China rising. We now live in a globalized world, inhabiting a new media-infused virtual space in which territory, nation, culture, and history appear in a very different light. Both Quebec and the rest of Canada have now reached the farther shore of identity transformation, and both communities exhibit a confidence about themselves that was missing in the 1960s and 1970s. The Canadian studies enterprise is in need of a radical re-think in this brave new world.

It is worth pointing out that the "comparative turn" of which I have been speaking has only been possible because the academic understanding of Canada is deep and thorough, rooted in a rich, fully-articulated scholarly tradition built up over four or five decades. The phrase employed in the quotation above is "learn from and contribute to." Students of Canadian politics don't just draw on the learning derived from comparative politics; they bring their knowledge of their own country to the international community of scholars and help to insert Canada's distinctive political experience into the international conversation about peace, order, and good government.

The Canadian studies movement from the 1960s to the 1990s played an indispensable role in fostering a broadly-based scholarly appreciation of Canada's life and times, in establishing Canada as a fit and fascinating subject of academic study, and in demonstrating its relevance both domestically and internationally. This is the foundation upon which the contemporary generation of Canadian scholars and scholarship rest. No one played a more substantial or creative role in establishing this foundation than Tom Symons. Throughout his long career, he has made an incalculable contribution to the fostering of an understanding and appreciation of Canada.

Many people would be content with their lives if they had done half of what Tom has done just in the field of Canadian studies. This volume has a dozen and a half chapters devoted to an appreciation of the many facets of Tom Symons's remarkable career and to the manifold contribution he has made in so many areas of Canadian and international life. Tom Symons is a conservative of the kind they don't make anymore, a man at once able to understand the importance of the past in shaping a full life and yet able to discern things in the future that need to be done, and do them. He is living testimony to the fact that an affection for the beloved, familiar things of life in no way precludes the most energetic pursuit of better things in the future, and to the truth that a rich knowledge of Canada does not impede, but sets the stage for an understanding of the big, wide world beyond.

Notes

1 I will rely on the Symons Commission's serviceable definition of "Canadian studies" in this chapter: "In general, the Commission considered as Canadian studies teaching or research in any field that, as one of its major purposes, promotes knowledge about Canada by dealing with some aspect of the country's culture, social conditions, physical setting, or place in the world. Within these terms, Canadian studies would include both work conducted along traditional disciplinary lines and work organized around a single theme or subject but drawing upon the knowledge and techniques of several disciplines." T. H. B. Symons, *To Know Ourselves: The Report of the Commission on Canadian Studies* Vol. I and II (Ottawa: Association of Universities and Colleges of Canada, 1975), 4–5.

2 A comment in his capacity as president of the AUCC in October 1975 upon the release of the first two volumes of the *Report.*

3 James E. Page, *Reflections on the Symons Report: The State of Canadian Studies in 1980* (Ottawa: Supply and Services Canada, 1981), x.

4 Fernand Harvey, claiming that the conclusions of the Symons Commission passed almost unnoticed in Quebec, notes several reasons for its differential reception. English-speaking Canada's effort to define itself in contradistinction to the United States collided with Quebec nationalism, whether of the traditional or new variety. The relationship of Quebec with the US is very different from that of English-speaking Canada. French Canada enjoyed a lengthy history, involving several academic disciplines, of reflecting on itself as a distinct society, something which English-speaking Canadians came to rather later. (*Pour une histoire culturelle du mouvement des études canadiennes.* [ACS *Newsletter*, Spring 1988], 15.)

5 Quoted in Thomas H. B. Symons and James E. Page, *Some Questions of Balance: Human Resources, Higher Education and Canadian Studies* Vol. III of *To Know Ourselves: The Report of the Commission on Canadian Studies* (Ottawa: Association of Universities and Colleges of Canada, 1984), 6.

6 David Cameron, *Taking Stock: Canadian Studies in the Nineties* (Montreal: Association of Canadian Studies, 1996).

7 Citizens' Forum on Canada's Future, *Report to the People and Government of Canada* (Ottawa: Minister of Supply and Services, 1991), 129. The Chairman, Keith Spicer, in his foreword exclaimed, "This country is dying of ignorance, and of our stubborn refusal to learn" (9).

8 The Standing Senate Committee on Social Affairs, Science, and Technology, however, stated in its May 1993 report, *Canadian Citizenship: Sharing the Responsibility*, that the situation of Canadian studies "still leaves much to be desired. The teaching of Canadian subject matters in postsecondary institutions remains inadequate and is taught in piecemeal fashion" (17).

9 "The State of Canadian Studies at the Year 2000: Some Observations," *Journal of Canadian Studies* 35, no. 1 (2000): 50. He does, however, as he acknowledges, speak of Canadian studies as a mission at the beginning of his paper: "To what extent has the Canadian Studies mission been accomplished? Has the character of this mission been altered by changing circumstances. . . ?" Ibid., 27.

10 In a 1991 lecture Michael Bliss wrote: "We are business historians, labour historians, Western, Maritime, Ontario and Quebec historians, intellectual historians, historians of women, education, law, cities, culture, crime, smallpox—historians of almost anything but Canada." Bliss argued that historians have turned away from the traditional themes of Confederation, federalism, English-French relations, commercial policy, Macdonald, Laurier, King, and how to govern

Canada—just as the understanding of them became the *sine qua non* of intelligent Canadian citizenship. *Privatizing the Mind: The Sundering of Canadian History, the Sundering of Canada* (Creighton Centennial Lecture, delivered as part of the University of Toronto History Department's 100th Anniversary Celebrations, October 18, 1991), 8.

11 "Visioning Workshop on Canadian Studies," Stoney Lake, Ontario, 11–14 June 1992, organized by the Association for Canadian Studies. Quotation from notes made during the proceedings.

12 "The State of Canadian Studies at the Year 2000," 28.

13 Ibid., 38.

14 Ibid., 47.

15 Linda A. White, Richard Simeon, Robert Vipond, and Jennifer Wallner, eds., *The Comparative Turn in Canadian Political Science* (Vancouver: UBC Press, 2008), vi.

16 Ibid.

CHAPTER 8

"It's All About Culture": The Cultural Perspective of Tom Symons

WALTER PITMAN

Michael Tait, a friend and colleague in my undergraduate years, remembers Tom Symons as a major figure in the life of Trinity College, the very Anglican institution on the University of Toronto campus. Though Tom was only a year ahead academically, it was from him that Michael received his introduction to the necessary information and expected undergraduate behaviour, along with an array of the many college myths and legends during the initiation week that dominated the early days of September 1948. He was impressed beyond measure by the contextual awareness of this second-year student who confronted him, a newly arrived secondary-school graduate now faced with the mysteries of postsecondary living and learning that lay ahead in this handsome college in the centre of Toronto. Here there was before him a natural leader and he could only marvel at the ease, the charm, and the integrity of the figure consigned to the task of making him feel comfortable and at home in his new academic space.[1]

I too first met Tom Symons at that Trinity that was to be our academic home throughout our undergraduate years in the late 1940s and early 1950s, perhaps from a more distant perspective. In spite of my obvious non-conformist religious background, I had been convinced by a wise and sensitive high-school guidance teacher that I should apply to a small college like Trinity rather than to the larger Methodist institution, Victoria College, or even University College, a secular institution that would have been my more comfortable route to an undergraduate degree. Certainly for an active Baptist, fortunately resident in Toronto and thus able to reach the university by streetcar, that would have been a more fitting venue. But that guidance teacher, a graduate of Trinity herself, had realized that I would miss the most valuable elements of university life as a day student in a large college and she was determined that this for me would not be the case. She knew I was coming from a family of modest financial means. Though I might feel somewhat intimidated by the considerable number of student colleagues from Ontario Independent Schools, who were comfortably ensconced in Trinity's residential accommodation, I could weather that first impression. With scholarship and bursary assistance and a part-time job, I would be able to enjoy my years at Trinity. I soon felt myself a part of the collegiate scene.

However, during these days of first impressions there was one figure for whom social class or religious denominational predilection meant nothing and for whom I developed a distant but intense respect. It was Tom Symons who seemed a constant presence and a force for civility and decency—even to the extent of welcoming awkward and nervous first-year students. In the midst of events for which the college football exhortation, "damn the dissenters, hurrah for old Trinity," seemed to be directed at my very person, I was encouraged by the attitude and warm welcome of Tom at any occasion we shared. I never came to regret that choice of learning, dining, and discussion at Trinity College. I was witness to the fact that even at this early age Tom exuded a comfort that I now realize was the blossoming of a world cultural view that affected both his own undergraduate learning and his warm relationships with his academic colleagues.

My next encounter with Tom took place many years later. After graduation, extended graduate work abroad, and a meteoric rise in University of Toronto ranks, he had been presented with a unique opportunity—that of being the founding president of a new university in the conservative south-eastern Ontario city of Peterborough. By that time, I had achieved a significant level of notoriety, having moved in 1956 to that city as a high-school history teacher and, in 1960, been selected by a not-yet-founded political party to be a candidate in an unexpected federal by-election prompted by the death of Peterborough's sitting MP. Surprisingly, I won the seat as a "New Party" candidate and became a member of Parliament in the fall of 1960. The victory had occurred in spite of the fact that the CCF, one of the founding participants along with the Canadian Labour Congress, would not be transformed officially into a formal political party until August of 1961, the timing of the Ottawa Founding Convention of the New Democratic Party.

It was a short two-year presence in the House of Commons, but by the mid-1960s a just-arrived Tom Symons saw a role for me at Trent as someone who knew the community of Peterborough into which his university had been dropped; who had worked in the local schooling system and knew its administrators, teachers, and students; and who might thus help find the linkages that he knew were essential if his institution was to be locally accepted and supported. To my surprise and delight, I was invited to join the staff of the registrar's office and to assume an academic role as a faculty member in the history department.

It was apparent that Tom's perception of the world would be deeply reflected in this new university, one that he had developed under the watchful eye of the mayor of Peterborough's Committee. Needless to state, there was enthusiastic support from an Ontario government aware of the burgeoning numbers of university places that would be required in the province as a result of the population explosion of the late 1940s and 1950s in Canada, and because of the large numbers of people who, after World War Two, had immigrated to Canada's shores.

However, in the heady decade of the 1960s, in the fall of 1964 to be precise, at the official Opening Ceremonies of Trent University, President Symons addressed the gathered dignitaries from other Ontario postsecondary institutions, the hosting students, faculty, and staff and members of the Peterborough community. He took the opportunity to outline his hope that this new university would become "a useful and significant centre for Canadian Studies. By this is meant the study of our Canadian civilization in its totality: its history, literature, art and institutions, its people and its sciences." In other words, a major focus was that of examining, defining, and expressing the nature of Canada's culture.[2]

Immediately upon its opening in the mid-1960s, Trent University pioneered perspectives of learning within a cultural context that older institutions were reluctant to approach. The legitimacy of multidisciplinary studies was addressed in programs of Native Studies and Canadian Studies, Environmental and Resource Studies and, yes, one defined as Cultural Studies. The last years of the old century and the first decade of the new century have witnessed additional programs in cultural studies in North American universities, but Trent was a pioneer in such offerings. Even more courageously, there was the expectation that academic departments would find common ground beyond the traditional styles of disciplinary autonomy, enhanced, in particular, by a strong college system that produced opportunities for continuing interaction among faculty from various disciplines. Thus, the traditional preoccupation with departmental autonomy and separation would be softened by an alternative that emphasized horizontal rather than vertical disciplinary-charged learning. It was this vision that made Trent University more than just a reflection of the already existing older and more tradition-bound universities in the province of Ontario. Succeeding years—including funding arrangements that celebrated the norm rather than the creative—revealed how courageous these initial steps had been.

There were some who thought that Trent, with its emphasis on tutorials and seminars as opposed to a reliance on lectures, along with the expectation that students would wear green gowns to the classroom and dining hall and feel a loyalty to a particular college within the university, was simply the working out of Symons's fevered memory of his years overseas at Oxford. But it was not that at all. These directions were a thoughtful Canadian's response to the needs of a postsecondary learning community in the context of a cultural understanding of what the educational system in the Canadian nation should include. Symons had carefully considered the unique alternative presented by this opportunity to start a new university and had the courage to follow his vision with positive action. For Ontario, Trent was to be a postsecondary learning option that promised students an intense developmental experience, one that also influenced a Tom Symons, deeply committed to his nation and its people, in his work on the Commission on Canadian Studies.

Tom Symons moved almost imperceptibly from his position as founding president of Trent, a position he brought to a conclusion in 1972 after more than a decade of leadership, to become chair of the Commission on Canadian Studies, sponsored by the Association of Universities and Colleges of Canada. This work could have been a non-controversial, "proper" and "traditional" study of the existing programs so designated by the country's colleges and universities, but Symons chose another course of action. He became consumed by the intense need to outline the unacceptable level of attention being paid to Canadian culture in the country's universities and the few scholars who were expressing its wonders and, in the process, inspiring a more appropriate response in the future. There had been years of controversy in Ontario universities over the dominance of newly-hired American rather than Canadian professors. Professors Robin Mathews and Jim Steele had led the charge, but this issue was overshadowed by what it meant in terms of teaching and research on the campuses of the province's postsecondary system.

The commission's report, *To Know Ourselves*, a record of the state of the postsecondary commitment to Canadian studies, turned out to be a massive undertaking requiring three years and more of Tom's life. In that time, as chair of the commission, he heard the response of two-hundred-and-fifty individuals in person, read some forty thousand letters and one hundred briefs, and produced a report of some three hundred thousand words in two sizeable volumes on the pathetic state of university and college commitment to any understanding of Canada's culture. *To Know Ourselves* was a signal that there must be change affecting courses, programs, and ultimately hiring processes. The report included recommendations that would transform the academic and social context of every campus.

Tom became the ambassador who then produced a paperback synopsis, *The Symons Report*, which clearly conveyed the central message and the accompanying recommendations of the Commission Report and, with this document in hand, he traveled across the entire county arousing a considerable uproar. He had critics on all sides. As commission chair, "I have been abused and clobbered from every conceivable direction," was how he once expressed his experience. The conservative elements wanted things to remain as they were, the intense nationalists wanted a document that blamed the American influence and could be used to drive it out of both the nation's community colleges and its universities.

The fact that his perspective had been worked out in Peterborough several years before its publication and appearance across the academic community gave it a relevance that only such a commitment could procure, thus making it a major influence on the minds of a broad sector of the Canadian educational community in the latter decades of the twentieth century.

For Tom Symons, this cultural perspective was the recognition of a broad, inclusive, multidisciplinary, interactive historical understanding of the political, social, economic, recreational, and artistic elements that make Canada a unique entity, capable of providing the basis for an abundant life for its citizens and able to make a contribution to a world in which peace and justice might possibly come to prevail. The narrow perception of "culture" as attendance at an opera house or symphony hall, or a preoccupation with mainstream economic and militaristic competition (the bane of past centuries) were and are today in total contrast, blatantly inadequate as guiding concepts, and, in the latter case, potentially destructive of human civilization altogether.

Thus, the "cultural" is a theme that carries through all of Symons's work of a lifetime. A cursory perusal of his curriculum vitae, or the entry under his name in the Canadian "Who's Who," reveals a staggering account of his participation in a plethora of committees, commissions, and government agencies on a wide range of public concerns. It leads to a false judgment of a man whose life work can seem to have been blighted as the result of his being an individual unable to say "no" whenever pressed to take on yet another communal task. Even before his retirement as president of Trent in 1972, he had associated himself with a number of these community issues; now in the twenty-first century, indeed, his involvement in public affairs continues unabated into the new millennium. This pattern of his life leads to a perception by some that Tom had scaled the heights in his early years and that the rest of his life was a long descent from those Trent mountaintops. Nothing could be farther from the truth!

It could be said that intellectually his entire life was of a piece. Even as a child he had been attracted to a family tendency to follow "conservative" values, and while a student at the University of Toronto, Tom was the founding president of the Macdonald-Cartier Club. He continued to pursue his interest in the philosophy of conservatism while he was president of Trent. During these years, he became actively involved with the Progressive Conservative Party of Canada and, at the invitation of Robert Stanfield, served throughout his leadership as chairman of the Policy Advisory Committee. This early involvement is an indication of his commitment to a belief that a politically active rather than passive life in the work of Canada's polity and governance is the appropriate style of one seeking to understand the nature of Canada's culture. (T. H. B. Symons is possibly the only president of a Canadian university to be the object of a student body protest against any electoral seduction of its leader that might threaten his absence from its midst—but that is another story.) His political allegiance in no way affected the choice of people, even some, like myself, democratic socialists, others openly Marxist, who found their way into the faculty and administration of a university whose members soon developed a reputation for numerous responses in the form of letters and petitions regarding the nation's major issues from a broad progressive, liberal, nationalist point of view.

One can be exhausted simply by the reading of an account of his many roles in public service, often as chair of this plethora of commissions and committees, all of them agents of policy and a challenge to make change. More important by far is the fact that one can trace the myriad strands of interrelationship within this endless list of commitments that reveal a cultural understanding that separation and specialization, rather than integration and inclusion, can only lead to wrong decisions and endless frustration at the policy implementation level. It is a lifetime trajectory that could be called totally consistent and relentless.

Throughout these many years since the 1960s, while continuing his active presence at Trent as Vanier Professor, Tom was asked to carry out this role as advisor to governments both of Canada and Ontario, his home province, and even to those engaged at the local or municipal level. Thus, my immediate task is apparent. It is placing a spotlight on what is generally perceived as the "cultural," when, in fact, every issue Symons confronted had a cultural element and a linkage with countless other public service roles he was playing on other commissions, committees, and agencies, as well as continuing his academic life at Trent University.[3] Those cultural preoccupations, identified often as "artistic," are but the most obvious and necessary mechanisms for the expression of that broad vision of Canada in all its varieties and richness that Symons desired to identify, defend, preserve, enhance, and extend. It is to a few of these significant roles that this chapter will be devoted. In a sense, the entire volume is a description of his working out of his interpretation of the word "culture."

The Symons Report, the paperback synopsis of *To Know Ourselves,* was funded, in part, by the Ontario Arts Council (OAC) at a propitious moment of its history.

While Tom was bringing to an end his presidency in 1971, composer Louis Applebaum had become the executive director of the Ontario Arts Council, the province's major arts funding agency and he too had a mission. His predecessor, Milton Carman, had been the founding director and was not willing to allow the OAC to be merely a funding agency concerned with satisfying the financial hopes of major arts institutions, for example, the Toronto Symphony Orchestra, then actively harassing the Ontario government for financial help. Carman placed his support behind individual artists and smaller arts organizations more committed to the new and experimental developments in the arts, somewhat to the surprise and despair of the government of the day. Louis found, after quieting down all the confrontation of council and provincial government, that he too wanted to move the OAC to a different level of commitment—that of supporting and encouraging the Canadian creative artist both collectively and as individuals with a vision for enhancing Canadian culture under enormous pressure from an aggressive American entertainment industry. It was inevitable that these two men, Symons and Applebaum, would meet and join their strategies and energies to a common cause. The appointment of Tom to the OAC board made possible an extraordinary initiative.

In a move that was both unique in its history and remarkable in its conception, Louis Applebaum, with Tom Symons at his side, was to set in motion an OAC "To Know Ourselves" (TKO) Committee, its designation based obviously on the title of Tom's Commission Report—a perfect mechanism for the linking of the Symons academic document with a clarion call to make the expression of the arts in learning apparent through the provision of directed OAC funding. Louis realized that the chair of this committee must be a prominent member of the council board; along with OAC chair, Arthur Gelber, he chose Sonia Koerner, who not only was a woman of enormous intelligence, commitment, and energy but who would also soon become the council's chair and who had a splendid reputation with artists and arts organizations as well as with prominent members of the corporate community.

Even before the launch of the "TKO Committee," Applebaum had invited Symons to address the OAC Board and staff on his findings as he was working towards the conclusion of his efforts on the Commission Report. Naomi Lightbourne, one of the original OAC staff appointees, was present and remembers to this day the almost hour-long dissertation that Tom provided, without a note, which ranged across the pathetic state of Canadian studies from coast to coast. She still considers it the most stunning learning experience she ever encountered in her time at the OAC.[4] This was to be the first and last such designated committee in the history of the council, and there were high hopes for its success.

The committee pursued efforts to bring the performing arts into the activities of campuses of colleges and universities, focusing its attention not on those with professional schools embracing drama, music, and dance but on those institutions that had no presence of fine arts at all. Making use of its mandate to "educate" about the arts as well as supporting performance, exhibition, and literary achievement, "Lou and Tom" brought a new focus to cultural development that continued for a number of years, beginning with Tom's determination to save the records of arts organizations—the very lifeblood for any research and writing about the expression of Canada's culture and creativity. The TKO Committee and Literary and Film Officer Ron Evans, in particular, produced a booklet on just how such archival material could be identified, classified, and protected. That Ontario has a rich and varied collection of such materials in several institutional archives can be traced back to that initiative, which came to include meetings and conferences with arts organizations that significantly increased their expertise in an area that had previously been ignored.

This effort connected itself to the realization that part of the reason for the lack of concern for Canadian cultural history came from the absence of curricular materials—the lack of books and periodicals on the cultural elements in the country's story. The degree to which the OAC's small budget could be used for the purpose of encouraging adequate research and writing was obviously minimal. However, as colleges and universities established their own committees on Canada's cultural reality, the interest in such contributions increased.

There was even an effort to engage universities directly. The University of Guelph Pilot Project provided funds particularly for the students and faculty engaged in agriculture that came to include the development of a band, a chorus, and a series of concerts in a space that linked the natural world to the sounds of quality music performance. A massive educational system placed demands far beyond the OAC's means, but it was a start in a process that was to bring a different response to arts expressions, not as hoped by involving every discipline but at least in certain corners of the postsecondary system. Tom's guiding influence as a member of the TKO Committee ensured that the emphasis was on the "comparative, the cooperative, and the connectional": in short, on the elements of the cultural that stressed their relationship to the total meaning of life in this country called Canada. At last, in the 1980s, the OAC was able to produce a history of its own first twenty years, which was written by Roy MacSkimming and included its changing directions in thinking culturally.

During this period of his OAC membership, Tom was asked to join the Canada Council. There was some resentment over this "raiding" of the OAC to secure a valuable member for the federal government's major arts funding body. It was plain that Tom could not sit simultaneously on both the Canada Council for the Arts and the OAC. Lou, in his diplomatic style, perceived the needs at the federal level as even more critical than his own and abandoned his efforts to keep Symons "on board" at the provincial level; Symons joined the Canada Council in 1976.

In these years of Canada's eleventh decade, Tom was also asked to join the Social Sciences and Humanities Research Council, and he served as its founding vice-president—but not before he had made a personal statement that had a significant influence. The functions of both the SSHRC and the Canada Council for the Arts had originally been included by the Massey Commission in its recommendations regarding the creation of the latter institution. Bowing to the perceived needs for greater attention expressed by the university community, the federal government created the SSHRC with special responsibility for the research interests of the university community. Symons very openly opposed this severance of the function of support for the postsecondary education and its research. He sensed that the living together of those concerned with funding research for all kinds of academic purposes with those providing support of cultural purposes that met the wishes of the arts community and the general public was a healthy combination indeed. It assured that research in Canada would be more relevant to a wider community and also that those cultural areas that needed a statistical and rational base for enhancement of their well-being would thus receive proper attention. These were joint needs arising from a single demand for a more vibrant social and intellectual life, as well as a basis for ensuring that Canadians were served by those attending to scientific and technological matters. Tom was responding to his long-held position that demanded a holistic understanding of Canada's culture.

Tom's appeal to Prime Minister Trudeau to reverse the policy of separating the academic and the artistic came too late—the deed was done and there was no turning back. Even the PM's realization that keeping the academic and artistic together would have been his own personal choice was of little significance.[5] In these crucial years, Tom served with both the Ontario Arts Council and the Canada Council as well as being the vice chair of the Social Sciences and Humanities Council. This gave him a unique position to make a difference, one that has kept Canadian universities closer to their communities than could otherwise been expected. He found that he took considerable abuse from both his academic colleagues—who thought their interests would be enhanced by separation—and those with artistic enthusiasms—who believed that the expansions of funding for the arts would be forwarded by the absence of their university colleagues on the Canada Council.

In 1979, Tom Symons was just fifty years old, but he had accumulated more than a lifetime of experience and expertise in the cultural field. He had founded a university and led it through half a decade of planning and preparation followed by a full decade of presidential responsibility. He had served with both the Ontario Arts Council and the Canada Council, as well as being vice-president of the Social Sciences and Humanities Council, and had been involved in the well-being of a number of major cultural institutions, many of which were tied financially and administratively to the federal government. He had seen the excitement and creative opportunities provided by the events preceding and during the Centennial Year based on a more generous support from the Government of Canada and had watched the loss of impetus when that funding had been reduced. He had witnessed beleaguered arts organizations in despair from the penury caused by obvious under-funding. The movement towards the self knowledge proposed in *To Know Ourselves* had continued, but with less intensity and focus than the report deserved. In spite of the awareness of this most eloquent statement—necessary to achieve sustainability for a nation facing internal division as well as threat of external pressures, at both federal and provincial levels, leadership was lacking.

However, there was an opportunity presented in 1979 that captured his sense of mission. It was in this year that the Conservative Party had come into power and Symons had every expectation that the policy directions he had proposed through the years would, in fact, become legislation. David MacDonald, a Red Tory "progressive" with little interest in pointless and self defeating partisanship, had been appointed secretary of state and minister of communications, and thus had captured the major departments with responsibilities for cultural institutions and their policies. He knew Symons well, and Symons was MacDonald's first choice as the chair of a new initiative, the creation of an Advisory Committee on Cultural Policy, one that would give advice to a Joint Committee of the Senate and House of Commons—a process he knew would move matters swiftly through the political maelstrom and ensure action in place of delay and disinterest. MacDonald inherited two strong deputies, Bernard Ostry and Pierre Juneau, who, in spite of their infection from years of Liberal association, knew the practical process of making things happen.

As much as the role of chair would have been the culmination of years of work in countless meetings and conferences, Tom knew he could not devote more time and effort to this cause of cultural policy. He was also aware that most of the federal institutions to which he had given his special attention would be under scrutiny, and his participation as chair of a body engaged in this cultural policy review might be suspect. Most important, he knew there was another person who shared his principles and values as well as his style of operating such a process—his friend and colleague from the Ontario Arts Council, Lou Applebaum. It was Tom's advice to the minister that Applebaum be appointed chair. MacDonald acceded and the cultural community was delighted. In making this recommendation, Tom knew he was providing the best possible advice. Lou had been the executive director at the OAC who had placed top priority on the giving of focus to Tom's report, *To Know Ourselves* by creating a committee by that name at the board level, in the hope it would result in policies that would move an entire province. It was apparent that Lou cared passionately about culture and the artists whose role it was to express that culture.[6]

In order to forward the cause, Tom agreed to be a member of the Advisory Committee on Cultural Policy, a commitment that both David and Lou appreciated enormously. Tom could not have foreseen the extent to which he would take on a leadership and judgmental role that would ultimately enable the successor to the committee to conclude its work. The story almost reached farcical proportions. The now fully operative Advisory Committee had met but twice before MacDonald's conservative government had fallen. Thus came immediately a period of delay, confusion, and partisan electoral rant, followed by the arrival of a new secretary of state, Francis Fox, a prominent Liberal member whom, unfortunately, neither Tom nor Lou knew personally. With the Fox accession came a totally new course of action. Even though both Lou as chair and Tom as a member were retained along with the handful of others who had been appointed to the original advisory body, the process was fundamentally changed.

Now, each of them was to be a member of a much larger Cultural Policy Review Committee, some appointed with Liberal credentials, others bearing particular expertise in one or more cultural areas under review. As well, the committee was expected to carry public hearings across the nation, with the public as a whole and with the arts community at the forefront, and present its advice to a Parliamentary Joint Committee on Cultural Policy in the form of a formal report containing recommendations affecting all the federal programs and institutions for which the new minister was seen to be responsible.

Amidst the change of minister, directions, and style of operation, Lou thought it paramount to appoint a small Chairman's Committee that included, besides Tom and himself, both the Deputy Minister Pierre Juneau and his assistant deputy, Léo Dorais, who were, rather surprisingly, still members of the reinvented policy review committee. The fear of conflict of interest was obviously present and the objectivity of the whole process was under deep suspicion, particularly by artists and arts administrators from coast to coast. Happily, the Chairman's Committee also included Albert Breton, a University of Toronto faculty member whose understanding of financial management and economic matters was invaluable, and whose integrity, like Tom's, was beyond question.

These changes made an enormous difference to the process to which Tom was now to give some three years of his life, traveling across Canada and ultimately being responsible for seeing that the Federal Cultural Policy Review Committee's Report was complete in particular areas where his enormous experience provided expertise. Lou Applebaum had been confirmed as chair but the minister intervened to appoint a co-chair, Jacques Hébert. Sensing his power was being eroded, Lou was ready to resign. However, he could not face the disappointment of leaving Tom and the lifelong commitment that both he and Tom had made to Canadian cultural enhancement and its financial well-being, including the support of all the artists who were depending upon their being rescued by this review, through the recommendations that would promise them a sustainable future. As well, such matters as the continuing commitment to principles of arms-length involvement in funding arrangements were essential, as was the maintaining of the pre-eminence of peer-evaluation as a basis of deciding excellence. Most essential was the establishment of commitment to the support of creativity as the dominant value throughout all the recommendations, a position that assured a recommendation that the federal government would be pressured to provide appropriate financial support. Tom and Lou were prepared to endure all kinds of inconveniences and frustrations that the Federal Cultural Policy Review rained down upon them in order to save these basic principles. The spectre of Canadian cultural funding becoming nothing more than partisan political manipulation was enough to keep both committed to the process.

The report of the Federal Cultural Policy Review Committee emerged in 1982. The process had a frantic conclusion—the minister was determined to have it as a public document no matter the cost of a few questionable solutions based on lacking or inadequate evidence. The hearings had come to dominate the severely limited time available, and little support was given to the research that could support the massive number of recommendations (one hundred and one in number) that came forth. Even more frustrating was the lack of time for the lengthy and profound discussion that might have led to fewer but more defensible recommendations.

Tom played a singular role. He undertook to see that federal attention to matters of "heritage" should retain its place in the priorities of the government. He had made the case for increased funding support and would do so in the 1990s and into the next century. He convinced his colleagues that it was essential that Canadians understand the major events that had shaped the country's past and would determine its future. As well, he was adamant that those Canadians who had contributed to its development be remembered and celebrated. Indeed, he produced a strategy that would ensure this result by including in the FCPRC's report a recommendation supporting a Heritage Council with increased financial support and a mandate to extend its attention and coordinate heritage activities across the entire federal government's menu of activities, which were then resident in several ministries.

As well, with all his experience in the international field, he realized that there was an imperative need for an international focus for those who considered that Canada's story, its values, and its public sector practices deserved to be better known throughout the world. He ensured there was a recommendation to establish an International Cultural Relations Agency to enlarge the amount of arts touring and provide more generous support for it. In doing so, of course, he was invading the territory held by the department of external affairs. But Symons knew that having more Canadian creators and performing artists and their sponsoring arts organizations, both English and French-speaking, able to go abroad and signal the presence of an exciting Canadian cultural reality would have a dramatic effect within the country as well. He had observed the British Council for the Arts as a free-standing body and admired the fine work it accomplished in extending the world's knowledge of the cultural life of the United Kingdom.

With all the commitment Tom had shown towards Aboriginal people, he had been assigned the role of chairing the FCPRC's public meetings in Canada's North, a task he had taken on with charm and aplomb. Indeed, Tom had become recognized as an advocate for the support of the cultural contributions Aboriginal people had made; he would also make that same case as a member of the Historical Sites and Monuments Board. Before it was a popular concept, he believed that their view of life could be a valuable segment of Canada's cultural expression as a whole. (In 1988, Symons was to take on the chair of the Canadian Polar Research Commission Study; in these years, the National Library Advisory Board also took advantage of his presence as a member to make use of him to chair its public hearings in Canada's North.)

Yet, what had seemed such a positive, non-partisan, politically-benign FCPRC process of reviewing and ultimately strengthening Canada's culture was to end in disaster. Most of the recommendations were not highly controversial, but behind the scenes there was a war going on that reflected political debates in Quebec in the 1970s and early 1980s. The Canadian Broadcasting Corporation, by far the most prominent of all the federal agencies under review, was in the midst of its normal ongoing battle over funding, but now the French-speaking broadcasting and cultural agencies were being accused of separatist tendencies, and Jacques Hébert was determined to punish the corporation employees for the perceived misdemeanors of misplaced loyalties. Tom Symons had had little connection with the CBC and, though Lou Applebaum had played a major role in its success on the English-speaking side of the ledger, Jacques Hébert was adamant in his determination to reduce its programming function and thereby argue for a reduced annual appropriation to the corporation's financial well-being. There was some rationale even to the recommendations that would have cut back both function and funding from the corporation—but in the context of the separatist fears, accommodation was not to be found. The result was a public uproar led by both the CBC and the National Film Board (a body also suspect and whose functions were also to be reduced) and encouraged by the electronic media that was prepared to undermine the entire process. The Parliamentary Committee's "review of the review" that followed played no significant role in rescuing the other recommendations that had nothing to do with diminishing the functions of the CBC and the National Film Board or their funding from the federal budget.

However, looking back after a quarter of a century, it is amazing how many of the recommendations have been followed in practice if not in complete accordance with specific details of administration and funding. No party wanted the responsibility for—or even wanted to take credit for—what had been achieved by a significant number of extraordinary members of the FCPRC, who had carried on in spite of the seeming chaos of political eruption going on around them. The intended solutions to the cultural life of Canada were abandoned, but the central determination to celebrate creativity and to defend peer evaluations and arms-length funding had an impact on all political parties.

In the latter stages of the review, Tom's role became crucial. He and a few committee members saved the Cultural Policy Review from becoming a total debacle. The report had been released and did indeed give support to such basic needs as that of increased support to the Canada Council and to several such organizations as the Canadian Music Centre, recommendations for support that were quoted in appeals for federal funds for decades after the report's demise. Indeed, the principles of peer evaluation and "arms-length" had been strengthened amidst all the havoc around national unity, which might have been perceived as a reason to end these defences of artistic and intellectual freedom and their essential roles on the Canadian cultural scene.

Tom's support for the report had gone even farther. After many arts enthusiasts had abandoned the report and everything to do with it, Tom had the courage to state openly that he believed the whole initiative, with all its confusion—amidst changes in government, changes in process and purpose—had been "a blue-ribbon effort" and once the dust had settled he wrote to Francis Fox, still secretary of state, indicating that "while much of the Committee's Report had proven controversial, I think it is a solid piece of work that will be of help to both governments and the cultural community for many years."[7] Ironically, one could argue that no report on cultural policy has surfaced in the past twenty-five years, and the presence of a strong, viable arts community has never been more assured and effective than since the arrival of the millennium. The recognition of Canada's cultural strength and integrity is now unquestioned, even in the shadow of a Federal Cultural Policy Review process that was politically undermined.

Lou Applebaum could not say enough about the role that Tom had played in making it all happen. Tom Symons remains, even in the twenty-first century, a chief advocate for an increased role on the part of federal institutions. And, while encouraging the support of the private sector on behalf of libraries, museums, art galleries, and the spectrum of agencies devoted to the care of all these activities, he has continued to support public involvement through democratically-elected governments at a time when conservatism has been equated with the privatization of those functions, in some cases even those that best allow Canada to be perceived as a civilized community.

In 1986, ten years after the publication of *To Know Ourselves*, and after serving on both the Ontario Arts Council and the Canada Council, and after participating as a member of the Applebaum-Hébert Committee on federal cultural policy, Symons was asked to give the keynote speech at a Canadian Society for the Study of Higher Education conference focusing on postsecondary involvement in the nation's cultural agenda. It was held at the University of Manitoba from the 30th of May to the 1st of June. Symons took the opportunity to express, in a comprehensive and controversial manner, the themes of culture and the arts that had already engaged his attention over several decades.

Perceptively, the faculty of education of the University of Manitoba published the main contributions to this conference in its *Monographs in Education* series. In the foreword to its initial volume, the editors, Alexander Gregor and Keith Wilson, described Tom's contribution to the conference as "splendid" and added that the address "builds on his earlier seminal studies to offer a definition, or rather a range of definitions; and then within those definitions he is able to outline, with compelling logic, the tasks and responsibilities that Canadian postsecondary institutions must assume. Indeed, his argument draws us to the conclusion that the cultural agenda is not an additional or optional role for those institutions; it is in fact their central and overriding mandate."[8] Of course, that was the very strategy that Symons had in mind when he had accepted the university's invitation.

Symons began his remarks by placing before his audience the reality that there are a broad range of definitions that the term "culture" attracts. Indeed, in his words, its definition is "a rather personal thing. . . . what it is, is what you yourself see or decide. . . it is in the eyes of the beholder."[9] He indicated that this "diversity" of definitions, rather than being "troubling," was indeed "desirable." He then went on from the narrow and conventional description of culture as "arts and letters" to that of "the totality of language, heritage and belief," and then on to one that included the "sum total of how one lives and what one values."[10] He indicated that this third definition was the one to which he himself was committed, as the most valuable and demonstrably as the most effective.

Tom's acceptance of the broad definition had encouraged him in his acquisition of the world view that had empowered his own career. It led him to warn his academic colleagues that "most of the great and fundamental problems in our society have far more to do with cultural affairs than with the state of the economy, or the constitution, or the armed forces."[11] This statement was a justification for the journey he had taken, both as founding president at Trent and as a continuing member of its faculty as Vanier Professor in Canadian Studies, a commitment to a horizontal approach to whatever he determined crucial to the future of the institution in question or the very nation itself.

However, he was speaking on this occasion to a roomful of academic leaders, and he took the opportunity to expose the implications of these definitions of culture for the unimpressive role universities had played in the past and the central role they must play in the future. He began by revealing how minimal had been the postsecondary commitment to even the most narrow interpretation of the term "culture" as merely a response to the fine and performing arts. By the twentieth-century's eighth decade, Canadian literature and thus its "letters" had attracted international attention and readership, yet authors like Margaret Atwood, Roberson Davies, and Margaret Laurence were faced with "a tenacity of some academics in denying or ignoring this fact," a position Symons termed as both "wrong-headed" and "unhelpful." The same could be said for other arts disciplines, and the resulting diminishing of Canadian writers and artists was quite shocking in its impact on how little Canadians knew of themselves. Reviewing a recent publication of the National Library on doctoral research on Canada and Canadians, Symons could proclaim that in the one hundred years of 1884 to 1983, there had been only twenty-two doctoral dissertations on the arts in Canada, eleven of which had been completed in American universities. In Canadian architecture, only five titles for doctoral studies could be found. Even more staggering was his discovery that "of the eighteen doctoral studies of Canadian musicians and composers, only two were completed in Canadian universities." The same disinterest and neglect in Canadian universities could be found in drama and theatre, film, and library studies. With caustic humour, Symons could claim that "more Canadian doctorates have been awarded on the subject of worms than on Canadian art, or architecture, or drama and theatre, or communications, or library studies." While conceding that attention through doctoral studies was not the only "way to heaven" in the understanding of Canada's cultural reality, these statistics gave some indication "of the paucity of attention as yet devoted to Canadian arts and letters at the highest level of the education system."[12]

Tom made the point that, during his time in the 1980s as a member of the Applebaum-Hébert Committee on federal cultural policy, he had been made aware of this same neglect and inattention to the arts in Canada's community colleges—a fact that he found even more distressing than these statistics about the lack of achievement at the doctoral level in the country's universities. The "Applebert" Committee—which had been reluctant to engage in any study of education as part of its research and seeking out of Canadian opinion—had found that it was nonetheless deluged by commentary about the lack of interest in matters Canadian to be found in the nation's schools, colleges, and universities.

Turning his attention to his second definition of "culture" as "heritage, language, and ethnicity," Symons made it clear that Canada's future as a bilingual and multicultural nation was at stake and that there were reasons to expect that colleges and universities should "develop some working proficiency in our two official languages." The seriousness of the issues facing the country's survival demanded such a course and, as well, there were good reasons for the expansion of activities at the postsecondary level providing "teaching, research, and service to the rich tapestry of our non-official languages." Given this cultural diversity of peoples, it was surely a ludicrous situation "that Canada had to rely on interpreters and translators from other countries" even in order to carry out its own official business. Symons demanded a postsecondary educational response that would result in "the creation of a national program from the federal government, the council of ministers of education, and the universities and colleges designed to meet this need."

With its diverse populations representing people from every corner of the planet, Symons saw Canada to be in a unique position to provide world leadership in this area along with programs that fostered understanding of ethnicity within the cultural agenda of the nation's entire postsecondary sector. Symons perceived this as a unique role that Canada could play on the international level, one he saw linked as well to regional studies. Indeed, speaking of a university system that had taken little cognizance of its presence in the life of the nation, he said, "Region-building is as significant a theme in the life of our country as nation-building."[13]

Symons considered the role of women as an element in any exploration of the implications of the second "heritage" definition of "culture" within the universities and colleges of the nation. He indicated, as well, the need for increased attention to the matters associated with human rights, a sensitivity that had emerged from his own work on the Ontario Human Rights Commission. It was clear that, for Symons, the age of the isolated ivory tower of academic separation from the issues that bedeviled the lives of the citizen on the street had ended. It was a demand for a caring and compassionate educational response to the problems that he felt threatened the quality of life of his fellow citizens and even the very survival of the nation.

In the course of these remarks, Symons also sounded the alarm that even the existing cultural values of the postsecondary system were at risk. In his view, the broadest definition of "culture" demanded attention to the very basic role of the university and college in a world that was being threatened by a government's preoccupation with science and technology, and an unsophisticated attitude toward the corporate power that accompanied this shift. The Speech from the Throne in Ontario had pointed to the government of the day's expectations that the province's postsecondary system would target and demand excellence in such areas as "science, technology, and innovation and business administration, marketing, and international trade." It was to be assumed that such an emphasis would provide greater "relevance" to a society faced with the forces of globalization that were on the horizon by the mid-1980s. Such "zeitgeist has often been wrong before as it is, I believe, in this instance." But given the fact that government was insisting on such targeting, and was the major source of funding of postsecondary education, it posed a particular threat. He put the case simply and strongly:

> Those who see the need to make a choice between technology and culture have simply not thought deeply enough. The two are not inherently in conflict. They are not necessarily opposites. And they are not of equal value. The choice is not between technology and culture, but about how best to make use of technology in the service of culture...[14]

It was the Symons tendency to expect this worldview from his political associates, those for whom the small "p" and small "c"—for progressive conservative—were relevant. As the twentieth century came to an end, there were few who perceived the dangers of the "sweetness and light" fantasies of a technological paradise, preferring to believe that technical solutions would save the planet and its inhabitants from climate change and all the elements of that crisis in human affairs. Symons was direct about his view that

> the cultural impact of technology is immense. In fact, the increasing role in society, makes it all the more necessary that increased attention be devoted to teaching and research about culture in our postsecondary institutions. . . . What is needed now is a reassertion of the fundamental role of the liberal arts and sciences to society and the individual.[15]

These deep and profound concerns came from Tom's broad understanding and articulation of the meaning of culture. Soon it was clear that the postsecondary system had joined in the unreflective and uncritical acceptance of all that technology promised of a global future that would benefit rich and poor, as well as resolve environmental problems that had remained unsolved for decades. It would be seen early in the new twenty-first century how important these warnings of Symons's had been.

Even the postsecondary institutions themselves were affected by the lack of critical response. The broad implications of the dominance of technological solutions soon reached into the very heart of the postsecondary system itself. The resulting presence of unhappy and unfulfilled academics and angry and frustrated students had led to a questioning by an entire society of the place of the college or university in the learning life of the total community of citizens.

Indeed, the university now shares the blame for the meltdown of the existing financial and monetary system in 2009 and, even more, for the lack of critical attention to the major factors and behaviours that led to it. (The Chicago School and its dominance of the post-war world economics is but a fraction of that involvement.) At its best, the university system's increased dependence on private sources of income has led to a lack of critical attention that can be seen as an unfortunate sharing in the general absence of sufficient analysis and understanding of the context of global economic disintegration. At its worst, it reflects postsecondary education's involvement in the context of greed and entitlement that formed the background of this worst economic crisis in three quarters of a century. This outcome has emerged from an uncritical stance that has accepted government pressure to gear curriculum and learning practices to the values of the corporate sector's determination to inflict globalization indiscriminately upon the world. It has been reinforced by a lack of sensitivity to the impact of diminished government support and the increased private funding on universities on the part of those providing leadership both in government, the private sector, and universities themselves.

The relevance of Symons's warning was evident to any professor in the trenches. In the words of an admittedly radical observer and participant in the Ontario postsecondary scene, Professor John McMurtry has this to say in regard to these decades since the 1980s:

> When it is believed that academics' work is at the leadership edge of the "global knowledge economy" none ask what the criterion of knowledge is. There is none except what reduces money costs and increases money revenues for many managers and professors. That is what "accountability" means in this value system. Thus teaching comes to mean only what produces graduates who make more money in the global market than they would have without their degree, with ever higher tuition fees at the cost of acquiring and selling their skills at a higher price.[16]

McMurty concludes his essay, "Nothing that does not pay off in more money to administrations is supported within the corporate university." This was the warning that Symons had placed before the postsecondary community in a more balanced and moderate language some twenty years before in the context of a universal understanding of what could transpire if cultural factors were neglected or ignored. Even Symons's reputation in the Canadian and international academic community could not make this prescient statement acceptable, nor could it advance a call to action that was heeded in any effective defence of critical academic and scholarly values.

Once again, it was within his broadest definition of "culture" as a holistic concept of all the values and visions that the postsecondary system could muster that Tom called for immediate action. He had seen in his work the devastating effect of social injustice in the failure to provide equal accessibility to, and comparable quality of, a postsecondary educational experience for all young Canadians (particularly those in the northern reaches and in the "have-not" provinces). He was determined to confront this scourge in the Canadian educational system.

Symons placed certain statistics before the audience (and later monograph readers) that gathered attention and, as a result, produced movement towards what he believed to be the esteemed and honoured Canadian values of equality of opportunity and of social justice. He expressed his concern for the obvious differences in educational opportunity in the various provinces of Canada, when the support for a full-time equivalent student could vary from five thousand three hundred and fifty dollars in one province and nearly nine thousand dollars in another. As dramatic were the contrasts in student support at the community college level. He also deplored the disparity in college and university library support from one province to another and the enormous contrast in tuition fees. All these numbers added up to reveal a contrast from province to province in the percentage of young people who were able to graduate from these institutions across the nation.

Symons called for a national strategy to overcome these differences. But such a strategy could only be devised and carried with the full support of the institutions across the country. Although governments would be the source of these funds, he knew it would not happen without the enthusiastic advocacy from the colleges and universities.

> Universities prosper best when they have some shared vision and concept of purpose which will energize them with a renewing sense of mission, of service, and of their own work.[17]

Calling for a "return to collegiality" and a "climate of scholarship," a new respect for humanity in education and "qualities of reflection, responsibility, wisdom and civility," he concluded his remarks":

> My highest priority for the postsecondary cultural agenda would call therefore for a re-dedication of the academic community to the learning of culture and the culture of learning.[18]

It could be assumed that the years of the 1970s and 1980s contained the ultimate statements of Symons's belief in the need for an acceptance of a broad understanding of the Canadian cultural reality as a basis for self-knowledge both at the individual and collective levels. However, Symons was not just committed to the rhetorical; he was determined to reveal his philosophy through yet other involvements in areas that needed recognition and support if the "cultural perspective" was to be advanced. He did so in four other areas: human rights, the National Library, heritage (especially the Historic Sites and Monuments Board), and the environment, especially the Trent-Severn Waterway.

In the 1980s, Tom Symons's attention in matters cultural was first drawn to what he realized to be a major aspect of the Canadian cultural reality—a commitment to human rights. For three years in that decade, Tom served as chair of the Ontario Human Rights Commission. Characteristically, in yet another area of perception, he brought the whole spectrum of human rights into a cultural context. It had once been considered the natural preserve of those concerned solely with equality before the law, with the focus inexorably trained on the legal profession on both sides of every issue. Tom saw a role for those outside the legal profession in developing public policy related to appropriate legislation and a concern for civil behaviour that should be the responsibility of every citizen. In Tom's view, intolerance, abuse, and violence perpetrated against citizens because of gender, sexual preference, colour of skin, or religious belief should be the concern of every member of the community. Eventually, enforcement of human rights must be the expectation of every person anxious to enhance Canada's culture.

As an involved and observant member of government committees, commissions, and agencies, Tom had seen lives demeaned and dismissed by cruel and inappropriate behaviour on the part of those in places of authority. Tom had no reluctance to speak in passionate terms about civility, decency, and tolerant behaviour as Canadian cultural norms that needed to be recognized as essential to the lifestyle of the country he loved. It was not just a matter of personal accountability related to the quality of life in each community. It must permeate public life and even a nation's foreign policy. It could be said that the greatest contribution Canada had made in the past and for the future was the presence of two nations, with a history of centuries of conflict, living together by finding the compromises and accommodations that made peace and non-violence the expected norm. For Canada to have achieved this level of harmony, while bringing in millions of people from every corner of the planet, was a miracle that deserved recognition and emulation. This miracle had taken place on a continent on which the conflict of black and white south of the forty-ninth parallel had never been resolved and had forced a civil war of enormous proportions and the continued souring of political life over a century and a half after. In Tom's view, the country's human rights record could stand proudly amidst that of other nations, but vigilance was a necessary complement to that proud record and this fact needed to be a part of every Canadian's cultural perception.

A second cultural area to which Tom devoted attention in the 1980s, consistent with *To Know Ourselves* and with his admonishment and encouragement of the formal educational sector, was the very basic materials that must be secured and, in some cases rescued, compiled and organized, protected and made accessible to scholars and the curious. In 1987, he became the chair of the National Library Advisory Board.

Symons was deeply impressed by the administration and staff of the National Library. He realized that the institution needed increased funding and the opportunity to develop a more visible commitment to outreach and public involvement in its affairs. The National Library Board was delighted to have someone who could share their enthusiasm, in particular, for the acquisition and protection of Canadian documentation of the country's history. This was a mission that Symons applauded and celebrated.

The advisory board had established a tradition of holding one of its meetings each year outside Ottawa, and when Tom arrived on the scene, it was time to travel to Canada's North with a formal meeting in Yellowknife and a number of informal exchanges with both Aboriginal people and more recent arrivals from the south in the Northwest Territories and the Yukon. One library staff member was staggered by the quality of Tom's chairing of these meetings, his capacity to include every person, to listen and to ensure there was understanding and consensus. Those who were not aware of his work with native people at Trent, on the FCPRC and in other settings, were astonished by his affinity, sympathy, and caring for this segment of Canada's citizenry.

In his role as chair of the National Library Advisory Board, Symons once again displayed his exceptional gifts and consummate effectiveness as a leader and board chair, especially of cultural organizations. As chair, he ensured every issue was addressed and the agenda was covered, because he saw that the clarity of the cultural context was never lost from sight in the myriad details of administering a great library.[19] "In the best interpretation of the term 'politician,'" a National Library observer remarked, "Symons was one of a kind."[20] Marc-Adélard Tremblay, the great Laval anthropologist, once described Tom's skill in chairmanship very perceptively. Symons's "extended knowledge in history, in the arts and humanities, in the social sciences," he remarked, "are some of the elements which constitute the fabric of his intellectual interdisciplinary culture. They become the perspective and part of the input process which regulate observations and discussions which occur among members of those organizations he leads. . . ." This great knowledge and understanding, together with "a very special know-how in the arts of human relations, in his skill in presenting topics being on the agenda. . . allowing everyone who has something to say to take the floor," combine to make Symons "a model" of a chair and a leader for educational and cultural organizations.[21]

A third cultural area to which Symons devoted attention in the 1980s and 1990s, consistent with *To Know Ourselves* and the Aplebaum-Hébert report, was the area of built and natural heritage. He served as chair of the Historic Sites and Monuments Board of Canada (HSMBC) from 1986 to 1996. In 1994, Tom was asked to give a keynote address at a conference to mark the seventy-fifth anniversary of the HSMBC. Tom had been a member of that board for many years, and he took the occasion as an opportunity not only to encourage a celebration of the board's three quarters of a century of accomplishments but to "reflect on where we should be going in the future." He had every confidence that his message would be heard, as no board member had attracted more respect that he had gathered both from board colleagues and staff.

Symons had given an enormous amount of his time to this enterprise over many years. Certainly, it was an opportunity to give advice and counsel on the nature of those personages and events from Canada's past that might attract the board's attention and recognition in the coming months and years. He was singularly expert on the criteria that had been employed to seek out the critical events and to identify the outstanding historical figures who had made a difference to the development of this country, thereby enhancing its cultural wealth of mind and spirit.

Over these years, a plethora of plaques revealing the important contributions of local citizens to the life of the nation, as well as to the events that had changed the course of the country's history, had appeared across the country. The text of these plaques carefully explained the reasons for their presence, and Tom had often joined in the many celebrations along with community history enthusiasts, often descendants of those being honoured, as well as with local politicians from every level of government, and with colleagues from the Historic Sites and Monuments Board and Administration. He reveled in this opportunity to move beyond the scholarly ranks of his university colleagues to citizens who often had a unique view of the individuals and events being remembered and celebrated.

However, as significant as these events were, erecting informational plaques was not the only role the board played. It was essential in every case to ensure the quality of the decisions in selecting the persons and events to be given a place in a dramatic visual presence. These plaques reflected the sage judgment and unassailable scholarship to which Symons was only too pleased to give his agreement. He demanded and received assurance from the staff that these moments of recognition were fully merited in the context of his understanding of the cultural reality of Canada's present and future. Nothing less would satisfy his expectations, and his colleagues associated with the board realized the importance of his support and assent.

As one might expect, military exploits and political developments held sway through these early years of board recognition as major subjects of appropriate provincial attention. A trip to Niagara-on-the-Lake, and the highway that wends its way along the river to the falls, contains visits to one after another plaque that commemorates both the beginnings of Canada's political efforts to achieve nationhood, and the battles along the Niagara River that dominated the failed attempted invasion by American forces in the War of 1812. It was the success of these early efforts to achieve self-governance and to defend the region that assured there would be a second nation north of the St. Lawrence and the Great Lakes. The survival of what became Ontario and Quebec in that war was the essential geographic base for the extension both east and west until Canada was indeed a Dominion from sea to sea after 1867. Niagara-on-the-Lake and the plaques that abound are a veritable history lesson accessible to every visitor.

However, time and new sensitivities led the board to realize that the preoccupation with the political and military was a distortion that failed to recognize the social, intellectual, and spiritual contributions and, even more disastrously, had failed to honour the part played by the female gender, to say nothing of the events that consumed the efforts of the members of Canada's Aboriginal people. That distortion had to be corrected. Symons ensured that this was the case and that "although the Board and staff are already making use of the device of convening special forums on such subjects, for example, the better recognition and commemoration of women and the Aboriginal peoples to Canadian history" it was not enough.[22] Symons continued, "We could also possibly make fuller use of the knowledge of people learned in a given subject by inviting them to participate in the Board's processes of research and evaluation." It was not to be about tokenism, but about full involvement. Indeed, though Tom abhorred huge committees and panels, he was prepared to see an enlargement of the board to accord wider representation of those who had received insufficient attention in the past.

Symons went on to make the case that there must be an acceleration of the overall process of "identifying, communicating, and maintaining our National Historic Sites." He noted that the cost to the taxpayer was at that time three dollars and sixty six cents per annum. Surely that was insufficient "to spend on the preservation of the national patrimony," especially in the light of the fact that

> heritage of value to Canadians is being lost or destroyed daily because of our inability to do what needs to be done. Once lost, it usually cannot be replaced and is gone forever. There is urgency in this race against time and it is a race in which heritage is too often the loser.[23]

Symons identified a strategy that might encourage a more generous level of private support. He dramatically underscored his point, but recognized yet another danger:

> Heritage is too important to be left in the hands of a few, no matter how expert. Nor should it be allowed to become a sort of middle-class conspiracy that promotes a cozy cream tea culture.[24]

A rational funding response could best happen, in Symons's view, if heritage was seen broadly as valuable and necessary to every citizen and could attract the support of the corporate sector, not as a strategy to lessen government support but to allow more to be done.

Symons seized on an even more progressive strategy, linking built heritage to a fourth area of Canadian and human culture that captured his attention in the 1990s: the environment. In the 1980s and 1990s, the crisis around environmental destruction, global warming, and the waning of sources of power to support an industrial society had broken upon public consciousness. Tom admitted that heritage might not ever attract the concern of the masses, but it was obvious that "the environment" had risen to the top of political interest for many people in his country. He realized "environmentalists have delivered clear, popular, well-understood messages." It was time for recognition that "environmentalists and heritage preservationists share the common concerns, the common values and the common goals that arise from the mutual commitment to a 'conserver' society. They have a near identity of interests. Surely they should make common cause?"

For Symons, the divide between the preservation of the results of human hand and the conservation of clean water and air—the delight of an unsullied landscape—were of a single passion and together represented the treasure to be handed down to future generations. In his words, it was paramount "for heritage conservationists to give more attention and support to the environmental dimension and its consequences."

How prescient in the circumstances—when the full measure of the environmental crisis was still a matter of concern to only a minority of Canadians—that Symons sounded the alarm. It was obvious to him that environmental conservationists who cared about the natural world must share cultural values with those seeking to preserve the remains of societal achievements. If Symons's alarm had been taken seriously, Canada's role in the coming millennium would have been very different. This country could have given leadership to the world through the Kyoto years—but it was not to be! Indeed, Canada became the scourge of developing countries, joining the United States in demanding the reduction of the national carbon "footprint" of the poorest countries when, in fact, their impact on the environment was comparably miniscule, at least in comparison to the industrial countries who had produced the crisis. His beloved nation had become the source of substantially increased pollution during the period of the Kyoto Accord. For Symons, it was transparent that "we will have to convey effectively the same message that the cultural world is part of our environment and that the natural world is part of our cultural heritage."[25]

As an aspect of the plan of action, Symons also felt it essential to confront those who—in opposing the board and its work—suggested that honouring the past only brought into focus the ongoing conflict of French- and English-speaking Canadians and made more apparent that the two nations seemed on a divergent path. Not so, in Symons's view. Our heritage must surely be, at base, "what we share." In Symons's view, heritage research must be characterized as "popular" in the best sense of the term. It is "not an abstraction" but is rather "dependent on people" in recognition "that heritage like culture is concerned with the sum of all we have and of the total historical experience of our society to the moment."[26] Symons was determined that a broad, horizontal, inclusive research be carried out within a context that safeguards "the values of imagination and creativity" and not be bounded by mere "logical analysis." Indeed, Symons approached these questions within the broadest perspective imaginable: "preservationists and environmentalists must co-operate to discover, to invent, to develop and improve a full array of tools, both technological and political to preserve and protect the world's natural and historic sites. . . We may well lose that balancing act and fall into a rootless condition like the tumbleweed if we do not soon discover our sense of history and our sense of purpose."[27]

After decades of working in the cultural trenches, his conclusion was that

> we need a new conceptual framework, one that sees the treatment of heritage as a totality embracing now the built. and cultural heritage and the natural heritage, both built environment and natural environment. We need a holistic approach to heritage concerns.[28]

It was an extraordinarily timely speech. The call for immediate action was apparent. The call for cooperation of all the players was obviously necessary. In every way, Symons was placing his life work before an audience made up of people who could make things happen, not least, the government of the day and the leaders of business and industry.

Tom also carried his concern for the environment as an expression and reflection of human culture into his subsequent involvement in what might otherwise have been perceived as merely a local process to protect and the Trent-Severn Waterway. As a Peterborough citizen for nearly half a century, he was eminently qualified both to care deeply and to comment knowledgeably on its past and future. He joined the panel of citizens who were to consider the waterway, which was, in every sense, a source of recreational, economic, and social development for a large area in which Peterborough was a major city presence. The report the panel produced was called *It's All About Water.*

In keeping with his own philosophy of cultural context, he found that although his views were accepted within the proceedings of the panel, the title was a problem. At a celebration of the release of the report in 2008, Canada's environment minister of the day, John Baird, made use of the title as the theme of his enthusiastic acceptance response to its successful accomplishment. However, Symons, in the audience with his panel colleagues, in a short interchange, brought the minister to a halt. "It's not all about water, Mr. Minister, it's about culture!"[29]

Of course, Symons was right. The waterway had everything to do with the daily life of those living in large and small communities lapped by its waves. It was how people in the large area drained by the waterway defined themselves and their neighbours. Even more, it was a way that connected those very people with the larger environmental challenges around the provision of clean water that this part of the country shared with others on the continent and the globe.

Perhaps water is the defining issue that every human shares with every other human. We have not been successful in reducing and ending the threat of war, violence, and, at its worst, the threat of nuclear annihilation. Nor have we confronted the injustice that deprives children of food, health, and shelter in a world in which that possibility remains within the providence of a planet that has had enough for all to share. Perhaps the cultural approach provides the most acceptable path to an end to war, violence, hunger, and homelessness as the major preoccupations of the planet's inhabitants, The fact remains that we all must share and nurture this world—or lose it as a species.

It could be said that Tom Symons's work of a lifetime has been that of promoting the role of a country that might well provide effective and sensitive leadership in the struggle for the survival, the enhancement, and the spiritual nurture of the planet's inhabitants. Ultimately, this is a large order demanding a complete shift in the values and lifestyle of all humankind. It is indeed "All About Culture." And Tom Symons made that reality his crusade, his passion, and his mission.

Notes

1 Interview with Michael Tait, 18 June 2009.

2 T. H. B. Symons, cited in A. O. C. Cole, *Trent, The Making of a University, 1957—1987* (Peterborough: Trent University, 1992), 42.

3 Interview with Gwyneth Evans, 10 September 2009. Symons had no desire to separate even his academic and his public contribution activities. In the late 1980s, while Symons was continuing his academic role as Vanier Professor in Canadian studies at Trent University, Gwyneth Evans, the secretary of the National Library Board to which Symons had been appointed as chair, was amazed by the extent to which he brought his students to that institution as a learning experience. Ms. Evans was even more surprised that he seemed to play the role of a mentor, who knew the name of every one of his "charges."

4 Interview with Naomi Lightbourne, 9 September 2009.

5 Interview with T. H. B. Symons, 27 April 2009.

6 Ibid. The Symons-Applebaum relationship is further explored in Walter Pitman, *Louis Applebaum, A Passion for Culture* (Toronto: The Dundurn Group, 2002).

7 T. H. B. Symons. Letter to the Honourable Francis Fox, Secretary of State, 7 March 1983. York University Archives, Louis Applebaum fonds, 2000—009/003[19], cited in Pitman, *Louis Applebaum, A Passion for Culture,* (Toronto: The Dundurn Group, 2002), 480 endnote 54.

8 Alexander Gregor, Keith Wilson, "Foreword," in Alexander Gregor, Keith Wilson, eds., *Monographs in Education* (Winnipeg: University of Manitoba, 1986), v.

9 T. H. B. Symons, "Canadian Postsecondary Education: The Cultural Agenda," in Alexander Gregor, Keith Wilson, eds., *Monographs in Education* (Winnipeg: University of Manitoba, 1986), 1.

10 Ibid., 2.

11 Ibid., 2.

12 Ibid., 5–7

13 Ibid., 11–15.

14 Ibid., 17

15 Ibid., 17–18.

16 John McMurtry, Canadian Centre for Policy Alternatives, *Monitor* (July–August 2009): 17.

17 T. H. B. Symons, "Canadian Postsecondary Education: The Cultural Agenda," in Alexander Gregor, Keith Wilson, eds., *Monographs in Education* (Winnipeg: University of Manitoba, 1986), 23.

18 Ibid., 28.

19 Interview with Marion Scott, National Librarian 1989–99, 10 September 2009.

20 Interview with Gwyneth Evans, secretary to the National Library Advisory Board 1981–92, 10 September 2009.

21 I am grateful to Katherine Berg, special advisor to the secretary-general of the Canadian Commission for UNESCO, for her kindness in sharing with me an introduction of Tom Symons by Marc-Adélard Tremblay.

22 T. H. B. Symons, "From Old Crow to New Bergthal: Opening Address" in Thomas H. B. Symons, ed., *The Place of History, Commemorating Canada's Past,* The Proceedings of the National Symposium on the Occasion of the 75th Anniversary of the Historic Sites and Monuments Board of Canada (Ottawa: Historic Sites and Monuments Board of Canada, 1997), 11.

23 Ibid., 12.

24 Ibid., 14.

25 Ibid., 14.

26 Ibid., 18–19.

27 Ibid., 21.

28 Ibid., 21–22.

29 Interview with T. H. B. Symons, 22 April 2009.

CHAPTER 9

Transformative Leadership: Tom Symons and a New Vision of Human Rights

ROSALIE SILBERMAN ABELLA*

When I was appointed as a Commissioner of the Ontario Human Rights Commission in 1975, Tom Symons was already its Chair. Other Commissioners included Bromley Armstrong, Lita-Rose Betcherman, Valerie Kaserac, and Bruce McLeod. We were very lucky because the chemistry between us was exceptional. Looking back, it was the most consistently collegial, joyful, and collaborative position I could have hoped for to launch a career in the public service.

The Commission's role was to receive and consider complaints under the Ontario Human Rights Code from the people of Ontario. At our meetings, the Commissioners would receive reports from the staff about these complaints. We decided which of these complaints was sufficiently important or serious that it needed the next step. And the next step was an adjudication. That meant a Board of Inquiry under an independent Chair, with the Commission lawyer on one side promoting a certain point of view on behalf of the complainant and the defendant, represented by his or her lawyer, on the other side.

The Commission didn't write the law. We didn't decide the cases. We only decided which cases should go forward to an adjudication. The Commissioners ceased to play a role the moment we sent a case off to a Board of Inquiry. But our lawyer—the lawyer hired to fight the case for the complainant—was arguing before a neutral arbitrator,

* This chapter is based on an interview with Ralph Heintzman, 29 April 2010.

and putting the commission's position forward. We would be the ones saying to the lawyer: "This is what we want you to fight for."

Even more than what I learned from Tom Symons about human rights—and I learned an enormous amount—was what I learned from him about leadership. He was the gold standard. He just did all of it masterfully. Even at the time, I was aware that something quite magical was going on whenever he presided. Now that I'm older, I appreciate those gifts even more. It is the leadership that lingers for me: intellectual, professional, and personal. Especially the way he was able to facilitate collegiality.

As Chair and leader of the Ontario Human Rights Commission, Tom Symons knew, above all, how to engender debate and discussion. Some people who lead come at a subject or an issue with their minds made up, and then they steer the discussion. He had a different way of doing it. Whatever his own views were, we always had the feeling that he wanted us to air our own.

He could be a wonderful conversationalist. I loved sitting beside him socially. But when he presided as chair—and that's the way I saw him most—he wasn't a conversationalist. He was *listening*. He was the facilitator, and he let the rest of us be the conversationalists. He made sure the discussion was vigorous, thorough, rigorous, and constructive. He knew when to intervene and was very careful about not derailing debate. None of us ever felt diminished because he disagreed with us. And the result was remarkable. He made all of us feel confident that he was genuinely interested in what we had to say. And so you were at your best. Or what you thought was your best.

I guess "generous" would be the right word to describe Tom Symons's leadership. He was so comfortable in his own skin that he was happy to let everybody else look good. He was interested in creating stars. We all felt his wind underneath our wings. He just said, "Go, fly! You have my blessing. Just be who you want to be." He wasn't a bit competitive.

As a result, the Commissioners themselves were all united behind Tom—we all adored and admired him. There was never a word from any of them that was anything other than utterly confident in and grateful for his leadership. Not even a hint of criticism. If anything, we thought he might have been overly solicitous.

And when I saw him with the staff, he was unfailingly polite. I never saw him criticize. He never said, "That's just not the way we do things." It was always an encouragement. "You may want to think about doing it in a different way next time, one that doesn't make the parties wait so long!" He always treated the staff as if they were Commissioners. There was no upstairs-downstairs with Tom. You could be staff, you could be Commissioner, or you could be the person clearing the table at the lunches at the Park Plaza. He treated you with the same graciousness.

Democratic is perhaps a good way to describe him, but I would not say he was a populist. He wasn't. He was a person who really cared about quality and he was discerning. He felt that distinctions should be made. There was a right way of doing things and there was a less right way of doing things. So he didn't say, "Well if that's what people want. . ."

The only way we knew that Tom was disagreeing with us was when he would, at some point, announce that it was time for lunch. He would then quietly talk to one or two of the Commissioners and explain that, from a public perception point of view, or from a ripeness of the issue point of view, or from a political feasibility point of view, perhaps we were heading towards a result that wasn't wise. He never did it at the table, because he didn't want to say anything that would cauterize our enthusiasm for the views we had been espousing. But he always ended up getting his way, because, of all of us around the table, he really was, in fact, the transcendently wisest. What I mean is that, even when he agreed with us, Tom was able to hover over the social and political landscape and see that some things were matters of timing. This wasn't about courage. He was a man of enormous courage. I came to see later that so much of it was about timing.

The clearest example was the Damien case in 1976. John Damien was a jockey who had been fired by the Jockey Club because, as they unabashedly said, he was "homosexual." And the Code at the time said you couldn't discriminate on the basis of sex, age, and so on. The question was whether we should send this matter off to a Board of Inquiry to determine whether discrimination on the basis of sex included "sexual orientation." Some of us were urging that we send the matter to a Board to test this proposition. The issue was not really on the public radar yet in any overt way, but it was certainly percolating. So some of us thought that the timing was right. Tom broke for lunch. It was 10:30 in the morning! And when we came back, votes changed, and the majority decided not to send it to a Board of Inquiry.

I think his view was, simply, it's not the right time. The very next year, we worked on a review of the Code to see how it should be changed to modernize it. Tom was determined that we include the recommendation that sexual orientation be part of the Code. Not only that, but he went to the press conference when we released our Report to make this pitch, knowing how incendiary it was going to be from a public relations point of view. I'm not sure it didn't cost him his renewal as Chair of the Commission. For him, it was the right thing to do and the right way to do it.

Another case raised the question of whether sexual harassment was included in the word "sex." Tom agreed that it was worth testing. This time we did send the issue off to a Board of Inquiry. The person hearing the case was Owen Shime, and his judgment that the word sex includes the concept of sexual harassment completely revolutionized the whole field of human rights in that area.

Tom was a quiet revolutionary. He was concerned about civility—profoundly. And he was also concerned about being effective. He understood that there were ways to be effective, and that you could lose out on something important if it didn't land in fertile ground. And if he thought the issue was important, then he thought it should land in fertile ground. He tried to ensure that when we did plant new seeds in the human rights field, it was in a way that took root.

Tom's visionary and courageous leadership of the Ontario Human Rights Commission was also demonstrated in the review of the Code I just mentioned, and in its historic report, called *Life Together*, one of his greatest legacies. It was an extraordinary process for me to watch. Tom had arranged a series of consultations across the province. It was a very public process to which the media were invited. Tom chaired every one of the hearings. He gave people the impression that they were really being heard, because they were. But he knew how to *communicate* that. He's such an exceptionally gracious and empathetic person. He can get into your shoes very easily.

After the consultations, we started the discussions among the commissioners and the drafting of the Report. Consideration of written drafts was preceded by discussion. Lots and lots and lots of discussion. I can't tell you how many weekends we spent at the Park Plaza Hotel discussing what should be in each chapter. When the drafting began, the heavy lifting was done by Tom and Bruce McLeod. If you look at it now, it's a pioneering and progressive Report, written in a very accessible style. This was still pre-Charter, so its broad inclusive approach to human rights was very bold and forward looking, especially the recommendation that sexual orientation be a prohibited ground of discrimination. Tom took a personal hit with *Life Together*, but he also changed the landscape of human rights in this country.

All the issues we were dealing with then were ahead of the curve. We were testing the boundaries. Tom presided over this expansion, and brought the rest of us along with him. His maturity about people, and his sophisticated appreciation for what people have to deal with, was really extraordinary. This was not a man who personally had experienced disadvantage, but he had a genuine concern for people and for eliminating unfairness. It wasn't *noblesse oblige* either. It was because he genuinely cared.

He was always the smartest person in the room. But he never showed off. It's not just what he knew. It's what he understood. Lots of people are smart and know lots of things. But he had judgment, wisdom, and understanding. Because he let us duke it out, he didn't impose his intellectual leadership on us. But we never doubted it. It was kind of there, as a safety net, for the rest of us.

You have to put Tom's leadership in the context of the time. At the time—less now, much less now—Ontario was a province that was quite comfortable with the status quo. Though he came from that same privileged background, Tom asked: is that the best we can do? Roy McMurtry was the same. I see him as the political analogue to Symons in many ways because, like Tom, he had the courage to change what needed to be changed to bring more people into the mainstream. In the 1970s, Tom was changing expectations, and therefore changing people's sense of entitlement. Inclusion was not exactly a watchword of Ontario in the 1970s. But you had all these groups making it very clear that they wanted in. And Tom said, "I agree with that." It was very courageous.

And he was authentic. He didn't play to the crowd. He was *aware* of the crowd, and he used that knowledge to help steer the issues he cared about, but he didn't play to it.

Tom was a transformative leader in many ways. He led each of us into our futures. He certainly led me into mine. I can't tell you how many times I've thought: I wonder what Tom would do? He was the best tutor a person could have, somebody you could watch and learn from, like a very good parent. He never had to say, "I want you to be a really good student." He never had to say, "I want you to work really hard." You just knew. That's the way he was. I knew, from watching him, that he expected us to be the best we could be. And so we tried to be. But he was the impetus and the inspiration.

Tom presided over probably the most dramatic reconfiguration of human rights since the beginning of Human Rights Commissions in this country. He started with what had been established: race and religion. And using the institutional respectability of the Ontario Human Rights Commission, he initiated public conversations that people hadn't had up until that point. He had willing Commissioners to do it with. We were so utterly respectful of his vision, and the chemistry between us was so good, that we all felt fearless. And we felt fearless because he made us feel safe.

Tom took the institution, which he could easily have left the way he found it, and opened it up to the public thinking about human rights in a much grander and more comprehensive way. By the time we got the Charter, five years later, there was much more receptivity to rights in part, I think, because we had started those very conversations at the Ontario Human Rights Commission—and they were conversations that the press largely endorsed. Tom created the fertile ground in which the Charter could grow. So when we got the Charter in 1982, the debate wasn't, "do we really need all these rights?" It was, "are the courts the best place to decide these important issues?"

So I give Tom—Tom's leadership of the Commission at the time—credit for making the public think about things they hadn't thought about before in a credible way. Across Canada, the Human Rights Commissions in the 1970s were really strong. They were all good. But the Ontario Human Rights Commission was definitely leading the pack at that time. We decided sexual harassment before anybody else. We were the first ones to take on sexual orientation. I don't think anybody would quarrel with the fact that we were probably a gutsy Commission. And, under Tom's leadership, we were the most visionary.

Tom Symons was a transformative leader. He transformed my own life. But he also transformed the landscape of human rights in this country, and so perhaps the country itself, because of the way—with grace, and dignity, and courage—he led us all to a new vision of human rights.

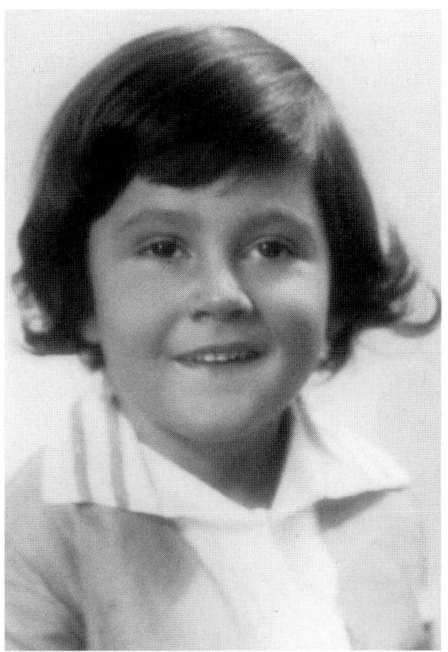

Tom Symons at four years old, 1933.
Photo Credit: Ashley and Crippen

Tom Symons as a teenager.
Photo Credit: Aage Serenson

University of Toronto graduate, 1951.
Photo Credit: Ashley and Crippen

President-designate of Trent University, 1962.
Photo Credit: Unknown

President Symons with the first Trent University Board of Governors, 1963.
Front row (left to right): Mrs. E. H. Zeidler, Miss V. Burgess, C. K. Fraser (Chair), W. G. Ward, Father J. F. Coughlin, President Symons, Dr. D. Whyte, N. J. Crook, Archdeacon R. P. Walker, Mrs. W. R. Philp.
Second row (left to right): S. J. Whitehouse, G. Dolan, S. R. Adamson, F. P. O'Connor, C. G. O'Donnell, I. Black, D. A. Loucks, G. M. Johnson.
Inserts (left to right): C.B. Neal, R. R. Faryon, Mrs. J. Holt, Dr. D. Aitken.

Photo Credit: Roy Studio

President Symons with the original Trent team, June 26 1964. To Symons's left is S. G. Denis Smith and to his right is Richard H. Sadleir, both later Trent Vice-Presidents. Others left to right are: John Anderson, J. D. P. Martin, John Pettigrew, and J. F. Brook.

Photo Credit: Nick Yunge-Bateman

Greeting Governor General Georges Vanier and Mme Pauline Vanier for the Official Opening of Trent University, October 17, 1964. On the left is the chairman of the Trent Board of Governors, C. K. Fraser.

Photo Credit: Parks Studio

Leading the academic procession for Trent's Official Opening, October 17, 1964, with William G. Davis, Minister of Education, later Premier of Ontario.

Photo Credit: Nick Yunge-Bateman

President Symons at his desk in Rubidge Hall, c. 1964.

Photo Credit: Unknown

Tom and Christine Symons viewing a model of Champlain College, c. 1964.
Photo Credit: Gerald Campbell

With Quebec Premier Jean Lesage (left) and Ontario Premier John Robarts (right) at the cornerstone-laying ceremony for Champlain College, October 20, 1965.

Photo Credit: Unknown

With Quebec Premier Jean Lesage (left) and former Ontario Premier Leslie Frost, Trent's first Chancellor (right), at the cornerstone-laying ceremony for Champlain College, October 20, 1965.

Photo Credit: Peterborough Photo Products

The Ontario Advisory Committee on Confederation, 1965.
Seated (left to right): Richard Dillon, Alexander Brady, R. Craig McIvor, H. Ian Macdonald, Chair, Ontario Premier John Robarts, Eugene Forsey, W.R. Lederman, D.G. Creighton, Rev. Lucien Matte.
Standing (left to right): John Conway, George E. Gathercole, Bora Laskin, John Meisel, Edward McWhinney, J. Harvey Perry, Tom Symons, Paul W. Fox, Roger N. Séguin.

Photo Credit: Unknown

President Symons outside the newly completed Champlain College, c. 1967.
Si monumentum requiris, circumspice.

Photo Credit: Bob Santen

Cornerstone-laying ceremony for Lady Eaton College, 24 February 1968. Left to right: Marjorie Seeley, first Principal of Lady Eaton College; Florence McEachern, Lady Eaton's daughter, President Symons.

Photo Credit: Parks Studio

President Symons with Thomas Bata at the opening of the Bata Library at Trent University, September 1969.

Photo Credit: Andy Turnbull

President Symons with Governor General Roland Michener and Mrs. Norah Michener on a visit to the Trent campus, 1969. To Mr. Michener's right is Richard Sadleir.

Photo Credit: Brian Parsons

As Chair, Tom Symons hosts a meeting of the Council of the Association of Commonwealth Universities at Trent University—the so-called "Council of Trent"—May 1972. To Symons's right is Sir Hugh Springer, Secretary-General of the ACU, later Governor General of Barbados. To his left is the Vice-Chairman, Sir Charles Wilson, Principal of the University of Glasgow. Third from the right in the middle row is Sir Douglas Logan, Principal of the University of London, whom Symons succeeded as Honorary Treasurer of the ACU.

Front row (left to right): Rayson Lisung Huang, Vice-Chancellor, Nanyang University; A. S. Adke, Vice-Chancellor, Karnatak University; A. A. Kwapong, Past Chair, Vice-Chancellor, University of Ghana; Sir Hugh W. Springer, Secretary-General, ACU; Tom Symons, Chair; Sir Charles H. Wilson, Vice-Chair, Principal, University of Glasgow; R. N. Dogra, Director, Indian Institute of Technology, Delhi; Phyllis Lawrence, Secretary to Sir Hugh Springer.

Middle row (left to right): F. J. Llewellyn, Vice-Chancellor, University of Exeter; J. Steven Watson, Principal, University of Aberdeen; D. R. Llewellyn, Vice-Chancellor, University of Waikato; B. R. Williams, Vice-Chancellor, University of Sydney; J. J. Auchmuty, Vice-Chancellor, University of Newcastle; D. H. Irvine, Principal and Vice-Chancellor, University of Guyana; Sir Douglas Logan, Honorary Treasurer, Principal, University of London; A. W. R. Carrothers, President and Vice-Chancellor, University of Calgary; Thomas Craig, Assistant Secretary, ACU.

Back row (left to right): Colin Mackay, Executive Director, Association of Universities and Colleges of Canada; H. N. Robson, Vice-Chancellor, University of Sheffield; F. Kalimuzo, Vice-Chancellor, Makerere University; Sir Fraser Noble, Vice-Chancellor, University of Leicester.

Photo Credit: Unknown

Chair of the Commission on
Canadian Studies, 1972.

Photo Credit: Roy Nicholls Photography

Inducted as an Officer of the Order of Canada by Governor General Jules Léger, 1976.
Photo Credit: John Evans

Vice-President of the Social Sciences and Humanities Research Council of Canada, with members and officers of the Council, September 16, 1983. Seated (left to right): Naomi Black (University of Toronto); William E. Taylor, Jr. (President, SSHRC); Tom Symons (Vice-President); Jean Cadieux, (Université de Moncton). Standing (left to right): James Lightbody (University of Alberta); Robert Crocker (Memorial University); Gerald Kristianson (Victoria); Douglas Kenny (UBC); Audrey Forster (Secretary, SSHRC); Denis Stairs (Dalhousie University); Elizabeth Arthur (Lakehead University); John Nicholson (Executive Director, SSHRC); Gaston Bouliane (Treasurer, SSHRC).
Photo Credit: Canapress Photo Service

As Chair of the National Atlas Advisory Committee, Tom Symons presents Prime Minister Brian Mulroney with a copy of the National Atlas, January 29 1986. Between Symons and the Prime Minister is Robert Layton, Minister of State for Mines in the Mulroney government, the minister responsible for the National Atlas.

Photo Credit: Unknown

Chair of the International Board of the United World Colleges at a meeting of the Executive Committee at London House, April 16, 1986.
Left to right (beginning third from left): Sir Ian Gourlay, Jack Matthews, Gianfranco Facco Bonetti, Sir Michael Parsons, Armand Hammer, Tom Symons, Kingman Brewster, Alec Peterson.

Photo Credit: Betty Arthur

Chair of the Historic Sites and Monuments Board of Canada, with other members of the Board, at the plaque unveiling for the Peterborough Lift Lock, 1988. Left to right: Charles Humphries (BC), Noël Bélanger (Quebec), Tom Symons, Andrée Désilets (Quebec), Shane O'Dea (Nfld.), David Smith (Sask.), Trudy Cowan (Alberta), Irene Rogers (PEI), John White (Ontario).

Photo Credit: Unknown

Chair of the National Library Advisory Board, November 1988.
Front row (left to right): Nancy-Gay Rotstein; Jessica Miller; Marianne Scott, (National Librarian); Tom Symons, Chair; Guy Cloutier; Catherine Bliss; Elizabeth Harris; Eileen Travis.
Middle row (left to right); Marian Wilson; Louise Dacquay; Phyllis Lerat; Peter Freeman; Erik Spicer, Librarian of Parliament.
Back row: Roseanne Runte; Graham Murphy; Elmer Smith; Jean-Pierre Wallot (National Archivist); George Story.

Photo Credit: Unknown

With Her Majesty Queen Elizabeth the Queen Mother, at the Church of St. Mary Magdalene, Toronto, July 3, 1989, for the unveiling of a national historic plaque honouring Healey Willan. Between Her Majesty and Symons is the Reverend Harold Nahabedian, rector of St. Mary Magdalene. Visible to the right of Symons is Sir Martin Gilliat, the Queen Mother's long-serving private secretary.

Photo Credit: n/a

The 75th anniversary of the Historic Sites and Monuments Board of Canada, Annapolis Royal, June 1992.

Left to right: Francis Bolger (PEI), Trudy Cowan (Alberta), André Lalonde (Sask.—hidden), Charles Humphries (BC—sunglasses), Margaret Conrad (N.S.), Marion Beyea (NB—hidden), Noël Bélanger (Quebec), unidentified soldier, Michael Kinnear (Manitoba), Tom Symons, George Macdonald (National Museums—hidden), Jean-Pierre Wallot (National Archivist), Raymonde Gauthier (Quebec), Christina Cameron (Secretary, HSMBC).

Photo Credit: Unknown

Chair of the National Statistics Council, November 1994.
Front row (left to right): Derek Hum, Noah Meltz, Susan McDaniel, Ivan Fellegi, Tom Symons, Ruth Getter, Madeleine Blanchet, Louis Berlinguet, Marc-Adélard Tremblay.
Middle row: Cliff Andstein, Erwin Diewert, Catherine Harris, Pierre-Paul Proulx, Andrew Alleyne, Harold Corrigan, John Palmer, Maxwell House, Edward Neufeld, Martin Wilk, Monica Boyd.
Back row: Bruce Petrie, David McQueen, Bruce Wilkinson, Tim O'Neill, Ian MacKinnon, Don Eastman, Rod Dobell, George Brinkman, Karol Krotki, Paul Bernard, John Grant, Ian Stewart.

Photo Credit: Unknown

Inducted as a Companion of the Order of Canada by Governor General Roméo Leblanc, 1997.

Photo Credit: Unknown

Symons the Teacher. The Vanier Seminar in the 1990s.

Photo Credit: Unknown

Tom and Christine Symons, November 22, 2003.
Photo Credit: n/a

Tom and Christine Symons with their children, November 22, 2003.
From left to right: Mary Symons, daughter-in-law Christine Symons, Jeffrey Symons, Ryerson Symons.
Photo Credit: n/a

With his cousin, Sir George Bull, at the unveiling of an Ontario Heritage Trust plaque honouring Symons's grandfather, William Perkins Bull, September 6, 2007. Symons was appointed chair of the Trust in 2010.

Photo Credit: Bryon Johnson, The Brampton Guardian

As chair of the Executive Committee of the British North America Committee, with Governor General Michaëlle Jean at Rideau Hall, October 2007.

Photo Credit: Unknown

With fellow members of the Board of the Fathers of Confederation Centre, PEI, presenting Quebec Premier Jean Charest with the Centre's Symons Medal, in Montreal, January 2010.
Left to right: Wayne Hambly (Chairman of the Board of the Confederation Centre [the Fathers of Confederation Memorial Buildings Trust]), Tom Symons, Quebec Premier Jean Charest, John Crosbie (Lieutenant Governor of Newfoundland and former federal cabinet minister), David MacKenzie (CEO of the Confederation Centre of the Arts), Claude Metras (Quebec representative on the Confederation Centre Board).

Photo Credit: Charles F. Scott

With the Governor General, the Premier of PEI and Symons grandchildren, Province House, Charlottetown, PEI, on the occasion of the presentation of the Symons Medal to the Governor General and the delivery of the Symons Lecture, 8 November 2010. Back row (left to right): Governor General David Johnston and Mrs. Sharon Johnston, Tom Symons, Robert Ghiz, Premier of Prince Edward Island. Front row (left to right): Ava, Wilson and Leighton Symons.

Photo Credit: PEI Government Photo—Brian Simpson

CHAPTER 10

Tom Symons and the Commonwealth

ALASTAIR NIVEN

One spring day in 1985, I was pottering in my front garden in Woburn Sands, a large village in Buckinghamshire, England, when Anastasios Christodoulou dropped by. I had known Chris, as everyone called him, for many years. He had been the founding secretary of the Open University, probably Britain's most successful and innovatory development in higher education since the Second World War. He was now Secretary General of the Association of Commonwealth Universities. Based in London, his private residence was just up the road from mine in the neighbouring village of Aspley Guise. Chris was as often as not overseas, not only in Commonwealth countries. When I heard that he had felt obliged to attend the nine-hundredth anniversary celebrations of the University of Padua in Italy, I realized that here was a man who simply loved to be on the move and would accept every opportunity to be so. It was therefore no surprise that, in chatting in the garden that day, he should say that he was on the lookout to recruit what he termed a special assistant to help him with some specific projects that he would not always be around to attend in person. Would I be interested?

Thus began my association with Tom Symons, for among the tasks that Chris Christodoulou asked me to undertake was to work with Tom on the ACU's seventy-fifth anniversary appeal. Professor Symons had been appointed chairman not only of the appeal, but also of the special projects, as they were termed, which were devised to celebrate the seventy-fifth anniversary. I was to help the former Secretary General, Sir Hugh Springer, then Governor General of Barbados, update the history of the Association, the first volume of which had been written by Sir Eric Ashby. I was also to manage a Tracer Study, which attempted to make contact with as many as possible former recipients of a Commonwealth Scholarship or Fellowship. Initially, I was taken on for two days a week, as I was experimenting with a freelance life and wanted to keep the decks clear for other projects; however, these were quickly assigned to a back burner, where sadly most of them quietly expired, because it had immediately become apparent that what was asked of me at the ACU would amount to a full-time commitment. I became a member of the Association's establishment and spent the next two and a half years happily engaged on the worthwhile initiatives that Chris had proposed in my garden. All of them were completed successfully. I drafted the text of *Commonwealth of Universities,* which was published in 1986; I produced a report for Commonwealth Ministers of Education, which summarised the experiences of over forty percent of former Commonwealth Scholars and Fellows (considered a good result by experts on questionnaire surveys); and I helped Tom Symons reach an appeal sum of two million pounds, twice its original target.

The aim of the ACU's seventy-fifth anniversary appeal was to raise one million pounds, so that a fellowship scheme could be set up that would allow Commonwealth academics and university administrators who were currently in mid career to have the chance to replenish their knowledge, skills, and experience in another part of the world. Tom Symons was in charge of the appeal; but, as he was himself based in Canada, he required someone to ensure that it would not be forgotten at the ACU headquarters in London. I was also required to research contacts in addition to the many that Tom already had, and it was assumed that I was literate enough to draft first versions of supplicatory letters. Our first—and looking back on it, wholly remarkable—achievement was to persuade Her Majesty The Queen to become Patron of the Association of Commonwealth Universities, which role she took on in 1986. The Queen had not exactly been looking for new patronages, having over six hundred and twenty already. Head of the Commonwealth and monarch of the United Kingdom, Canada, and her other realms since 1952, she was much the most suitable person on the international stage to be the titular head of the appeal. The problem was that Her Majesty could not be directly linked to so coarse an activity as raising money, even for as ethical a cause as professional development in the universities. We did not pull any wool over the eyes of the officials at Buckingham Palace who dealt with the matter of the patronage; they were perfectly aware that we were enticing funds from suitable sources around the world. By accepting to be Patron of the whole association, The Queen was implicitly Patron of the appeal itself, since its launch was the high spot of the year in which she took on the role.

Tom's influence in securing the patronage of The Queen was no doubt helped by the fact that, whenever he was in London, he would visit the Prince of Wales, then president of United World Colleges, with which Tom too was involved as chairman of the board for two three-year stints between 1980 and 1986. More incidentally, he had a vicarious link with the prince's popular grandmother, Queen Elizabeth The Queen Mother, in that both considered the Stafford Hotel, close to Green Park in central London, the best hotel in town, especially for afternoon tea. I had cause on a number of occasions to agree with them. Tom would invariably have a catching up session there rather than in the offices of the Association of Commonwealth Universities: "better tea and quieter" was his justification, though my Calvinist background caused me to exclaim more than once at how much could be charged for a combination of a tea leaf and some hot water. I suspect that Dr. Christodoulou tore his hair out at the matter of Tom's expenses, but he was a hirsute fellow and it did not show. It was Tom's style, when possible, to do business in gracious surroundings because so often it led to the outcome he sought. I am certain that we would have been only half as successful in our fundraising strategy if we had met potential donors in mean settings. It would be wrong, though, not to record that eyebrows were sometimes raised, and not just Chris Christodoulou's exceptionally bushy pair.

The ACU's seventy-fifth anniversary appeal set itself a target of one million pounds. In the event it achieved double that. Our ambition was to establish a new level of fellowships, aimed at refreshment of middle managers and mid-career academics. It was becoming apparent by the 1980s that the energy that had generated the new universities in the late 1960s, and had seen the recruitment of bright academic and administrative staff, was becoming slightly dimmed as the potential for continuing expansion was halted. Staff once young and adventurous had become fixtures in their institutions. Inevitably, they were not only blocking the path for the next generation but also were often themselves blocked by more senior people than themselves who had been appointed at the same time and who still had plenty of years of service ahead. By creating a new fund, fellowship placements could be created that would give university staff—those who might be feeling slightly trapped and possibly undervalued—a chance to travel and to have their batteries recharged. We envisaged that the scheme would be especially helpful to personnel based in developing countries because they would, by spending time in a so-called developed nation, have the chance to re-skill and to have access to new technologies and systems.

It is for others to evaluate how successfully our goals were realized; but, by skilled diplomacy, Tom undoubtedly led a visionary project to the point where it could actually happen. Corporate companies, Commonwealth alumni, universities themselves, and wealthy individuals were tactfully approached. Few declined Tom's blandishments. The largest commitment was from a Nigerian prince, while the smallest was from me. Everything raised came down in the end to Tom. He flourished without the backing of a professional team of full-time fundraisers, such as is routinely deemed necessary today. I have no doubt that the appeal would have fared much less well, and also been far more expensive to administer, if it had been run as it would be now. One eminent Canadian, with a part-time assistant and the backing when required of the Secretary General, was enough to bring in twice the figure we had set for ourselves and to see the scheme properly launched.

To see Tom Symons outside his comfort zone of Canadian and British academia was a revelation. I particularly recall the ACU council meeting in Penang in June of 1986. Malaysia is a friendly country and the Rasa Sayang Hotel, where we held the conference, was luxurious and friendly. It had state-of-the-art provision for an international gathering of this sort, excellent cuisine, and a nearby beach. ACU meetings in tropical environments tend not to be too formal in terms of attire, but every day Tom would appear looking well groomed and refreshed. His slow, bulky walk reminded me at times of a well-hewn statue being moved slowly and with dignity to the place where it would be erected. Life always appeared to move faster around Tom than he did, but invariably it was the tortoise that delivered the goods. Nothing ever seemed rushed in Tom's company. His manners were never less than perfect. I was in Penang with my wife and very young children. Tom and Christine always had time to greet them in a friendly manner and to make them feel as though they mattered, although in reality he would invariably have a very full schedule of meetings ahead of him.

I unashamedly used these opportunities to observe Tom's technique with people, for I could easily see how he had become the founding president of Trent University when only thirty-four. His erudition was worn lightly, his sagacity was evident in every comment he made, and his charm was unforced and engaged. Already by 1986 there was hint of another age about him, not because he had failed to keep pace with developments in higher education—he had manifestly done so, as his support for the fellowship scheme indicated—but because his courteous manners seemed slightly out of step with the pushiness that was replacing it as the norm in social intercourse. Perhaps he slightly played on this olde-worldliness because it made people listen to him and respect what he invariably said with deliberation.

Symons's enthusiasm for the Commonwealth went back to his Oxford days, where he had encountered fellow students from many countries. He recalls a conversation in 1956 with Dr. Sidney Smith, president of the University of Toronto, where two years before he had been given a fellowship and started teaching.[1] Smith advocated what he termed a "Grand Britannic Plan" for the circulation of students around the Commonwealth. The idea was no more than a gleam in his eye, but he recognized in Symons's response the possibility that it could make headway. He invited Symons to write a short synopsis of what it might entail to move students around the Commonwealth, not just between the former dominions but between developed and developing countries and even between developing countries, by-passing Britain, Canada, Australia, and New Zealand. Crucial to the proposed plan was that it should not be centred on the United Kingdom. Symons proposed that each participant country in the scheme should be responsible for funding the students who went to study there. There should, in other words, be no big centralised mechanism holding together this potential network of students and scholars. "Each tub on its own bottom," as Tom graphically put it to me.[2] Dr. Smith was appointed minister of external affairs (as the cabinet position was then called) of Canada in 1957 and could therefore help to ensure that his idea, as written up by his young colleague at the University of Toronto, came to the attention of the first Commonwealth Education Conference, held in Oxford in 1959. From this gathering was generated the Commonwealth Scholarship and Fellowship Plan, remarkably akin in the way it was drawn up to the concept outlined in the Symons synopsis. Although Symons had at this stage no institutionalised role in the management of the scheme, his fingerprints were clearly on it from the start.

If one has held a Commonwealth Scholarship or Fellowship at any time in its history, it is apparent that one has been selected by a rigorous process and identified as a person of promise. Living up to that promise is perhaps a different matter—I speak from experience as I was a Commonwealth scholar at the University of Ghana between 1966 and 1968—but recipients have always felt a sense of privilege in being part of such an innovative scheme. In my time, too, it was more generously funded than comparable awards. Circumstances changed over the subsequent decades. Some countries had to withdraw from the Plan because it was too expensive to remain within it and, as recently as 2008, the British Government arbitrarily announced that it would be discontinuing funding of scholars from eight "developed" nations, among them Canada, thus creating a storm of criticism that has not yet subsided. The plan has recently celebrated its fiftieth anniversary, with the Prince of Wales attending a reception in its honour at Marlborough House in London on 5 May 2010, hosted by Kamalesh Sharma, the Commonwealth Secretary General.

All this jumps the gun, however. In 1985, as part of Tom's vision for the seventy-fifth anniversary of the Association of Commonwealth

Universities, it was agreed to conduct the Tracer Study of former Commonwealth Scholars and Fellows to which I referred earlier. The twenty-fifth anniversary of these awards had been acknowledged the previous year with only low-key attention. There was not yet sufficient documented evidence of whether the Plan was proving effective or not. Tom was in the forefront of those who saw the need for it to prove itself by seeing what had become of those who had received awards under its auspices. By contacting as many of these people as we could, we were able to nail a major misconception. It had often been asserted, without supporting evidence, that there was a tendency for Scholars and Fellows from developing countries to stay in the countries in which they had held their award and not to return back home. This turned out to be a calumny. Over ninety percent of students and fellows from Africa, the Indian sub-continent, and the Caribbean went back to their places of origin and contributed from that moment to the development of their homelands. Ironically, if there was any proclivity toward staying put and not returning home it lay with those from "first world" nations. From time to time, I would share our Tracer Study findings with Tom and with Chris Christodoulou, and both would say something along the lines of "I always suspected that was so." Some of the study's findings were more predictable, but no less valuable for having hard evidence to prove them. An example was confirmation that women academics would, on return from holding a scholarship or fellowship abroad, do quite well professionally for a few years but then hit a barrier, which meant that very few of them ended up in top positions.

Tom Symons's engagement with issues of this sort has kept him involved with the Commonwealth Scholarship and Fellowship Plan for its entire history. From 1983 to 1987 he was chairman of the Plan's Canadian committee, charged with selecting those who would hold awards abroad. He was an enthusiast for the establishment of a fiftieth anniversary Commonwealth Scholarship endowment fund, announced in Kuala Lumpur in 2008, an initiative to raise partnership funding to sustain the Plan where governments have been either unable to, or simply recalcitrant about, maintaining existing levels of financial commitment to it. He serves until at least 2012 as one of the fund's trustees on a board of nine.

My encounters with Symons in the mid-1980s were for him, of course, just the start of another professional relationship in his long-standing role at the Association of Commonwealth Universities. The ACU had evolved from a grouping called the Home Universities Committee, which met for the first time on 19 November 1910. Eric Ashby, in his history of its early years, records that this "was a red-letter day in the history of Commonwealth universities, for out of that meeting grew the Congress which gave birth to the Association of Universities of the British Commonwealth."[3] Here is not the place to trace the pre-Symonsian era of the Association, except to note that its original name, bespeaking much about the period in which it was founded, was the Bureau of Information for the Universities of the Empire. It was only in 1948 that it became the association using the appellation by which Ashby describes it. In 1963 a Royal Charter was granted, and it took the opportunity, as was now customary in Commonwealth terminology, to drop the word "British" from its title and to become the Association of Commonwealth Universities. It was shortly after this, in 1967, that Symons's links with the Association became formalised when, as president and vice-chancellor of Trent University, Peterborough, Canada, which he had helped to found in 1964, he took his fledgling institution into membership. He made an immediate mark on its deliberations.

Symons was an active and fully committed part of the ACU from the moment Trent University joined it. He attended all the meetings for which he was eligible. Detecting too much British domination of the Association, as well as seeds of disaffection for other reasons, and threatened drop-outs by some member institutions, he advocated from the start a more representative internationalism in the council of the Association. In 1970 the appointment as the ACU's Secretary General of Hugh Springer, formerly registrar of the University of the West Indies, was a fillip to Tom particularly. Here was a fellow internationalist, someone with recent experience of Commonwealth affairs through being based for four years at the Commonwealth Secretariat. They were allies and later close friends, right up to the time of Sir Hugh's death in 1994.

In 1971 Professor T. H. B. Symons, as he was officially cited in all ACU documents, was elected chairman of the council of the

Association in succession to the great Ghanaian classical scholar and university vice-chancellor, Dr. A. A. Kwapong. Symons set about organising a council meeting in Canada, held partly in Peterborough and partly in Ottawa in May 1972. Inevitably destined to be known as "The Council of Trent," it was a hugely influential event that led to the transformation of the council itself, with much more varied and representative membership than before. Only two years later, Symons was asked to become the honorary treasurer of the Association, taking over from one of the great figures in its history, Sir Douglas Logan, former vice-chancellor of the University of London. Symons spent fourteen years in this office and oversaw the great improvement in the ACU's financial standing, accompanied by expansion of its institutional membership, which took place under Springer and more so under the next Secretary General, Dr. Anastasios Christodoulou.

Chris Christodoulou had been the founding secretary of the Open University, generally regarded as the most innovative initiative in higher education in post-war Britain. As I have indicated, he and Symons sometimes had a wary relationship. Though it was mutually respectful, I never detected quite the degree of warmth in it that undoubtedly existed between Symons and Springer. Nevertheless, they planned the seventy-fifth anniversary as though it were a military operation. Many an organisation would have been content to have a drinks reception at the Association's headquarters in London, perhaps with royalty present, and leave it at that. Chris and Tom had much more ambitious ideas, as I have outlined at the start of this chapter, and to their enormous credit, they achieved them all.

No account of Tom's connections with the Association of Commonwealth Universities can be complete without mention of the Symons Award. He himself has always stayed out of the selection process, leaving it to the Association's council to make an annual choice of someone it wishes to honour for their outstanding service to the universities of the Commonwealth. This may have been through the ACU itself, but it can also be given to an appropriate person elsewhere in higher education. The award, which Tom endowed because he wanted there to be recognition of the academic, intellectual, and administrative achievements of outstanding individuals in

Commonwealth higher education, can be shared. This was the case in its first year, 1973, for its recipients were Sir Douglas Logan and Sir Charles Wilson, principal of the University of Glasgow. The first Secretary General of the ACU, Dr. John Foster, was given the award posthumously in 1975. Although no one received it in 1977, or again between 2004 and 2007 when the Association was going through a period of painful malfunctioning, it has honoured thirty-seven people in its thirty-seven years. They include some of the outstanding servants of the Association itself, among them Sir Hugh Springer, Tom Craig, Dorothy Garland, and Peter Hetherington, as well as great figures in the story of Commonwealth education, such as Lalage Bown, professor emeritus of the University of Glasgow, Geoffrey Caston, vice-chancellor of the University of the South Pacific, Walter Kamba, a legendary figure in the story of Zimbabwe's higher education, Colin Maiden, Tom's successor as honorary treasurer of the ACU and a former vice-chancellor of the University of Auckland, and Anirik Singh, secretary of the Association of Indian Universities. On some occasions, the ACU council has made some imaginatively unpredictable choices: Michael Kelly, for example, honouring his outstanding work on HIV/AIDS in all levels of education, or Asantahene Otumfo Osei Tutu II, who received the Special Millennium Award in 2000. Symons was present in London when the award was presented in 2010 to Professor Crispus Kiamba, formerly the vice-chancellor of the University of Nairobi, who had then gone on to become a keen advocate of Commonwealth higher education within the Kenyan government. The Symons Award has been truly pan-Commonwealth in its reach, reflecting its founder.

In establishing the Symons Award, Tom was keen to ensure that those who received it should have a thing of beauty that would hopefully bring them joy forever. He commissioned the distinguished artist, Dora de Pédery-Hunt, to design a medal made of bronze. She was Canada's foremost miniaturist in metal, an example of her work being the effigy of The Queen that adorns Canada's coinage. Is it too much to hope that the ACU itself, which owes so much to its former chairman and treasurer, might commission a metal portrait of Tom Symons, either in the form of a bust or a plaque? Sadly, Dora de Pédery-Hunt died in 2008, but a young metallist on the threshold of his or her career would be an appropriate person to ask to undertake the work, which would be a fitting tribute to someone who has been, for nearly sixty years, at the epicentre of Commonwealth higher education.

In 1996 Tom Symons, at the invitation of the then Commonwealth Secretary General, Chief Emeka Anyaoku, produced the Symons Report, the findings of a commission on Commonwealth studies. It was entitled *Learning from Each Other: Commonwealth Studies for the Twenty First Century.*[4] He had been invited to chair this commission partly as the result of his own nagging. He had felt for some time that the Commonwealth Secretariat could play a more vigorous part in the promotion of knowledge and understanding of the Commonwealth itself within higher education. Initially reluctant to take this on, Chief Anyaoku eventually saw the light and appointed Tom to oversee an enquiry into the state of Commonwealth studies. Although presented to the Commonwealth Heads of Government Meeting in Edinburgh the following year, there was, by the year of the millennium, considerable criticism in unofficial Commonwealth circles that the report had been allowed to gather dust. Concern about indifference to the Commonwealth had been manifesting itself at all levels of education. A key recommendation was for an association of academics, archivists, teachers, even musicologists, to get together to promote the teaching and research of Commonwealth concerns. In particular, the report identified a lack of formal recognition of Commonwealth studies in most higher education institutions—the Institute of Commonwealth Studies in the University of London being an exception.

Faced with the inertia of the Commonwealth Secretariat to stimulate a response to the report after Chief Anyaoku retired, Tom decided to take matters in hand by bringing together interested academics to form a new Association for Commonwealth Studies. After an initial meeting in Halifax, Nova Scotia, in 2003, when health issues provided the focus, there were two more meetings at Cumberland Lodge in Windsor, England. The first meeting, in 2005, examined the literatures of the Commonwealth; the second meeting, two years later, was entitled "Educating the Commonwealth about the Commonwealth." It was opened by a long-time associate of

Tom's, Lord Moore, formerly Private Secretary to The Queen. It was a typical Symons touch to invoke the support of so apt a person at a meeting taking place within a foundation of which Her Majesty is a much-engaged Patron. At the earlier of the Windsor meetings, it was formally agreed that the new association would exist to raise the profile of the Commonwealth in universities, particularly by focusing on key successes in the Commonwealth, such as its ecological policy and its burgeoning creative literature. Symons was made president of the ACS. Its work since then has been sporadic, but the flame is flickering. A group set up to review the Institute of Commonwealth Studies in 2005, of which I was a member, concluded that the discipline of "Commonwealth studies" had academic legitimacy and prospects. As usual, Symons was inspiring a worthy cause, though it is now for others to take forward the vision that was expressed in his report and that led to the setting up of the association.

Although I have not had personal experience of it, I cannot leave this summary of Symons's Commonwealth interests without further reference to the United World Colleges, whose board he chaired for the first six years of the 1980s. Having been one of the founders of Pearson College in Victoria, British Columbia, Canada's national monument to its former prime minister, Lester Pearson, it was natural for Tom to accept an invitation to be on the international board of the United World Colleges, a network of thirteen schools around the world, of which Pearson College became a constituent part in 1974. Others will know better than I of Symons's commitment to the educational ideals of the UWC. My reason for including mention of it in this chapter is to underline the fact that he was drawn to the enterprise by three motives that have informed everything I have been describing: admiration of the internationalism of the United World Colleges, determination to raise the organisation's sights intellectually, and pleasure in the attainment of young people. He sees his years at the helm of UWC as "a repeat and parallel performance to what I did at the ACU a decade before."[5] During his time as chairman, his close association with Prince Charles, president of the colleges, was greatly beneficial and led to a friendship that has been maintained in the subsequent quarter-century.

There have been many other Commonwealth connections over the years. From 1982 to 1988, for example, Tom was a member of the Commonwealth Standing Committee on Student Mobility. In 2002, he joined the council of the Institute of Commonwealth Studies in London, of which he is still a member. A checklist of his publications will show how many articles he has written on aspects of Commonwealth culture and education. He has visited the majority of Commonwealth countries. From youth to age there has been remarkably little deviation from a trajectory that might almost have been designed beforehand. The young historian who went to the University of Toronto in 1947, and who in the 1950s spent time discovering how other people live in Oxford, Paris, Leyden, Rome, and Boston, became the *doyen* of Commonwealth studies, his passion for student interchange and educational cooperation undimmed in old age.

2012 will see the Diamond Jubilee of the accession of Queen Elizabeth II, Head of the Commonwealth. The following year will celebrate the one hundredth anniversary of the Association of Commonwealth Universities. Symons looks ahead to these and other Commonwealth milestones with the same enthusiasm that set him on the road at the start of his career. The extraordinary thing about him is that he has the same energy of mind and unflagging commitment to Commonwealth principles that informed his authorship, back in the late 1950s, of that influential two-page synopsis of how a Commonwealth scholarship scheme might be devised. If only such stamina, coupled with wisdom, were the general rule in Commonwealth higher education today, then many of the issues raised by the report of the Commission on Commonwealth Studies would be unnecessary. Tom is a pragmatist, however, as well as a man of principle and vision, and when he sees a problem or evidence of dilatoriness he does not berate the perpetrator. Instead, he goes quietly about making them see the matter from a different perspective. Only when that does not work is there a glint of steel. I see him in his ninth decade, when surely he must wind down a little, as the Indian poet Vikram Seth envisages the retirement of a venerable Chinese civil servant. It seems appropriately of the Commonwealth to cross the continents and end with this oblique tribute to a great servant of higher education and of the global community:

The Humble Administrator admires a bee
Poised on a lotus, walks through the bamboo wood,
Strips half a dozen loquats off a tree
And looks about and sees that it is good.
He leans against a willow with a dish
And throws a dumpling to a passing fish.[6]

Notes

1 Tom Symons in conversation with Alastair Niven at the Royal Over-Seas League, London, 4 May 2010.

2 Ibid.

3 Eric Ashby, *Community of Universities* (Cambridge: Cambridge University Press, 1963), 5.

4 T. H. B. Symons, with Suma Chitnis, et al., *Learning from Each Other: Commonwealth Studies for the Twenty First Century*, Report of the Commission on Commonwealth Studies (London: Commonwealth Secretariat, 1996).

5 Tom Symons in conversation with Alastair Niven at the Royal Over-Seas League, London, 4 May 2010.

6 Vikram Seth, "The Humble Administrator's Garden," from *The Humble Administrator's Garden* (Manchester: Carcanet, 1985), 11.

CHAPTER 11

Peace and International Understanding through Education: Tom Symons and the United World Colleges

RALPH HEINTZMAN

Tom Symons's role in the Association of Commonwealth Universities—including as honorary treasurer from 1974 to 1988—was paralleled and complemented by his growing involvement in another international movement: the United World Colleges (UWC). There was often a good deal of overlap between his roles in these two organizations. And because he was actively involved with both of them, he was often able to draw on the ideas, networks, and relationships of one to respond to challenges the other was also facing.[1]

Symons had already been following the development of Atlantic College in Wales, which was the mother college of the later UWC system, and he was excited about this new educational venture from the start. He thought the international concept that was being developed there—creative, dynamic internationalism at the senior secondary and junior university level—was immensely promising. Atlantic College had pioneered an approach to secondary education that was profoundly international: not just taking international courses, or studying international affairs, or mixing in a few students from various parts of the world, but a college with an international mix both of faculty and of students; and international in its curriculum, as it adopted what was then emerging as the International Baccalaureate (IB), a standard Symons himself had helped to develop. The UWC educational philosophy also emphasized the ideal of service to local communities, a driving force in Symons's own life.

So it was natural and perhaps inevitable that Symons should become involved from the start with the movement to establish the second United World College in Canada. There was already another college in Singapore, but it had not been created specifically as a UWC and had only later been brought into association with the UWC movement, eventually becoming a full UWC college. The Canadian college was to be the second UWC established expressly for that purpose, with the UWC educational philosophy as its driving force from the beginning. Establishing a Canadian UWC would also help to extend the international spirit underlying the UWC approach, making the Canadian college another important step toward developing a genuine international network of UWC colleges in a variety of locations and cultures around the world.

Symons was also attracted by the proposal to name the Canadian college in honour of Canada's former prime minister, Lester Pearson, winner of the Nobel Peace Prize. He was a strong admirer of Pearson, whom he considered an outstanding international statesman, a great commonwealth man, a great Canadian, and a "very, very special person." So he thought it entirely fitting that the new college should become a national memorial to Canada's "most remarkable international figure."

There were also circumstantial reasons for his involvement. One of the moving spirits behind the establishment of what was to become Pearson College was Jack Matthews, then the head of Lakefield College School, located just north of Peterborough and Trent University. Later to become the first head of Pearson College, Matthews had been a strong supporter of the establishment of Trent University while at Lakefield. As Trent's first president, Symons had become a member of the Lakefield board, and a friend and admirer of Matthews. So when Matthews and others began to draw together potential support for establishing a Canadian UWC, it was natural that they should turn to Symons.

Following an initial informal meeting in Toronto in 1972, Senator John Nicol and Major General George Kitching formally invited Symons to join the Canadian National Committee working to establish a Canadian UWC. Symons not only accepted but soon became chair of the Foundations Committee for the fundraising effort, enrolling canvassers and approaching numerous Canadian and US foundations. One of the focuses of his fundraising efforts was to endow scholarships for a college that was to be entirely self-funded, with no tuition fees, so there would be no financial barriers to excellence or to international students from less developed countries. By October 1973, Symons was already receiving praise for the "extremely well organized program" he was carrying out in his fundraising role.[2]

By 1976, the fundraising campaign and the work of the National Committee had made Pearson College a reality. Symons was elected to the board of trustees for the new college in November 1976, attending its first meeting in April of the following year.[3] Almost from the start he took an active interest in the international dimensions of the new college, and its links with the broader UWC movement. By November 1978, for example, he was recommending to John Nicol, the first chair of the Pearson board, that the new Canadian college should take the initiative in proposing to UWC's international board that it establish an academic committee, and also that Pearson should increase its own financial contribution toward the work of the UWC International Office.[4] Not surprisingly, at the beginning of February 1979, the Pearson board formally elected Symons as the chair of its own international committee, thus making him Pearson's official representative on the UWC international board, a role he seemed already to be playing informally.[5]

The UWC international board had three types of members. In the first category were the official representatives, like Symons himself, from each of the constituent colleges. In the second were the academic heads of the colleges. And in the third were some individual members of the international board, elected at large.

The international board had a variety of roles. It was the place where general matters of policy were discussed and standards established for the individual UWC colleges, in addition to the IB academic standard. It also provided an opportunity for exchanges between the heads of the colleges, who also held separate meetings of their own. And it was the venue for developing the overall UWC concept and vision, the development of the UWC network, and the creation of new colleges.

Relations between the international board and the boards of the local colleges were often delicate. It required a very deft hand to steer an international venture involving a variety of cultures and different parts of the globe. Contrasting values and approaches, differing points of view and priorities, and competing ideas about what to do with scarce resources meant that it was a constant challenge to keep every one in step and to ensure creative results rather than conflict.

There were also, inevitably, problems about money. On the one hand, the individual colleges were naturally very cautious about money going to the international board and office, at the expense of the local colleges and their own budgets and priorities. But at the same time, the international UWC movement was also critical of generating a local and international constituency that provided financial support for the individual colleges and for the movement as a whole. Keeping a healthy, creative balance between the international movement and the local colleges was an enduring challenge.

In this kind of atmosphere, Tom Symons was in his element, and his singular diplomatic gifts were soon recognized and appreciated. Few people can pour oil on troubled waters as Symons can, or create harmony and common purpose among diverse impulses and personalities. He had been Pearson's official representative on the international board for scarcely a year when the possibility of him assuming the chairmanship of the international UWC board began to be bruited. The current chair, Professor Alec Peterson, was a great Scottish educator, a specialist in pedagogy, who had played a key role in developing both the IB and the UWC movement. Peterson was already seventy and wanted to step down after a two-year term, and he soon identified Symons as the best person on the international board to succeed him.[6] In addition to Symons's obvious personal and leadership gifts, Peterson apparently felt that it would be helpful for the UWC movement to enjoy a period of leadership from outside the UK. Symons informed his Pearson board colleagues about this proposal, and received strong encouragement from them to take on the international chairmanship.[7] By January 1980, Symons had agreed to do so.[8]

As the new chair of the UWC international board, Symons had some six major priorities to which he wanted or needed to devote his time. The first—reflecting the challenges and tensions of which he had already become aware—was developing a sense of common interest and good relationships among the colleges in the UWC network. The second was enlarging the UWC network by planning and founding new colleges. Partly as a result of his work, four new colleges were established during his time as chair, and another three were in the planning stages, initiated during his term of office and nourished by his efforts. The third and, as it proved, very rewarding focus was relations between the board and the UWC president, Prince Charles. For six years he was in touch weekly—by phone or letter or meeting—with the Prince of Wales in this capacity. The fourth priority was relations with the IB headquarters in Geneva. While the International Baccalaureate movement was much broader than the UWC colleges alone, nevertheless, as a system that was totally IB, the UWC occupied a special place in the IB universe. There were also problems arising from UWC's exclusive IB focus, since the IB curriculum and approach did not always work well for all the UWC students. The fifth priority sometimes had to be support for the survival of some of the UWC colleges. One or two of them were in serious jeopardy during Symons's time as international chair, and the international board was their necessary lifeline. The sixth and final priority was helping to find and encourage leading citizens in countries around the world who might become interested in the UWC movement, and bringing them into active participation either with a local college or with the movement as a whole. Even many countries that did not yet have their own UWC colleges might nevertheless have a UWC committee or association. The role of these committees was to support the UWC movement both locally and worldwide, and to select and support students from their countries to attend UWC colleges, often located elsewhere in the world. The chair of the international board had to maintain liaison with these committees and help them prosper. And he also had to develop relations with other possible sources of financial support for the individual colleges, or for the whole UWC system.

As chair of the international board, Symons was responsible for the ongoing business of the international board and its office. The president occupied a more honorary position, somewhat like that of a university chancellor or a college visitor. But Prince Charles had no interest in being merely an honorary head. He was a very active president for the UWC movement. He had inherited the role of president from his great-uncle, Lord Louis Mountbatten, and there was probably an element of filial piety—honouring the memory of a favourite uncle and mentor—in Prince Charles's devotion to the UWC cause.[9] But there was also genuine personal conviction.

Prince Charles had been a student at Gordonstoun, and some of the educational philosophy of the United World Colleges had grown out of Gordonstoun and out of the thinking of the educational leader who started Gordonstoun, Kurt Hahn. Prince Charles had been attracted to the UWC movement by his interest in that kind of education, with its emphasis on the outdoors, by the international dimension of the UWC approach, and by a strong concern for the development of the whole person. So when he was called on to succeed Mountbatten, he responded with interest and energy. He believed strongly in the diversity of the UWC colleges, and would often try to visit one of them on his international travels. During Symons's tenure, the prince played a leading role in the establishment of colleges in the United States, in Italy, and in Venezuela. Indeed, without his active involvement, at least two of them might never have gotten off the ground.

Every time Symons went to London for a meeting in these years, he met with the UWC president. They would review the UWC board agenda, and Prince Charles would express views on items the board would be dealing with. He sometimes suggested items. From time to time he would attend a meeting. Symons enjoyed working with him tremendously. He found Prince Charles a thoughtful, imaginative, caring president. "I can't tell you how lucky we are to have a person of such talent, and such capacity, and such resilience," Symons says now. "We don't quite know it. . . . But I had six years of it. And I want to tell you he's an absolutely A++."

In addition to the Prince of Wales, there were many other strong personalities on the international board with whom the chairman needed to maintain good relations to ensure their continued commitment to the UWC movement worldwide. Developing the network and attracting new interest and participation on the board was one of his chief challenges. During his two three-year terms as chair, Symons recruited many new board members, including Kingman Brewster, the former president of Yale University, later US ambassador to the United Kingdom; Prince Sadruddin Aga Khan, former UN commissioner for refugees; Sir Hugh Springer, secretary general of the Association of Commonwealth Universities from 1970 to 1980; Sir Jack Cater, chief secretary of Hong Kong from 1978 to 1981; Sir Shridath Ramphal, secretary general of the Commonwealth from 1975 to 1990, and many others.

Managing large personalities from diverse backgrounds and many parts of the world could be a big challenge. An international movement like UWC, with an inner ethos or spirit, naturally attracts people who feel strongly about it—and who sometimes believe they are the only custodians of the true faith. There were rival camps (sometimes even within the same country) that had to be kept working harmoniously together.

One of the strongest personalities Symons recruited to the international board was Armand Hammer, the flamboyant Russian-American tycoon who controlled Occidental Petroleum. Hammer had made both his initial fortune and his fame (or infamy, in the eyes of some) through his business dealings with the Soviet Union, starting soon after the 1917 Revolution. Symons got to know Hammer through his work in the creation of the UWC of the American West, and found he liked the controversial tycoon and was able to work with him. So he invited Hammer to join the international board at the beginning of his own second three-year term as chair, in the spring of 1983.[10] There was a genuine affection and mutual respect between Hammer and Prince Charles. Hammer had a fleet of some thirty aircraft, the largest of which was his own master control centre. He would often lend one of them to Prince Charles and Symons for UWC business.

In this way and in many others, Hammer soon confirmed his great value to the UWC international board, as he had already done in the US movement. The very next year, for example, he provided funds to cover the deficit of the UWC international office.[11] But this was only a stop-gap. The effort to find a more permanent solution for the financial problems of the UWC central operations led to one of the most colourful incidents in Symons's time as UWC international chair.

At a board meeting, shortly afterward, Symons expressed concern about the need for some substantial funding, including to endow more scholarships for the colleges. After the meeting Hammer took Symons aside and said: "Now, really, what do we need here?" Symons replied: "Well, I'd really like $5 million, and it would make it possible to get the costs of the Board off the back of the colleges"—to ease relations between the central UWC administration and the individual colleges, who sometimes felt they were being taxed to support the UWC international office—"and also to create more scholarships at different colleges." "OK, $5 million, leave it to me, I'll see that you get it," Hammer answered. "I'll have to have you, I'll have to have the Prince of Wales, and I'll need a three-day weekend."

So for a weekend in November 1985, Hammer took over an entire hotel in Palm Beach, Florida, to which he invited enough friends to fill the hotel, at the cost of $10,000 each. A smaller number were invited at the price of $50,000. The drawing card was to be the presence of Prince Charles and Princess Diana, as well as entertainers like Victor Borge and many other attractions. Combining the two admission categories, Hammer managed to raise $5 million net for the UWC movement, after expenses. But that wasn't all: one of the guests, a Japanese businessman, insisted on bringing his bodyguard, including to the gala banquet where Borge was to perform. It then turned out that several other guests—not to be outdone—wanted to bring their bodyguards too. So Symons and Sir Ian Gourlay, the UWC director general, came up with an ingenious solution that gave Prince Charles a big laugh. Alright, they said, you can bring your bodyguards—at a fee of $10,000 each! But it still didn't end there. Because when Prince Charles spoke at the end of the dinner, reporting the remarkable financial results of the weekend to great applause, the Japanese businessman leapt up, and said, "This has been so special, I give five hundred!" Five hundred what? "Five hundred thousand!" And then two or three others in the room followed suit. It was certainly a colourful incident in the life of the UWC movement, but also a very important shot in its financial arm.[12]

The first college to join the UWC network after Symons became the international chair was the Waterford Kamhlaba school in Swaziland. It had been founded as a multi-racial school in 1963 by a group of South Africans who wanted to create a school where all races could study together.[13] Located in Mbabane, the capital of Swaziland, because such a school would have been illegal in South Africa at that time, it had become a UWC Associated School in 1978.[14] In 1981, with Symons's support, it became a full member of the UWC network, as the United World College of Southern Africa. The Swaziland college was a wonderful addition to the UWC family because it was a multiracial school at a time and in a place when it was badly needed. The Mandela family, for example, had sent members over the border to attend the college, and so did many white South African families who wanted their children to have a wider interracial experience at a time when South Africa was still in the grip of apartheid.

Symons made it a policy to visit every UWC college at least once. Christine joined him on these visits, and on almost all his UWC travels. She was a true partner in this as in so many other parts of his life. In the case of the UWC of Southern Africa, they spent an entire week there in February 1984. They lived in the college, and Symons taught a number of classes, spoke to the school assembly, to the IB students, and gave other talks, including one on Canadian Prime Minister Pierre Trudeau's then current international peace initiative.[15] Symons liked the students immensely and felt he learned a great deal from them.

When he and Christine left the college, they received a rude lesson in the political realities of South Africa at the time. They had planned to spend a day or two in Johannesburg and to visit other parts of South Africa. But when they arrived at the airport, they were immediately interned by the South African security forces. Symons was, after all, the international chair of an organization whose Swaziland college was attended not only by the children of black South African families but even by those of influential white families too, in open defiance of South African apartheid policies. The South African authorities were not going to let this defiance go unnoticed. The

Symons were locked in a room at the airport and were not allowed to leave except to board a plane out of the country the next day. For Symons it was a revelation. The sight of soldiers parading around outside, wearing Nazi-style boots and carrying Sten guns, was a chilling reminder of human brutality and injustice that he never forgot. The existence of the Swaziland UWC seemed more important than ever.

The second new UWC college, established during Symons's chairmanship, was the UWC College of the Adriatic, in Italy. It was to be the fifth college in the UWC network and the first outside the English-speaking world. Italy was a priority because there was a very strong Italian community in UWC, who were eager to establish a UWC there and willing to play a strong leadership role. They developed impressive support, not only from the Italian government but also from the regional governments, and then from individual donors. The campaign was so successful that the Italian college was able to be established, like Pearson College, on the basis of one hundred percent scholarship funding.

The site selected for the college was the little town of Duino, just outside Trieste. It was a superb site on the Adriatic shore, tumbling down to the sea, right on the cultural fault line between Italians, Croats, and Serbs. The location helped shape the distinctive focus of the Italian UWC, which was to be Mediterranean and intercultural studies, with also some outreach to the nearby countries that were still, at that time, behind the Iron Curtain.

The only problem was that the site selected was Duino Castle, the very place where Archduke Franz Ferdinand of Austria had spent his last night, on 27 June 1914, before setting out for Sarajevo and his appointment with destiny. The castle was owned by an Italian archduke, Prince Raimondo della Torre e Tasso. And the archduke—whose lineage went back to the Hapsburg or even to the Holy Roman Empire—couldn't get along with the local UWC leader, who was a communist mayor! The key to unlocking this puzzle turned out to be—not for the last time—Prince Charles. The archduke, living in somewhat reduced circumstances, could no longer maintain the building. But he couldn't quite make up his mind to sell it either, at least not to the local UWC committee. So when the negotiations had reached a crucial stage, Prince Charles was brought into the picture. He came to stay with his fellow prince. They were related in a very distant way—generations back—and they called each other cousin. They genuinely respected each other. And the deal was done.

By June 1982, Symons was corresponding with the chair of the new governing body for the College of the Adriatic, Corrado Belci and, during the summer, arrangements were being made for the staffing of the college.[16] The first students entered the college in September 1982.[17]

Meanwhile, work was going rapidly forward for a new college in what proved to be one of the trickiest and most challenging countries for Symons to deal with during his time as international chair of the UWC: his own neighbour, the United States! The problem was not lack of interest, but possibly an excess, and a huge cultural gap, between two regional factions. There was a long-established, socially prominent, well-to-do Atlantic seaboard UWC support group. But there was also a less long-established, even more well-to-do, but perhaps less "cultured" Pacific coast group, with other supporters scattered in between these two. Reconciling the two groups was always a challenge for the international chair.

Armand Hammer was a prominent member of the western group. But someone like him was persona non grata to the Atlantic coast elite from New York, Washington, New England, and Maryland. The impasse between these two groups had prevented agreement on how to establish an American UWC and where it should be located.

Once again, it was Prince Charles who was able to break the logjam. In May 1981, he was on a semi-state visit to the United States and agreed to chair a meeting of the American UWC committee at the British embassy in Washington. The meeting was to include representatives of the two American groups together with some international board members, such as Kingman Brewster, in order to help the various American groups achieve agreement on an action plan. As international chair, Symons opened the meeting by suggesting it might be time for the American initiative to move forward and to begin the search for a college site. Right on cue, Prince Charles looked around the room, especially at the east coast group, and said, "That's agreed, eh?!" When nobody dared disagree with the Prince of Wales, Armand Hammer chimed in, "I will put a plane and pilot at your disposal, and you can go and look at sites." Once again, Prince Charles looked around the room and said innocently, "Oh, aren't we lucky! Thank you, thank you, Dr. Hammer. That's agreed?!" It was a superb performance, and there was now no turning back for the American UWC committee.[18] Hammer clinched the agreement by making three commitments: he would purchase the site when found, he would cover any deficit for the college during his lifetime, and he would leave an endowment in his will.[19]

The meeting at the British Embassy was the occasion for one of the most amusing incidents in Symons's time as UWC international chair, and perhaps in his whole life. After the meeting, there was tea for the thirty or so UWC committee members and officials. During tea, it was discovered that in front of the embassy there was a hostile crowd demonstrating against Prince Charles and shouting, "Go home." It was still the time of the troubles in Northern Ireland, and some of the demonstrators were Irish Americans. But some were what the American secret service agents traveling with the prince referred to as a "rent-a-mob," available for almost any kind of demonstration. The prince was amused, and said he would like to go outside and mingle with the demonstrators. The British ambassador said, "Certainly not!" But Prince Charles wanted to go out anyway. So, finally, he put on an old raincoat and fedora, and Symons put on something else, and they went out a backdoor and around the side of the embassy, mingling with the crowd that was demonstrating loudly against Prince Charles. The crowd didn't recognize him, and Prince Charles soon joined the shouting, "Charles, go home! Go back! Go home!" The demonstrators were carrying signs that said things like "Limey go home," and Prince Charles eventually succeeded in getting one of the signs to hold too. Symons wished he had a camera. The prince said, "If only I'd thought of it, I would have arranged for [his secret service bodyguard] to get it on film."

After the success of the meeting at the British embassy, Symons arranged for the American UWC committee to strike a search committee to consider some thirty potential sites for the new college. These were eventually whittled down to three, and the final choice was to be made by Symons, as the international chair, and by Hammer, who was going to buy the site selected for the UWC. They were to visit all three sites together in one day in the summer of 1981. Symons was very concerned. He didn't want to get into a disagreement with Hammer, who was being so generous. But he didn't want to agree to a bad site for a UWC college either.

The first location they looked at in the morning was a land-locked site in San Diego. Symons didn't say anything, but he was getting even more worried now, because he didn't want to be part of choosing a site that was really nothing more than three or four city blocks and that would not give students the outdoor opportunities they had at other UWC sites. The second site was on the sea, and was certainly an improvement over the first. But it still wasn't right either. The seacoast site was not really attractive or usable, nothing like the wonderful seacoast location of Pearson College. And there was no nearby community to provide historic or cultural interest. It was only a marginal improvement.

Then they flew over the mountains to visit a site at Montezuma, New Mexico, where they discovered a magnificent old hotel at the western terminus of the Santa Fe railway. It was right on a mountainside, with a fantastic view and marvellous forested mountains around it. At the foot of the mountainside was a community called Las Vegas. Not the famous Las Vegas, but a small Hispanic-American village with a hot spring. The old hotel was a marvel and might be fixed up for a college. Symons could easily see where other buildings would fit into the landscape. And there were obvious opportunities for mountain-climbing, as well as for woodcraft, and for community service, an important feature of the UWC educational philosophy, with a rich mixture of Hispanic and Pueblo as well as Euro-American cultures. And nearby—just on the other side of the Santa Fe National Forest—was Santa Fe, the beautiful cultural centre of the American southwest. Symons was thrilled. He thought, "God, this would be great!" But he wasn't ready to tip his hand to Hammer, who wasn't tipping his either.

So they flew back over the Rockies without talking about the three sites. Symons was wondering how to broach the subject, because he would rather not have a college at all than agree to the first two sites. As they got into his car at the airport, Hammer asked, "Well now, what do you think?" Symons started very gingerly, saying all the sites were very special, but very different. Very different, yes, Hammer could see that. What did Symons think the differences were? So Symons started carefully again, alluding to some of the disadvantages of the urban site. Hammer readily agreed. "It's a pity about San Diego," he said. "I was hoping I would like that. I already own that property! You know, it cost me several million, but there'll be lots of development opportunities for that." So they went on to the second, seaside site. Symons said, "You know, it disappointed me a little. It wasn't as suitable for marine activity. And it wasn't a place of great aesthetic appeal. It just was a bad bit of shore. And the mountains weren't near." He was really scrambling for arguments. "Uh-huh," said Hammer. "What did you think of the one up in the mountain?" "Well," Symons replied, "I thought it was pretty attractive." "Of course you're right," Hammer exploded immediately. "It's the only possible choice!" So it was settled.

But there was one more step to be taken—one that played out a bit like a scene from an old-fashioned gangster movie. The site had still to be purchased for UWC. And it turned out to be owned by the Catholic Church. The old hotel at Montezuma had been used as a training centre for Mexican priests during the years, earlier in the twentieth century, when Catholicism was outlawed in Mexico. Postulants would be smuggled out of Mexico to be trained here, then smuggled back across the border. The site was now abandoned, but was still part of the church properties managed by an ecclesiastical office in Washington. Hammer and Symons had to make a pilgrimage to Washington.

They agreed to meet at a Washington hotel the night before their appointment with the church authorities, to discuss how the meeting should be conducted the following morning. Hammer told Symons, "You do the bit about UWC, and why we believe in it, and why this would be such a wonderful site. Then, when we get to the business side, I'll do that part." It was a perfectly logical division of labour. So they went in to see the relevant authority responsible for all church property.

It turned out the Catholic Church had no less than a bishop whose sole job it was to look after properties like the one UWC wanted to buy. And so there was a bishop to greet them. He had a pleasant enough demeanour, but was steely-eyed. Not a dear old boy at all, thought Symons to himself. But after all, the elderly Russian-American tycoon and his young Canadian academic colleague were a bit of an odd couple too. After Symons had done his part—explaining the plans for the American UWC college and why the site was so ideal for it—the bishop said: "Well, very interesting, Professor Symons. I applaud your educational ideals. We've learned something about you. And I respect what you've done. And I know this was a very carefully considered thing, coming from educational people. But, you know, it's not for sale. We have never advertised it. How did you learn of it?" Well, Symons explained, it was just word of mouth, and the possibility that this abandoned site might be available. The bishop said, "Well, we've had no intent for selling it. We're just holding it. Who knows when it might again be. . . "

Symons began to sense the door was not completely shut. The bishop then asked, "If it were for sale, what sort of price would you offer?" Symons was dumbfounded. He thought, "How impossible that is!" But the canny Hammer seemed to have anticipated exactly this turn of events. He had said nothing at all so far. He had sat perfectly silent throughout the forty minutes of the interview. But he now lifted up a battered old briefcase. Symons had noticed the briefcase because it was very unlike Hammer to carry one. He never carried anything. But now Hammer put his briefcase on the table, and tapped it. "Bishop," he said, "would you sell it for what's in here?" Symons couldn't believe what he was watching. Hammer and the Catholic bishop just eye-balled each other for what seemed like an age. After a very long silence, the bishop seemed to have made his calculation, and made up his mind. He obviously knew about the Armand Hammer legend. And he probably guessed how badly Hammer wanted the property. He finally broke the silence and said, "Yes, Dr. Hammer, we'd sell it for what's in there." Only then did Hammer open the briefcase. It contained precisely $1 million, in new American bills. The asking price was later reported to be $1.8 million.[20] But the Montezuma site now belonged to the UWC.

The problems with the American UWC committee were not ended by this success. The two regional groups continued to feud, especially over fundraising turf, for the rest of Symons's term as chair, sometimes requiring his characteristically tactful and "diplomatic" but also "firm" interventions to sort out respective roles.[21] Nevertheless, the Armand Hammer United World College of the American West was officially opened in a ceremony on 28 October 1982, at which Symons, as the UWC international chair, was one of the speakers.[22] Considering Symons's crucial role in launching the American college, this was more than usually appropriate.

Another UWC college Symons played a key role in launching was Simon Bolivar UWC in Venezuela. Partly due to Prince Charles, Venezuela had been a UWC priority even before Symons became the international chair.[23] Within months of taking office, Symons was already responding to the prince's enthusiasm by suggesting to him that Venezuela should be UWC's top priority.[24] The UWC network was spontaneously looking to the English-speaking world and western Europe. Prince Charles wanted to break out of this limited focus. And he apparently also thought a Latin American college offered an opportunity for an agricultural vocation that would relate closely to the needs of its own surrounding region.[25] The prince was himself a farmer, who loved the land and believed strongly in agriculture. He saw the establishment of a United World College of Agriculture in Venezuela as "a contribution, however small, to tackling the problem of world hunger."[26] And this natural bent of his own connected with the plans of the local Venezuelan committee.

Like Italy, Venezuela had emerged as a priority because of the strength and leadership of the UWC national committee there. The Venezuelan committee had been a financial contributor to the UWC movement and had regularly sent students overseas to UWC colleges. It was well-connected, both socially and culturally, and had succeeded in getting the support of the major Venezuelan foundation. But it was also important to secure the support of the Venezuelan government, especially to acquire the proposed farm site for the college at Ticoporo in the Venezuelan interior. It was a settled area, but it also had a frontier flavour, which responded well to the outdoor dimension and challenge of a UWC college, in which Prince Charles also believed strongly.

This was another occasion when the prince played a critical role. It was agreed that his presence and prestige would greatly help to clinch the deal. But that wasn't easy to arrange, because an official visit to Venezuela by the Prince of Wales would entail all kinds of protocol and formal social obligations that would distract from what he wanted to do: have quiet discussions with the Government of Venezuela, with donors, with the Venezuelan foundation, and with the potential donors of the land for the proposed college site. So the plan eventually adopted was that the prince's plane would touch down unofficially in Caracas on his way back from an official tour in the South Pacific. Officially, he would simply be en route but, unofficially, he would be in Venezuela conducting UWC business. Tom and Christine Symons would meet him there. And together they would fly out to look at the proposed college site, about two hundred miles from Caracas in the Venezuelan interior.[27]

It didn't quite work out that way. In fact, the prince's unofficial visit to Venezuela led to another one of the amusing adventures with which Symons's tenure as UWC chair seems to have been peppered. The night before Prince Charles—quite unknown to the local media—was to arrive, there came a knock at the Symons's hotel door. When Tom opened the door, an obviously British man introduced himself and said, "I'm from the British Secret Service." Symons invited him in, and the secret service agent began: "You know, tomorrow Prince Charles and you are flying out to the site, and the arrangements have been made that you would go in Air Force One (the president of Venezuela's air force plane)." Symons said, "Yes, we're doing that. It's two hundred miles." And the British agent said, "I'm sorry, Prince Charles can't fly on that plane." Astonished, Symons asked, "What's this about?" The agent explained that, unknown to the Venezuelans, the British agents had secretly inspected the president's plane to ensure it was suitable for Prince Charles. The British agent said, "We don't think it's flight worthy." Symons thought to himself, "Well, what are we going to do about this? How do you go to the president of Venezuela and say: we're not going to use your plane? And the secret service of another country has outwitted your guards and inspected your plane, and your private plane won't do?" It seemed to be an impossible situation. But when he asked the secret service man what they were to do, the agent only replied firmly, "I don't know. But the Prince simply cannot fly on that plane."

The next morning, Symons had still not come up with any real plan. But he had to go out to the airport and wait for the prince's arrival anyway. There was a line-up on the tarmac, with Symons fourth in line, behind the Venezuelan foreign minister, the British ambassador, and a third person. Prince Charles's plane landed, and the prince himself emerged at the top of the airplane stairs, looking in the pink of health, bronzed from his South Pacific tour. On the spur of the moment, Symons broke ranks and rushed forward to the airplane stairs, as if he were overcome with pleasure at seeing The Prince of Wales! Prince Charles ought to have been startled, but he just looked at Symons and murmured quietly, "What's wrong, Tom?" Symons whispered, "You're sick. You don't feel well!" And between the top step and the next one, the vigorous young prince began to look as if he were failing fast. By the time he reached the bottom, he was obviously worse, not at all well. The foreign minister forgot all about Symons's faux pas and said to the prince with concern, "Your Royal Highness you had a long flight. You must. . ." And Prince Charles said, "Yes. You know I've had a bit. . . it must have been the water." That was all Symons could do for the time being. Prince Charles would have to figure out how to handle the situation on his own. He continued looking sick all the way to the British embassy in the motorcade.

When they met up again at the embassy, Prince Charles said, "What the hell is this?!" Symons explained the situation, and they had a good laugh about it. But there was no way Prince Charles could fly to the proposed college site the next day. They couldn't arrange for another plane without creating an international incident because the British secret service had secretly inspected the president of Venezuela's own plane. So the prince stayed at the embassy in Caracas, while the Symons, the British ambassador, and Ian Gourlay flew out to the site in the un-flight-worthy plane. Flying through a patch of thunder and lightning didn't enhance their peace of mind. But they made it. The whole town had turned out. And because Gourlay looked every inch the British general that he actually was, Symons guessed they got pretty well through the whole ceremony before many people figured out Prince Charles wasn't actually there!

With the help of Prince Charles's secret visit to Venezuela, plans for the college moved forward. The following year, Symons was able to congratulate Mrs. Maria de Burelli Rivas, chair of the Venezuelan UWC national committee, on the acquisition of the farm and college site at Ticoporo.[28] The college was ultimately launched in 1986, just as Symons was completing his term as international chair, but it didn't become a full member of the UWC network until 1988.

Early in Symons's first term as chair, the UWC international board had set a five-year goal to establish UWCs in Swaziland, Venezuela, Italy, India, and the United States.[29] By the end of his two terms as chair, in 1986, Symons had almost done it all. The only exception was India, where there were several false starts. But even there, his hard work eventually paid off when the Mahindra UWC of India was approved in 1993 and opened in 1997.

Symons also led the early planning for two other UWC colleges that were opened after his term of office. The UWC in Norway, for example, took years of groundwork before it was finally opened in 1995. The choice of Norway for a Scandinavian UWC was determined, like Italy and Venezuela, by the existence of a particularly strong UWC national committee there. For the Scandinavian college, the UWC entered a working partnership with the Red Cross, which gave the college (again, like the Venezuelan UWC) a special flavour and orientation that Symons thought valuable and positive.

Symons also laid the groundwork for a UWC in Hong Kong. He made several trips to Hong Kong during his two terms as chair, to strengthen relations with the UWC committee there. The Hong Kong UWC committee was a strong one, very successful in fundraising, including for scholarships to Atlantic College and to other UWCs. The leading member of the local committee was Sir Kenneth Ping-Fan Fung. Another, with whom Symons developed a special friendship, was Sir Q. W. Lee, the head of the Hang Seng Bank and the Hang Seng Index. "Q. W.," as he was known, would even fly halfway around the world to have breakfast with Symons in London in order to bring him up to date on progress in Hong Kong. Symons discovered the Hong Kong group liked to do business at the Happy Valley racetrack in Hong Kong, where Fung had a huge box in which meals and drinks were served. Once, when Symons got back from Happy Valley, he found a cheque waiting for him at his hotel: a cheque for $50,000 for UWC! Because of these friendships, Symons was well positioned to push forward planning for the Li Po Chung UWC of Hong Kong that finally opened in 1992.

Not everything succeeded, of course. At various times during his tenure, proposals were made about possible UWCs in Bermuda, the Bahamas, Australia, and Nigeria, among others. None of these bore fruit. The biggest disappointment for Symons was Nigeria. He had longed to see a second UWC established in Africa and considered Nigeria the ideal location. The first African UWC was in Swaziland, in the foot of Africa. The second, he thought, should be in the north and west. And Nigeria would be a natural place for it. It was the richest and most powerful black African nation, supporting a network of good universities, of which the leading ones were world class. Through it flows the huge river Niger, which offered a marvellous physical setting for a college. Symons even had a name for a Nigerian UWC college: the "College of the Niger." But it was not to be. Nigeria was then torn by civil war, making conditions in the country too problematic for establishing a UWC. Symons still looks forward to the day when it may be possible.

Throughout the first half of the 1980s, Symons devoted a huge portion of his professional life to the UWC movement. In the first six months of 1985, for example, he calculated that he had spent fifty-one full days on UWC business, and had devoted some time to UWC correspondence telephone calls and brief meetings on virtually *all* the other days in that period—more than half of a normal working life.[30] A similar period the following year included fundraising events and other work for major financial campaigns for the UWC colleges in Canada and the United States and for the international operations fund; a visit to the Singapore UWC and follow-up talks with Singapore government officials; meetings in India, and with half a dozen other UWC national committees; two visits to the United Kingdom, where he met with the UWC president, with other UWC board members, and with the staff of the international office; not to mention a heavy daily load of UWC mail, daily calls from and to UWC people around the world, and weekly or biweekly telephone conferences with the UWC international office in London.[31]

Obviously, given his other commitments, Symons could not have sustained this kind of workload and pace without first-class support. And he got it. Especially in the form of the remarkable director general of the UWC international operations, Sir Ian Gourlay. Gourlay had been commandant general (the professional head) of the Royal Marines from 1971 to 1975. Upon retirement from the Marines, he had been "recruited" by Lord Mountbatten. On reaching the age of seventy-five, Mountbatten had wanted to hand over the UWC presidency to his great-nephew, the Prince of Wales. But before he did so, he felt he needed to provide Prince Charles with strong support. He regarded Gourlay as "the best Commandant General the Royal Marines had ever had."[32] So he persuaded him to become director general of United World Colleges, a position in which he served until 1990. To this role Gourlay brought both the competence and the distinction of a four-star general. He had immense knowledge and broad experience of many parts of the world. An ability to inspire, to bring people together, to get teams working together on common projects. And an ability to make do with practically nothing. He was an excellent judge of character, who was himself a model of decency and integrity. Symons adored him and depended on him. They seem to have got on superbly from the start.

Symons's father had served in the First World War and he himself had been in the officers training corps. He had always had a respect for the people and the best traditions of the armed forces. But working with Gourlay was a revelation to him, not just about integrity and decency but also about the depth of culture, kindness, and caring of the very best soldiers. For Symons, his working relationship with Gourlay was very special, not just a matter of total mutual respect but a genuine and very substantial friendship. The feeling was mutual. Gourlay considered himself "extremely fortunate and indeed privileged" to have the "memorable" experience of serving as UWC director general right through Symons's six years of service as chair of UWC's international board.[33] For his part, Symons was so impressed by Gourlay that he enrolled him again, a decade later, as a key actor in the Meta Incognita project, described in another chapter of this book. To this day, a trip to London would not be complete for Symons without a breakfast meeting with Gourlay. His accomplishments as the UWC international chair were joint accomplishments, which would have been impossible without Gourlay as a full partner in the enterprise.

Symons's immediate predecessors as international chair had served only two years each.[34] But as Symons approached the end of his initial three-year term, there had been pressure from many quarters for him to accept another. Jack Matthews (who had replaced John Nicol on the international board in 1982) argued that, under Symons's leadership, the UWC was "taking a step into a new level of world statesmanship" and that it continued to require his "experience and diplomacy for guidance."[35] As his second three-year term drew to a close and the search began for a successor, praise for his accomplishments continued. Corrado Belci said that Symons's term of office had been a period of "significant development of the movement and the establishment of new schools."[36] The chair of the Nigerian national committee spoke of Symons's "outstanding contributions. . . to the development of the UWC as an international concept."[37]

Perhaps the most significant assessment of Symons's role as UWC international chair came from his predecessor. Alec Peterson thought his choice of Symons as international chair had proven a "triumphant success." In Peterson's eyes, the qualities that had made Symons so valuable to the UWC movement, and had "won him so many friends in it," were not just his "unrivalled and continuing experience of the world of international education"—which made him "ideal for the post"—but, even more, his qualities of wisdom and humanity and, above all, his ability to exercise the virtue of patience. "To watch Tom steer a meeting through to conclusions, which in the early stages seemed impossible to achieve within the allotted time, without appearing to hurry anyone" said Peterson, admiringly, "has been an unforgettable experience."[38]

There can be no doubt that Symons brought immense talents to his role as chair of the UWC international board, and that the UWC movement was greatly strengthened by his leadership during a significant period of expansion. But it can also be said that the

UWC movement deeply appealed to something in Symons's own make-up and values. Once again—as at Devonshire House, at Trent University, and in so many other roles—he was seeing through to the inner, animating idea of something and trying to bring the outer reality into closer approximation with the inner form. The UWC idea that appealed so deeply to him—and to many others—was that of international understanding and peace through education.

For Tom Symons, the growth of the United World Colleges in Canada and elsewhere had "great implications in the long term for human rights and peace." The UWCs, he said in 1984, were promoting

> knowledge and understanding amongst peoples and nations by bringing together young people from diverse cultures and background in a shared educational experience with an international orientation. With their multinational, multiracial, and multicultural approach, these colleges are already making an important contribution to a better international knowledge and understanding both of human rights and of the conditions making for peace, and of the interrelationships between the two.[39]

Perhaps the last word on the great ideal that drove Symons in his leadership of the international United World College movement can and should be given to his esteemed partner in that enterprise. For Sir Ian Gourlay, the joy of their six-year collaboration was rooted not only in their growing friendship but also in the fact that they "shared an ever strengthening conviction that what the United World Colleges were seeking to do was hugely worthwhile." With the heart of a poet that sometimes beats in the breast of a four-star general, Gourlay describes the idea that inspired both of them, in these fine words:

> Here was a unique international educational movement which had been developed in the aftermath of a World War to promote the cause of global peace. . . peace, without which our most cherished hopes and dreams, arguably, could all too easily be frustrated. There is surely no doubting that men and women everywhere need an attachment to some larger purpose, as opposed to the pursuit of merely selfish interests, and there was a general

> perception in UWC that nowhere was there to be found a more desirable and challenging educational purpose than the search for international understanding through international education, through the instruction of young people drawn together at an impressionable age, from a limitless range of nations and different cultures, right across the globe.
>
> UWC can now boast more than 40,000 alumni, veritable candles of enlightenment, shining out across a dark world in a hundred and more countries: active, inspiring multipliers of the UWC ethic, and touching the hearts and minds of everyone they meet. All this in a world of nations still waking up to their interdependence, and of men and women still waking to their common humanity. There can be little doubt that peace is UWC's ultimate goal. It may be that those who have not experienced war cannot discern its utter futility. But listen to Bertrand Russell: "It's either co-existence, or no existence." He had his eye on nuclear war, but whether this occurs or something else lies ahead, it is Mahatma Gandhi who movingly sums up the action we need to take, in some inspiring words: "If the world is to survive, we must start with the rising generations and help them to love one another!"[40]

To which Tom Symons, I am sure, would say amen, and amen.

Notes

1 Unless otherwise indicated, the information and quotations in this chapter are drawn from an interview with T. H. B. Symons, 2 October 2009.

2 Kenneth Rotenberg to T. H. B. Symons, 5 October 1973, Symons Papers, Trent University Archives, Fonds 01-003, Box 25: UWC correspondence, 1972–81, Folder #1: Pearson College- Foundation UWC 1973–75. I am grateful to Kathryn McLeod for her invaluable research assistance in the preparation of this chapter.

3 Correspondence re: election to Board of Trustees of Pearson College, November 1976. Symons Papers, Trent University Archives, Fonds

01-003, Box 25: UWC correspondence, 1972–81, Folder #5: Pearson College of the Pacific 1976–77.

4 T. H. B. Symons to John Nicol, 29 November 1978. Symons Papers, Trent University Archives, Fonds 01-003, Box 25: UWC correspondence, 1972–81, Folder #6: 1977–78 Pearson College.

5 Jack C. Matthews to Sir Ian Gourlay, 13 February 1979. Symons Papers, Trent University Archives, Fonds 01-003, Box 25: UWC correspondence, 1972–81, Folder #7: United World Colleges and Pearson College, 1978–79.

6 T. H. B. Symons to Alec Peterson, 4 December 1979. Symons Papers, Trent University Archives, Fonds 01-003, Box 25: UWC correspondence, 1972–81, Folder #9: United World Colleges and Pearson College of the Pacific, 1978–79; A. D. C. Peterson, *Schools Across Frontiers: The Story of the International Baccalaureate and the United World Colleges*, 2nd ed., revised and updated (Peru, Illinois: Open Court Publishing Company, 1987, 2003), 172.

7 Letters to T. H. B. Symons from R. B. Hutchison, Kenneth Rotenberg, John R. Yarnell, December 1979: Symons Papers, Trent University Archives, Fonds 97-019, Box 41: United World Colleges, Folder #1: UWC 1979–81.

8 T. H. B. Symons to John Nicol, 10 January 1980. Symons Papers, Trent University Archives, Fonds 97-019, Box 41: United World Colleges, Folder #1: UWC 1979–81.

9 Peterson, *Schools Across Frontiers*, 124.

10 T. H. B. Symons to Armand Hammer, 30 May 1983; Armand Hammer to T. H. B. Symons, 20 June 1983. Symons Papers, Trent University Archives, Fonds 01-003, Box 26, Folder #4: UWC: some correspondence notes and documents, 1982; Fonds 97-019, Box 41: United World Colleges, Folder #2: UWC 1982–83.

11 Armand Hammer to Prince Charles, 14 August 1984. Symons Papers, Trent University Archives, Fonds 01-003: Box 26: UWC correspondence etc. 1981–85, Folder #16: UWC: some correspondence, notes, and documents, 1984.

12 Letters from T. H. B. Symons to Prince Charles and Armand Hammer, 25 November 1985. Symons Papers, Trent University Archives, Fonds 01-003, Box 26: UWC correspondence etc., 1981–85, Folders #18 & 19: 1985.

13 Peterson, *Schools Across Frontiers*, 122.

14 Ibid., 125.

15 Symons Papers, Trent University Archives, Fonds 97-019, Box 41: United World Colleges, Folder #3: UWC 1984 key Folder.

16 T. H. B. Symons to Corrado Belci, 22 June 1982; Antonin Besse to Ian Gourlay, 30 August 1982. Symons Papers, Trent University Archives, Fonds 01-003, Box 26: UWC correspondence etc., 1981–85, Folders #3: UWC: some correspondence, notes and documents, 1981–82; and Folder 4: UWC: some correspondence, notes, and documents, 1982.

17 Peterson, *Schools Across Frontiers*, 129.

18 Notes on meeting held in the British Embassy, Washington, DC, 1 May 1981, presided over by Prince Charles, to discuss plans for establishing UWC in USA. Symons Papers, Trent University Archives, Fonds 01-003, Box 26: UWC correspondence, 1981–85, Folder #1: 1981.

19 Peterson, *Schools Across Frontiers*, 176.

20 Ibid., 177.

21 Armand Hammer to Prince Charles, 20 June 1985; Ted Lockwood to T. H. B. Symons, 10 July 1985; Draft directive of the executive committee of the international board of UWC, 6 August 1985; Annotated telex from Ian Gourlay, 16 August 1985; Notes for remarks to US National Committee of UWC, 23 August 1985; Ted Lockwood to T. H. B. Symons, 26 August 1985; George S. Franklin to T. H. B. Symons, 23 October 1985. Symons Papers, Trent University Archives, Fonds 01-003, Box 26: UWC correspondence, 1981–85, Folder #19: 1985; Box 27: United World Colleges, correspondence, etc. 1985–86, Folder #1: 1985.

22 Notes for remarks at Opening Ceremonies of Armand Hammer UWC, 28 October 1982. Symons Papers, Trent University Archives, Fonds 01-003, Box 26: UWC correspondence, 1981–85, Folder #5: United World Colleges, some correspondence, notes, and documents.

23 1978 paper re: consultations in the UK on proposal for agriculturally oriented UWC in Venezuela discussed by Prince of Wales, 27 June. Symons Papers, Trent University Archives, Fonds 01-003, Box 25: UWC correspondence, 1972–81, Folder #8: United World Colleges and Pearson College of the Pacific.

24 T. H. B. Symons to Prince Charles, 14 October, 1980. Symons Papers, Trent University Archives, Fonds 01-003, Box 25: UWC correspondence, 1972–81, Folder #14: UWC and Pearson College, 1980.

25 Notes on Venezuelan Agricultural College project meeting, 21 May 1980; Notes on Venezuelan Agricultural College curriculum meeting, 3 September 1980. Symons Papers, Trent University Archives, Fonds 01-003, Box 25: UWC correspondence, 1972–81, Folder #15: UWC and Pearson College, 1980.

26 Peterson, *Schools Across Frontiers*, 169.

27 Brief to Prince Charles for visit to Venezuela, 28–30 April, 1981. Symons Papers, Trent University Archives, Fonds 01-003, Box 25: UWC correspondence, 1972–81, Folder #18: 1981.

28 Telex to Sra de Burelli on occasion of handover of farm and college site at Ticoporo. Symons Papers, Trent University Archives, Fonds 01-003, Box 26: UWC correspondence, 1981–85, Folder #4: UWC: some correspondence, notes and documents, 1982.

29 Agenda: UWC international board chairman's meeting for Canadian and UK visitors to New York, 17 February 1981. Symons Papers, Trent University Archives, Fonds 01-003, Box 25: UWC correspondence, 1972–81, Folder #18: 1981.

30 Hand-written note. Symons Papers, Trent University Archives, Fonds 01-003, Box 26: UWC correspondence, 1981–85, Folder #19: 1985.

31 T. H. B. Symons to David Sutcliffe, 7 May 1986. Symons Papers, Trent University Archives, Fonds 01-003, Box 27: United World Colleges, correspondence, etc. 1985–86, Folder #4: 1986.

32 Peterson, *Schools Across Frontiers*, 124.

33 Communication from Sir Ian Gourlay, 13 October 2010.

34 Peterson, *Schools Across Frontiers*, 172.

35 Jack Matthews to T. H. B. Symons, 7 March 1983. Symons Papers, Trent University Archives, Fonds 97-019, Box 41: United World Colleges, Folder #2: UWC 1982–83.

36 Corrado Belci to T. H. B. Symons, 19 November 1985. Symons Papers, Trent University Archives, Fonds 01-003, Box 26: UWC correspondence, 1981–85, Folder #18: 1985.

37 Dr. Ebo Ubahakwe to T. H. B. Symons, 15 October 1986. Symons Papers, Trent University Archives, Fonds 01-003, Box 26: UWC correspondence, 1981–85, Folder #19: 1985; Box 27: United World Colleges, correspondence, etc. 1985–86, Folder #1: 1985.

38 Peterson, *Schools Across Frontiers*, 172.

39 Thomas Symons, "Human Rights and Peace—Some Canadian Priorities? An Overview of the Colloquium," in Michael R. Hudson, ed., *Human Rights and Peace—Les droits de l'homme et la paix*, A report on the proceedings of a colloquium which took place in Ottawa, Feb. 10–11, 1984 (Montreal: Canadian Human Rights Foundation, 1985), 93.

40 Communication from Sir Ian Gourlay, 13 October 2010.

CHAPTER 12

Tom Symons, Independent Schools, and the Canadian Educational Standards Institute

JOHN STEVENSON

Tom Symons has been a lifelong supporter of independent schools in Canada and has played a leading role in their continuing development and response to challenges. Over forty years ago, in 1965, in an address to the Annual Conference of the Canadian Headmasters Association, he paid tribute to the important contribution of independent schools in Canada and expressed the hope that future changes and developments in education would be assisted by the special contribution for which the schools are equipped and of which they are uniquely capable. He impressed those present with his detailed knowledge of the history and development of independent schools, including examples of academic improvements initiated by independent schools and later adopted by public schools.

Fourteen years later, in 1979, Tom Symons delivered another address to the annual meeting of the Canadian Headmasters Association in a joint meeting with the Canadian Association of Principals of Independent Schools for Girls and also the Founding Conference of the Canadian Association of Independent Schools. He noted that at his last address to the Headmasters Association in 1965, he had pointed out the need to work more closely and suggested that it would be a natural and constructive step if the separate organizations could join in one association and how pleased he was to be speaking again on the day this recommendation was adopted, although he "would not comment upon the somewhat less than breathtaking speed with which this proposal was implemented." He noted that changing conditions, such as declining dollars and declining birth rates and the role of technology in society and the growth of cultural pluralism, presented challenges for change and experimentation and offered exciting developments in education. He looked to independent schools to assume their responsibility and to take a leadership position in resolving these issues. He stated that the arguments for diversity and freedom of choice needed to be put forward loud and clear and that there were many valid arguments to be made in support of independent schools: their existence ensures, for example, that the educational system is not a monopoly in control of the state and also provides a significant opportunity for educational experiment and for the search for excellence. This address was such a source of inspiration and practical ideas that the conference made the formal recommendation that all members read it. Over the years, the contents of this address have provided a working "blueprint" for the future of independent schools in Canada.

Dramatic times followed the announcement in 1984 by then Premier William Davis of Ontario that Catholic schools would be fully funded to the end of the secondary level. On 12 June 1984, Premier Davis also announced the creation of three independent educational commissions. The first would establish the system under which the Catholic schools would be funded, the second was to enquire into the financing of all elementary and secondary education in Ontario, and the third was to examine the position of private schools in Ontario. On 2 August 1984, the minister of education announced the appointment of Dr. Bernard Shapiro, then director of the Ontario Institute for Studies in Education, as a one-man commission to enquire into the role and status of private schools in the province's educational system. Shortly after this appointment, the members of the Conference of Independent Schools of Ontario (CIS) met and unanimously agreed to retain Tom Symons to prepare a submission to the Shapiro Commission on behalf of all twenty-three schools in Ontario.

A submission was prepared by Symons, who spent countless hours reviewing and discussing the positions taken on behalf of the schools, which had much in common but had not been accustomed to being so actively associated with one another. The independent schools were not in the habit of preparing joint submissions to government. There was a need at the outset to convince everyone that presenting to the Shapiro Commission was important and necessary. Symons's powers of persuasion were much in evidence as the schools debated what to do and what positions to take.

The brief submitted to Dr. Shapiro on 27 November 1984 stated the belief that it was very important that there be an independent option in education, not just a state monopoly. It emphasized that there ought to be variety and diversity in education, just as there is in society in all its aspects. With that in mind, the brief called for less government regulation and for more freedom for independent schools to develop innovative programs and standards of excellence. Concern was also expressed that direct public funding would likely lead to more restrictions and loss of independence. Recalling that "he who pays the piper calls the tune," the conference recommended that the province not develop any proposals for direct public funding of independent schools.

During this time of major educational reviews, suggestions emanating from the Ontario education ministry indicated that the status quo and the ways of the past for independent schools would come to an end soon. Regulation of private schools was required to avoid various alleged abuses and, furthermore, Ontario ministry inspectors no longer needed for inspection of Catholic schools were available to assume new responsibilities.

In December 1984, a group of chairs and heads met with Dr. Shapiro to discuss the basic philosophy and approach of conference schools regarding government policy in the field of private education. Special mention was made of the conference's statement of four freedoms for independent schools and of the recommendation against direct public funding.

Also, in late December 1984, the government of Alberta received two reports regarding private education in that province. One was prepared by Woods Gordon and was entitled "A Study of Private Schools in Alberta"; the second was the final report of the Committee on Tolerance and Understanding. This latter report was released to the public in February 1985. Each of these reports recommended greater government control over private schools. Draft legislation was presented during the 1985 spring session of the legislature but was subsequently deferred pending the Alberta election then underway. Ontario's independent schools needed to be mindful of what was happening in other provinces.

In October 1985, Dr. Shapiro presented his report to the Ontario government. It was released to the public in early November. In December 1985 and January 1986, Dr. Shapiro carried out a series of public information meetings around the province. During the course of those public meetings, Dr. Shapiro stressed that the status quo relationship between the government and the private schools would be ending. Whether the government decided to fund the private schools or not, there was a need for new legislation and/or regulations. Concerns respecting alleged abuses in some private schools, as well as the growth and expansion of private education over the past decade, were driving this new policy direction.

At its meeting in November 1985, CIS schools agreed to incorporate the Canadian Educational Standards Institute (CESI) and to engage Charles Beer, then assistant headmaster of Pickering College, as interim director for the period 1 January to 30 June 1986 to carry out research and prepare a proposal on the possible operation of such an institute. A working group was created consisting of Barry Wansbrough, headmaster of Hillfield-Strathallan College in Hamilton; Angus Scott, former headmaster of Trinity College School in Port Hope and the executive director of CIS; as well as Tom Symons, John Stevenson, and Charles Beer.

Symons took the lead in strongly encouraging the CIS schools to make this decision since implementation of the Ontario government plans to regulate private schools was delayed. It was his view that this delay created an opportunity for the organization of an independent educational authority, the Canadian Educational Standards Institute (CESI). The purpose of CESI would be to encourage the highest academic standards and a system of evaluation and accreditation of independent schools.

On 3 February 1986, the working group met with Sean Conway, the minister of education, for a broad discussion of the Shapiro Report and its implications. In the course of his remarks, the minister underlined that the status quo could not continue, and thereby confirmed government policy intentions to bring closer regulation to the private education sector. Symons advised that it was clear from this discussion that the independent schools had to move as quickly as they could to establish the proposed new accreditation body.

On 26 March 1986, the institute's Letters Patent were issued dated 22 January 1986, which was the date of application. The CESI board was made up of four representatives from member schools and four educators not directly associated with the schools; at the outset, it consisted of Tom Symons as chair; Walter Pitman, director of the Ontario Institute of Studies in Education; Marnie Paiken, chair of the council for university affairs; and Dr. Ronald Watts, former principal of Queen's University. All of these distinguished educators were recruited by Tom Symons.

On 20 April 1986, the CIS heads met at Appleby College. They reviewed the material prepared by the interim director based on his visits to member schools in February, to independent schools associations in the United States, and in discussions with the executive board of CIS. The formal establishment of CESI was approved, and it was agreed that two pilot evaluation and accreditation projects should be undertaken. CESI proceeded to evaluate Ridley College in June 1986 and Crescent School in November 1986 and accreditation was first granted to these schools.

The role of Tom Symons in these early years following the 1984 announcement of the Shapiro Commission was to lead in articulating and developing the call for the independence of accredited schools from government regulation. He continued to play a vital role in the deliberations of CESI as the chair of the board and subsequently as honorary chairman.

CESI has grown and prospered over the past quarter century. It now includes member schools from all regions of the country and overseas. Over the past year, further changes have taken place, and CESI has been merged with the Canadian Association of Independent Schools, which will then result in one national organization that both supports and accredits independent schools.

The directions and guidelines set forth in the blueprint address given by Tom Symons at the founding conference of CAIS in 1979 for the freedom to engage in educational experiment and to search for excellence remain key elements of the new body. His views and policy directions have continued to shape and support Canada's independent schools for more than forty years.

CHAPTER 13

The Sum of All We Are: Tom Symons and Heritage

CHRISTINA CAMERON

In 1986 Thomas H. B. Symons was appointed chairman of the Historic Sites and Monuments Board of Canada by the Hon. Tom McMillan, then federal minister of the environment. Symons's background and experience made him eminently qualified for this appointment. Yet what made it predictable was the friendship between the minister and the chairman. The two men had worked closely together through much of the previous fifteen years and shared a progressive conservative political philosophy. They had collaborated in the 1970s at the federal Progressive Conservative Party's Policy Advisory Committee (Symons as chair from 1968 to 1976 and McMillan as executive assistant to the committee), at the Ontario Human Rights Commission (Symons as chair from 1975 to 1978 and McMillan as executive officer), and at the Commission on Canadian Studies (Symons as commissioner and McMillan as a senior research associate), which produced the pioneering report on Canadian education, *To Know Ourselves* (1975). Each man believed passionately in a distinctive Canadian culture rooted in its unique political, social, and cultural development.

Appointed to the board at age fifty-seven, Symons brought decades of experience and a grand vision to the job. An academic bureaucrat, he had chaired or been a member of several national commissions dealing with education, Canadian studies, native rights, multiculturalism, Northern studies, and human rights. He therefore had a sound understanding of public policy and Canadian issues as well as finely-honed skills in chairmanship.

Of particular relevance to the work of the Historic Sites and Monuments Board of Canada was his participation from 1980 to 1982 in the Federal Cultural Policy Review Committee, known as Applebaum-Hébert. It is clear from the briefs presented to the committee that historic sites had gained in importance since the Massey Commission thirty years earlier.[1] The final report highlights strong public interest and concern among Canadians, noting "the importance of heritage as a distinct and vital component of Canadian culture."[2] While its formal recommendations dealt only with impact studies for historic sites and a heritage preservation act for the Northwest Territories, the report itself set out a robust policy agenda that included federal heritage legislation for historic buildings and archaeological sites under federal administration, a "heritage first" policy for government accommodations, comprehensive heritage preservation legislation for the Northwest Territories, and compulsory heritage impact studies before altering or disposing of federal historic sites. It also identified the need for leadership and coordination of federal heritage activities, recommending the creation of an arms-length Canadian Heritage Council that—while not operational—would serve as champion and clearing house.[3]

This comprehensive vision influenced Symons's approach to the board. Not deeply interested in the day-to-day operations of the National Historic Parks and Sites Branch, or in the more operational aspects of the board's work, he focused his attention on building the public profile of the board and updating its policies in order to play the role of national champion for heritage. He envisaged a well-known public institution that would be seen as a professional and scholarly body in tune with the current preoccupations of Canadians.

Historic Sites and Monuments Board of Canada

The Historic Sites and Monuments Board of Canada is a seventeen-member statutory advisory body to the minister of the environment on the commemoration of nationally significant aspects of Canada's history. Since its creation in 1919, the board has been supported operationally by a secretariat located in the government organization responsible for parks and sites, currently known as Parks Canada.

When Symons was appointed to head the board, he became the latest in a distinguished roster of chairmen who advocated tirelessly for the preservation of Canada's past. Without exception, his predecessors were historians. The first person who presided over the board from 1919 to 1939 was Brigadier General Ernest A. Cruikshank, a soldier and historian with the Department of National Defence, who had a particular interest in the War of 1812. Subsequent chairmen usually came from university history departments or provincial archives, including Fred Landon, librarian and professor of history at Western University (from 1950 to 1958); Bruce Fergusson, provincial archivist and professor of history at Dalhousie University (from 1960 to 1967); Alan Turner, historian and provincial archivist of Saskatchewan (from 1967 to 1970); Marc La Terreur, professor of history at l'Université Laval (from 1970 to 1978); Leslie Harris, professor of history and dean of arts and science at Memorial University (from 1978 to 1980); and J. M. S. Careless, professor of history at the University of Toronto (from 1981 to 1985).

In *Negotiating the Past* (1990), historian C. J. Taylor describes the evolution and changing focus of the board over time.[4] Its establishment just after the First World War in 1919 signalled a heightened awareness of the important contribution of historic places to the construction of a Canadian identity. It was Canada's first institution dedicated to historic place, although from the outset the board also included persons and events within its scope of interest. In the early years, the board focused on those people, places, and events that helped to define Canada, principally related to territorial exploration, the fur trade, defence, and interaction with Aboriginal communities.[5] The board's main activity was the marking of sites with stone cairns and bronze tablets to commemorate these significant moments in Canadian history.

After the Second World War, when the Massey Royal Commission studied developments in the arts, letters, and sciences, it criticized the board's narrow interest and sphere of action, observing that historic sites were not just forts and battlefields. Remarking that this "appears to be a curious emphasis in a country that boasts not infrequently of the longest undefended border in the world," the Royal Commission urged the Historic Sites and Monuments Board of Canada to broaden its perspective to better reflect Canada's national life and its common achievements. It set a course for the board that was still relevant thirty-five years later when Tom Symons took the helm. It specifically recommended a redesign of the commemorative markers, greater emphasis on preservation, expanded board membership, systematic protection of federal heritage property, and a national leadership role for the board. It called for new funding to enable the board to undertake this expanded program.[6]

Foreshadowing Symons's concerns decades later, the Royal Commission also recommended that the "drab, melancholy, and unreadable" markers be revamped with shorter texts and imaginative designs to match the "excitement and colour of the events or persons commemorated." It encouraged greater emphasis on the preservation and restoration of historic sites, adding architectural design to a consideration of historic significance, because such places offer information about Canadian history in an emotional and striking fashion. The Royal Commission was particularly taken with the urgency of preserving sites that "still have the history of the past written on the very surface of the land, but this history is threatened every day with obliteration." It called for a larger board with more historical scholars and representation from all parts of Canada, a recommendation that was soon carried out with the passing of the *Historic Sites and Monuments Act* (1953). In an effort to protect federally-owned heritage buildings, the Royal Commission called for no further alienation of such properties to other authorities.[7]

In the ensuing decades, the board gave priority to the commemoration of Canada's political and economic history. For example, it spearheaded a program to acquire homes of former prime ministers and Fathers of Confederation. It also supported Prime Minister Diefenbaker's new vision for northern development by recommending a major commemorative program to mark the Yukon gold rush and its surviving steamboats, dredges, goldfields, and historic buildings. By the mid-1980s, when Symons took over the chairmanship, the board was focused on economic history, a priority of the first National Historic

Sites System Plan (1981), and architecture, under the influence of the Canadian Inventory of Historic Building (begun in 1970).

Symons observed early on that Parks Canada lacked enthusiasm for the historic sites sector. He noted that the organization spent most of its time on national park issues, in particular on the Rocky Mountain parks in Alberta and British Columbia. It gave priority to properties that it administered directly, a reflection of its deeply rooted "we are what we operate" culture. The board, on the other hand, was in the business of recognizing national historic sites not necessarily in federal ownership. In this context, the involvement of Parks Canada in supporting national historic sites was seen by some within the organization as a waste of scarce financial and human resources. In the field, the board's plaque ceremonies were grudgingly carried out as modestly and quickly as possible. The year of Symons's appointment was also a time of transition in the senior ranks of Parks Canada. Following the successful celebration of the National Parks centennial in 1985—one hundred years after the establishment of Banff National Park—1986 saw the retirements of the assistant deputy minister, Al Davidson, and of the director of National Historic Parks and Sites, Henri Têtu. It was an opportunity for renewal.

Dealing with Ministers: The Symons Decade, 1986–1996

Prior to the appointment of Tom Symons, interaction rarely occurred between the minister and the chairman of the Historic Sites and Monuments Board of Canada. A notable exception concerned the issue of commemorating Canadian prime ministers at their birthplaces. It is a case that clearly demonstrates the scholarly standards of the board as well as its tenacity in the face of political pressure. The issue arose in 1981 under the chairmanship of Maurice Careless, a professor of Canadian history from the University of Toronto whose prodigious scholarly and intellectual achievements were widely recognized and respected.

The specific matter was the proposed commemoration of the Right Honourable W. L. Mackenzie King at his birthplace in

Kitchener, Ontario. In keeping with its established policy, with very rare exceptions, not to commemorate prime ministers at their birthplaces, the board made a negative recommendation to the minister, the Hon. John Roberts. In 1982, following a request from the minister to reconsider the matter, the board reaffirmed its position on the grounds that "seldom in the course of history have the accomplishments of outstanding individuals been directly linked with their place of birth." The next year a new minister of the environment, the Hon. Charles Caccia, was appointed. He came to the job with the passionate conviction that any person who reached the position of prime minister of Canada should automatically be recognized as having national historic significance. He insisted on meeting the board to discuss the issue. Despite a command performance on Parliament Hill on 18 November 1983, during which Minister Caccia forcefully made his case to the entire board, a flushed and uncomfortable Careless displayed extraordinary intellectual and policy talents in defending the board's stance on the grounds of historical scholarship. He made a peace offering by agreeing to review the board's policy. Following "exhaustive discussion" at two subsequent meetings, the board nonetheless refused to budge. It did offer a consolation prize by suggesting that "should the Minister feel that the Federal Government must make a commemorative gesture at the birthplaces of Prime Ministers of Canada. . . it might do so by means of small bilingual plaques of a standard design, similar to those which have been erected at the gravesites of the Fathers of Confederation."[8] The issue evaporated with a change of minister in September 1984.

Tom Symons reported to seven different ministers during his tenure as chairman. At the beginning of his mandate, he enjoyed an easy and open relationship with his friend and former colleague, the Hon. Tom McMillan, minister of the environment from August 1985 to December 1988. From the outset, Symons made it clear that his line of communication would be directly with the minister, assuring board members that he would raise important or urgent issues immediately. By all accounts, the minister and the chairman frequently discussed board matters, often without departmental staff present—not a customary practice in the federal bureaucracy. At the

November 1987 meeting, Symons "noted that the Minister had a great personal commitment to the work of the board and that he met with the Chairman regularly to discuss heritage matters of mutual interest and concern."[9] This interaction is confirmed by staffer Edna Hall, then working in Prince Edward Island and witness to many discussions between the two men at Brackley Beach, where they both spent their summer vacations.[10]

Minister McMillan's interest in cultural heritage was substantive and genuine. He (and Symons) held the view, not necessarily shared within Parks Canada, that the built and natural environments were one and inseparable.[11] This understanding of heritage was evident when the minister announced his intention to establish a new national park in the South Moresby area of the Queen Charlotte Islands. In the context of confrontations between the Haida people and loggers over land use, the board was asked to review its previous recommendations related to the cultural components of the area. Symons informed the board members that he had requested that this matter be placed on the agenda "both as a result of his intense personal interest in the future of the South Moresby Archipelago and the increasing number of enquiries, directed to him and to the Minister, on this issue."[12] While recognizing that site protection would require cooperation with the Haida, the board advised the minister that "Ninstints, Tanu, and Skedans are certainly outstanding sites, perhaps the most outstanding aboriginal sites in the Pacific Northwest, and failure to protect them and their integrity will result in a profound cultural loss to Canada, and indeed, the world."[13]

The clearest demonstration of the close relationship between the minister and the chairman occurred at the June 1988 meeting in Peterborough. Not only did the minister meet face to face with his board—a rare occurrence—but he also invited an eminent American expert, Professor Robin Winks of Yale University and a former chairman of the American National Park Service Advisory Board, to address the board. Dr. Winks spoke about the parallels and differences between Canadian and American approaches to commemoration and protection of the built heritage.[14] The minister and the professor joined the board for a memorable festive dinner in the garden of the Symons historic residence in Peterborough.

It would never be like this again. Following the Hon. Tom McMillan's electoral defeat, Tom Symons worked with six subsequent ministers. They included three ministers of the environment, the Hon. Lucien Bouchard (1988–90), the Hon. Robert de Cotret (1990–91), and the Hon. Jean Charest (1991–93); one minister of communications, the Hon. Monique Landry (June to November 1993); and two ministers of Canadian heritage, the Hon. Michel Dupuy (1993–95), and the Hon. Sheila Copps (1996–2003).

Symons had little access to Minister Bouchard, remarking to his board colleagues in June 1989 that after half a year he still had not been successful in arranging a meeting with the minister to discuss board business.[15] The most significant exchange between the board and Minister Bouchard occurred over a plaque text to commemorate French-Canadian nationalist and founder of *Le Devoir*, Henri Bourassa. Bouchard thought that the board's text failed to capture the essence of the man. In an unusual gesture, the minister took it upon himself to rewrite the inscription and had the plaque cast and erected in Montreal without consulting the board. In a curious foreshadowing of his own political path, Minister Bouchard changed the text to emphasize Bourassa's "fierce independence" and to underscore his break with the federal party and its leader, Sir Wilfrid Laurier.[16] The board was furious, though the message it sent back to the minister was couched in diplomatic language:

> The Board recognized that it is an advisory body to the Minister and as such it is the Minister's prerogative to accept or reject inscriptions approved by the Board. . . Nevertheless, the Board expressed deep concern that its integrity as an independent and impartial body would be compromised if the Board's empowered function of reviewing and approving plaque texts (plaques which are in the final analysis erected under the Board's auspices and with its imprimatur) is circumvented in a similar manner in the future. Accordingly, it was recommended that no revisions be made to Board texts without reference to the Inscriptions Committee and, further, that in all cases where changes are proposed, appropriate documentation be supplied for Committee review.[17]

The next minister, the Hon. Robert de Cotret, treated the board with benign neglect, or as Symons diplomatically expressed it, "although genuinely interested in the heritage side of his portfolio, Mr. de Cotret was quite understandably consumed at the present with other issues, such as the Green Plan."[18] Nonetheless, it was during de Cotret's watch that the Edmonton Heritage Conference was held in October 1990. Initiated by his ambitious colleague, the Hon. Marcel Masse, then minister of communications with an eye on expanding his heritage responsibilities, the federally-sponsored policy conference brought together hundreds of heritage experts, officials, and advocates from across Canada. Symons scrambled to respond to the hastily-organized initiative, convoking an extraordinary preparatory meeting of the board in September.

Ironically, Minister Masse did not even show up in Edmonton, leaving his colleague Minister de Cotret to represent the federal government. Symons's report to the board after the Edmonton meeting illustrated the breadth of his vision as well as some feistiness with regard to the predatory behaviour of the Department of Communications. In a veiled reference to the simmering turf war between the two departments, Symons noted that Minister de Cotret's presence emphasized "the very real responsibilities which his Department has in the field of heritage in Canada." He pointed out that "despite some initial confusion [i.e., short notice] it had been extremely well attended and could only be termed a success. He expressed some concern that, as the policy evolved, it would focus narrowly on federal heritage policy rather than on a truly national policy, the latter being what was clearly needed."[19] Indeed, he subsequently criticized the final report because it "did not adequately reflect the consensus that there was a clear need for a national heritage strategy based on broad-based consultations."[20]

Symons's relationship with the next minister, the Hon. Jean Charest, was marked by mutual respect. One of the minister's first gestures in the spring of 1991 was to renew Symons's appointment as chairman for a second five-year term. Symons reported that he had regular access to Minister Charest and that they shared an interest in heritage matters and an understanding of the mandate of the Department of the Environment as it related to the commemoration of significant aspects of Canada's natural and cultural heritage.[21]

Together, the two men presided over several high profile events, including the commemoration of the national significance of Queen's University in the presence of His Royal Highness, the Prince of Wales, and four thousand other attendees, as well as the remarkable arrival of the replica Viking ship *Gaia* at the Vineland Revisited ceremony at l'Anse-aux-Meadows National Historic Site in Newfoundland. A mark of the minister's interest was his hosting of a dinner in honour of the board at its November 1991 meeting.[22] This promising start was dampened by the overriding imperative of the 1992 Rio Summit, Canada's Green Plan, and intensification of the national unity debate.

In June 1993, Prime Minister Kim Campbell undertook a major restructuring of the federal government, including the creation of the Department of Canadian Heritage. The transfer of Parks Canada to this large, disparate department inadvertently spared the national historic sites program from disappearing into oblivion. Just prior to the change in government, Environment Canada had been in the process of aligning its programs with the priorities on Canada's Green Plan. Senior officials in the department had concluded that historic places made no contribution whatsoever to the Green Plan and were preparing to recommend cancellation of the program and disposal of national historic sites from the federal inventory. The final decision was to have been taken in July 1993 at a management retreat at the Chateau Montebello. The sudden creation of Canadian Heritage at the end of June, and the transfer to it of Parks Canada (including the historic sites program), had the unintended consequences of stopping this decision as well as repositioning national historic sites and the board in the new department as valuable contributors to Canadian identity.

Following the October 1993 election, Symons, although clearly identified as a Progressive Conservative politically, nonetheless established cordial working relationships with the new Liberal minister of Canadian Heritage, the Hon. Michel Dupuy. Reporting to the board on his meeting, Symons said that Minister Dupuy "had stressed that he was mandated to build Canadian heritage awareness, unity and community and that he had indicated an interest in meeting the members of the board as soon as it was feasible." The minister also committed himself to meet Symons regularly to discuss the board, its work, and its membership.[23] Despite this early enthusiasm, the minister did not show up for the opening of the board's seventy-fifth anniversary symposium in November 1994.

As soon as the Hon. Sheila Copps was named minister of Canadian Heritage in January 1996, she made her priorities clear to the board. She intervened directly in a longstanding board issue about the commemorative focus of Grosse-Île by unilaterally renaming it "Grosse-Île and the Irish Memorial National Historic Site." She assigned a member of her staff to attend board meetings to improve communications. Through her staff representative, she asked the board to examine the tax implications relating to heritage buildings that fell within federal jurisdiction and to advise the minister on what changes might be made to the income tax system to better preserve heritage buildings. She also asked for advice on how to better conserve national historic sites and on a reasoned approach to the devolution of federal heritage properties. Although their interests were well aligned, Symons and Minister Copps had little interaction and he was replaced by a new chairman, Richard Alway, on 10 September 1996.

Enhancing the Profile of the Board

At his first meeting in June 1986, it was evident to an outside observer that Tom Symons came to the board with an agenda. As its new chairman, he clearly intended to transform the board from a quiet debating society to a visible federal institution that would provide national leadership for heritage. He was well aware of the comprehensive roadmap set out by the Federal Cultural Policy Review Committee a few years earlier. He wanted to bring the board out of the shadows and into the mainstream of Canadian life. Often slipping in a phrase that unofficially expanded the board's mandate beyond its specific advisory role on persons, places, and events of national historic significance, Symons habitually introduced the board as the advisory body to the minister, and through him to the government of Canada on all historical matters.

At the June 1987 meeting, Symons initiated a review process by creating an ad hoc board committee to discuss its role and mandate.

Board members agreed that "now was the time. . . to determine whether it should strive for higher public profile and greater visibility and to determine how these ends could be achieved, if found to be desirable."[24] The discussion at the next meeting revealed the ambitious scope of the review. Consideration was given to moving from a traditional advisory role to another administrative and operational model. It was essentially a complete review of the existing system, as recorded in the minutes:

> These discussions would touch on, but not be limited to, the composition of the Board, its role and responsibilities and those of its Chairman, its Vice-Chairman, its members and its Committees. In the course of this exercise the Board would also examine its relationship with, and responsibilities to, the minister, the Department, other levels of government, non-government organizations, UNESCO World Heritage, the heritage community generally and the international dimension to the Board's work. Finally, the Board felt that it was important that it take a hard look at its delivery system and discuss such matters as staff and professional support, marketing and publications (an annual report, a policy document, brochures, etc.) ceremonies and commemorations generally, communications and public relations.[25]

While such discussions continued over the years without major structural change, many incremental measures succeeded in enhancing the board's profile. Symons, like earlier board chairmen, invested time and political capital in ensuring that his recommendations for new board appointments met the highest scholarly and professional standards. It was a standard that also applied to research reports. At this time, the board began to send research papers back for revision, with requests that staff researchers "make every attempt to bring a national perspective to bear in their discussion."[26] Symons also contributed to raising the profile of the national historic sites program within Parks Canada by pressuring the assistant deputy minister to meet face to face with the board as "a regular part of the agenda."[27] In 1987, as an external member of the hiring board to select a new director general of National Historic Sites, he insisted on the professional and scholarly qualifications of the candidates. In 1989, with not-so-subtle prodding from Symons, the Public Service Commission agreed to upgrade the board's "Assistant Secretary" position to the more prestigious title of "Executive Secretary" in order to reflect the increased workload and importance of the role.

As part of his strategy to raise the public profile of the board, Symons relentlessly pursued a robust plaque ceremonies program. He understood the potential value—hitherto unexploited—of unveiling commemorative plaques as a means of involving local communities and interested Canadians in the work of the board. To reinforce the pan-Canadian aspect, he called for board members to preside over ceremonies "in provinces other than their own, in order to underline the national dimension of the Board."[28] New wording was proposed for ceremony invitations, the main change being to create a link between the board and the minister. A vetting process for plaque texts was initiated as a means of involving more Canadians. Prior to this period, Parks Canada usually followed a practice of installing Historic Sites and Monuments Board of Canada plaques with little or no ceremony. It suddenly found itself challenged to produce large public events involving many stakeholders, senior officials, and elected politicians. Symons noted considerable improvement in his 1989 report to the board:

> Professor Symons then spoke at length of the ceremonies that had been held across Canada over the past summer. He characterized the more than 30 ceremonies that had been held in that period as "a solid record of achievement." The Chairman was especially pleased by the great success of the five ceremonies that had been held in Metropolitan Toronto and by the positive reaction by civic and provincial heritage bodies to that strong federal presence. This positive reaction served as an indication of what can be achieved if efforts are made to strengthen ties to sister organizations. He then thanked his colleagues for all they had done to make the 1989–90 ceremony year such a success and was especially pleased to note that a number of members had moved out of province in order that the Board's national scope might be reinforced.[29]

For the same reason, Symons and the board actively supported Heritage Day activities and the short-lived Heritage Awards program of Parks Canada. In a gesture of outreach to other heritage organizations, the Heritage Canada Foundation was invited to make annual presentations to the board. Closer ties were developed with the National Capital Commission, highlighted by a dinner at Kingsmere, the Mackenzie King estate, where the host, NCC Chairman Jean Pigott, gave her inspirational "yellow bus" speech on Canada's capital.[30] When the board held its spring meetings outside Ottawa, site visits were supplemented by ceremonies and receptions as means to connect with local heritage groups.

Symons's sustained effort to produce an annual report is further evidence of his desire to build the board's profile. While his longed-for annual report never materialised due to lack of resources, the 1994 national symposium to celebrate the seventy-fifth anniversary of the Historic Sites and Monuments Board of Canada was a benchmark event that did much to enhance its national leadership role. Symbolically held on Parliament Hill, the meeting brought together over two-hundred-and-fifty participants for three days to debate the future direction of the heritage field. The impact of the symposium went well beyond the actual meeting, since it aired across the country for several months on CPAC (Cable Public Affairs Channel) and eventually made its way into *The Place of History: Commemorating Canada's Past*, published by the Royal Society of Canada in 1997 and edited by Symons with support of a board editorial committee.

Outreach was not limited to Canada. Symons encouraged involvement with international heritage agencies and groups as a means of bringing new ideas and concepts into the work of Parks Canada and the board. He reported regularly to the board on his own contacts with heritage trusts and committees in other countries including the United Kingdom, Italy, Australia, New Zealand, and Mauritius.

This deliberate outreach strategy bore fruit if one judges by the dramatic increase during the Symons period in the workload of the board. It dealt with approximately fifty proposals for designation each year, with agenda documentation rising from about three hundred pages of documentation per meeting at the beginning of the period to one thousand five hundred pages or more. Part of the increased workload stemmed from the recent passage of the *Heritage Railway Stations Protection Act*. But the agenda was also driven by public demand. Applications for designation came from a broad range of proponents, including non-governmental organizations, corporations, members of Parliament, other levels of government, universities, and individual citizens.

Influencing Heritage Policy Renewal

With regard to the development of board policies, the relationship between the board and Parks Canada was a symbiotic one. Once a policy need was identified, the board and the program worked together to develop options. The board then made its decisions on what policies it would recommend to the minister for approval. Each body within its sphere of responsibility could initiate policy discussion; each had an obligation to comment upon the other. Between 1986 and 1996, the years that Symons chaired the board, heritage policy development flourished. Some policies emerged directly from the board's commemorative activities; others came from Parks Canada's renewal of its cultural heritage policies; still others were part of an emerging national framework for historic places.

Policy development took place against a backdrop of government restructuring and budgetary upheaval, which often diverted resources and attention away from the grinding routine of policy work. From 1979 to 1993, Parks Canada (or the Canadian Parks Service, as it was called from 1987 to 1993) was part of Environment Canada; in 1993 it was transferred to the new Department of Canadian Heritage. In March 1996, the federal budget announced that Parks Canada would be transformed administratively into an agency, thereby creating uncertainty about lead responsibility for policy. The Historic Sites and Monuments Board was directly affected by these changes, since it automatically moved in lockstep with Parks Canada to a new minister. Following the 1993 election, the Liberal government undertook a program review exercise to reduce government operations by twenty-five percent as part of its deficit reduction strategy. The future of the board itself was addressed at this time and, as was the case with the Nielsen task force review of the mid-1980s, the board's important role was confirmed by the review. This is worth noting, since a number of other boards, agencies, and commissions were wound up at that time. Overshadowing both departmental change and downsizing was the national unity crisis that followed the failure of the Meech Lake agreement. The ensuing tension influenced the board and Parks Canada through the perceived need to construct and reinforce a strong Canadian identity.

Policies that grew out of the board's work at this time often reflected general trends in the heritage field and occasionally broke new ground. For example, the development of definitions and criteria for historic districts, a painstaking two-year process, resulted in a solid foundation for considering subsequent proposals. In the context of an expanding notion of what constituted built heritage, the board recognized that the significance of some properties went beyond individual monuments or even streetscapes to encompass large districts. It created a definition for the identification of historic districts of national significance:

> Historic districts are geographically defined areas which create a special sense of time and place through buildings, structures and open spaces modified by human use and which are united by past events and use and/or aesthetically, by architecture and plan.[31]

The board added criteria to flesh out this definition. A group of buildings, structures, and open spaces need not individually have national significance but, taken together, the group should present a harmonious representation of one or more styles or constructions, building types or periods; should comprise an outstanding example of structures of technological or social significance; or should share uncommonly strong associations with individuals, events, or themes of national significance. Above all, a historic district must have a "sense of history"—intrusive elements must be minimal, and the district's historic characteristics must predominate and set it apart from the area that immediately surrounds it.[32]

The first historic district to meet this fledgling standard was "a contiguous group of commercial structures. . . representative of the mercantile establishments built in St. John's in the mid-19th century, by those associated with the Newfoundland fisheries and the Atlantic trade." The district included buildings on Water Street as well as the Murray Premises and the open spaces that surround them.[33]

The case of Old Town Victoria revealed the limits of the board's policy. In a decision that displayed a bias towards unity and visual appearance, the board deferred discussion of Old Town Victoria in 1987 in order to consider "sections within the sub-areas of the district, as defined in terms of 19th century commercial activity, in which harmonious groupings of 19th century buildings predominate, thereby creating a special sense of history." The following year, the board rejected the proposal outright on the grounds that it "could not be seen to meet the criteria recently established to identify historic districts." While the board did concede that at some future date it might need to develop a designation category to encompass large and heterogeneous areas like Victoria, it wanted to experience firsthand any "sense of history" that such a diverse collection of buildings and open spaces might have, at an upcoming meeting on Vancouver Island.[34] Concerned with maintaining high standards, the board was uneasy about setting a benchmark for culturally diverse areas. It took nine years for it to finally recommend a reduced commemoration focused on Victoria's Chinatown, arguing that its cohesive group of historical buildings associated with Chinese immigrants created the sought-after sense of history.[35]

One of its key policy decisions came from consideration of the Prince and Hollis Buildings in Halifax, a contemporary development that retained facades of eight pre-Confederation buildings as part of a new shopping and office tower known as Founders Square. The board ruled in 1986 that facades integrated into modern developments were not suitable subjects for commemoration because the integrity of the buildings that once existed had been destroyed.[36] In spite of a passionate appeal from its Nova Scotia member, the board refused to soften this decision, choosing instead to clarify its thinking by explaining that the tower "differs from the historic fabric of the buildings so significantly as to dramatically lessen the cohesiveness of the streetscapes below," that "the traditional functional links between the Prince and Hollis Buildings have been diminished quite dramatically in that they are no longer eight separate premises with eight separate entrances," and that "the new development causes one to experience the buildings from the inside, where spatial and structural elements appropriate to the buildings' exteriors no longer exist."[37] This important decision on the then-popular façadism set the standard for Canadian conservation practice at the time and continues to be the rule today both in Canada and in other countries.

In terms of broad policy development, the board had significant influence on the renewal of the National Historic Sites System Plan, a policy framework that set priorities for thematic research and the selection of historic places. By the time Symons came to the board, implementation of the 1981 System Plan was well underway, with research and site selection on industrial themes like forestry, pulp and paper, fisheries, manufacturing, and petroleum as well as on architectural styles and building types like Queen Anne revival, schools, and drill halls. Both Parks Canada and the board realized that this focus on economic development and architecture was out of step with the current interests of Canadians, who were proposing different kinds of sites for consideration. As a result, three new priorities were chosen to better reflect the diversity of Canadian experience: historic places related to women's history, cultural communities, and Aboriginal history.

The board was instrumental in guiding Parks Canada's strategies to develop these thematic areas, insisting on a combination of academic research and community involvement. One can readily see the influence of Symons's experience in Aboriginal and multicultural issues, and his conviction that heritage discussions required community participation.[38] Addressing a small but significant irritant, the board first changed the name of its committee for Aboriginal matters from the Native Peoples and Natural Resources Committee to the Cultural Pluralism Committee (it later migrated to the Cultural Communities Committee). On approaches to commemorating Native history themes in the North, the board advised caution in the context of land claims negotiations. Rejecting Parks Canada's proposal for one large comprehensive summit with government officials and native organizations, the board recommended a low-key consultative approach through a series of meetings with separate Aboriginal groups in recognition of differing perceptions of what constituted nationally significant aspects of history and in an effort to ensure that discussions regarding commemoration were interactive and focused.[39]

The board also took an important decision regarding the kinds of Aboriginal sites that might qualify for national recognition. In a bold move away from the view that authenticity is necessarily rooted in physical fabric (enshrined in the 1979 Parks Canada policy), the board recognized the subtlety and associative value of historic places in Aboriginal cultures. Indeed, this position differed little from the board's approach, evident from the very beginning, to the commemoration of battlefields and other vestigial sites. In 1990 the board recommended that

> sites of spiritual and/or cultural importance to Native peoples, generally, should be considered to be eligible for designation as national historic sites even when no tangible cultural resources exist providing that there is evidence, garnered through oral history, or otherwise, that such sites are indeed seen to have special meaning to the culture in question and that the sites themselves are fixed in space.[40]

This Canadian recognition of associative values in historic site commemoration was at the forefront of an international trend in heritage policy that was coalescing within UNESCO's World Heritage system. In 1994, the World Heritage Committee also moved toward the intangible in its revised guidelines for cultural landscapes and authenticity. Defining cultural landscapes as "a diversity of manifestations of the interaction between humankind and its natural environment," the committee justified the inclusion of associative cultural landscapes "by virtue of the powerful religious, artistic, and cultural associations of the natural element rather than material cultural evidence, which may be insignificant or even absent."[41] In this same period, global discussions among experts at Bergen, Norway, and Nara, Japan culminated in a shift towards intangible values as part of a World Heritage property's authenticity.[42]

Not all board members were at ease with the implications of the new System Plan priorities related to women's history, cultural communities, and Aboriginal history. In a provocative paper presented to the national symposium marking the seventy-fifth anniversary of the Historic Sites and Monuments Board of Canada, in 1994, British Columbia Board member Charles Humphries regretted the subdivision into "studies history" and the development of "exclusive language" to the detriment of the broad picture of Canadian history.[43] His remarks were hotly contested by many of the symposium participants.

During the Symons era, the board was called on to develop policies to implement the *Heritage Railway Stations Protection Act*, a private member's bill that successfully passed through Parliament without government support in 1988. The work required the board to develop definitions and evaluation criteria, to create a process for developing heritage character statements, and to produce methodologies to assess the acceptability of proposed interventions and disposals. The extraordinary workload was delegated to a new committee chaired by Alberta board member Trudy Cowan. The massive task of assessing several hundred railway stations began in 1989 and lasted for about six years.[44] The real test of the law and the professionalism of the board's work came with a proposal from Canadian Pacific to demolish parts of Windsor Station. In compliance with the law, and at the request of the minister, the board held public hearings in November 1991 to assess the appropriateness of the proposed interventions and formulate its advice to the minister. The Windsor Station case validated the board's capacity to develop and implement operational policy and enhanced its public profile in the Canadian heritage field.

On rare occasions, Symons did not agree with the policy stance taken by his board. One example was the proposal to commemorate postsecondary institutions. While the majority of board members were opposed, on the grounds of the "increasing number and complexity of post-secondary institutions which have been established in recent decades, and the consequent difficulty of assessing their significance to Canada in a rigorous and equitable manner," the minutes record that Symons chided them with a courteous rebuke:

> While the chairman agreed that the Board's recommendation above respecting the commemoration of institutions of higher learning was undoubtedly the way to go for the next leg of the journey, he expressed the hope that the board would be prepared to revisit the matter at some future date, should it become obvious that re-examination would be helpful.[45]

But Symons did not yield quite so graciously to the board's entrenched position on the question of the twenty-five-year rule. This policy originated in a 1990 discussion about business leaders. The existing rule, adopted in 1983, allowed for consideration of individuals five years after their death, with the right to defer consideration for another five years if the board felt that a fair assessment could not be made. Because deferrals were frequent, the board replaced it with a new criterion to apply to business leaders, as follows:

> With the exception of Prime Ministers who are eligible for commemoration immediately upon death, twenty-five years must pass following the demise of an individual before the Board will, under normal circumstances, consider the possible national significance of that person.[46]

The twenty-five-year rule was in a sense reinforced when the board was asked to consider Arthur Erickson's house in Vancouver. Although it agreed that the house had provided a contemplative haven to one of Canada's pre-eminent living architects, the board twice refused to consider it on the grounds that the board lacked distance and perspective.[47] The disagreement came to a head when Symons proposed commemoration of Glenn Gould on the tenth anniversary after his death in October 1982, for he was convinced that the extraordinary achievements of this world-renowned pianist would meet the criterion's wiggle room as an exception to "normal circumstances." The board, however, concluded at its March 1991 meeting (when Symons was absent) that it saw "no compelling reason" to exempt Gould, recommending that "consideration of the possible national significance of Glenn Gould be deferred until such time as he would conform to the board's criterion respecting individuals recently deceased, that is to say until the year 2007."[48]

Symons mounted a considerable campaign to convince his colleagues. At the next meeting, he asked for reconsideration of the twenty-five-year rule, only to be rebuffed by the board, which reaffirmed its position on the grounds that a long waiting period "allowed controversies surrounding an individual to subside and was more likely to result in the commemoration of a person's achievements rather than of his/her memory." The minutes record that "members of the Board thanked Professor Symons for asking that the '25-year rule' be tabled for further consideration as it had provided an opportunity for them to ensure that as a Board they felt comfortable with what was clearly a policy decision of major importance."[49] The saga continued. After a briefing from the chairman, then Minister Charest took advantage of a formal dinner to scold the board on its inflexibility with regard to the twenty-five-year rule.[50] A last-ditch attempt to reverse the decision before the Gould anniversary occurred in June 1992, when the policy was once again put before the board. It stuck to its position.

While much of the board's work was uncontroversial, the case of Grosse-Île was an exception. The island first came to board attention in 1974 as part of a study on lighthouses. In considering its other merits, the board recommended designation for its role as a quarantine station. No reference was made to the general theme of immigration. The catastrophic typhus epidemic suffered by mainly Irish immigrants in the summer of 1847 exemplified the island's role as a quarantine station. The roots of the controversy are perhaps best understood as originating with the 1981 National Historic Sites System Plan and its theme of immigration. The fact that Grosse-Île was rich in in-situ resources (a system plan priority), even if these resources focused primarily on quarantine, led the board to impose a grand historical theme on a place of more limited thematic or historical specificity. The interpretive focus shifted to the long period of immigration from 1832 to 1939. A decade later, controversy was sparked by an insensitive planning proposal that characterized the island as a place of hope and welcome. Following a vociferous public outcry, with letters and petitions from mainly Irish-Canadian groups and individuals, Parks

Canada undertook national public consultations in 1993. In more than one hundred and twenty briefs, participants insisted that, because of the importance that Grosse-Île holds for the Irish in Canada, the primary commemorative theme at the site should relate to the epidemic and not to immigration generally.

The board deliberated on two options: whether to recommend the relocation of the immigration theme to Québec City, thereby allowing Grosse-Île to concentrate on the quarantine theme and the "Irish dimension" of the site, or to propose giving greater emphasis to the "Irish dimension" within the existing commemoration. The board chose the second option, believing that the island's cultural resources were related not only to the island's evolution as a quarantine station but also to its role as the first point of contact for many immigrants to Canada for over a century. It recommended balancing the Canadian immigrant experience with that of the Irish in the tragic epidemic years. While accepting this recommendation, Minister Sheila Copps who, as an opposition member of Parliament, had written a letter to the board to support the Irish-Canadian groups, nonetheless gave greater focus to the Irish dimension by changing the site's name to Grosse-Île and the Irish Memorial National Historic Site on St. Patrick's Day in 1996.[51]

During the period of Symons's chairmanship, the idea of developing a national heritage policy was in the air. It had been recommended in 1982 by the Federal Cultural Policy Review Committee (Applebaum-Hébert) of which Symons was a member. In October 1986, an editorial by the executive director of Heritage Canada, Jacques Dalibard, took up the cause. Symons and the board were not enthusiastic. "While a national inquiry into heritage may, at some point be called for, it is the board's view that it is premature to propose such a review now, as the findings of a number of recent federal Task Forces on heritage and culture have yet to be digested."[52] Nonetheless, elements of a national heritage strategy were periodically discussed by Parks Canada and the board. The secretary reported in 1989 on formal discussions with the provinces to create a Canadian Register of Historic Places.[53] In 1991, Professor William Neville, then chairman of the Manitoba Heritage Council, called on the board to support tax incentives for the preservation of built heritage, noting the difficulty of sustaining heritage programs in an unfavourable tax climate.[54]

But there was little momentum until the Prince of Wales came to Canada in May 1996. During a tour to Fredericton, New Brunswick, in the company of the Hon. Sheila Copps, then minister of Canadian Heritage and deputy prime minister, he remarked on the sorry state of Canada's built heritage and the need for something like the United Kingdom's National Trust. The minister quickly reacted by asking the board to examine current disincentives in the income tax system to the preservation of heritage buildings and to forward recommendations to her regarding changes that might help to improve the situation.[55] This was the beginning of the Historic Places Initiative, a visionary strategy that proposed a suite of measures organized under two general themes: engaging Canadians (registry, conservation standards, fiscal incentives, and a National Trust), and putting the federal house in order (legislation, funding). It was only at the end of Symons's chairmanship that the stage was set for the development of a national heritage policy. He did not actively participate in this phase since his board mandate ended in the summer of 1996.

Conclusion

In reviewing Tom Symons's role as chair of the Historic Sites and Monuments Board of Canada, one is struck by his broad vision and deep conviction. There is a consistent—though gradually widening—vision of the importance and place of heritage in the lives of all Canadians. This conviction is rooted in a lifetime of experience that began in his formative years under the influence of his family. It is evident in his work on the Applebaum-Hébert report in 1982, and is even more explicit in his chapter in *The Place of History* in 1997. Calling it a "fundamental aspect of our national life" and a race against time, Symons argued that "now, more than ever, we should be paying attention to heritage in our country. It is what we have in common. It is what we share."[56]

Symons has a strong sense not just of history and culture but also of place. He brought to the board a holistic view of heritage that grew even wider through his experiences with board work. At the 1994 symposium, he summed it up by stating that heritage is "the total environment inherited from the past. It includes our tangible legacy of physically touchable things. . . as well as our intangible legacy of customs, values, knowledge and beliefs. It is the sum of all we have and are, of the total historical experience of our society to this moment. It is the context into which we have been born and in which we now live. It provides us with our sense of identity and our bearings for the next journeys into coming generations."[57]

Symons held the view that heritage was the business of everyone, and by extension it had to be relevant. During his tenure, the board began to deal with less iconic, more representative sites, partly under the influence of the systems plan approach. It was wrestling not simply with persons, places, and events that were representative of the best but also with the challenge of including the "average," the commonplace, or the community landmark in a system of national historic sites. Because of its transcendent importance, Symons believed in the need for broad public engagement in heritage matters—hence his emphasis on public ceremonies and meetings with stakeholders. He contended that heritage was too important to leave in the hands of a few experts. He bluntly made this point to the mainly expert audience at the 1994 symposium, stating that heritage should not be allowed to become a "sort of middle-class conspiracy that promotes a cozy cream tea culture" and that it needed to be pried loose "from the sometimes dead hand of antiquarians and professional historians and other groups who have tended to monopolize the field, however good their intentions."[58] This is a vision that emphasizes not only the importance of heritage to community and culture but also a very broad (and broadening) idea of what heritage means or should mean.

Symons brought to the Historic Sites and Monument Board of Canada a vast experience in Canadian educational, social, and cultural issues. A networker par excellence, he sought out national and international experts as well as ordinary citizens to discuss and debate heritage conservation work. A leader, a visionary, and a quintessential chairman, he espoused a broad view of Canadian life, scholarship, and a thoughtful consideration of all issues. Behind his soft-spoken, dignified, and extraordinarily gracious demeanour was a man who could be courageous, tenacious, and manipulative when a point of principle was at stake.

His personal quirks are well known. How could one forget the tiny scraps of paper containing vital information that spilled out of his papers? Or documents heavily annotated in black felt pen with lines, circles, arrows, question marks, and exclamations? Or his crumpled old hat that he wore on field trips? He enjoyed visiting historic places, although he never quite got the hang of dressing casually. When challenged by the executive secretary as to why he was formally dressed for a bus tour, Symons responded quietly, "You never know when you will need a blue suit!" Accompanied by his wife Christine, Symons enthusiastically participated in the board's site visits, never failing to thank his hosts and guides with courteous speeches and small gifts.

His ten years as chairman are marked by his efforts to enhance the profile of the Historic Sites and Monuments Board of Canada and to develop policies for the expanding field of heritage conservation. His contribution is well reflected in the 1994 symposium and its legacy, *The Place of History: Commemorating Canada's Past.* It is a mark of his continued interest that, in 2010 at the age of eighty, he accepted an appointment as chair of the Ontario Heritage Trust, the Historic Sites and Monument Board's Ontario counterpart.

Notes

1 Canada, *Summary of Briefs and Hearings: Federal Cultural Policy Review Committee* (Ottawa: Department of Communications, 1982), 63–83.

2 Canada, *Report of the Federal Cultural Policy Review Committee* (Ottawa: Department of Communications, 1982), 107.

3 Canada, *Report of the Federal Cultural Policy Review Committee* (Ottawa: Department of Communications, 1982), 346–47.

4 C. J. Taylor, *Negotiating the Past: The Making of Canada's National Historic Parks and Sites* (Montreal & Kingston: McGill-Queen's University Press, 1990).

5 Parks Canada, Directory of Designations of National Historic Significance of Canada http://www.pc.gc.ca/apps/lhn-nhs/index_e.asp (consulted 14 Nov. 2009).

6 Canada, Royal Commission on National Development in the Arts, Letters and Sciences, 1949–1951, *Report* (Ottawa: King's Printer, 1951), 4, 127–28, 347. http://www.collectionscanada.gc.ca/massey/h5-400-e.html (consulted 14 Nov. 2009).

7 Canada, Royal Commission on National Development in the Arts, Letters and Sciences, 1949–1951, *Report* (Ottawa: King's Printer, 1951), 346–50.

8 Historic Sites and Monuments Board of Canada, *Minutes* (June 1984).

9 Historic Sites and Monuments Board of Canada, *Minutes* (Nov. 1987).

10 Edna Hall, former area superintendent for National Historic Parks and Sites in Newfoundland and Labrador, was district superintendent for Parks Canada in Prince Edward Island from 1986 to 1991.

11 Historic Sites and Monuments Board of Canada, *Minutes* (Nov. 1988).

12 Ibid.

13 Ibid.

14 Historic Sites and Monuments Board of Canada, *Minutes* (June 1988).

15 Historic Sites and Monuments Board of Canada, *Minutes* (June 1989).

16 The most significant change that Minister Bouchard made to the Henri Bourassa plaque inscription is the replacement of the phrase "Il débuta en politique comme libéral mais, à l'occasion de la guerre des Boers, il commença se détacher de Laurier. La rupture devint définitive en 1910" with " Foncièrement indépendant, il s'est éloigné du Parti libéral et de son chef Wilfrid Laurier à l'occasion de la guerre des Boers." Historic Sites and Monuments Board of Canada, *Minutes* (Nov. 1988).

17 Historic Sites and Monuments Board of Canada, *Minutes* (Feb. 1990).

18 Historic Sites and Monuments Board of Canada, *Minutes* (Nov. 1990).

19 Ibid.

20 Historic Sites and Monuments Board of Canada, *Minutes* (March 1991); Department of Communications, *Heritage in the 1990s: Towards a Government of Canada Strategy* (Ottawa: 1990).

21 Historic Sites and Monuments Board of Canada, *Minutes* (June 1991).

22 Historic Sites and Monuments Board of Canada, *Minutes* (Nov. 1991).

23 Historic Sites and Monuments Board of Canada, *Minutes* (Nov. 1993).

24 Historic Sites and Monuments Board of Canada, *Minutes* (June 1987).

25 Historic Sites and Monuments Board of Canada, *Minutes* (Nov. 1987).

26 Historic Sites and Monuments Board of Canada, *Minutes* (Nov. 1986).

27 Ibid.

28 Historic Sites and Monuments Board of Canada, *Minutes* (Nov. 1987).

29 Historic Sites and Monuments Board of Canada, *Minutes* (Nov. 1989).

30 Historic Sites and Monuments Board of Canada, *Minutes* (Nov. 1991).

31 Historic Sites and Monuments Board of Canada, *Minutes* (Nov. 1987).

32 Ibid.

33 Historic Sites and Monuments Board of Canada, *Minutes* (June 1987).

34 Historic Sites and Monuments Board of Canada, *Minutes* (Nov. 1987).

35 Historic Sites and Monuments Board of Canada, *Minutes* (Nov. 1995), 46.

36 Historic Sites and Monuments Board of Canada, *Minutes* (Nov. 1986).

37 Historic Sites and Monuments Board of Canada, *Minutes* (June, 1988).

38 Symons served as president of the Canadian Association in support of Native Peoples (1972–73); was co-chairman of the Canadian Conference on Multiculturalism (1973); and was chairman of the Canadian Arctic Polar Research Commission Study (1988).

39 Historic Sites and Monuments Board of Canada, *Minutes* (Feb. 1989).

40 Historic Sites and Monuments Board of Canada, *Minutes* (Feb. 1990).

41 *Operational Guidelines for the Implementation of the World Heritage Convention*, WHC/2 Rev. (Feb. 1994), 14.

42 Knut Einar Larsen, ed. "Nara Document on Authenticity," in *Nara Conference on Authenticity* (Paris: UNESCO, 1995), xxi–xxiii; Christina Cameron, "From Warsaw to Mostar: the World Heritage Committee and Authenticity," *Bulletin of the Association for Preservation Technology* 39, no. 2–3 (2008): 19–24.

43 Charles W. Humphries, "The Past and the Culture of Compliance: My History, Your History, No History," *The Place of History: Commemorating Canada's Past*, ed. Thomas H. B. Symons (Ottawa: Royal Society of Canada, 1997), 119–26.

44 Historic Sites and Monuments Board of Canada, *Minutes* (Feb. 1989; June 1993); ibid. (June 1996), 2.

45 Historic Sites and Monuments Board of Canada, *Minutes* (Nov. 1992).

46 Historic Sites and Monuments Board of Canada, *Minutes* (Nov. 1990).

47 Historic Sites and Monuments Board of Canada, *Minutes* (June 1992, June 1993).

48 Historic Sites and Monuments Board of Canada, *Minutes* (March 1991).

49 Historic Sites and Monuments Board of Canada, *Minutes* (June 1991).

50 Historic Sites and Monuments Board of Canada, *Minutes* (Nov. 1991).

51 Historic Sites and Monuments Board of Canada, *Minutes* (June 1992; June 1993; Nov. 1993; Nov. 1994).; ibid. (June 1996), 47.

52 Historic Sites and Monuments Board of Canada, *Minutes* (Nov. 1986).

53 Historic Sites and Monuments Board of Canada, *Minutes* (Nov. 1989).

54 Historic Sites and Monuments Board of Canada, *Minutes* (June 1991).

55 Historic Sites and Monuments Board of Canada, *Minutes* (June 1996), 51–52.

56 Thomas H. B. Symons, "Commemorating Canada's Past: From Old Crow to New Bergthal," *The Place of History: Commemorating Canada's Past*, ed. Thomas H. B. Symons (Ottawa: Royal Society of Canada, 1997), 15.

57 Ibid., 19.

58 Ibid., 13, 22.

CHAPTER 14

Tom Symons and the National Statistics Council

IVAN FELLEGI

The National Statistics Council (NSC) played a subtle but crucial role in the evolution of Statistics Canada as probably the best regarded national statistical agency in the world. And, as its founding chair, Tom Symons played a crucial role in the development of the council. Indeed, not only was Tom its founding chair, but he provided leadership to it for some twenty years. In order to appreciate his contribution, it is important to understand the subtle role of the council as it evolved under Tom's chairmanship.

The National Statistics Council

Statistics Canada is a highly centralized national statistical agency, operating under a strong Statistics Act. The act, among its other features, provides unlimited subject matter scope for the agency while also spelling out twenty specific areas in which it must be active—such as population, agriculture, health and welfare, education, labour and employment, prices and the cost of living, manufacturing, commerce with other countries, etc. By statute, the agency operates under a minister. The chief statistician, "under the direction of the Minister, supervise(s) generally the administration of this Act and control(s) the operations and staff of Statistics Canada." The act assigns the legal mandate for the preservation of statistical confidentiality to the chief statistician, not to the minister.

In addition to these legal provisions, a strong tradition has evolved in this relationship: Statistics Canada is treated at arm's length by the minister and the government. Successive governments confirmed and reconfirmed that statistical information should be free of political interference. So, while the government establishes the total budget for Statistics Canada, statistical priorities within the budget are set by the chief statistician following extensive consultation with key users in governments (federal and provincial), the private sector, academics, and other key users. As an additional safeguard, all statistical information is made available by Statistics Canada to all members of the public at the same time. A so-called pre-release of less than twenty-four hours is made of a handful of key economic series to designated senior officials for purposes such as the orderly management of money markets. The very limited time available to them ensures it is visibly impossible to alter either the statistics themselves, or, indeed, their analysis.

So, while the chief statistician reports to Parliament through a minister, the agency's professional independence is unquestioned. Although nowhere stated in its mandate, council sees as its fundamental role to protect this independence.

In the early 1980s, Statistics Canada embarked on a conscious program of strengthening its active consultative mechanisms with key clients and broadly-based representatives of the national interest. This included the establishment of a series of bilateral senior committees with key federal departments and the setting up of some ten to fifteen professional advisory committees. The latter consisted of experts (typically from outside government) in such areas as demography, labour, national accounting, price measurement, and service industries.

Coincidentally, in 1985, the government established the National Statistics Council, by Order-in-Council, at the apex of the agency's consultative mechanisms. Its formal mandate is very brief: it is to "advise the Chief Statistician in setting priorities and rationalizing Statistics Canada programs." In line with other aspects of Canadian public policy on statistics, a careful balance was attempted between strengthening the policy relevance of the agency while maintaining its professional independence: members of the council are appointed by the *minister*, but their duty is to advise the *chief statistician.*

There are about forty members. While there are no rules for representation, the following practice evolved in discussions with Tom Symons and has generally been adhered to:

a. All members serve in their individual capacities—there are no formal representational appointments.
b. Members are interested and prestigious analysts of some aspect of Canadian life, but few are professional statisticians.
c. Some members from Statistics Canada's various professional advisory committees serve on the council. This ensures the availability of a wide range of subject matter knowledge within the council, as well as linkage with the agency's other advisory bodies.
d. At least one senior journalist on social or economic affairs is a member.
e. Membership is selected in such a fashion as to ensure appropriate knowledge of the different provinces and territories of Canada.
f. No federal official is a member of the council (except as in (g) and (h) below). This enhances the *de facto* independence of council to "speak up" should it be necessary.
g. The chief statistician is an *ex officio* member.
h. An assistant chief statistician serves as secretary.

Most of the initial members, including Tom Symons as its chair, were appointed by the minister from a list of persons recommended by the chief statistician. Subsequent appointments have been proposed to the minister by the chief statistician following discussions with the chair of the council.

As a result of these measures, the council is a very knowledgeable, influential, and broadly-representative group. Given its strictly advisory role, its influence derives from the individual prestige of its members.

The council normally meets twice a year, each time for a day and a half. There are two regular agenda items: "Statements by Members," in which council members may raise questions or concerns either for immediate response or subsequent discussion, and an in-depth report by the chief statistician on recent developments at Statistics Canada (including new substantive initiatives, forward planning, budgetary expectations). Other agenda items usually deal with major statistical or policy issues, such as census content, environment statistics, longitudinal data, issues in social statistics, national accounts, dissemination practices, pricing policy, privacy and record linkage, contingency planning in the face of expected budget cuts, the provincial component of the national statistical system, and significant statistical information gaps.

Each meeting's agenda is selected from matters raised by members during previous meetings, and from issues identified by Statistics Canada in discussions with the chairman. From time to time, a subgroup of the council has been formed to deal with certain particular issues in greater depth between council meetings (e.g., access to historical censuses, research access to Statistics Canada data, public communications during census operations.).

The council generally provides feedback to the chief statistician through a discussion among its members. Consensus is usually (though not always) achieved. Resolutions and formal recommendations are rare, although the chairman has been authorized by council on a few occasions to write to the responsible minister—and on one occasion to key deputy ministers. Topics included securing funding for testing the 1991 Census, the impact of potential additional budget reductions on the outputs of the agency (and hence on its clients), and non-budgetary administrative hindrances to the agency's cost-recovered service functions. In general, these rare external interventions were thoughtfully received and, undoubtedly combined with other considerations, were favourably dealt with on more than one occasion.

While strictly speaking, these external demarches went beyond the council's formal mandate to advise the chief statistician, members of the council, under the gentle guidance of Tom, felt an obligation to act as guardians of the public good in respect to statistical information. By so doing and through the power of precedent, they extended their formal function in a subtle but important way.

Having been associated with council for over twenty years, I can assert that it played a major role in the evolution of Statistics Canada. And, as its founding chair, a role in which he also continued for some twenty years, Tom shaped the council. I want to detail his role under the following headings: Tom, the statesman; Tom, the consummate chairperson; and Tom, the incredibly thoughtful friend.

Tom, the Statesman

Tom had a clear set of principles for the functioning of council. But Tom, the statesman, would never articulate them as rigid rules. These are, therefore, *revealed* principles identified by observing his behaviour and gentle guidance:

1. Council derives its influence from the eminence of its members.
2. It advises the chief statistician about major program priorities and with respect to appropriate responses to external challenges to Statistics Canada's funding, mandate, or non-political objectivity.
3. It does not involve itself in internal management issues.
4. It provides its programatic advice without necessarily seeking consensus and certainly avoids voting.
5. It is guided by its very brief formal mandate, but if need be it is ready to stretch this mandate within reason.

Each of these principles had significant implications for the functioning of council. The first principle turned out to be particularly wise: as has been mentioned, council derived its mandate from a cabinet decision that gave it modest direct authority so its weight at any rate could only be based on the eminence of its membership. But I would go as far as suggesting that even if cabinet had devolved major substantive powers to the NSC, Tom the statesman would have felt more comfortable in basing its standing on the substantive merit of its discussions, which in turn depended on the intrinsic quality of its members. But given the fact that the appointments were made by the ministers responsible for Statistics Canada, this principle had associated with it some potential hazards. To avoid them, Tom would try to meet each and every minister during his long period of chairmanship—and there were numerous ones. He actually succeeded in impressing on each of them the absolute necessity of quality choices. Anyone who knows Tom will instantly recognize how effective he must have been in these situations: he has a unique combination of friendliness and gravitas about him. And, of course, his exceptional personal reputation was of major help here as well. As a result of his demarches, every minister at least tacitly accepted the principle that he or she will receive nominations jointly from the chair and the chief statistician and that, with rare exceptions, the appointments would be made from people on these lists. During Tom's tenure there must have been something like a hundred council appointments; and, though in a handful of cases our nominations were not accepted, I can recall only two instances when a person not so nominated was actually appointed. In these two cases, Tom certainly went out of his way to make each one feel welcome by extending every personal and professional courtesy. In the first case, after perhaps two meetings, the person asked to be relieved; in the second case, he quietly served one term and then was replaced.

While the first principle established the credibility of council, the second principle determined its modus operandi. Meetings of council were carefully prepared: agendas were partly determined by members voicing issues that they thought could usefully be discussed, and by the chief statistician flagging other ones that he particularly thought would benefit from the advice of council. Tom and I would then discuss between meetings what the actual agenda should be. Most agenda items would be initiated by a brief presentation from Statistics Canada outlining the issues and the options; this would be followed by a wide-ranging and typically exceptionally enlightening discussion by members. Reflecting upon the exceptional standard of these discussions, I have often referred to council only half jokingly as my "permanent Royal Commission."

The third principle is self-explanatory, but making it effective required the proverbial Symons tact. With the best of will all around, it was a periodically recurring temptation to start acting like a board of directors. But Tom would, with characteristic gentle firmness, remind members of the wisdom of avoiding such attempts.

The fourth principle required perhaps the gentlest touch to make it effective. Yet urging council to avoid the need for voting and formal decisions was one of the most important contributions that Tom made to the effective functioning of council. These meetings are *advisory* in nature: by avoiding the constraint of having to channel the discussion to a consensus, he encouraged and guided the discussion in such a manner that all views got fully expressed and the richness of different perspectives was fully articulated. It is, perhaps, difficult for non-members to realize just how illuminating and stimulating council discussions have been, in spite of the fact that there were typically over thirty members of council present. Tom had a unique ability to create an environment in which everyone felt not only that he or she could contribute freely but that each person's views were genuinely appreciated. I do not remember a single meeting or agenda item whose discussion did not generate truly insightful contributions. Just as important, at every occasion just about all members spoke, typically several times.

Finally, as far as the fifth principle is concerned, Tom the statesman was certainly guided by the formal mandate of council. But he was equally seized with the importance to Canadians of relevant public goods—such as good national statistics. The essence of his statesmanship was to know just when and how it is appropriate to take a flexible interpretation of the formal mandate to safeguard and further develop these public goods. Potentially damaging large budget cuts qualified. Even more importantly, it was Tom who impressed on council that perhaps its single most important task was being vigilant about any sign of politicization of Statistics Canada—although there is no mention of this task in any of the documents defining the formal role of council. He clearly realized that nothing could cause greater damage to this source of public goods.

There is no doubt in my mind that Tom was the dominant personality shaping the National Statistics Council to become the uniquely effective body that it has become; at the same time, his influence made membership in this unpaid activity a source of prestige and, indeed, pleasure for its members: in spite of each member's busy schedules, meetings were extremely well attended. Indeed, as one of the members put it, "We should be paying for the privilege of attending."

Tom, the Consummate Chairperson

I have already touched on Tom's unique ability to get the very best out of a large group of people. I have spoken to many members of council about this special gift that all admired. In fact, we used to say that he could provide graduate-level instruction on chairmanship. I am still not sure I understand every aspect of it, but here are a few insights.

First and foremost, he felt and showed respect for every speaker: he truly was interested in their views and this communicated itself to everyone.

Second, he was always prepared. Sometimes he asked for help in preparing his introductory comments, but one way or another he always had them. And they were always both substantive and graceful.

Third, in all the years I observed him, I can think of no occasion when he had to cut off discussions due to time constraints—and this in spite of charged agendas and lots of speakers on every topic. Sometimes he asked that people be concise, but this was never a polite signal to withdraw their wish to comment. Yet, and here is the magic, agendas were always completed and always within approximately the allotted time. This was because everyone genuinely liked and respected him.

Fourth, he was particularly attentive to people who had greater difficulty socialising. He sought out such people during coffee breaks and dinners and not only involved them but arranged for others to engage them as well. He was particularly appreciative when they subsequently intervened in the discussions.

Fifth, he was singularly attentive to personal developments involving members and made sure the others were as well. He was aware of any honours or decorations that anyone received and he genuinely celebrated the recipients. Less publicly, but just as genuinely, he kept track and discretely followed up on health or other personal problems.

Finally, he truly managed to become friends with all the forty-odd members of council. And this brings me directly to my final point—Tom, the incredibly thoughtful friend.

Tom, the Incredibly Thoughtful Personal and Institutional Friend

I am particularly fortunate to count Tom among my friends. He has the rare ability to be always there when one needs him, yet his awareness of life's major events is never intrusive. He will literally go out of his way to share the moments of joy of his friends. I will never forget how he turned up, unexpectedly, when I received a major award, even though this occasioned a special trip for him from Peterborough to Ottawa.

Tom is not only a personal friend, but he is also a friend of Statistics Canada. Just one example will suffice. He had already retired from the chairmanship of the NSC when the government was looking for members for an external panel constituted to review the programs of Statistics Canada and make recommendations for significant reductions. Tom's name naturally emerged. Over a period of several weeks, he worked tirelessly not only to familiarise himself with all of Statistics Canada's major outputs, but also to ensure that others on the panel shared his insights. While his enormous personal integrity prevented him from keeping me informed of the activity of the panel, I felt that the fate of the organisation was in good hands because of Tom's presence there—not to frustrate the government's intent but to help implement it in the most intelligent manner possible.

It should be obvious that I am not an unbiased observer of Tom's activities over his twenty years as the chair of the National Statistics Council. As I mentioned previously, he has been a good friend of Statistics Canada and of mine. I have a great fondness for Tom and a deep admiration for all that he has done both for my organisation and for Canada.

CHAPTER 15

Unexplored Frontiers: Tom Symons and the Arctic Landfall of an Elizabethan Adventurer

STEPHEN ALSFORD

If fortune is kind, one may have occasion, during the course of an education or career, to come under the tutelage of giants—or at close enough quarters to observe and learn from them. When, as a history undergraduate, I was exposed to the Symons report, *To Know Ourselves*, I hardly imagined that later in life I would work closely with its renowned author, over the course of more than a decade, on the Meta Incognita Project: something I look back on as one of the most rewarding and self-developing experiences of my career.

The project took its name from a term approved by Queen Elizabeth I for the Arctic region (southern Baffin Island) to which the adventurer Martin Frobisher had led three entrepreneurial expeditions between 1576 and 1578. Beginning as an attempt to find a northwest passage through to fabled Cathay, it was repurposed into an ambitious mining and (abortive) colonization venture after alchemical analyses of ore deluded potential backers into the belief that it contained gold. Just how this mistake came about, and how maintained—leading to considerable investment not only in the sizable third expedition but also in the construction of extensive smelting facilities in England—was one of the mysteries on which project researchers hoped to shed light. As is often the case, years of research were not to solve the mystery definitively, but narrowed down the range of possible solutions and left much better understood the circumstances surrounding it—circumstances that included the preparedness of Frobisher to do whatever necessary to win fame and fortune, the similar ambition and flawed science of alchemist-assayers active in Elizabethan England, the interplay of international competitiveness for empire and of gold fever on leading members of Elizabethan society, and a desire to expand the boundaries of the civilized world as it was understood by Europeans. The Meta Incognita Project has rehabilitated that episode in history from the status of a dead-end side-street to one that prefigures key themes in the stories of European maritime exploration and of the Old World exploitation and colonization of North America, particularly Canada's North.

The project began, to be frank, with a squabble between researchers: that type of competitive scholarly energy which, if harnessed and channelled, can prove all the more fruitful. To set the scene for that, we must look back to 1861, when American explorer Charles Francis Hall, searching for traces of the Franklin expedition in the Baffin Island region, had identified an islet[1] off the north-eastern coast of Frobisher Bay as the base camp established by Martin Frobisher on his second expedition. Some of the "relics" brought back from Kodlunarn Island, as Hall rendered the Inuit name for the place (Qallunaan now being more politically correct),[2] were deposited with the Smithsonian Institution. Interest in this strand of the history of Elizabethan maritime ventures, of initial attempts to establish colonies on future Canadian territory, and of early contact between Europeans and Native North Americans revived under the approach of the four hundredth anniversary of the Frobisher expeditions, when the Royal Ontario Museum sent historical archaeologist Walter Kenyon to survey the island (1974). Ten years earlier, the Historic Sites and Monuments Board of Canada (HSMBC) had mooted whether investigation and/or protection of the historic remains on the island—symbolically significant, but visually unspectacular—was warranted. The board made a positive recommendation in this regard, also recommending historical research be undertaken, and declared Kodlunarn a site of national historic importance; but it stopped short of designating it the national historic site that would have entailed a specific governmental responsibility. Consequently, no concrete action followed at that time.

In 1981, the Smithsonian showed new interest by conducting its own survey of Kodlunarn and other sites in the area suspected as having some connection with the Frobisher voyages; it also worked with Canada's National Historic Parks and Sites (NHPS) on analysis of some of the Hall artifacts. Dr. William Fitzhugh, director of the Smithsonian's Arctic Studies Center, followed up his initial survey with a return visit in 1990, as part of his wider search for Arctic sites of historical interest. The stimulus was not solely the Frobisher expeditions but the fainter prospect that evidence might come to light of even older cross-cultural contact: Viking and Inuit.[3] He was now seeking an archaeological permit from the Prince of Wales Northern Heritage Centre (PWNHC), the authorized permitting agency, with a view to a more detailed investigation of sites believed to contain Frobisher-related materials, and had assembled a team of American and Canadian scientists. At the same time, Arctic archaeologists in Canada, notably Dr. Robert McGhee of the Canadian Museum of Civilization (CMC) and Dr. James Tuck of Memorial University of Newfoundland, had similar interests and had paid a visit to Kodlunarn during the ice-free season in 1990, reporting on their return that the historic sites there were better preserved than anticipated but in urgent need of protection for the future. The significance of the Frobisher sites to Canadian history (and, further, ramifications for the sensitive issue of Canadian sovereignty in the Far North) engendered some concern as to whether any investigation of the sites ought to be an initiative directed from the United States. A further concern was for the potential harm to the heritage character of the island, if archaeological excavation was not carefully managed.

To assure Canadian involvement in any such initiative, and to avert any risk that rival claims to direct investigation might sour relations between the Smithsonian and the CMC, the latter's executive director, Dr. George Macdonald, felt there was need for an advisory or steering committee with high-level representation from key Canadian institutions having mandates for archaeological investigation and site management; such a committee would be tasked with making sound recommendations to those same, and other interested, institutions on appropriate actions in matters of research and site preservation, as well as with coordinating some of those efforts. He asked Tom Symons if he would chair this Meta Incognita Project Steering Committee. It was a shrewd and fortuitous choice. As an ex officio member of the HSMBC, Dr. MacDonald had direct experience of the statesmanlike leadership of Professor Symons, as chairman of the board, and had been able to discuss with him the challenge faced. He knew that Symons had not only a reputation that commanded respect but also the political acumen and diplomatic skills to steer a research project through anticipated murky waters of professional jealousies and institutional jurisdictions.

The committee was put in place in November 1990. Besides Professor Symons and Dr. MacDonald, the membership comprised the directors of the Archaeological Survey of Canada,[4] National Historic Parks and Sites branch of Parks Canada,[5] and the Northern Heritage Centre.[6] These were to be augmented by voices from the Frobisher Bay region: an archaeologist from Arctic College in Iqaluit[7] and a member of the Inuit community.[8] Between 1990 and 2005, the committee held seventy-four meetings, the majority by teleconference but a number face to face in Ottawa or, occasionally, farther afield.

At the inaugural meeting, members identified the immediate issues the committee would have to address. One was how urgent archaeological research on Kodlunarn might be. It was known that the island was subject to severe temperatures, to wave action produced by high tides with strong currents, to violent winds and occasional storms, as well as to grating of sea ice along its shores; but the extent and rapidity of the resultant coastal erosion, and whether it jeopardized historical remains, were unknowns. At the same time, there was awareness of increased interest in Arctic sites on the part of tour operators, creating the prospect of another source of damage to the heritage landscape (fragile in an environment that lacks potency in self-repair) from group visitation and even souvenir hunting. On the other hand, encouraging archaeology in the face of such threats had to be balanced against the damage to the landscape that excavation itself might cause. There was thus not only a need for research but also for historic resource management into the future. An additional complication was the impending resolution of Inuit land claims and their effect on jurisdictional decisions (such as archaeological permits), as a territory of Nunavut moved toward becoming a constitutional entity. A second question was that, if research were to proceed, who should take the lead, while a related third was the role of the steering committee. To help it come to terms with these issues, the committee invited briefings at its initial meeting from Dr. Tuck and Dr. Fitzhugh, the latter bringing several members of his proposed team, including archaeologist Dr. Réginald Auger of Université Laval, who was now taking the lead in seeking an archaeological permit and a funding grant, and geologist Dr. Donald Hogarth of the University of Ottawa.

Tom Symons, recognizing that there was both a valid national interest and a natural international one in researching the Frobisher expeditions, favoured a cooperative effort by the various interested parties and a multidisciplinary approach that might encompass initiatives not envisaged by those researchers currently interested. At the same time, there was general agreement that, as far as work on Kodlunarn was concerned, it was advisable to proceed cautiously until more data could be collected on erosion and until closer consideration had been given to the full scope of research and appropriate investigative mechanisms and techniques. The "full steam ahead, damn the torpedoes" approach of the Fitzhugh team was worrying to the committee. Yet at the same time it did not wish to dampen the ardour for a worthwhile research initiative that already had momentum.

The second meeting of the committee continued its fact-finding efforts, with briefings from Dr. McGhee and Dr. William Taylor (Canada's first professional Arctic archaeologist and Dr. MacDonald's predecessor as director of the national museum of human history), the latter relating the experience of the L'Anse aux Meadows project, another program of international research focused on a Canadian site and directed by a steering committee. The Meta Incognita Project Steering Committee was conscious that it had no formal authority, only informal influence over the institutions represented by its membership. However, it was shortly to receive authorization from the Government of the Northwest Territories to advise it on what permits should be issued for research on Frobisher sites.

A further need was felt for someone with suitable expertise to have closer oversight of the overall project than was possible for a committee that met at intervals; that is, who could gather information about issues impacting on the project, liaise with researchers, explore possible funding sources, and report to and advise the committee on planning for a research program. Tom Symons pursued a suggestion by Dr. Charles Arnold (the Northern Heritage Centre representative on the Steering Committee) for a project coordinator, pointing out that what was needed was not just a good scholar but someone able to work constructively with the project researchers. With the committee's agreement, he recruited the well-respected Dr. Taylor for the role;[9] the two men had a prior working relationship through the Social Sciences and Humanities Research Council (SSHRC), were both energetic champions of Canadian studies, and shared a deep respect for the Aboriginal cultures of Canada.

After Dr. Taylor reported on his consultation with various of the researchers on the Fitzhugh team, the committee felt sufficiently well informed to endorse a two-pronged expedition for the summer of 1991 that was aimed primarily at gathering information to feed into the longer-term planning for research. Drs. McGhee, Tuck, and Auger visited Kodlunarn to conduct a careful surface survey and to examine selected site features using small test excavations and non-intrusive methods (notably ground-probing radar).[10] Dr. Fitzhugh took a second team to survey other sites of potential interest in Frobisher Bay and to initiate excavations at several historic Inuit sites, the latter work conducted primarily by Canadian Lynda Gullason and American Anne Henshaw. Dr. Hogarth spent time with both teams, helping to identify off-Kodlunarn sites with Frobisher associations, assessing the threat of erosion to the island, while at the same time pursuing his own geological survey. A conference of researchers and scientists was held at the CMC in October, for collegial sharing of information on what had been accomplished and on preliminary findings, as well to inform the steering committee as it gave thought to longer-term goals for research and site management. Shortly thereafter was set in motion an oral history component of research, to probe the survival among Inuit elders of traditions concerning early contact with Europeans.[11]

The committee's immediate preoccupation was with the long term. Symons was concerned that Kodlunarn not be excavated and then abandoned. With the assistance of Dr. Taylor, the committee produced a position paper as a milestone on the road towards a management plan, and in mid-1992 distributed this to project researchers, for comment, with copies to several federal and territorial ministers of pertinent jurisdictions, in the hope of obtaining greater or more explicit commitment (particularly in terms of assuming long-term responsibility for Kodlunarn). This was followed up with a presentation by Dr. MacDonald to the HSMBC Cultural Pluralism Committee, and then a presentation to the full board; the former made a recommendation to the latter, which accepted it to go forward for the consideration of the minister of the environment. Yet while this recognized the historical importance of Kodlunarn, it did not go so far as to give the NHPS a clear mandate to manage the site. It remained uncertain whether the Department of Indian and Northern Affairs ought rather, as land manager, to be the lead agency or what would be the role of the Inuit Heritage Trust, then in process of being established as part of the emerging Nunavut.[12]

Noting the unique character of the Kodlunarn site and its significance to Canada, both in regard to the history of European exploration and to early European-Inuit contact, the position paper stated the belief that Canada should take the lead in any research efforts there and in protecting the fragile heritage resources; it saw in situ preservation and protection of those resources as the primary concern, with research interests secondary, though valid. This position led the committee to withhold approval for further work on the island in 1992, beyond putting markers in place to help measure the erosion rate, although it supported the completion of excavations at the Inuit encampment sites examined in 1991—in part because erosional damage some had sustained called for a rescue strategy—and continued off-island work by Dr. Hogarth. The restrictions placed on excavation in 1992 did not sit well with Drs. Fitzhugh and Auger but, although frustrations had bubbled up during presentations and discussion at the Canadian Archaeological Association annual meeting in May, the committee's balanced approach to opposing needs was for the most part managing to keep matters contained yet moving forward.

The position paper reflected the steering committee's belief not only that researchers should make every effort to share their data, and interpretations thereof, in a collegial and professional manner but also that results from research ought to be communicated to wider audiences and through a range of media. Apart from one press release about the 1991 field research, the committee was holding off on public announcements, not wishing to draw too much attention to sites still unprotected. And yet, at this time, the first fruits of this dissemination goal appeared. Under the auspices of the committee, the findings of the 1991 expedition and subsequent laboratory analysis of excavated materials were published.[13] Hard on its heels, a second publication presented more detailed analysis of geological evidence from the Arctic sites, contextualized by archival research into the mining, assaying, and smelting aspects of the Frobisher expeditions.[14] Dr. McGhee prepared a video that could prove useful, in due course, for public viewing[15] and began to give thought to a public exhibition (a process typically requiring several years from gestation to fruition).

Meanwhile, a new research front was being opened up. At the first meeting of the steering committee, Tom Symons noted that researchers interested in the project were mostly pre-historians whose experience of Arctic archaeology had pulled them into the historical period. One of the issues discussed at several meetings was whether it would be better for historical research to precede archaeological investigation, in the hope that the former might reduce or focus the need for excavations at historic sites. Since, however, the impetus for archaeology was already strong, it became apparent that to address some of those key questions surrounding the Frobisher expeditions called for a hand-in-glove relationship between archaeological and historical researchers, each side informing the other. The 1992 position paper stated that archaeological research ought not to be conducted in isolation from other lines of enquiry. But the Frobisher expeditions were not then the subject of any coherent program of historical investigation, the episode having been relegated to the position of an example of European maritime exploration that had not been productive. But it turned out that not all historians were of that mind. The committee shouldered the new challenge of initiating a program to seek out undiscovered or little-known sources of archival information, define and research topics under which those sources could be fruitfully exploited, and provide related guidance in response to queries from researchers in the archaeological wing of the project. Thus, it was to be responsive both to the information needs of existing research efforts and be able to use its own discretion in pursuing new lines of enquiry.

To bring together a group of experts, Symons called on the organizational and leadership skills of Sir Ian Gourlay, KCB CVO OBE MC, one-time commandant general of Britain's Royal Marines. The two men had worked together in the context of the United World Colleges project and are both still accorded honorary vice-president status within that organization. They had formed a close bond, based on mutual respect, and it required only a brief courtship on the part of Symons before Sir Ian accepted, in February 1992, the further imposition on his retirement of a leading role in the Meta Incognita Project.[16]

This branch of the project, dubbed in quasi-military tradition the Archival Task Force, or ARTAF, began to take shape in the weeks that followed, holding its first meeting that summer. Dr. Taylor had travelled to England to meet with Sir Ian, and between them the pair had established contact with the National Maritime Museum, Royal Geographic Society (with which Hall had deposited some of his finds, later gone missing), Hakluyt Society, Royal Archives and Library at Windsor, as well as several universities. Symons followed on his heels to discuss with Sir Ian the formation of the team of historical and archival experts.

The short-term outcome was communication with several British historians highly familiar with archival sources pertinent to Elizabethan England. Of these, Ann Savours Shirley, Dr. Helen Wallis, and (for a short time) Nicholas Rodger were soon brought on board; a leading expert on Elizabethan maritime exploration, Professor David Beers Quinn, was added. After Symons learned of a living descendant of Martin Frobisher, Sir Ian made contact to ascertain whether the family might have any records or heirlooms that had been handed down. The assistance of the National Archives of Canada was enlisted, its Canadian headquarters designating an officer to act as liaison and to provide a list of documents in British repositories that made reference to Frobisher.

Around this nucleus of personnel, in meeting space kindly supplied by the Royal Geographic Society (where Sir Ian had an influential contact in the person of Sir John Hunt), and with a small operating budget furnished by the CMC, Sir Ian gradually assembled a volunteer team of young bloods and veterans as research associates and consultants, their combined expertise covering a number of specialized fields, such as historical cartography, medicine, shipbuilding, and navigation. Most were based in Britain with others in North America and France.[17]

As an historian chairing a committee made up largely of archaeologists, Symons took a particular and direct interest in the work of Sir Ian's squad. He made a point in attending a number of ARTAF meetings, particularly during a period of sabbatical from Trent University in 1992–93, but also on several subsequent occasions, offering advice and encouragement, and he kept in close touch with Sir Ian between meetings.

Despite the original anticipation, on the part of both the steering committee and ARTAF itself, that historical research would serve primarily to contextualize and elucidate matters arising from archaeological investigation—Drs. Auger and Fitzhugh having met with ARTAF at the earliest opportunity and submitted lists of questions they hoped could be researched (although their expectations of ARTAF were overly optimistic)—it became clear as ARTAF's work progressed that much could be done to add to the known story and to reinterpret some of what was already known. As research papers drafted by several of the members grew in number, it was evident that the volume and quality of output warranted a conference or a publication—ideas mooted as early as spring 1993.

However, at that time, the steering committee was preoccupied by events unfolding on the archaeology front. Dr. Auger had been successful in obtaining an ample SSHRC grant for further excavations over the next couple of years, contingent upon him being guided by the committee as to what work might be permissible. The committee now had to make difficult decisions on what it should recommend. In this it was influenced slightly by reports of unrestricted tourist visitation to the island and by growing public awareness of the project—a radio documentary on the Frobisher expeditions, incorporating interviews with project researchers, aired in 1992 as part of a circumpolar series produced by the BBC.[18] Dr. Auger was hoping to undertake fairly extensive and intrusive excavations, which made the committee uncomfortable; yet within the committee itself, opinion was divided on how much, if any, excavation ought to be allowed, for against the preservation need had to be weighed the desire not to discourage Canadian-led research conducted responsibly and purposefully. A period of negotiations followed, with the committee urging Dr. Auger to moderate his expectations, by focusing on specific research goals and accommodating the committee's stated position regarding protection of the heritage landscape and in situ preservation of archaeological resources. This was perhaps one of the most challenging periods of Symons's chairmanship, as he sought to foster discussion of the diverse perspectives on the complex issues, while looking for a middle path balancing needs that often seemed irreconcilable.

From this challenging process emerged a definition of work that was acceptable both to the researchers involved and to the steering committee. Limited further sampling excavations were to be carried out on a couple of selected features. Where vegetation was disturbed as a result, steps were to be taken to restore it before leaving the island. Follow-up work was to be done in monitoring erosion. Although Dr. Fitzhugh provided some logistical support, his own program of research had concluded and he and most of his associates were engaged now in cataloguing and analysing their finds; continued work on Inuit sites in the vicinity of Kodlunarn he had turned over to Daniel Odess. In the event, Dr. Auger's field season in 1993 proved brief, in part because of poor ice conditions. For the 1994 season, the steering committee felt able to recommend test excavations at additional features. This loosening of restrictions was partly the consequence of new information from an NHPS scientist indicating that those features might provide unique evidence on sixteenth-century pyrotechnology and therefore shed important light on the assaying mystery at the heart of the Frobisher mining venture; and partly also because the committee now had greater confidence in the prospect of restoring excavated areas to close to their original condition. The CMC furnished a senior conservator to accompany the Auger team, to assist with site restoration and the safe retrieval of fragile materials. Of these, perhaps the most striking find, visually, was a largely complete, though flattened, wicker basket used by Frobisher's excavators to carry ore from the surface mines to boats for transport to expedition ships. In the conservation labs at the CMC it proved possible to restore this basket close enough to its original condition to warrant its public display.[19]

In May 1995, with archaeology having given way to laboratory analysis of the finds (a process for which CMC and NHPS were providing conservation support), and with ARTAF's work proving productive, Symons proposed to the steering committee that serious thought be given to a multi-day symposium to bring together researchers and scientists from all disciplines and countries involved in the project, and open to other interested parties, to be followed up with a publication of the reports. Other members were fully supportive but torn between whether a symposium should be held in a more convenient southern location or in the more appropriate one of Iqaluit. Although a committee initiative in 1993 had resulted in a grant of ten thousand dollars from the Donner Canadian Foundation, earmarked for dissemination of project findings, the committee still faced mounting the symposium on a shoestring budget, and this favoured a southern venue.

Arrangements for the symposium became, throughout 1996 and into 1997, the most prominent matter of business for the steering committee. Symons had taken the tiller in this matter, steering the vessel through some choppy waters. His office at Trent served as the operations centre, and he persuaded the university to make conference facilities available and to provide logistical and financial support. The event's budget was bolstered by a financial contribution from Parks Canada, to honour Professor Symons's recent retirement from the chair of the HSMBC, and others from the Prince of Wales Northern Heritage Centre (PWNHC) and CMC, while a smaller amount had come from a private anonymous donor. By the opening of 1997, some ninety percent of the replies to explicit invitations sent to interested parties had indicated an intent to attend—this including a contingent from the Roanoke project—and the event ended up slightly over-subscribed.

The symposium took place over the course of three days in May 1997.[20] ARTAF members were enthusiastic about the opportunity to share the results of their research, and Sir Ian brought his entire team; even the senior statesmen of the group, in fragile health, made the Atlantic crossing, Professor Quinn giving the keynote address. On the archaeological side, there was some concern that analytical results were still at a preliminary stage, but most of the principal researchers gave individual presentations or participated in panel sessions. It was even possible to bring in a delegation from the North, which included an Iqaluit-based researcher who would talk about Inuit terminology in relation to place names. A side-trip was arranged for ARTAF researchers to Ottawa to view the Frobisher basket and other archaeological and geological finds from Meta Incognita sites. By all accounts the symposium was a resounding success.

Accounts of the 1993–94 excavations and subsequent finds analysis were not yet ready for publication, but the research completed by ARTAF was sufficient to fill a book, and the steering committee decided to proceed with that. In fact, a two-volume work proved necessary, and Symons took on the chief editorial duties in order to bring it to realization.[21] About half the cost was covered by the CMC and the PWNHC, and the remainder was covered through sponsorship money raised by Symons. He also arranged for the book to have added prestige in the form of a letter of support, in both English and Inuktitut, from the Northwest Territories minister of education, culture, and employment, and of a brief signed foreword written by the Prince of Wales, with whom he had worked closely during the years he was chairman and Prince Charles was president of the international board of the United World Colleges. The prince's wide-ranging interests included archaeology and history, and Symons had kept him informed at intervals about the progress of the project; the prince had also lent his name as an honorary chairman of the 1997 symposium.[22]

Significantly, release of the publication was timed to coincide with the inauguration of Nunavut (April 1999)[23] and Symons's dedication of the book was "to the People of Nunavut, past, present, and to be."

Although the 1997 symposium had been opened with an Inuktitut prayer by an Inuit elder from the Baffin region, and closed with a few comments by the same, it could not fulfill the recognized need to include the northern community in the dissemination of information. Symons was, from the beginning of the project, concerned to have northern involvement, not simply on the principle of inclusivity but prompted by his own strong consciousness that the Arctic has an integral, though too often neglected, part in Canadian history. It had, after all, been the Inuit who led Hall to Kodlunarn and communicated to him oral traditions regarding the island's European visitors and their encounters with locals, while one of the research goals of Dr. Fitzhugh's team was to assess whether the influx into Inuit settlements of European materials left on Kodlunarn by the Frobisher expeditions had any economic or political ramifications for the development of Inuit society. Not long before the Meta Incognita Project was initiated, Symons had written that he was troubled by "the persistent sense of remoteness and alienation of Northern Canadians from most Canadian polar research."[24] The committee's 1992 position paper stated, "It is in the general interest that activities be conducted with local participation where possible, with meaningful consultation in Iqaluit and with respect for regional sensitivities."

To that end, efforts had been made to bring northern, particularly Inuit, representation on the steering committee; this met with limited success,[25] but the committee was fortunate to include an Iqaluit resident in Dr. Douglas Stenton, while Dr. Arnold also had good connections with that community. The former had, in 1992, suggested a briefing of community leaders and was able, on several occasions, to brief key individuals in the community on the Meta Incognita Project. He reported back to the committee that the project was not seen there as community based and so the community was rather ambivalent towards it, although the elders, while seeing the project as relevant only to non-Inuit history, had no objection to research proceeding. Symons, who had been enthusiastic about receiving input from the Iqaluit community, was concerned, though not wholly surprised, by its lack of interest. He hoped to improve the situation through a more formal and structured presentation that might stimulate a bi-directional exchange of information. In its early years, the committee had held off on a community briefing in the hope that long-term responsibility for Kodlunarn would be assigned to some agency. With that still elusive, and spurred on by the success of the Trent symposium, a more modest gathering was mounted at Iqaluit in November 1997, with Dr. Stenton its organizer and fundraiser, using facilities at the community hall and Nunatta Sunakkutaangit museum. With committee members in attendance, joined by Drs. Auger and Fitzhugh, videos were shown, presentations were given on various components of project research, and Inuit and non-Inuit members of the community talked about aspects of local oral history and topography; Dr. Arnold spoke about the issues related to long-term management of the historic sites and conveyed the committee's wish for feedback from the community. Simultaneous translation between English and Inuktitut was provided and ample time allocated for audience questions and discussion.

At the dawn of the new millennium and the second decade of the Meta Incognita Project, the steering committee had accomplished most of its goals. Archaeological investigation of the Frobisher sites had been managed in a way that showed due consideration for protection of the heritage resources. The historical research program had been wrapped up, with Symons ensuring the unpublished documentation of that component would be preserved through Trent University archives. Research findings had been communicated to scholarly and general audiences through a variety of media. Two ambitions in particular remained. One was to publish final reports from the archaeological investigations. The second was, in the continued absence of a lead agency, to draft recommendations for a site management plan.

The intended publication was planned to include reviews of the historical and geographical contexts of the Frobisher expeditions as well as reports on the following: the archaeological investigations of the 1990s, analysis of finds,[26] conservation of the Frobisher basket; consideration of Inuit-European interaction and societal impact as evidenced from Elizabethan materials found on Inuit sites, and evidence for such interaction from Inuit place names and other terminology. As well, the committee's recommendations for a site management plan would be published. Regrettably, publication plans were, after several years of effort, finally thwarted by a combination of adverse circumstances, some unforeseeable and others difficulties plaguing the project from the outset. The latter included funding.

As may be surmised from references already made to aspects of project funding, much had to be cobbled together from various sources, sometimes on an ad hoc basis. A modest operating budget for the steering committee had been put in place from the outset by the CMC and was subsequently expanded to cover ARTAF; it also provided most of what was needed for the early Mercury publications. At a rough estimate, this budget amounted to no more than half a million dollars over the lifetime of the project,[27] no great sum for running an international, multidisciplinary research program over an extended period. The other agencies represented on the steering committee also contributed resources in the forms of staff time and cash. Major initiatives, such as the 1991 archaeological expedition, the symposia, and the final publication were financed, to a large degree, through fundraising efforts by the committee, with Dr. Taylor initially taking the lead in this and, after his departure, Professor Symons. Private donors with a strong interest in Canadian heritage, organizations such as the Donner Canadian Foundation and Celanese Canada, and the T. H. B. Symons Trust Fund, administered by Trent University, helped make such initiatives financially feasible. The work of Drs. Auger and Fitzhugh had been funded by SSHRC, National Geographic, and the Smithsonian, the last of which had also made a contribution toward publication of the first Mercury volume. Federal belt-tightening as the 1990s progressed took its toll on CMC's fiscal resources, which trickled down to the Meta Incognita Project budget; from 1999, following the retirement of Dr. MacDonald from his position as CEO, that budget dried up almost entirely.

The steering committee pressed on, regardless, working toward a final report that could guide any agency having future responsibility for Kodlunarn Island toward development of a site management plan. In 1997, it had distributed to interested parties a consultative draft, seeking feedback on questions such as which sites should be under a plan's umbrella; how to control activities, whether human or natural, that posed a potential threat to those sites (and whether preservation considerations or scientific investigation should be given precedence); what concrete measures might be taken to monitor the sites and enforce protection; and where artifact and archival materials related to Kodlunarn should be cared for. Over the course of 2000, the committee, having taken into consideration responses to its consultative draft and feedback received at the public meeting in Iqaluit, finalized its recommendations for a management plan for Kodlunarn Island and related archaeological sites in Outer Frobisher Bay. At the opening of the following year, copies (which included French and Inuktitut translations of the executive summary) were submitted to the federal ministers of Canadian Heritage and of Indian and Northern Affairs, and to Nunavut's ministers of culture and of sustainable development, as well as to the HSMBC and several Inuit associations active in the heritage field.

This report, which included an appendix extracting germane comments from the public consultation, made the following principal recommendations:

- That the sites requiring integrated management include not only those where Frobisher's expeditions were intensively active (Kodlunarn Island, Countess of Sussex Mine, and Winter's Furnace Mine), but also Inuit settlement sites occupied at the time the expeditions were present (Tikkoon Point and Kamaiyuk).
- That, with a view to protecting the historic remains, a panel of experts be available to review, from a needs-benefits perspective, any future applications to conduct archaeological research on any of those sites, with provision for exceptions should sites become at imminent risk of damage from erosion (which should be monitored regularly) or other causes.[28]
- That an authorization process be put in place to control inevitable tourist visits and that visitation impacts on the sites be limited by designating landing areas, walking trails (coordinated with an interpretive plan), and areas where activities should be prohibited. There should be two tiers of monitoring: that carried out by local residents on an ongoing basis (which would require the stimulation of local

interest, both intellectual and economic) and periodic official inspections.

- That plaques or other interpretive markers at the historical sites be limited and unobtrusive, with interpretation focused more on alternatives, such as an exhibit at the museum in Iqaluit, printed brochures, and videos for use by tour operators, and information be made available on the Web. Interpretive tools should emphasize the significance of the Frobisher expeditions not only to European (and thereby Canadian) history but also to Inuit heritage, and should present both perspectives on the historical episode.
- That Parks Canada develop a commemorative integrity statement (covering all sites identified above for inclusion), as the basis for identifying inter-agency authorities and responsibilities.

This account of the work done by the Meta Incognita Project Steering Committee[29] does not need to conclude with an assessment of the significance of the Frobisher expeditions—for Canada and for an incipiently imperialistic England—since that has been more expertly presented elsewhere,[30] although their significance may yet remain to be fully appreciated by Canada's political leaders in the context of looming international disputes over Arctic sovereignty. This paper is instead about the management of the human endeavour to understand such episodes in our history and to preserve the surviving material evidence of those episodes, while at the same time ensuring that the knowledge stemming from both facets is accessible to Canadians at large, and indeed to humanity in general. Underlying the formation of the steering committee, and the sustained shared efforts of its members, were the beliefs that, as Tom Symons himself said, in other contexts: "Canadians have an obligation, which the rest of the world expects us to honour, to play the leading role in scholarship relating to Canada."[31] And that "what we choose to save, or to destroy, reveals our values as a people. . . . Heritage conservation is important to the health and vitality of our country."[32]

For a decade and a half an ad hoc committee, under Tom Symons's leadership, held the fort for the protection and investigation of Frobisher-related sites in the Arctic. In retrospect this was perhaps the best thing to have happened. For, had a duly-constituted governmental organization been assigned responsibility for Kodlunarn, the likelihood is that it would have placed an indefinite moratorium on archaeological research while it conducted an environmental assessment and developed principles and mechanisms for site management; nor could it have been expected to pursue the historical research that proved so fruitful. The steering committee did its best with very modest resources and little formal authority; what was achieved within those limitations has been remarkable.

Keeping the diverse interests represented within the steering committee and the research teams on board and on target was no mean feat, which is testimony to the diplomatic skills of the chairman. It was thanks largely to Tom Symons's farsighted appreciation of the scope of the project that it developed from what began as an arbitration between rival researchers into a wide-ranging interdisciplinary investigation that has been able to re-evaluate the Frobisher expeditions and cast their historical significance in a new light. Effective leaders, while able to lead by example and through the combined force of energy and determination, also appreciate the advantages of associating with others capable of achieving. They prefer to empower than to control. Such leaders tend to be persons to whom their supporters can refuse nothing, not out of fear or hope for gain, but out of respect and admiration. Such qualities Tom Symons possesses in abundance.

Notes

1 Its longest dimension being barely three hundred metres.

2 Qallunaan is part of the trend to convert names derived from Aboriginal terms to an orthography more accurately reflecting Aboriginal pronunciation and meaning. The Inuit name for the island was an important piece of evidence, for it means "white man's," representing the survival of Inuit memory of the English visitors centuries earlier. Frobisher had named the island for the Countess of Warwick, one of the investors in

his venture. For consistency, and avoidance of confusion, Kodlunarn will be the form used throughout this paper.

3 As indeed it now appears to have done. See Patricia Sutherland, *Dorset-Norse Interactions in the Canadian Eastern Arctic.* <http://www.civilization.ca/cmc/explore/resources-for-scholars/essays/archaeology/patricia-sutherland/dorset-norse-interactions-in-the-canadian-eastern-arctic> [last accessed 22 October 2009]. Dr. Sutherland, it should be noted, was a close colleague of Dr. McGhee at the CMC. Dr. Fitzhugh went on to curate a travelling exhibition, "Vikings: The North Atlantic Saga" (2000–03).

4 Initially Dr. Roger Marois and later Dr. Donald Clark.

5 Dr. Christina Cameron, although due to demands on her time she was increasingly represented at committee meetings by her director of archaeological services.

6 Dr. Charles Arnold, an Arctic archaeologist and educator.

7 Dr. Douglas Stenton, who would, during the course of the project, go on to become executive director of the Inuit Heritage Trust, and later chief archaeologist and director of heritage for the Government of Nunavut.

8 Initially Tommy Owlijoot, one-time director of the Inuit Cultural Institute at Arviat; later, another former director of the institute and a deputy minister of culture, Peter Irniq, who was soon to become the second commissioner of Nunavut. Inuit representation on the committee was, however, not continuous, and although the committee discussed on several occasions expanding representation from the northern community, it proved impossible to find suitable candidates with the time to serve. Maintaining representation proved challenging, given a relatively small pool of heritage-oriented persons from which to draw, the division of authority among different groups within the community, the demands on time of an Arctic lifestyle, and the well-known reticence of Inuit, partly a reluctance of individuals to speak for the entire community.

9 Sadly, after completing his work coordinating the earlier archaeological investigations, ill health obliged Dr. Taylor to withdraw from the project in 1994; he died later that year. Thereafter, Tom Symons took upon himself much of the responsibility of liaising with project researchers.

10 An undertaking made possible thanks in part to private donations from several Albertan sponsors.

11 However, the researcher engaged to undertake this, unable to find all the necessary funding (although CMC had provided some support) and uncomfortable with the politics within the project, made but little

headway and eventually bowed out. Regrettably—not least because oral traditions are nowadays less well transmitted to younger generations—the committee's later subsequent efforts to revive this component also met with difficulties.

12 Pending ministerial review, however, NHPS at least requested the NWT Department of Economic Development and Tourism to include, as a standard clause on cruise ship permits, an embargo on landing passengers on the island. The lack of a lead agency at once obliged the steering committee to take a hand in affairs for so much longer than originally envisaged yet hindered it from pursuing definitive and resourced steps either to protect the historic sites or to engage the local community in such an undertaking.

13 *The Meta Incognita Project: Contributions to Field Studies*, ed. by Stephen Alsford, Mercury Series, Directorate Paper no. 6, (Hull: Canadian Museum of Civilization, 1993). At about the same time was published a volume summarizing earlier research: *Archeology of the Frobisher Voyages*, ed. by William Fitzhugh and Jacqueline Olin (Washington: Smithsonian Institution Press, 1993).

14 D. D. Hogarth, P. W. Boreham and J. G. Mitchell. *Martin Frobisher's Northwest Venture, 1576–1581: Mines, Minerals, Metallurgy*, Mercury Series, Directorate Paper no. 7 (Hull: Canadian Museum of Civilization, 1994). One of the more curious findings was that the ore mined by Frobisher had, in fact, an abnormally low gold content, although ironically Dr. Hogarth subsequently identified diamond-bearing ore in the vicinity!

15 Indeed, it soon began to receive regular showings at the Nunatta Sunakkutaangit museum in Iqaluit.

16 Sir Ian Gourlay had in fact agreed to a less demanding liaison role the previous June, before the concept of ARTAF had been fully formulated by the steering committee, and had thereafter been briefed periodically on developments. Declining an offered honorarium, he served as ARTAF's leader on a purely voluntary basis.

17 A good idea of the scope of the central players is given by the list of contributors to the project publication *Meta Incognita: A Discourse of Discovery* (see note 21). A paper by Ian Gourlay in the same publication discusses in more detail the formation, membership, and activities of ARTAF. A number of other historians provided assistance on a more informal basis. Links between the two branches of research tended to focus on Professor Hogarth and Dr. Bernard Allaire, an associate of Dr. Auger.

18 While the steering committee did not relish the publicity, it recognized the inevitability, and the CMC accordingly supplied the episode's producer with Arctic field kit for his time on Kodlunarn with the archaeologists.

19 The process of conservation, in the field and in the laboratory, is described in the *Inuit and Englishmen* virtual exhibition: <http://www.civilization.ca/cmc/exhibitions/hist/frobisher/frbas01e.shtml> [last accessed 22 October 2009].

20 A report from the conference can be found in an article by Peggy Berkowitz, "Martin Frobisher's Quest for Gold: a Search for the Northwest Passage Quickly Turned into a Gold Hunt, and a Scandal to Rival Bre-X," *University Affairs* 38.9 (November 1997): 19–21.

21 *Meta Incognita: A Discourse of Discovery. Martin Frobisher's Arctic Expeditions, 1576–1578*, ed. by Thomas H. B. Symons, 2 vols, Mercury Series, Directorate Paper no. 10 (Hull: Canadian Museum of Civilization, 1999). The book met with strong demand and, unusual for Mercury publications (which target specialized audiences), had all but sold out its print run within a couple of years.

22 As had the aforementioned Northwest Territories minister and the federal minister of Canadian Heritage.

23 As part of that commemoration, the Canadian Museum of Civilization also opened its temporary exhibition, *Inuit and Englishmen: The Nunavut Voyages of Martin Frobisher*, curated by Dr. McGhee; its run to January 2000 was extended by several months and it was subsequently scaled down into a more modest, longer-running exhibit. The exhibition combined archaeological data and conjecture by including a reconstruction of the small house that had been erected on Kodlunarn as a prelude to colonization, and a scale model of the island at the time of the presence of the final Frobisher expedition. An exhibition review by Jeffrey Murray can be found in *Archivaria*, 48 (Fall 1999): 244–47. A virtual version of the exhibition, enhanced with additional information from the Meta Incognita Project, was launched in November 1999 on the Canadian Museum of Civilization Web site: <http://www.civilization.ca/cmc/exhibitions/hist/frobisher/frint01e.shtml> [last accessed 22 October 2009].

24 *The Shield of Achilles: The Report of the Canadian Polar Research Commission Study* (Ottawa: Department of Indian Affairs and Northern Development, 1988), 5.

25 See note 8. Also of limited success was an attempt to issue an Inuktitut version of the press release about the 1991 fieldwork; difficulties in

engaging a qualified translator resulted in that version being released late. Translation continued to be problematic as efforts were made to have available in Inuktitut the draft, for public consultation purposes, of the committee's recommendations for a site management plan.

26 These included stove tiles and other ceramics, slag, and other ironwork from site features confirmed to have been workshops for testing ores, and foodstuffs.

27 Not including the value of staff time, which took in personnel in the areas of project management, research, conservation, communications, and administration, and excluding the cost of the exhibition, *Inuit and Englishmen,* a product developed independently of the project per se.

28 After visiting Kodlunarn in August 2002, Dr. Stenton reported that the erosion monitoring grid put in place on the island's east coast in 1992 was still largely intact and that measurements from it suggested an erosion rate of a couple of centimetres per year (lower than previously estimated rates). He also reported extensive regeneration of vegetation on the sites of excavations and that no post-excavation disturbance of sites was evident, except at the Frobisher house, where someone had removed some of the rocks used to secure a (now deteriorating) tarpaulin placed by archaeologists over the site. *Qallunaan Island (KeDe-1) Site Inspection Report,* Government of Nunavut Department of Culture, Language, Elders and Youth (unpublished document), March 2003.

29 Except where otherwise noted, the basis for this paper is the author's own recollections (bolstered by consultation with Tom Symons) and project documentation held at the Trent University Archives (Meta Incognita Fonds 03-012) and at the Canadian Museum of Civilization.

30 Thomas H. B. Symons, "The significance of the Frobisher expeditions of 1576–1578," in *Meta Incognita: A Discourse of Discovery* (see note 21), vol.1, xix–xxxiv.

31 T. H. B. Symons. *To Know Ourselves: The Report of the Commission on Canadian Studies.* 2 vols. (Ottawa: Association of Universities and Colleges of Canada, 1975), I, 17.

32 Thomas H.B. Symons, "Commemorating Canada's Past: From Old Crow to New Bergthal," in *The Place of History: Commemorating Canada's Past.* ed. by Thomas H. B. Symons (Ottawa: Royal Society of Canada, 1997), 15.

CHAPTER 16

Tom Symons and Massey College

JOHN FRASER

I caught sight of him from my handy vantage point in the Master's Office walking slowly from the entranceway of House II, through the quadrangle, ostensibly heading toward the main entrance to the college's Common Room. I believe it was in pre-walking-stick days still for the "Founding President and Vanier Professor Emeritus" of Trent University, possibly 1999 or 2000—maybe earlier, possibly slightly later. As the years push on, it gets hard—irritating actually—to distinguish incidents and people from one year to the next, and doubly irritating that everyone at the college of a day doesn't know the people I have known through all the days. An aging administrator's gripe!

But I remember this particular perambulation because it produced a classic Tom Symons moment. The sun was out, the water garden my wife had lovingly made of the central pond at Massey College was at its full late spring glory, with irises and water lilies proclaiming life renewed in bellicose profusion. Several Junior Fellows were either studying on the benches or simply taking in the welcoming warmth of the sun. In short: a college idyll, so long as you didn't probe the anxieties of the students or the pain the Founding President probably had with each considered step.

He stopped to take in the scene and that's when Dr. James Orbinsky came from seemingly nowhere right up to him. Oh, of course, I thought, they must know each other. James was an undergraduate at Trent and after that went on to do his medical degree and follow his extraordinary career as a doctor with Médecins Sans Frontières. It was with MSF that he found himself, famously, at the vortex of horror during the Rwandan genocide, only to return home spiritually wounded and politically angry, and also very determined for the rest of his life to do more than bandage wounds. He wanted to understand why people were pushed to such extremities and what could be done to prevent such horrors in the future. So, quite humbly, he came back to school and through the good offices of Professor Ursula Franklin, he became a Massey College man: first as a Senior Resident (during which time, as president of MSF, he accepted the Nobel Peace Prize on behalf of the organization), then a very special graduate student at the Munk Centre for International Studies, then a professor of emergency medicine at the University of Toronto, then a Senior Fellow of Massey, then the founder of Dignitas (his remarkable foundation created in 2008), and then—and now and most recently—as a member of the governing Corporation at Massey College. At this meeting, though, it was still early days in the dramatic career of young Dr. Orbinsky.

So from that office window perch, I could see these two were well met. Tom's face had broken out into one of those all-embracing smiles that could light up the universe and enveloped one in such instant and commodious affection that there was no other place you wanted to be but in conversation with this man. James was talking animatedly—later I learned he was merely explaining himself and his presence at the college—and I realized I was watching two Trent guys, however indirectly, reliving their Trent days in the Massey quadrangle. Perhaps this was the first time I realized how important Massey had become in Tom's life. In our own way, we were keeping true to a concept of academic community that he had given much of his life to experience, savour, create, build upon, and defend, but at a time when this concept was under severe threat at the very institution he had helped to found in Peterborough.

So this is an account of Tom Symons, the Massey College man, and it comes first of all with a remarkable set of coincidences. Consider just these:

- Tom Symons transformed the Trinity College and University of Toronto residences on Devonshire Place into a multidisciplinary, residential prototype of Massey College, which would be built directly across the street.
- When Prince Philip laid the cornerstone for Massey College in 1962, there was Dean Symons at the staging post.
- When Tom came to oversee the creation of Trent University, the architect of choice was Ron Thom, the troubled genius who built Massey College.
- When he sought out a home in Peterborough from which to preside as the founding president, whose house would serve better than that of the departing editor of the *Peterborough Examiner*, who had moved to the master's lodging at Massey just across the street from the domain of the departing Dean of Devonshire House.

Nothing in life follows a straight trajectory, so it was not until Tom had retired from Trent and had gone on to his task-filled post-university life that he became a Senior Fellow of the college, but I knew from the instant of his first visit as a fellow that we had lucked into a very special relationship. In the midst of his conversation with Dr. Orbinsky, for example, a Junior Fellow approached James and quietly stood a little way off hoping to nab James after he was finished with Professor Symons. Instead of staying aloof, which neither man seems genetically capable of doing, James introduced him to Tom, and you knew that the student was about to undergo one of those Symons's inquiries that left you thinking that you really were going to make it through to a life of achievement and contribution.

That was his special gift to all the Junior Fellows he encountered at Massey, either by chance in the quadrangle or relaxing the common room or sitting down for a shared meal in Ondaatje Hall. His ability to fix a generous eye on whoever he was talking to, to summarize their often jumbled and possibly embarrassed explanations of themselves into a hugely positive précis fed directly back to them; his instant warmth coupled with an undeniable seriousness of purpose; his genius for community and *fellowship*—all these things conspired to make the lucky Junior Fellow feel on top of the world. However brief the subsequent euphoria, the moment remained an indelible juncture point, worth infinitely more than any number of ticks on a term paper or the congratulatory handshake from a gilt-braided Chancellor on graduation day. Even if Junior Fellows could not—and would not—describe it as a kind of academic apostolic blessing, passed on from a succession of sympathetic and inspiring college worthies stretching back to...to...to the misty past, they knew they had been put in the path of both history and the best part of their own ambition. And in the serendipitous way of the Founding President, one of those young Junior Fellows—a classical scholar, no less, who made it into the twenty-first century—ended up in a post at Trent University and helped to set up a conference on "College community renewal" featuring, amongst others, Dr. Donald Markwell, the Warden of the Rhodes Trust at Oxford and a bemused Master of Massey College. Three rows back from the front and to the side sat Tom Symons. You could see the glimmer of patient hope in his eyes.

I have seen that glimmer at the two other institutions of which Tom Symons and I are members, although he has been the crucial member (and the chief recruiter). These are the Association of Commonwealth Studies (ACS) and the British-North America Committee (BNAC): the first is academic and the second is hoi-poloi.

The ACS grew out of Tom Symons decades-old faith in the Commonwealth and its potential, yet again, to bring people together in academic fellowship. It is not yet a happy story, having been the chief recommendation of the 1993 Symons Report on Commonwealth Studies and yet, because of poor funding from an economically pressed Commonwealth Secretariat in London, only having managed two not entirely successful meetings. The reason for the shaky start (the tale is not over yet) has as much to do with contemporary academic politics as it does with currently ambivalent views on the future of the Commonwealth. Nevertheless, I will always remember, and cherish, the patient, slightly withered smile on the face of T. H. B. S. every time a presented academic paper referred to "post-colonial" rather than "Commonwealth" studies. You could read everything into that thin smile: a complete understanding where the loathsome term had sprung from; an infinite patience to wait for its eventual demise; something much deeper and certainly sadder than irritation; and almost complete forgiveness, because, after all, the chap had bothered to do "a pretty decent paper and was prepared to take part in the conference and his key points were really rather good, I thought. What did you think?"

The BNAC is something else again: a distinguished gathering of "top people"—key figures from the worlds of politics, the civil service, academia, international finance, and business. They gather at least twice a year, in fellowship and out of a concern to understand global issues, especially as they affect, or might affect, the venerable Atlantic triangle of Britain, Canada, and the United States. The organization easily commands the attention of government, university, and business leaders—you could call them Tom's people—who are invited to make significant, off-the-record presentations of importance. Each country has its own organization, all of them quite small and very distinguished, and then there is an international chair and for over a decade that chair was sat upon by Tom Symons. Watching him at the few meetings I have attended, working his way through this plummy crowd—titles galore in Britain, gazillionaires from America, and the humble (sort of) from Canada—is like having a front row seat to see one of the great diplomats of our day. The key thing I noticed is a kind of egalitarianism Tom brings to these occasions. It's not that he doesn't have a due regard for rank, title, and economic status in society and life generally, but it is not rank, title, or economic status that gets this man's interests and sympathies vibrating: it is a wonderful mixture of fellowship and ideas, and for these the rankings take different forms, as do titles and economic status. I have seen him occupy the same territory again and again at Massey College, through both happy occasions and those imbued with the sort of suffused tension that is a specialty of tenured academics.

On days of high importance and great academic pomp, for example, he was always able to bring a human touch. Two notable examples make the point well. Tom listened in near rapture—that's my surmise from examining his facial muscles a few feet away—when Professor Ursula Franklin received one of the first Clarkson Laureates in Public Service in 2004. He loved that this famous and still feisty octogenarian was still an active fellow of the college and that in her acceptance words was saying exactly the sorts of things that resonated with what he felt community and academic life should be. Afterward, of course, he sought her out and I know for a fact he left her feeling much the same way he left the Junior Fellows.

On another high occasion, when the King and Queen of Sweden came to the college to a special high table in their honour following the awarding of the annual Polanyi Prizes (created two decades earlier by the Government of Ontario to honour the Nobel Prize in Chemistry awarded to the college's founding Senior Fellow, Professor John Polanyi), I watched Tom down "below the salt" regaling his end of a table, which included Junior Fellows, Senior Fellows, and an assortment of Swedish court officials and business luminaries. From my august but decidedly stiff and uncomfortable perch between the King and Queen, I knew where I'd rather be. Later, a Swedish baroness—one of the Ladies-in-Waiting to the Queen—asked me the name of that "large courtly gentleman" and I knew the Symons magic had transcended court, country, and Scandinavian dourness. It was the same for the somewhat academically lonely MA student from North Bay studying the annals of Canadian bush pilots in northern Ontario during the Great Depression.

All of which amounts to what? To nothing in some ways and paradoxically to everything in other ways. To nothing if nuances of encouragement mean little, if unblinkered commitment to fellowship leave you cold, if deep understanding of tradition and history (including instant traditions and potted history, which have their own place in college life) seem silly, and above all if the ripples of affection felt for wise and humane mentorship do not affect you. Nothing learned, nothing gained. To those for whom such things have the opposite effect, however, for whom the Symons magic continues to cast its spell and impel the admiring and grateful disciple to carry on a life of evolving emulation, it amounts to almost everything.

CHAPTER 17

Summer Islander: Tom Symons and Prince Edward Island

EDWARD MacDONALD

Over time, the experience was polished into a story, shorter and longer versions, depending on the company and the occasion. Yet the story never seemed to lose its freshness nor the teller his own sense of discovery.[1] It began in 1953 with a young student, "an Ontario lad," out to discover his country in a way that would only become fashionable in the ensuing decade. He was hitchhiking, to Halifax, with all of twenty-eight dollars in his pocket, when a kindly farmer detoured him to Prince Edward Island. The farmer left him off in Hunter River, and he made his way to the North Shore near Brackley Beach. "Dusk was falling," he remembered, "and I saw a light at the end of a long lane." He had come to Shaw's Hotel, the province's oldest tourist resort, just outside the boundaries of the Prince Edward Island National Park. When he asked the innkeeper, Gordon Shaw, about a bed, he got far more than he bargained for: "Gordon was kindness itself. There was supper in the kitchen and a bed in the barn, and I was not allowed to pay any money. I did odd jobs, stayed three days, never did get to Halifax." Tom Symons had discovered Prince Edward Island. "I fell in love with Shaw's," he said. The next year he was back. And the next. In fact, he has returned every year since, and over the ensuing decades has become something of an institution at Shaw's.

The happenstance visit of the footloose student began a love affair with Canada's smallest province that has now stretched into its seventh decade. Two anecdotes from his early years at Shaw's suggest how Tom Symons found his way with Islanders—although they certainly don't account for Tom's affection for Prince Edward Island! On his second visit, this time as a paying customer, some female pranksters filled the bottom half of his bed with horse manure. Next morning, they asked innocently how he had slept: "I replied, clearly to their amazement, that I had slept very well indeed, and made no further comment."[2] It was absolutely the right response! On his third visit, he was met in Hunter River by Alix Shaw, "driving a small truck loaded with potatoes. Alix already had two passengers so Jim and I were instructed to sit in the back of the truck with the potatoes. In this way, we learned early on that potatoes are more important than tourists on Prince Edward Island and that people from 'away' should expect no coddling."[3] Tact, then, and wry good humour, and a becoming absence of self-importance: the young Tom had an instinctive grasp of the appropriate behavior for a mainlander on Prince Edward Island. Even after he had become a rather important person, he never forgot that early lesson.

So, how do you come to love so deeply a place that puts manure in your bed and loads you in the back of a truck like a sack of potatoes? In a man much attached to tradition, the annual sojourn at Shaw's would become a cherished tradition—cherished by his hosts as much as by their guest. But Prince Edward Island also appealed to Tom Symons's roots and his sensibilities. It was beautiful, of course, a gentle conjunction of land and sea that everywhere bore the marks of human habitation. And its ruralness appealed to the city boy with the farm roots. Quoting his father and adding his own addendum, Tom reflects,"'Country people journey to the city to make enough money to live in the country.' There's a wisdom in that and a wisdom that's always marked life on Prince Edward Island."[4] The province also embodied, sometimes to the point of cliché, old-fashioned virtues, and in certain ways, even as a young man, Tom has always been old fashioned. Emotionally and intellectually, the culture reached out to his sense of community and human conduct:

> There is a quality about the life and the pace of life, and the civility, the extraordinary but honest consideration with which they treat one another. . . . It's also related to the more thoughtful

> way people proceed about things. And that's a product of the generations of self-dependence, inter-dependence of the people of the Island. They developed habits of knowing how to cooperate and be collegial, yet how in the close quarters of a small island to retain their personal identity.[5]

Even on his first visit to the region, he says, "I had a feeling of coming home."[6] And, finally, there is the matter of scale: "It's a very outstanding example of a smaller community that has developed the identities that go with detached, more substantial territories and political entities. The fact that it is a small community and yet that it has experienced self-government and continues to have a very large degree of self-dependence and self-government."[7]

In Prince Edward Island, Symons could also actualize his deep convictions about Canada. For him the country's smallest province matters for its own sake, a feeling he shares with thoughtful Islanders. It matters, too, for Canada's sake, and not just as the "Cradle of Confederation," much as he likes to remind Canadians of that claim. In Tom Symons's Canada, each part matters equally. Each part contributes its distinctiveness to his vision of the country. In reflecting on the province's importance, he always avoids qualifiers, never prefaces statements with "despite" or "although" or "for its size."[8] In his mental map of Canada, where the sum always exceeds the parts, each province is of equal size. Canada is, at the same time, the pieces in the mosaic and the picture that they form.

A genuine appreciation of the place, then, underwrites Tom Symons's concern for Prince Edward Island. The Island's culture and Tom Symons's character are perfectly matched. But how does a summer resident—even a distinguished one—contribute to the progress, preservation, and cultural well-being of a place that nourishes a sharp distinction between "us" and "them," "home" and "away," "here" and "there"? The answer appears to be "diplomatically, delicately, circumspectly, and, wherever possible, on invitation." In Tom's words, "It's not at all helpful for people from away to tell Island folk things that they know better anyway. But you can be supportive. You can be encouraging. You can occasionally facilitate."[9] And that is exactly what he has done.

In the beginning, Tom's engagement with Island affairs was strictly informal and predictably channeled along educational lines. As an educator and university administrator, the Trent president had pleasurable dealings with his Island counterparts, Rev. George MacDonald, rector of St. Dunstan's University ("We had many good cups of tea—and beverages of sorts!"), and the redoubtable Frank MacKinnon, principal of Prince of Wales College (which achieved university status in 1965), a fellow innovator with big dreams for his institution. The connection soon extended to the University of Prince Edward Island, which replaced the existing schools in 1969. Tom took a lively interest in university affairs in the province, and his informal involvement spread out on either side of presidential relations to invited participation as guest lecturer and seminar participant and occasional conversations with the provincial government.

The impact was tangible, if difficult to measure. Certainly, the creation of a Canadian Studies program at UPEI in 1981 was a logical, knock-on development from Tom's 1975 Commission on Canadian Studies report, *To Know Ourselves*, for the Association of Universities and Colleges of Canada (AUCC).[10] In 1983, the University of Prince Edward Island recognized both his larger achievements and his relationship with the province by awarding him an honorary degree (the third of his fourteen to date). After lauding his diverse achievements, the citation referenced his "deep and sensitive understanding of our Province and culture."[11] After Wade MacLauchlan became UPEI's fifth president, it was Tom and Christine Symons who organized a dinner in his honour at the University Club in Toronto in 2002 with a guest list that artfully included potential partners in MacLauchlan's vision for his "Great Small University."[12]

By then, of course, Tom's engagement with the Island had long since spread beyond formal education to culture and heritage, partly from simple interest but partly because he considered them vital components of identity. "Concern for heritage and education are absolutely, inextricably entwined," he argues. "They are two legs under the table of my experience of Prince Edward Island, my affection for the Island, and anything I've been able to contribute to the Island."[13] Over the years, as time and circumstances allowed, he has been able to put his heritage principles into practice.

Paradoxically, it was a national appointment that gave him one of his first opportunities to act locally. As chairman of the Historic Sites and Monuments Board of Canada between 1986 and 1996, he took a special interest in Prince Edward Island. Of the province's fifty-six "Designations of National Historic Significance" since the 1930s, nineteen were designated and/or plaqued on Tom's watch.[14] While as chair he would never subvert the process of designation, there was no disguising his pleasure each time an Island site was honoured, and he loved to preside in person whenever possible. Local Parks Canada staff used to joke that he favoured Island nominations because he enjoyed coming to the province so much. Tom stoutly denies the accusation, yet:

> I felt that, you know, it happens sometimes things fall a little bit behind and a little catch-up is needed. And I would just say with respect that there was a little catch-up needed in terms of Prince Edward Island. And I was very lucky because Father Francis Bolger [the unofficial "Dean" of Island history during the 1970s and 1980s] was on the Board of the Historic Sites and Monuments Board with me as the Island representative, a man for whom I have profound respect and high affection, and we worked very closely together to see that there was a bit of catch-up activity in terms of recognition of Island sites. And I believe that. . .we were very successful.[15]

Ever the diplomat, he is careful to add, "It was not done at the expense of any other part of Canada, I assure you." Indeed, notwithstanding the bloom of designations during Tom's tenure, Prince Edward Island still has a third fewer designations than any other province.[16]

If presiding over an active HSMBC raised Tom's heritage profile on Prince Edward Island, other events would quietly raise it further. From time to time, Island premiers had invited his views on educational and heritage matters, but the first to give him a formal undertaking was Liberal premier Joe Ghiz, who shared Tom's synthesis of the local with the national. In the summer of 1990, he invited Tom to his office "for a visit and a cup of tea and a good chat." The chat concerned Ghiz's plans for a commission that would investigate the development potential, culturally, politically, and economically, of Charlottetown's historic role as "cradle of Confederation." Tom has turned the encounter into a good story: "He explained to me, he said, 'I'd so much like to ask you to serve on this, but, you know, it's quite impossible. First of all you're from away and secondly, you're a Tory! Nonetheless, I'm going to ask you. Would you?"[17]

Tom would. The Birthplace Explored Commission was chaired by Wendy MacDonald, and its membership was a judicious blend of occupations and interest groups. As the only non-Islander among the commissioners, Tom was the soul of diplomacy, but he was high-minded about their mission, convinced of its importance, and tactically shrewd about how to go about it. He had a knack for steering without dominating, and one of the directions in which he steered was a national perspective on the importance of the birthplace—not instead of, but in addition to, its provincial significance.[18]

The commission worked quickly. Released in 1991, its report both affirmed the Island's potential "birthplace" role and provided a template for action.[19] Among its recommendations was the creation of a Capital Commission in Charlottetown, twinned with the National Capital Commission. It was duly established, although it has since been absorbed into larger, tourist-oriented bodies.

In the half-decade after its release, the Birthplace Explored Commission report seeded a number of projects, most of them through the Capital Commission. One of the first fruits of its labours was the Confederation Landing Park, which converted an abandoned oil tank farm on Charlottetown's historic waterfront into a splendid green space. Symons was named to the National Design Competition Committee for that project, and while he regrets that lack of funds prevented the winning design from being completely implemented, he was pleased with the result. (And so are the thousands of Charlottetonians and visitors who use the park each year). He is more ambivalent about the next major heritage development on the Charlottetown waterfront, Founders Hall.

The Founders Hall project (1999–2001) set out to save an historic building, the former CNR Car Shop, by converting it into a heritage attraction—with the emphasis on "attraction"—that would entertain visitors with the story of Canadian Confederation. Again, the responsible agency (the Charlottetown and Area Development Corporation, working through the Capital Commission of PEI) bolstered its credibility by naming Symons to its National Heritage Advisory Committee, along with such other luminaries as historians Michael Bliss, Jean-Claude Robert, and John Herd Thompson. Local heritage organizations bemoaned the "mis-direction" of scarce heritage dollars, even while admitting that they were dollars that were likely unavailable for local heritage anyway. Meanwhile, historical purists decried the Hall's occasionally flippant trivialization of a complex and sometimes conflicted past (the media-heavy displays were provided by the same creative team responsible for the *History Bites* television series).[20] Tom's assessment is characteristically even-handed:

> It isn't everything that I might have hoped for. It's wonderful in that it has preserved a heritage site, and it has helped with the preservation of an open space not otherwise used on the waterfront. And it's served a moderately useful role for education. One would have to look at the figures, but I think it's been some help for tourism. I can't help but think that possibly the money that went into that, if it had not been trying to serve so many different purposes, if it had been focused more specifically on heritage education, . . . would have been more effective, but that's a hard thing to judge.

Risky, too, he might add, especially for someone sensitive to his status as summer Islander: "I never forget, I assure you, that when all is said and done I'm from away."[21]

But if Tom had trouble with the often uncomfortable marriage between tourism and heritage preservation represented by the Founders' Hall project, he warmed to its topic. Prince Edward Island and Confederation—Confederation itself, that great, ongoing, ever-evolving project—was a subject dear to the heart of the man who had once planned a dissertation on the Pacific Scandal and still keeps a statue of John A. Macdonald in his study. And the Prince Edward Island institution that best mirrors his appreciation of Canada as a dynamic dialogue between past, present, and future is the Confederation Centre of the Arts, Canada's only national memorial to Confederation. By the turn of the new millennium it had become the main focus of his intellectual investment in Prince Edward Island.

The Confederation Centre of the Arts was the brainchild of two stubborn, visionary "do-ers," Prince of Wales College principal Frank MacKinnon and Calgary oil tycoon Eric Harvie. Working through allies, intermediaries, and partners, they convinced Ottawa and the ten Canadian provinces to cost-share (at the rate of fifteen cents per capita) the construction of the Fathers of Confederation Memorial Buildings, an art gallery, theatre, archives, and library complex on Charlottetown's Queen Square, to mark the centennial of the Charlottetown Conference of 1864. The complex opened on time and on budget, quickly simplified its name to the Confederation Centre of the Arts, and soon coined its durable tag-line, "a living memorial to Confederation," which mantra it quickly wore out as it joined the Darwinian struggle for fiscal survival that defines the state of the arts in Canada.[22]

In the beginning, Tom was more or less an innocent bystander in the story of the Confederation Centre. He was present when Queen Elizabeth gave the building her Royal blessing in the fall of 1964, and for the variety concert that provided a taste of things to come in the centre's theatre. Among the entertainments, Don Harron and Norman Campbell auditioned part of a musical they'd been developing about an orphaned redhead. Tom tells the story with relish:

> And when Her Majesty was introduced to the creators of *Anne*, she was talking to Norman. . .and she said, 'That was a wonderful number, Mr. Campbell, but tell me, where is the rest of it?'. . . .
>
> 'The next time you come, Your Majesty [Campbell promised], 'we'll have more.'[23]

Tom has never forgotten the first time he saw the complete version of *Anne of Green Gables, the Musical*: "[I]t was magnificent, and you knew right there that this was an extraordinary moment in the history of musical theatre, anywhere, and in the history of Canadian theatre." In Anne, as in Prince Edward Island, Tom saw a reflection of *his* Canada: "*Anne of Green Gables* [the musical] deserves a lot of thought as an expression of part of Canadian experience and Canadian values. Its significance goes way beyond a piece of entertainment."[24] And like the person who never tires of their favourite foods, Tom has never tired of seeing the play in its half century of performance at the Charlottetown festival.

The Confederation Centre Art Gallery and Museum, with the largest art collection east of Montreal, has also drawn Tom and Christine's interest. "On several occasions," he notes, "we've had the good fortune to be able to facilitate major presentations of worthwhile additions to the collection there. That has given us a lot of pleasure."[25] In this case, the dictum "art for art's sake" might be modified to read, "art for Canada's sake." In 2000, for example, the Celanese Canada Company presented a trio of fine paintings to the Confederation Centre in appreciation for Tom's long-time service as a director and founding chair of the company's Social Responsibility Committee.[26]

Tom's interest in the centre did not go unnoticed and, in 1985, he was appointed to its board as one of its national directors. It was no sinecure, at least not in the way Tom went about his duties. By 2003, he was one of the board's longest-serving members. The *longue durée* gave him a unique perspective on the centre's mandate and its prospects. Among other things, he gradually became concerned at a perception among federal agencies, private donors, and the general public that the Confederation Centre was—or had become—just another regional arts centre. With an event horizon dominated by next year's shows and last week's bills, the centre was itself in danger of forgetting what it was all about, that it had been conceived as a national shrine and constructed through a national effort.

In the mid-1970s, acting on that vision (and fiscal need), the centre's executive director had launched an arduous but largely successful campaign to convince each province to make an annual contribution to the institution's operating expenses.[27] But the funding arrangements were held together more by good faith and expediency than any sense of permanent obligation. One by one, financial exigencies had forced most of the provinces to reduce or abandon their support. As if to symbolize the blurring of national purpose, board positions reserved for off-Island provincial appointments went unfilled. Metaphorically speaking, the centre seemed to have entered a mid-life crisis.

As the national mission lapsed more and more into lip service, it did not help that local cultural producers railed against precisely that national mandate, pressing for more time and more space in the centre's programs. It was not as if the centre had to choose between one or the other identity; they were not inherently contradictory. But maintaining a "proper" balance between local needs and national mandate was as difficult to do as it was to define, and the tension between the two roles had been present from the genesis of the Confederation Centre project.[28] What was at stake went well beyond an abstract argument over mission statements. Recognizing that the economic—if not cultural—benefits of the complex were largely local, the Government of Prince Edward Island had long been its principal external funder.[29] But the limits of provincial support had clearly been reached by the turn of the century, and if the centre was to survive and prosper—or at least make ends meet—it must look elsewhere for new monies. Logic dictated that "elsewhere" should be Ottawa (already a major funder, albeit through certain generic programs) and the other provinces, the original partners in the whole enterprise.

Tom was the main driver behind the "National Vision Task Force" that the board of the Confederation Centre of the Arts created in the summer of 2003. He was named its chair, and he framed its agenda. The mission statement is worth quoting in full:

> The National Vision Task Force seeks to enlarge an understanding of the Trust's national significance and to contribute further to Canadian community and unity. Fortified by the findings of the research project, the Task Force will draw upon the lessons of the past and its precedents to devise a strategic plan for confronting the challenges facing the Confederation Centre. The plan will seek to re-capture the concept of the Confederation Centre as a trans-Canadian national memorial the responsibility for which does not rest almost entirely on the shoulders of one province and one federal department. To that end, it will seek to re-engage the financial support of each Canadian province (and even its three territories) for the Fathers of Confederation Buildings Trust and the Confederation Centre of the Arts as a relevant, enriching national resource; and it will seek to re-structure the support

> arrangements with the federal government in such a way as to recognize the Centre's special status as a national memorial to Canadian Confederation, including, especially, the creation of a significant endowment that would help fund the operations of the Centre.[30]

The first phase of the task force's work was to commission "a careful investigation of the consensus on which the Confederation Centre was constructed."[31] Tom supervised and facilitated every stage of the report, "Cradling Confederation: The Origins of the Confederation Centre of the Arts," which was delivered to the centre's board at its semiannual meeting in Montreal in February 2004.[32] As Tom hoped it would, history provided a moral (and morale) boost as well as an evidentiary foundation for the task force's next step, a patient, delicate campaign (supported by the Island's premier) to re-engage the financial support of Canada's provinces and territories for Confederation's national memorial. In keeping with the centre's renewed sense of national vision, the principle of provincial support was put above any rigid funding formula. The results have been encouraging, but the campaign is ongoing.

For obvious reasons, the courtship of the provinces was done quietly, but the next initiative of the National Vision Task Force needed as much fanfare as possible. Concerned that what the Confederation Centre *does* match what it *is*, Tom and Christine provided a generous financial gift to grubstake a new initiative. In addition to showcasing Canada's art and culture, Tom felt that Canada's only memorial to Confederation should orchestrate an intellectually rigorous conversation about the state of Canadian Confederation through a high-profile series of annual lectures. The topics could be as various as the many faces of Confederation, but the tone should be formal, the speakers should be distinguished figures, and the event should command national attention. The Confederation Centre, Tom reasoned, should be the place where Canadians came together to talk about their country.

Catching fire from Tom's vision, the Confederation Centre, led by the board chair Wayne Hambly and the executive director David MacKenzie, soon moved to name the lecture program in his honour. The inaugural Thomas H. B. Symons Lecture on the State of Canadian Confederation took place in the Mainstage Theatre of the Confederation Centre in November 2004 and featured Tom's friend, Quebec Premier Jean Charest, speaking on the financial implications of federal-provincial relations. In an inspired choice (again, Tom's idea), Denis Fentie, the premier of the Yukon, inaugurated what would become a standard feature of the event—a substantive, thoughtful response to Charest's remarks.

Naming the lecture series after the man that conceived it was a fitting honour, but it was also an honest reflection of Tom's central role in its early progress. He fussed over details like a mother hen, imbued the concept with much of its gravitas, and underscored its aspirations by inspiring a coterie of his off-Island friends to attend each year. He also used his own personal connections to recruit the Symons Lecture's first seven speakers! It has been a remarkable performance.

As new universities and new countries well know, creating traditions is not just an oxymoronic exercise; it's a challenge. Now entering its eighth year, the Symons Lecture seems on its way to becoming a staple of Canadian intellectual life. Tom deflects the credit to the Island's political leaders, Confederation Centre staff, and fellow task force members, such as George Kitching, but there is no mistaking his pleasure at the lecture's early progress: "It has become. . .a significant event for Island folk, I think, for Island leadership, but also for Canada, to have this national series of events in which Canadians are invited to join in discussing broad themes about the way in which the country is unfolding, the way our Confederation is evolving."[33] As if to set the seal on that significance, the Confederation Centre commissioned a handsome medal, which is now presented to each year's featured speaker.

Naming a national lecture series for Tom Symons was a recognition of his national stature as well as acknowledging his role in its creation. But the decision, taken by Islanders and widely endorsed in the province, also suggests that, after almost six decades, Tom Symons had himself become something of an institution in his summer haven. The informal desire to contribute had over time found formal expression in ways that brought his name to the lips of people that had never met him, never been touched by his courtesy and kindness, never benefited from the shrewd intelligence that age re-labels "wisdom." At the end of a long interview, Tom asked permission for a final testament:

> If we're closing I'd just like to end with the thought that my association with the Island has been one of the richest and most rewarding and happiest themes throughout the last fifty years of my life. It's taught me so much, given me so much: friendships, and experience, and visual pleasure and adventures. I'm very, very grateful to Prince Edward Island and its people."[34]

And we to him.

Notes

1 The version here was committed to paper: "Remarks of Professor Thomas H. B. Symons, . . .at the Plaque Unveiling Ceremony Commemorating the National Historic Significance of Shaw's Hotel, Brackley Beach, Prince Edward Island," 6 August 2005 (Personal coll. of Thomas H. B. Symons).

2 Remarks Commemorating Shaw's Hotel.

3 Ibid.

4 Interview with T. H. B. Symons, 2 November 2009.

5 Ibid. It is precisely such qualities that Ian McKay has famously denigrated as fabricated identities in *The Quest of the Folk: Antimodernism and Cultural Selection in Twentieth-Century Nova Scotia* (Montreal & Kingston: McGill-Queen's University Press, 1994), yet in Prince Edward Island's case there is substantial truth in Symons's perceptions/projections. See Edward MacDonald, *If You're Stronghearted: Prince Edward Island in the Twentieth Century* (Charlottetown: Prince Edward Island Museum & Heritage Foundation, 2000), especially chapters 1, 7, and 8.

6 Ibid.

7 Interview with T. H. B. Symons, 2 November 2009.

8 In extended references to Prince Edward Island in a recent interview, the only concession he made to the power imbalance among provinces was an assertion that the Island "punched well above its weight in terms

of its contribution to conceptual thinking about Confederation issues." (Interview with T. H. B. Symons, 2 November 2009).

9 Interview with T. H. B. Symons, 2 November 2009.

10 Thomas H. B. Symons, *To Know Ourselves: The Report of the Commission on Canadian Studies* (Ottawa: Association of Universities and Colleges of Canada, 1975). For the creation of the Canadian Studies program at UPEI, see *1981–82 Calendar, University of Prince Edward Island,* UPEI Archives, Robertson Library, University of PEI, Charlottetown (henceforth UPEIA). The trickle-down effect of *To Know Ourselves* is noted by UPEI Professor Emeritus Andrew Robb (Telephone Interview with Andrew Robb, 13 May 2010).

11 "Citation for Thomas H. B. Symons," UPEIA, UPEI-Convocation-Citations-Vertical File, Item #46.

12 Wade MacLauchlan to Tom and Christine Symons, 6 December 2002, Private Collection of T. H. B. Symons. A seating plan for the evening also survives.

13 Interview with T. H. B. Symons, 2 November 2009.

14 "Directory of Designations of National Historic Significance of Canada," Parks Canada, http://www.pc.gc.ca/apps/lhnnhs/page3_E.asp?locateinp=&nhsprov=Prince+Edward+Island&nhschoice=alldesig&list4=Generate+List (accessed 13 May 2010). The proportion is even higher (twelve of twenty-two) if one looks only at National Historic Sites.

15 Interview with T. H. B. Symons, 2 November 2009.

16 Saskatchewan is next at eighty-nine. At last count, there were two thousand and seven Designations of National Historic Significance. See http://www.pc.gc.ca/apps/lhnnhs/page3_E.asp?locateinp=&nhsprov=Prince+Edward+Island&nhschoice=alldesig&list4=Generate+List (accessed 13 May 2010).

17 Interview with T. H. B. Symons, 2 November 2009.

18 This is the assessment of the author, who was secretary to the Birthplace Explored Commission.

19 *Powerful Memories, Powerful Dreams: Report of the Confederation Birthplace Commission* (Charlottetown: Queen's Printer, 1991).

20 For two divergent takes on Founders' Hall, see Edward MacDonald and Sasha Mullally, "On National Heritage, Grand Narratives, and 'Making History Fun': Founders' Hall, Prince Edward Island, and the Story of Canada," *International Journal of Heritage Studies,* 13 (2007) 3: 288–94.

21 Interview with T. H. B. Symons, 2 November 2009.

22 For the story of the centre's origins, see Frank MacKinnon, *Honour the Founders! Enjoy the Arts! Canada's Confederation Memorial in Charlottetown*

(Charlottetown: Fathers of Confederation Memorial Trust, 1990); and Edward MacDonald, "Cradling Confederation: The Origins of the Confederation Centre of the Arts," Report prepared for the National Vision Task Force, Confederation Centre of the Arts, Charlottetown, February 2004.

23 Interview with T. H. B. Symons, 2 November 2009.

24 Ibid.

25 Ibid.

26 Telephone interview with T. H. B. Symons, 27 July 2010. The paintings were: Robert Pilot's *Farmhouse Piedmont*, an oil on canvas; Maurice Cullen's *Spring Break-up on the Cache River*, chalk and pastel on paper; and Adam Sherriff Scott's *Winter Morning in the Laurentians*, also an oil on canvas.

27 MacDonald, "Cradling Confederation," Appendix D.

28 Ibid., 3–4.

29 As evidenced by copies of financial statements from the centre in possession of the author.

30 "Renewing the Vision: Project Outline for the National Vision Task Force," collection of the author.

31 Ibid.

32 Edward MacDonald, "Cradling Confederation: The Origins of the Confederation Centre of the Arts," Report prepared for the National Vision Task Force, Confederation Centre of the Arts, Charlottetown, February 2004.

33 Interview with T. H. B. Symons, 2 November 2009.

34 Ibid.

CHAPTER 18

Tom Symons and Peterborough

SYLVIA SUTHERLAND

In the autumn of 2005, as my penultimate year as Mayor of Peterborough was ending, I received a call from Tom Symons.

"Sylvia, as you know, I've been working on a lot of national and international projects. Well, I think I now would like to do something for my city."

My initial, unspoken, reaction was that the establishment of Trent University four decades ago would surely qualify as "doing something" for his city. My spoken response was to suggest a spot on the Peterborough Architectural Conservation Advisory Committee.

Tom hesitated. He had not long before stepped down after several years as chairman of the Historic Sites and Monuments Board of Canada and wanted a bit of a change of pace.

A spot would be opening up on the Peterborough Lakefield Police Services Board. In fact, the board would soon be in need of a chairman. How about that?

"Yes, that might be good. I have always been interested in social justice issues."

I was then in my fourteenth year on the Police Services Board, and I didn't want to disillusion Tom regarding the exact nature of the board and its rather peripheral involvement in social justice issues. I did know, having served with Tom on the board of Broadview Press, that he had the business acumen the Police Services Board needed and the experience and personal skills to make a superb contribution to the board. That he has done. But his experience there was not without incident, and there may have been times when he wished he had opted for the Architectural Advisory Committee instead.

Trent University changed Peterborough forever, and for the better. The chief architect of that change was Tom Symons, and his influence to the cultural, civic, and institutional life of the city is to be felt in Peterborough to this day—well beyond the parameters of the university. Robertson Davies, who did not much care for Peterborough, would have undoubtedly been happier there had he followed rather than preceded Tom and Trent to town.

It would be highly unfair to Peterborough to declare it devoid of cultural or intellectual pursuits before the coming of Trent University. Indeed, as Tom well recognized and frequently acknowledge, the city had a rich literary and artistic heritage dating back to the Strickland sisters scribbling away in the woods of Upper Canada just north of Peterborough. And it was, after all, the initiative of the community leadership itself that brought the university to the city. The Davies—Robertson and his wife, Brenda—had enhanced and improved an already active community theatre group, and an enormous engineering talent, with its own particular inventiveness and creativity, was to be found at Canadian General Electric. The Community Concert series had a high subscription rate in Peterborough, and several of the local churches had remarkably talented choirs.

What the city lacked was a postsecondary educational institution, along with all the enhancements to the local community that such an institution could bring if its leadership acknowledged the importance of the interrelationship between the community and the university, and appreciated the community in which the university found itself. This Tom most assuredly did. He was the perfect founding president for a university located in Peterborough.

Tom will tell you that he loves Peterborough now, and did when he came here in the spring of 1961 as the thirty-two-year-old president-designate of Trent University and member of its founding board. It was the city's physical setting and its built environment that attracted him—the buildings and their expression of old Ontario that was, in his words, "neither souped-up nor spoiled."

"I had no commitment to accept the Trent position when I first came," Tom recalls. He had been offered a similar position in Oshawa, which was also seeking to establish a university. Which community would get the university depended to a large extent upon which invitation Tom decided to accept. It was Peterborough that won him and, through him, the university.

Speaking at Trent's opening ceremonies on Saturday 17 October 1964, Tom explained to those assembled the special relationship the university had to the community—to Peterborough, to the Valley of the Trent, and to Eastern Ontario.

"No new university," he said, "has received a greater measure of support from its home community—for which heartfelt thanks—as well as from many friends across the nation. It was this support and in the final analysis the dedicated service given by men and women here in this community—many of whom are present here today—which made Trent University possible and brought it into being.

"It also gave Trent much of the special character and outlook which already make it distinctive. Located in the historic Valley of the Trent, and in this old Ontario city of Peterborough with its long tradition of interest in the arts and letters, it is natural that this University should feel a particular interest in the study of the history and culture of its community and of our nation."

It was Tom's innate understanding of the history and culture of Peterborough that led in those early years to such a happy synergy between town and gown. As a result, the city benefited from the university in ways that its citizen founders probably did not foresee.

Two years after he spoke at Trent's opening ceremonies, Tom contributed an article on the university to *Land of Shining Waters*, a particularly fine anthology of essays about Peterborough and its region by local authors, assembled to celebrate Canada's centennial in 1967. In his piece, Tom outlined what he saw as the contribution the university would make to the city, which, because he understood its importance, was in no small way Tom's contribution to the community in his role as president of Trent. Another president may not have been so perceptive, or so determined, in having the university serve the community that gave it birth.

He wrote:

> On the most basic—but nonetheless important—level, the University will be an enormous economic boon to the whole region. In the not far distant future the University will be one of the largest employers and largest consumers of goods and services in the region. Not only will it pour money into the local economy in the form of wages, and therefore, increased buying power, but it will demand merchandise and maintenance in large quantities, not only in new buildings and new equipment, but food, fuel and supplies of every sort, as well as increased services such as buses, telephones, water and electricity. In addition to the goods and services required by the University itself, the economy of Peterborough will be stimulated by the need to supply the needs of the many hundred members of the university faculty and staff (and their families) and several thousand students who will consume everything from clothing and books, to haircuts and entertainment.

All of which is a given for any community hosting a university. It certainly proved true for Peterborough. But Tom saw the other side of the coin as well. He understood that Trent would make continuing economic demands on the community, and that, "if it wishes to be anything more than mediocre" it will have, among other things, "to depend upon the continued generosity and far-sightedness of government and citizenry in it own locality." Certainly, the community had been generous and, not least, so had the labour unions, then a formidable force in Peterborough, numbering more than fifty. Organized labour turned out to be the largest single benefactor of the university. No other university in Canada had such support. It was something Tom Symons, child of Rosedale, scion of one of the country's most established of establishment families, made happen.

"They had every right to be suspicious of a young person from Rosedale who was a member of the Macdonald-Cartier Club," says Tom. "I never tried to disguise what I was, but we got along wonderfully well together. Gerry Dolan was their liaison and together we talked to each union, some of them definitely Communist. We developed a constructive, happy relationship. It was almost a magical thing. Every union endorsed the university, and supported a wage deduction of 25 to 50 cents a week for 25 years."

When asked why his relationship with the members of the unions worked so well, Tom replies simply, "I liked them." Despite Rosedale, he also understood them, having worked on summer jobs in lumber camps and meat packing plants.

For many in the labour movement, Tom's approach helped them realize the benefits Trent would have for their children and grandchildren. This was no small contribution to the future of the community and the country.

In that same article in *Land of Shining Waters*, Tom asked the question, somewhat rhetorically, "What kind of community do we wish (Peterborough) to be?" His own response laid down some challenges for Peterborough, many of which remain challenges today. His very expression of them put them into focus. He stated, "The day has surely passed in which we can afford to allow our cities and towns to expand and change in an entirely haphazard manner." Yet, cities and towns, and to some extent Peterborough, have continued to do exactly that; although I am happy to say that there remains an awareness here that bigger is not necessarily better and that we must struggle to hang onto those very features that attract people such as Tom and Christine to Peterborough and keep them here.

He spoke of the importance of municipal and regional planning, and of the necessity of resisting what was being done in other cities, of attempting to become "just a. . .stunted edition of Toronto."

He spoke of Peterborough as "a city of immense character in an historically significant setting of remarkable physical beauty," and he said, "developed with imagination and care, it can and should be one of the most attractive communities in Canada." He spoke of Peterborough and the surrounding county as being able to "lay claim to a cultural and literary tradition almost unrivalled by any other Canadian community." He spoke of the architecture of the city and of the surrounding communities.

And then he threw down a challenge, noting "the shockingly mis-used Market Hall, which is the heart and symbol of both the City and County of Peterborough" and the lack of an appropriate plan for downtown re-development—re-development "that could well make or break Peterborough."

"The wrong decision, a decision to favour some proposal to destroy important parts of the colourful and historic core of the City and to replace it with some common-place construction, could spell the end of Peterborough as a community of any particular distinction or consequence." Within five years, the city's Bradburn Opera House, along with other old, distinguished buildings, was torn down to erect a non-descript downtown mall, Peterborough Square, which turned its back on the street and has been a challenge to anyone looking at a downtown master plan ever since.

Tom urged the development of a park along the river in the city's core –something that has been done—and vigilance against the pollution and misuse of the surrounding lakes and rivers. He was truly prescient as he looked ahead to the challenges that would face the community in the years ahead, and he would contribute directly in helping to meet some of them.

For the "continued generosity" to happen, Tom knew that Trent would have to become part of and contribute to the community in a myriad of ways not directly related to economic benefit. Beyond economics, it was the other impacts Trent would have on Peterborough, and Tom's fostering of these, that would make such an enormous contribution to the community. Tom saw Trent attracting to the city "a whole range of persons whose artistic sensitivity, intellectual discipline, and technical competence is bound to broadened and deepen the consciousness of the entire community."

Gwen Brown is ninety now. For many years, before Trent came to Peterborough and for all the years since, she has been an active member and talented contributor to the theatrical life of the city. She recalls the boost that the arrival of Robertson and Brenda Davies with their professional theatrical experience brought to what was then the St. John Players, which became the Peterborough Theatre Guild. "But, oh Trent! Mrs. Brown exclaims. "The talent it brought to town! The wonderful Terry Mellors, the Gallops, Gillie and Paul Wilson, Finn Gallagher, Gordon Johnson, John Pettigrew, Michael Sidnell. . .the list just goes on and on. How lucky we were."

The list does go on and on, and not just in areas related to theatre. There was the musical talent of Joe Wearing, full-time professor of political science and part-time singer who brought renewed vigor to the Peterborough Singers. There were the artistic talents of Professor John Wiseman and of Jean Nind, wife of Trent's second president, who, in addition to her own pursuits, would serve on the board of the Art Gallery of Peterborough as it was establishing a permanent home. There was Jean Cole, author and historian who, with her husband, Trent's first registrar, Alf Cole, would produce the award-winning Historical Atlas of Peterborough County. There was Martha Anne Kidd—married to Kenneth Kidd, a professor of archaeology—whose research and books would raise the consciousness of the city to the richness of its built environment. And there was Elwood Jones, a history professor, who would write a history of the city and who continues a weekly newspaper column on Peterborough's past. Indeed, the list goes on and on.

It includes Harvard-educated professor of history, Christopher Greene, who would spend years until his death in 2006 serving as a member and chairman of the Peterborough Architectural Advisory Committee, lending his knowledge and talents to the identification and preservation of Peterborough's architectural heritage. His story is an interesting and not an unusual one as it relates to Tom's contribution to Peterborough.

His wife, Janet, recalls Professor Greene's decision to come to Trent in the spring of 1966:

> We had been at the University of New Brunswick for two years, and Christopher was looking to move on. We thought most likely to New Hampshire. He was invited to come to Peterborough for an interview for a position at Trent, and accepted the invitation somewhat reluctantly. He said it would be a waste of the university's money to bring him there because he was not the slightest bit interested in going to Peterborough.
>
> Then, he had tea at Tom's house and was very taken with the culture and civility that Tom had brought to the university. So, we came to Peterborough and found here a very congenial group and a lively social life. There were wonderful dinner parties and a real interaction between the townspeople and the faculty, which Tom encouraged. Christopher saw Tom's vision as highly idealistic, but he also saw it as working.

Christopher Greene would stay at Trent University for thirty-two years, until he reached the mandatory retirement age of sixty-five. He probably would not have come at all had it not been for tea with Tom. Like so many of the others who came to the university and the city because of Tom's vision, and because of his courtesy, hospitality, and civility, Christopher Greene enriched the civic as well as the educational life of the community.

Christopher Greene's and Martha Anne Kidd's interest in the architectural heritage of Peterborough was no greater than Tom's own. Tom saw both its beauty and its value. Rubidge Hall, Sheedy House, Abbott House, Scott House, Stratton House, Bradburn House—all beautiful, historic buildings—were acquired by Trent in the early days, restored and adapted, and remain part of the fabric of the community although, unfortunately, the role of most has changed in recent years.

It was not just the old; it was also the new. It was Tom's determination that Trent would be a physical as well as a social, cultural, economic, and educational adornment to the community. Architect Ron Thom made that happen with the buildings that now grace the west bank of Symons Campus—Champlain College, the Bata Library, and Lady Eaton College. They are among the finest and most beautiful, if not the finest and most beautiful, twentieth-century academic buildings in the country. And, thanks to Tom, they are in Peterborough.

Tom and Christine opened their home, as they have continued to do, to many residents of Peterborough when they hosted distinguished academics, scholars, writers, and public figures from across the country and the globe. They exposed Peterborough to these visitors, and these visitors to Peterborough.

Daryl Bennett was thirteen years old when Trent came to Peterborough and took away his ski hill to put in a sewer. A decade later, he would drive Tom (who gave up driving after he drove a tank through the gates of Camp Borden when he was in the ROTC in university), to various events.

"What really impressed me then, and has continued to, is how he reached out to young people. It didn't matter how dumb the question, he took you seriously. And then, the next thing you knew you, he would be talking on the car phone to the president of some world body, a premier, or the Prime Minister. I felt elevated by my association with him."

He continues to feel that way. Now a highly successful businessman and mayor of Peterborough, Mr. Bennett has grown increasingly close to Tom as the years have passed and, because of that association, has served on the British North America Committee, something he would never have visualized himself doing as he bemoaned the loss of his ski hill. "Great people from around the world have come to Peterborough," he says. "They would not have been here if Tom had not been here. He has, through them, promoted the city to a broad community. Tom has a vision of a better way, and he always insists on doing things right. He has a correct way of approaching things. And he is the consummate teacher."

"There was another, very concrete thing Tom did for Peterborough when he and Christine arrived in town," Mr. Bennett recalls. "I remember the guy in the LCBO store telling me that all of a sudden they were selling good Scotch and wine. 'We never sold any of that stuff before,' he said."

With Tom as honorary chair, Mr. Bennett would serve on the Committee to Save Market Hall, one of several projects Tom took on for and in the community both before and after he retired as president of Trent University.

In 1966, Tom was appointed to the board of Sir Sandford Fleming College, one of the nineteen Colleges of Applied Arts and Technology then being established in the province. He was part of a two-man search committee to find and recommend a president to the board. On his committee's recommendation, David Sutherland was chosen, and between them the two founding presidents established a working link between their institutions that was perhaps unique in Ontario. That link was to benefit both Trent and Sir Sandford Fleming—and the community both served.

Post retirement, Tom served on a committee exploring the future of the Trent-Severn Waterway; on an advisory committee on the building of the Evinrude Centre, a local arena; on the board of Broadview Press, then a fledgling publishing company located in Peterborough; and on the Peterborough-Lakefield Police Services

Board. It was perhaps this experience that led Daryl Bennett to observe, "Tom has adopted the community, but I wonder if he has been fully adopted by the community."

Following that initial phone call to the mayor's office in 2005, and following a requisite interview by a selection committee of council, Tom was duly and unanimously appointed to the Police Services Board in late 2005. In May of 2006, the board elected him its chairman. Under the terms of the Police Act, his term on the board expired with the term of council, and he had to reapply in January 2007. The new council appointed him for a two-year term.

This should have been the first clue. Normally, the city's appointment to the board runs the term of council—in this case, and for the first time in Ontario, for four years. Why then, only two for Tom? The answer was that the mayor, Paul Ayotte, had another person in mind for the seat, Dave Paterson, former head of Johnson & Johnson, which had left Peterborough. Earlier, as a councillor, the mayor had served with him on the board of the Civic Hospital and had been impressed with his performance. He wanted him on the Police Services Board. Two years for Symons, two years for Paterson. And then maybe four more. He encouraged Mr. Paterson to apply for the position. Innocently, not knowing that Tom would reapply, Mr. Paterson did.

Late in 2008, having been unanimously reelected chairman of the board in January; having brought an atmosphere of collegiality and cooperation to the board and the service where one was perceptively lacking before; having presided over the hiring of a new chief and the expansion of Police Headquarters; having a service with a continuing successful clearance rate amongst the highest in the province; and having a policing operation amongst the most economical in terms of cost per citizen, Tom was once more interviewed by the selection committee of council.

The press and the public were told that the selection committee recommended Dave Paterson to fill the seat. That was not the case. In caucus, it was the mayor who convinced council that Mr. Paterson, because of his business experience, should be selected, ignoring the fact that it took a certain amount of business acumen to establish a university and to, among other things, chair the private sector board of Bata Shoes. In a 7-4 vote, council, sitting in caucus as Committee of the Whole, decided to appoint Paterson. Then, to put it bluntly, all hell broke loose.

The Police Service Board members were stunned. Board member Ken Armstrong, known for choosing his words carefully, said he was "outraged." A lot of other people in Peterborough thought it was outrageous, too.

Retired RCMP officer, Ralph De Groot, wrote to the *Peterborough Examiner*:

> It is almost impossible to believe that city council, with the exception of four of its members, is prepared to dismiss Dr. Tom Symons from the Peterborough Lakefield Police Services Board. Dr. Symons was appointed as the citizens' representative. He served as chair of the board with uncommon distinction. . . .Citizens are not dumb. They recognize there must be another agenda in play. It appears to be the quest for power. . . . Dr. Symons's candidacy was supported by other members of the Police Services Board (which combined has a wealth of experience in matters financial, including raising and managing multi-million dollar budgets and appropriations), the Peterborough Police Association and our new police chief, who, by the way, himself holds a masters degree in business administration.
>
> Over and against these circumstances, the mayor claims 'there is nothing unusual; changes like this happen all the time.' I beg to differ and I hope that all citizens will feel the same and say so. What happened here is most unusual. It is the worst of politics and it surfaces just at that time of year when the spirit of goodwill toward all men ought to be foremost in our mind.

Striking a somewhat different note, another local lawyer, Joel Moldaver, wrote to council:

> In my view, this is a reprehensible error in judgment that poorly reflects on our Council and City. T. H. B. Symons is one of the most educated, enlightened and respected citizens of our city. It is indeed

> an honour to have him residing in our community. . . .A review of his remarkable career and accomplishments would obviously dispel any thought of his so-called 'lack of financial background. It will indeed be a sad and embarrassing day for our city to arbitrarily terminate one of Canada's most accomplished citizens from this local board.

In an editorial, the *Peterborough Examiner* declared, "This city deserves better. When someone with the intelligence, experience and integrity of a Tom Symons volunteers for community service, you say yes. Gratefully. And you certainly treat them with the respect they have earned and deserve."

A few of the councillors who had voted for Tom in caucus spoke out publically against the decision taken in caucus. Others, including the senior member of council, Jack Doris, changed their vote. On 12 January, sitting as Committee of the Whole, council reappointed Tom to the Police Services Board and confirmed the reappointment a week later. The next day, the members of the board reelected him its chairman.

For Tom, the overwhelming support for him from all sectors of the community had to taste sweet. It was support so well deserved, not simply for his role on the Police Services Board but for all that he had contributed to his adopted city. In various ways, his city had recognized his contribution. It has awarded him both the Peter Robinson Award, its equivalent of the Order of Canada and the Order of Ontario, and the Key to the City. A citizen's committee voted to place him on Peterborough's Pathway of Fame. One suspects, however, that the words spoken by so many and so vigorously in his defense when he was under siege meant more to him than the other local tributes. It is good that he heard them.

As is so often the case with such episodes, the entire incident quickly receded in the public memory as Tom continued to chair the Police Services Board with skill, wisdom, and dedication. What has not diminished for the citizens of Peterborough and the Trent Valley is the memory of the young man who came to their community to establish a university and who stayed to leave a lasting legacy in modern concrete, in the preservation of some of the best of their historic domestic architecture, in an appreciation of those who peopled their past, in community service, in education, in civility—and in the availability of a decent Scotch.

CHAPTER 19

Tom the Radical Tory

MARCO ADRIA

This chapter offers some reflections on Tom as teacher, scholar, and citizen. I'm a former student, now a colleague and friend. Tom was my thesis supervisor at Trent University when I completed my MA in what is now called the Frost Centre for Canadian Studies and Indigenous Studies, which he helped found.

A year with Tom Symons the teacher was full of auspicious occasions. I remember sitting across the dinner table from Robert Stanfield in a Hull restaurant. I recall discussing human rights with Max Yalden, who was then the federal chief commissioner of the Canadian Human Rights Commission. I spent time in the cottage that Tom occupied as his university office at Trent's downtown campus, where I could hear and be part of incoming and outgoing telephone calls with business and political leaders from across Canada. "Hamilton Southam on the line," would cry Tom's capable and quite hard-of-hearing secretary. My thesis committee was invited for tea to the cottage every few months; eventually I received my degree.

My thesis topic was only modestly within Tom's area of experience, although his expertise in relation to what I was studying was, I felt, of a particular quality. I had been writing about popular music and in particular the tradition of singer-songwriters that had grown up in Canada around figures in the 1960s and 1970s such as Joni Mitchell, Neil Young, and Gordon Lightfoot, and then later with Bruce Cockburn and k.d. lang. I wanted to complete my thesis on the life and work of Leonard Cohen. I felt that Tom would give me the latitude to look at Cohen in full context—not simply as a folk singer and not exclusively as a poet or novelist but as a figure on the ground of a Canadian mythology. I sensed some bemusement in Tom's voice when he called me from Peterborough in early 1990 to ask about the thesis proposal I had sent him. Tom has a deep knowledge of Canadian culture and the powers of the poet. He knows Canada's musical folklore. He knows that Cohen possesses an artistic stature to be reckoned with. But I would not say he was a folk song aficionado. In spite of his love of Canadian letters, he was never able to finish reading Cohen's cryptic novel *Beautiful Losers,* with its amorphous structure, profanity, and undulating repetitions of theme and language.

I mention my thesis, the cottage, and conversations with eminences in the nation's capital because the lived experience is at the core of Tom's approach to learning, the status of patriotism and citizenship in Canada, and the role of the university in our society. My study of Leonard Cohen became a study of Canada and a study of Tom Symons too. I doubt my experience was unique. Tom has shaped many people's way of thinking about Canada and Canadians. He continues to stimulate new ideas about and approaches to the meanings of Canadian identity. This influence is more profound than it would be if it depended on finding sympathetic ears for any particular set of opinions or judgments. Instead, Tom's life has an attractive exemplary character in itself. Those of us attuned to constant change and variation in current affairs and in our disciplines have much to gain from trying to understand the embodied mode within which he lives.

I want to suggest that Tom is a Radical Tory.[1] Radical Tories are difficult to name and locate because they have no manifesto. They are loosely tied together only by their experiences and by their lived expression of an ideal. We know that time and timelessness are always in view for the Radical Tory. The university and the church in western societies have created spaces and places for regarding and assessing the changes of historical time, alongside the contemplative attitude towards the timeless. Tom's vantage point as a teacher has been from his seat at the university he created. His vocation is history, the art of measuring and assessing changes in time. He is a generalist and not a historicist or specialist. The generalist loves architecture, visual arts, folklore, geography, science. The Radical Tory can learn to love the songs of Leonard Cohen.

The broad perspective sets Tom apart from his disciplinary colleagues, for whom specialization defines scholarly identity. The larger view of the Radical Tory is in harmony with that of Northrop Frye, who calls the university the "engine room of the world."[2] For Frye and for Tom, the university at its best is full of people measuring, commenting on, and discussing how the world compares with our professed designs for it—showing us what is, in contrast with what might be. In Sean Kane's gentle parody, entitled *Virtual Freedom*, there is a comment made to the effect that in the university people are content to live in a constant state of awareness of their position outside of history, but insist on talking about it anyways. They talk endlessly about themselves and about others.[3] (This is my paraphrase, and not a quotation from Sean's book, whose imagery and style are not immediately subject to summary descriptions.) Something of this sentiment can be read in *To Know Ourselves*, Tom's most famous publication. The study that gave rise to the scholarly area of Canadian Studies has the resonance of the existential note ringing through its title. We reflect on ourselves just because that is what we are bound to do.

One of the two worldviews from which historians write is materialism. History can be offered from this perspective as an account of power and the consolidation of economic strength. That's not Tom's perspective on history. His worldview gives precedence to understanding the transcendent values of societies over time. The values of historical idealism are not reducible to linguistic codes. Words cannot fully capture the visions of the ancient philosophers. Yet the Radical Tory is linked through an unbroken ancestry to these visions, to the inexpressible truths that so many words have been devoted to expressing.

The life of the Radical Tory can take rather different forms. In the public and political sphere, Michael Ignatieff invokes the tradition of the Radical Tory in his family lineage.[4] His uncle, George Grant, was the author of *Lament for a Nation*. Tom's brother Scott created in his own life what we would today call a mashup, a dramatic joining together of disparate pieces. He wanted rights for gay life but decried the loss of the Union Jack in Canada as the succumbing of a national culture to the easy comforts of pop art. He mourned the incremental loss of the significance of the Holy Eucharist not for the church, or even for the religious among us, but for Canadian society. The author of *Place D'Armes* (1967) was given a high Anglican mass for his funeral in 2009.

The family and the family compact are as important in the shaping of Canadian society as we have often suspected them to be. In childhood and youth, the Radical Tory is offered a choice of life-modes. One is the inward journey, implying the acceptance, without continuous comment, of the inexpressibility of the truth of the visions. Those Radical Tories who choose this journey might become well known in commerce or law. The alternative life-mode for the Radical Tory is to live the embodied life, to exist in a state of continual mindfulness and expressiveness. That is Tom's path. He has spoken and written through what I would call indirect communication and what others have called virtual communication.

The existence of the life-modes of silence or of indirect communication would suggest that there are indeed Radical Tories among us in Canada. They remain invisible most of the time. We are not conscious of their existence except in moments of social crisis—throughout World War I, during the Defense Crisis of 1962, when John Turner exhorted Brian Mulroney not to give up the "economic levers" in 1988, or in the several days leading up to the 1996 referendum. I am not referring to the political weight of these moments but to their ontological meaning. Communications theorist Briankle Chang argues that embodiment and mindfulness take on critical importance during such moments:

> Communication becomes virtual only when its space is heterogeneous, when it is invaded by an alien, an inscrutable other that embodies a void, a nothing as the I-know-not-what, which I, having been invited into that space, cannot ignore. It is this alien invasion that creates a crisis in me, and it is this crisis that causes the event of communication to occupy me, to take its place in me—in spite of its nothingness, in spite of the void it induces in me.[5]

The worldview of the Radical Tory is expressed through the "invasion" of communication spaces and the articulation of a sense of loss, which is experienced by others as a "crisis" or "void." This is indirect communication. In philosophy, the indirect method is not unprecedented. Kierkegaard communicates indirectly by creating a series of fictitious characters, each of whom speaks with a distinctive ontological voice. Kierkegard's own life was full of momentous events. These included a fateful romance early in life and hidden agonies later. Such events are part of the philosophical work. But Kierkegaard wants others to reflect on their own lives, not on his. By communicating indirectly, he creates a reverse image of the existential philosophy with which he is now associated. Tom's persuasive method, too, his rhetoric of ontology if you will, is enacted through being. His philosophy is embodied in the life and work of T. H. B. Symons.

Consider an important contribution that Tom has made through his involvement in higher education. Tom's leadership gave rise to the interdisciplinary area of Canadian Studies. This was accomplished, I would say, through embodiment rather than through persuasion. Tom *lives the life* of a Canadianist. He himself constitutes the argument for what we now understand to be the scholarly area of Canadian Studies. It's instructive to remember that in the tradition of Canadian thought on social identity, knowing and loving one's own is the first responsibility of the patriot. Loving our own must give way to loving others. George Grant describes the irreducibility of "knowing ourselves" this way:

> Love of the good is man's highest end, but it is of the nature of things that we come to know and to love what is good by first meeting it in that which is our own—this particular body, this family, these friends, this woman, this part of the world, this set of traditions, this civilization. At the simplest level of one's own body, it is clear that one has to love it yet pass beyond concentration on it.[6]

Tom once asked me, as he has done many times of others, "Who are your people?" We must know. We must love our own first. In loving the good by first loving one's own, the Radical Tory's sensibility creates a lens on the social world that reveals some things and obscures others. Among those things seen by the Radical Tory are communal ties, particularly as these ties are strengthened over time, while maintaining their essence outside of history. Tom's Trent University is saturated with markers and signifiers to the university's own history and that of the region—when college houses were purchased or built and in what circumstances, and the lineage of those who donated or sold them.

I mentioned that the Radical Tory has received a keen spiritual sensibility. Religion is not an occasion for testimony, but the ground on which the figure of the life-mode is configured. The Radical Tory also possesses the gift of a rich and intuitive physical sense. Viewing and living with, but also handling, the objet d'art is prominent in experience, memory, and knowledge. The Radical Tory, and Tom, therefore sees *idealism in the mundane.* Our world is not to be lived only for itself but within a consciousness of the traces of the unseen and the timeless. Forgive me if I hear Tom's voice in the words of his then-twenty-nine-year-old brother Scott:

> After dinner, the Queen Mother asks [Scott Symons] when his people came to Canada, and from where. "Two centuries ago, Ma'am, from the Thirteen Colonies, as Loyalists to your Crown," Symons replies. "We are still loyal to your Crown, Ma'am. We are your Majesty's Royal Americans."[7]

Our dear Queen is at the centre of a symbolic order in Canada. We respect and treasure the offices of our appointed, hereditary, and elected leaders, even Mr. Mulroney. Radical Tories, it must be emphasized, do not express allegiance to a particular territory, worldly empire, or political order. We know that the Loyalists gave up the territory they could not possess in order to keep what they could not lose. Radical Tories cannot live other than as subjects of the eternal and unseen crown.

Tom loves heraldry and ritual, both of which reflect the ideal in the mundane. Tom the Radical Tory lives immersed in a *sensuality rooted in daily life.* Scotch for the guests before bed; vintage port at Christmas. By participating in ritual, the Radical Tory continually enlivens and draws out the thread between the mundane and the eternal. College life at Oxford and Trent Universities—singing, conversation, eating together, living in daily fellowship and friendship.

But the Radical Tory also loves the written word, which takes us away from heraldry and ritual. The written word creates the critical faculty, as Marshall McLuhan reminds us.[8] It allows us to develop the critical point of view and to speak and act as individuals. In doing so, it takes us out of the world of physical sense, pageantry, and colour. The famous exhortation from the Duke of Gloucester to Edward Gibbon on being presented a volume of *Decline and Fall of the Roman Empire* was, "Another damned, square book. Always scribble, scribble, scribble! Eh! Mr. Gibbon?" Immersed as he was in the sensuousness of the peerage, the written word for the duke was ephemeral. Radical Tories, on the other hand, tack briskly between the colour and sense of daily life and the ecstatic remove of the written word. On the one hand, the Radical Tory lives within the cleavage between the written word and its ideal of transcendence; on the other hand, there exists the word's potential to create a new heaven and a new earth. The boundary between the two is always at contest. Radical Tories must return continually to St. John's teaching and hope that the word is continually becoming flesh.

I think of Tom and Christine living in their beloved Park Street home for almost fifty years—while all the other university presidents I've known have retired to somewhere other than the city in which they held high office. When he was appointed master of Massey College, the previous resident of the house, Robertson Davies, wouldn't give it up; in fact, he briefly considered moving the house to Toronto before he realized the idea implied engineering challenges that were likely insurmountable. The house must be inhabited by guiding spirits. The notion is not mine: Davies played a parlour game he called "Homicidal Maniac" in the house in the 1950s with a group of friends that included the journalist Scott Young.[9] Davies wrote much of the Salterton Trilogy in the same study in which at least some of *To Know Ourselves* would have been conceived.

The observant reader will note that I have invoked the tradition of the Radical Tory and not that of the more commonly discussed Red Tory. The *Red* Tory represents a set of political preferences, believing that with honest effort, clean living, and a bit of ingenuity, a gathering of followers can be accomplished, perhaps as many needed to inspire a popular political movement. While Red Toryism was born in Canada, the Radical Tory lives without attachment to a territory, except as that territory exists under the sovereignty of the crown.

At the beginning of my biography of another Radical Tory, the late radio broadcaster and chancellor of Trent University, Peter Gzowski, I wrote an epigraph to Tom suggesting that he provide evidence that someday Canada would be inhabited by Canadians.[10] When I expressed that sentiment, I was reflecting on the latent Canadian Radical Tory tradition. Perhaps Tom is the firstborn of a new nation for a world in which expressions of the ineffable are in short supply.

Notes

1 Charles Taylor, *Radical Tories: The Conservative Tradition in Canada* (Toronto: Anansi, 1982).

2 Northrop Frye, "Speech at a freshman welcome," in *Northrop Frye's Writings on Education,* eds. Jean O'Grady and Goldwin French (Toronto: University of Toronto Press, 2000), 280.

3 Sean Kane, *Virtual Freedom* (Toronto: McArthur, 2002).

4 Michael Ignatieff, *True Patriot Love: Four Generations in Search of Canada* (Toronto: Viking Canada, 2009).

5 Briankle Chang, *Deconstructing Communication: Representation, Subject, and Economies of Exchange* (Minneapolis: University of Minnesota Press, 1996), 223.

6 George Grant, "Canadian Fate and Imperialism," in *Technology and Empire* (Toronto: Anansi, 1969), 73.

7 Charles Taylor, "Scott Symons," in *Six Journeys: A Canadian Pattern* (Toronto: Anansi, 1977), 191.

8 Marshall McLuhan, *Understanding Media: The Extensions of Man* (Corte Madera, CA: Gingko Press, 2003).

9 Judith Skelton Grant, *Robertson Davies: Man of Myth* (Toronto: Viking, 1994), 324.

10 Marco Adria, *Peter Gzowski: An Electric Life* (Toronto: ECW Press, 1994).

CHAPTER 20

A Canadian Life

RALPH HEINTZMAN

The chapters of this book lead gradually to an inescapable conclusion: that Tom Symons must be considered one of Canada's pre-eminent educational and cultural statesmen in the second half of the twentieth century—a role that continues in the early years of the twenty-first, in his own ninth decade.

An educational and cultural statesman of this kind has a special but very necessary function. He or she may not always do the creative work of an artist or scholar, but they share their values. And they create the conditions in which such work can be done. They establish, lead, manage and nourish institutions. They make connections between institutions and people. They create and lead communities: communities of practice and of values. They represent institutions and communities to others. They build bridges. They develop support and encourage funding. They point direction. They advise and give counsel to public officials. They provide leadership to public bodies or initiatives and influence public policies. They create trust and establish legitimacy. They are sought out not just for their knowledge or imagination but for their wisdom and judgment. Without leaders of this kind, the educational, scholarly, and cultural life of the country could not be carried on, nor could it reach out to the wider public community or help to shape it.

What sort of people are we talking about? Well, in Canada, to be specific, this community might—in the second half of the twentieth century—have included people such as Vincent Massey, Georges-Henri Lévesque, Sidney Smith, Norman MacKenzie, Davidson Dunton, Alphonse-Marie Parent, Tom Patterson, Alex Corry, Claude Bissell, John Deutsch, Jean Boggs, Clément Cormier, Paul Lacoste, Larkin Kerwin, Harry Duckworth, Andy MacKay, Shirley Thomson, Fernand Lindsay, Lou Applebaum, Phyllis Lambert, Ron Watts, David Johnston and so on. You can probably add to this list. It is no disservice to such a distinguished group to suggest that Tom Symons must be considered in this kind of company. Nor that, considered in such company, the range and depth of his public roles become even more striking. Very few of these other, comparable statesmen and women can have played such a wide range of leadership and institutional roles, nor can have influenced so many areas of Canadian and international life so profoundly.

Tom McMillan recalls Tony Lovink's observation that Symons was Canada's best "academic diplomat." There is obviously much to be said for this assessment. Symons's accomplishments clearly owed a great deal to his remarkable gifts of diplomacy, described in most of the chapters of this book. But the rather weak connotation of "diplomat" may do justice neither to the range of Symons's roles, nor to the quietly energetic and creative way he played them. For this kind of leadership the term of statesman seems more adequate.

For many people the accomplishments described in any one of the chapters of this book would have been quite enough to justify a lifetime. Most of us would have been content to have planned, established, and led one highly distinctive university. For others it would have been more than enough to have led one major public commission. For still others it would have been quite enough to have led one major public body. But Tom Symons did it over and over, and over again. There are twenty chapters in this book, and even they do not exhaust the range of his professional life. There is nothing here, for example, on Symons's active involvement in several major business enterprises. As these chapters illustrate, Tom Symons has done enough to fill many very rich lives. And he has never been content to do it routinely, simply as a time-serving office-holder or file-pusher. Almost every one of the many areas in which he has worked has been transformed by his leadership. Sometimes to his own cost.

For a man consistently described by the contributors to this book as notoriously gracious, kindly, discreet, courteous—even courtly of manner—it seems at first surprising to notice that two of the qualities that emerge routinely from the accounts of Tom Symons's professional life are vision and courage.

Tom Symons's visionary leadership appears, however, less like the banal quality of "vision" hyped by modern books on leadership and rather more like an exercise of old-fashioned moral imagination. Symons was never content to let things go on as they were. In whatever situation he found himself—beginning with his very first roles at the University of Toronto—he could always imagine some better future: more fulfilling, more rewarding, higher quality, more humane, more just. And he was not content until he had started some process or other to bring that better future closer to reality.

Another way to put it would be to describe Tom Symons as an idealist, in the old philosophical meaning of that word. He seems to have been inclined, instinctively, to see through to the "idea" of things. An idea, in this sense, is "the conception of a thing, which is not abstracted from any particular state, form or mode, in which the thing may happen to exist at this or that time; nor yet generalized from any number or succession of such forms or modes; but which is given by the knowledge of *its ultimate aim*."[1] By knowledge of its inner form, the thing or state it points us toward, or which it is trying to be. Tom Symons seems to have approached each area of human life with which he became involved by looking through it to the *idea* it embodied, or was trying to embody, or should embody. The ideal form to which the current reality was just an approximation. And then he tried, as far as was practical in that time and place, to bring the existing reality closer to the ideal form.

The obvious first example was the university. From a very young age—indeed while he was still an undergraduate—Tom Symons seems to have developed a clear idea of what university education should be: a powerful conviction about what John Henry Newman had already called the *idea* of the university. First at Devonshire House and then at Trent University, he boldly sought, against very long odds, to bring that idea into being.

That might have been enough. But it was just the start. Symons then went on to pursue, in similar manner, the idea of the political party; the idea of the modern state; the idea of Ontario; the idea of linguistic, Aboriginal and human rights; the idea of culture; the idea of heritage; the idea of international education; the idea of national self-knowledge; the idea of Canada; and the idea of the Commonwealth, to name only a few of the "ideas" to which he tried to give more adequate form and concrete reality.

For some of his colleagues this idealistic inclination was tiresome or even dangerous. It was too romantic or old-fashioned or unrealistic. People inclined to think of themselves as "realistic" and "practical" are often the least genuinely realistic of all. They are content to remain on the surface of things, to accept the world as it seems to be. They do not see beyond the surface to the life of forms. So they cannot see what is really there, or what things mean, or where they are going or should be going. To them, Symons seemed much too ready to rock the boat. It made them distinctly uncomfortable. They sometimes dug in their heels, or found ways to put sticks in his spokes. So this idealistic approach to leadership necessarily required the other quality that is repeatedly evident in these pages. It took courage.

Courage seems to us a flashy virtue. We associate it with Achilles and other such heroes. But real courage is often a much quieter, everyday kind of virtue. It is simply the choice to do something rather than something else, to aim higher or farther than there is any need to do, especially when nobody is pushing to go there, or when caution or self-protection might suggest the opposite course. Tom Symons did not need to establish a university based on residential colleges and small-group teaching, against prevailing North American models and funding formulas. He did not need to be an early advocate for the Aboriginal peoples nor establish the first Canadian university program of Native Studies. He did not have to become an early champion for French-language rights in Ontario, an architect of Ontario's own "Quiet Revolution" and of a modern partnership between Canada's two largest provinces. He was not obliged to stick his neck out for greater attention to Canada in the university curriculum, earning sneers from many of his university colleagues. It was not a career-enhancing move to lead the way toward a new and broader vision of human rights. No one required him to become an early and life-long champion for heritage preservation or develop a much broader, holistic notion of what heritage should mean, even an alternative vision of what North American communities could become if they really took their built, natural, and human heritage seriously. It was not fashionable during his lifetime to devote oneself to the development and life of the Commonwealth, much less of Commonwealth studies.

If Tom Symons had been a more calculating man, he might have chosen to serve as chief policy advisor for a different federal political party. In the 1970s, when the Liberals held power in Ottawa and the Conservatives at Queen's Park, he had an encounter in the Ottawa airport with a famous Canadian architect. You know, said the famous man, I'm a provincial Conservative, but in federal politics, I'm a Liberal. "Why, John," responded Symons, no doubt with the usual, disarming twinkle in his eye, "how sensible!" Tom Symons was not a sensible man. He was, instead, a visionary and courageous leader.

It is commonplace to describe Tom Symons as a conservative, or even a Tory. And there are obvious reasons for this. But the Symons case invites us to reflect on what those terms may mean.

One way to do that is through the two lenses of the community and the individual. A conservative, properly so-called, starts from the community. A liberal, properly so-called, starts from the individual. For a liberal, the community is composed of free individuals who have entered into a social contract based on a cost-benefit calculation: free individuals agree to limit their own absolute freedom in order to secure the benefits from living in society. For a conservative, it works the other way around: liberties come instead from a concrete community and can only be understood or enjoyed within that community, within its traditions, institutions, practices, and well-being. For a conservative, the community comes before the individual and creates the possibility for individual liberty and fulfilment. For a liberal, the individual comes before the community, and should only surrender to that community the minimum of freedom necessary for a common life.

Three things are immediately evident from this distinction. The first is that the labels of modern political parties have often been reversed. In the twentieth and twenty-first centuries, Conservative parties have often (or even usually) been liberal parties, and Liberal parties (except in continental Europe) have often been conservative. The second thing is that, since the perspectives of the individual and of community are both legitimate—both necessary to each other—the only really reasonable thing to be is a conservative liberal or a liberal conservative.

And the third thing is that, from this perspective, Tom Symons truly is a conservative. But not in the way that term—in its upper case, political manifestation—is increasingly understood in Canada today. Symons has always started from the community, and his distinctive genius has been to build community. If there is an "idea" linking all the other ideas to which he tried to give more adequate form, it is the idea of community. Wherever he found himself, his first instinct was to see it *as* a community, and his second was to help it achieve a better, richer, more satisfying form *of* community.

The obvious starting point, both conceptually and in time, was, again, the university. For Symons the university can only be a truly civilising and humanizing influence, offering a higher education worthy of the name, if it is and aims to be a genuine community: a community of scholars and a community of learning. The university he planned and established is—or was—one of the few in the world designed from the ground up—in all of its architectural, organizational, academic, administrative, and human details—to create community.

Symons's devotion to heritage preservation is another obvious manifestation of his conservative instinct for community. But if Tom Symons's commitment to heritage reflects his conservatism, his championing of rights might justifiably be called an expression of Symons the liberal. The modern "rights" agenda is largely a liberal creation, a product of liberalism's emphasis on the individual person and his or her inalienable rights. So Tom Symons's role as a pioneering champion of Aboriginal, linguistic, and human rights can quite properly be seen as a reflection of his very liberal conservatism—though, again, in senses opposite to those in which the two words are often used, politically, today.

But even Symons's bold championing of rights can also be viewed as an expression of his authentic conservatism. There are, after all, two kinds of community.[2] We might call them "horizontal" and "vertical." The horizontal community is the community of today, the community of Canada, or Ontario, or Peterborough, or Trent University, or the Commonwealth, in all their current manifestations. But there is another kind of community, the vertical community, which is instead a "community of memory."[3] This community is the historical experience out of which the horizontal communities of today have emerged, and without which they could not be what they are—the traditions that help us understand the "future possibilities which the past has made available to the present."[4] This kind of community is what G. K. Chesterton called "the democracy of the dead." Why, he asked (in effect), should the community only include "those who merely happen to be walking about"?[5]

It is plausible to speculate that Symons's Canadian conservatism leads him to place himself and his country within a community of memory that extends all the way back—as his mentor, Chester Martin, might have said—to Magna Carta, a tradition of liberty broadening slowly down from precedent to precedent, in the framework of parliamentary institutions, under the authority of the Crown. In this kind of vertical community, the recognition of Aboriginal, linguistic, and human rights is not necessarily a liberal innovation but simply the logical next step in the tradition, in such a broadening down of liberty, a step without which the tradition would be unworthy of the inner idea it embodies, and to which it is striving to give ideal form. To do any less would be to fall short of the tradition of which you are a part.

Tom Symons is notably proud of his Loyalist forebears. And one of the things of which he is most proud is the fact that many minority communities chose to leave their homes and emigrate to the northern colonies—in one of the largest mass migrations in history—believing (not entirely without reason, as it turned out) that their liberties would be better protected under the Crown than under an intolerant democratic majority. Ensuring the tradition remains faithful to that inner idea it embodies is the highest form of loyalty: loyalty to the good. Ontario's own motto might serve for Symons as well, even—or especially—in what outwardly would seem his boldest innovations: *sic semper fidelis.*

Despite his UTS teacher's encouragement to embrace Voltaire's motto ("Écrasez l'infâme!") and make it his own—advice he clearly took to heart—Symons's instincts about rights probably derive less from Voltaire and Jean-Jacques Rousseau than from the alternative tradition represented by Edmund Burke, or perhaps, even more, from the simple human compassion that moved an old Tory like Samuel Johnson. To those who muttered that he was going too far, or too fast, Symons could easily have responded with Johnson's rejoinder to Whig laissez-faire some two hundred years earlier: "I am always afraid of determining on the side of envy or cruelty. . .lest I should be yielding to the suggestions of pride, while I persuade myself that I am following the maxims of policy; and under the appearance of salutary restraints, should be indulging the lust of dominion and that malevolence which delights in seeing others depressed."[6]

Liberals often start from abstract principles and from a utopian or outside perspective, or what John Rawls has called an "original position," developed behind a deliberate "veil of ignorance" about any concrete, existing community, or real life.[7] For conservatives, in contrast, there can never be any such veil of ignorance. They start from the inside rather than the outside, from the concrete reality of the existing community and its culture. Instead of abstract principles, the conservative takes as a starting point the moral obligations that arise from and sustain a specific, existing community, or what Hegel called *sittlichkeit*. The critical feature of *sittlichkeit* is that it "enjoins us to bring about what already is."[8] It expresses the inner moral idea of the community in whose life we already participate, and which makes us what we are. The institutions and practices of a given society are the bearers of implicit norms that call upon us to develop and live them out, not in abstract theory but in practice. In this perspective—largely opposed to the modern—we start not from the universal but from our own: from our own horizontal communities of today and our own vertical communities of memory.

But here there is a paradox, of which Tom Symons is perhaps the limiting case. Because in truly loving your own, you open yourself up, paradoxically, to others. Loved deeply enough, the particular leads right through itself and out the other side. It leads outward, not inward. If it is not intercepted by the opposing principle of self-assertion from which liberalism proceeds,[9] an innate sense of "loyalty to one's fellows *reaches out*," as Bernard Lonergan put it, "through kinsmen, friends, acquaintances, through all the bonds—cultural, social, civil, economic, technological—of human cooperation to unite ever more members of the human race in the acceptance of a common lot, in sharing a burden to be borne by all, in the building of a common future for themselves and future generations."[10]

Dennis Lee recalls George Grant's exuberant reaction to Lee's confession of his deep love for his boyhood Muskoka cottage: "How marvellous, Dennis!" Grant boomed. "It's what Plato meant, isn't it? . . .That we're made to love the Good. . . . And the way we come to love the Good is by first loving our own."

> By first loving our own! I still remember the little click with which that phrase slid into place, and I realized I actually knew what he was talking about. Grant was giving me back my instinctive, closer-than-breathing love for those pines, that rocky shoreline, the ramshackle cottage: giving it back to me in a luminous further dimension. For cherishing this childhood place—that was not just something I did by accident. It was what I was fitted for. Humans are being human when they love their own. I'd always known that. And at the same time, loving the cottage was a necessary first step, something to grow ahead from—it schooled me to love less immediate forms of 'the good.'[11]

If there were ever a Canadian who illustrates Plato's and Grant's point, that Canadian is Tom Symons. (Another is André Laurendeau, with whom Symons, fittingly, established a warm, spontaneous bond in the 1950s.[12]) Symons was raised by his family, especially his father and grandfather, to have a profound attachment to his own: to his own family, his own community, his own traditions, his own institutions, his own party, his own landscape, his own tastes, his own people. But instead of closing him off to others and to other communities, as you might expect, it opened him up, opened him up more fully than almost anyone you can think of. Many of the authors in this book remark on Symons's highly distinctive personal mannerisms, reflecting his own family and social background, a style with which he was entirely comfortable and felt no need to compromise. Yet almost all of them remark also on his extraordinary interest in—and empathy for—people from other backgrounds, traditions, languages, cultures, conditions, and places. When you really, truly love what you are, and where you come from—in the widest sense—you can't help responding to the same instinct in others. A genuine Upper Canadian Tory (as John A. Macdonald showed in the famous Brown Chamberlin letter, for example[13]) can readily understand why French-speaking Canadians—or people in or from other countries or cultures—might be as deeply attached to their own language and traditions as he or she is to theirs. Because Tom Symons is so deeply comfortable with his own identity, he is not threatened by difference. He welcomes and values it. Because he is so strongly attached to Canada, he is not limited by or to Canada. He sees Canada instead in the context of its wider loyalties, traditions, institutions, and new international opportunities. When you are truly at home in your own skin, as I said at the beginning of this book, it seems to open you up, paradoxically, to the whole world.

Robertson Davies once remarked that in order to understand Vincent Massey, you had first to understand that he was an artist. But an artist who worked in an unusual medium: his own life.

I believe something similar could be said of Tom Symons. And his artistic temperament is linked to the idealist impulse I already noted. In both his personal and public lives, he seems to be gifted in—and motivated by—the creation of form. Whether it is the giving of form to an "idea"; recognizing the presence of form in communities, buildings, painting, and objects; or the giving of form to everyday life, in the shapes of gracious courtesy, ceremony, celebration, friendship, and fun.

Symons's temperament is also artistic in its concreteness. He is not normally given to abstraction or to theory. Like an artist (and a historian) he is drawn instead to the particular: particular places, people, objects, institutions, and so on. The particular can be an intuitive door to the universal, but it remains stubbornly particular, individual, concrete. Symons's own preference for the concrete is especially pronounced, even material and physical.

One of the modes in which this aesthetic physicality combines with his conservative instinct for community is in Symons's tender delight in the careful stewardship of the Perkins Bull Collection, the artefacts, *objets d'art,* and paintings assembled by his grandfather.[14] It is also evident in his profound sense of place, his deep loyalty to specific communities and landscapes. But it can perhaps best be seen in his lifelong commitment to heritage preservation in all its many forms, especially architectural heritage. "Being the point of conjunction between art and life," he argued as early as 1967, "architecture is the pre-eminent expression of the sensibility of a cultural community." The buildings of a community express its "historical essence." They are the "vital records of a nation which represent a living tradition, and accumulating inheritance, which can and should be passed forward to succeeding generations as their birthright." Four decades ago he already deplored the "naïve and unconsidered approach" to urban development which was destroying the distinctive character of communities all across North America and producing nothing but "more supermarkets, more parking, and an indefinite expansion in the amount of plate glass and chrome." This was a dead end: socially, culturally, and even economically. The best way for communities to achieve real and worthwhile development, Symons argued—and would continue to argue for the next forty years, and more—is to emphasize the "special character" that distinguishes them from others. And the "most obvious, the most fruitful and yet the simplest way" for a community to do that is "to preserve and enhance its architectural heritage."[15]

While Tom Symons's artistic temperament and aesthetic physicality are everywhere present in his professional and public activities, they are perhaps most evident in his own life. As he himself once wrote, "life is an art."[16] And nothing illustrates that better than the one he has led, and how he has led it. No one who has witnessed the zest and care with which Tom Symons plans and organizes a social event—from the smallest, most informal cup of tea in front of a fire to a major reception involving the Royal family—can be in any doubt that they are in the presence of a consummate artist, a creative genius in the endowment of everyday life with significant form.

Symons's gift for creating form in everyday life no doubt has many roots, but one of them must surely be his huge capacity for enjoyment. This too can be seen as another aspect of his natural conservatism. Michael Oakeshott, for one, has argued that the "disposition to be conservative is. . .warm and positive in respect of enjoyment." It is a disposition to "enjoy what is present," a disposition "to enjoy rather than to exploit."[17] No one embodies this disposition more vividly than Tom Symons. From his youth, his friends recognized his zestful gusto for the stuff of everyday life. It was one of the things that drew them to him, and made him a natural focus of social activity. It is simply fun to be with someone who is so much *in* the present: who is enjoying it and himself enormously. Symons takes deep delight in the things of everyday life: in physical surroundings of all kinds—objects, paintings, buildings, streetscapes, landscapes—in people and encounters, in new discoveries and old familiarities, in prodigious work and in equally relished play, in hospitality and occasion, in dignified ceremony and spontaneous tomfoolery, in wit and laughter, in music and singing, in food and drink, and so on. This is clearly something deep in his own nature, but no doubt also absorbed, like so many other things, from the example of his family. In his natural capacity for enjoyment Symons certainly echoes his maternal grandfather's outsized appetite for life, and for all it holds of pleasure and adventure. In his own autobiographical notes, Perkins Bull expressed puzzlement at "those who cannot understand a man doing anything [simply] for sheer joy in the task. . . . I have made money and given most of it away, or lost it, studied, travelled. . . all for the same reason—the reason for which I have eaten more pumpkin pie and blackberry roly-poly than was good for my figure—because I enjoyed myself in the doing."[18] Something very similar could surely be said of his grandson.

Oakeshott remarks that the conservative disposition is most evident in certain kinds of activities—"where what is sought is present enjoyment and not a profit, a reward, a prize or a result in addition to the experience itself"—and that one of the chief among these is the activity of friendship: "Friends are not concerned with what might be made of one another; but only with the enjoyment of one another."[19] Whatever the validity of the generalization about the conservative temperament, of Tom Symons it could scarcely be more apt. He has a singular gift for friendship, and that gift is a clue not just to the private man but also to his professional success. His instinct, where possible, is to turn his professional colleagues into something more like friends, to make work a kind of friendship. This is one of the qualities that makes him such a successful leader and chair of innumerable boards, committees, commissions, and so on. His colleagues normally feel the friendliness of this outlook and are warmed by it. They feel valued and appreciated. They feel as if they have their place, and have a contribution to make. They usually respond in kind, with loyalty and constructive engagement.

Tom Symons's gift for friendship is also closely connected to his ideas about higher education. For him, a university is at its best when it is something like a circle of friendship, a place of mutual interest, support, guidance, and even affection. That partly explains his commitment to a vision of higher education based on the concept of the residential college. Because it is only within the smaller scope of the constituent college that university education is able to approach closer to something like a model of friendship. Only within the structure of a residential college—where people not only learn together but also eat, drink, and live together—can professional colleagues become something more like friends, across all the boundaries of discipline and background, and offer friendly interest, guidance, and human example to their students.

The spirit of friendship is also related to Symons's parallel belief in small-group teaching. Because it is only in small groups that real conversations can take place. And conversation is at the heart of learning. Since Socrates and Plato, we have known that genuine learning takes place in the intensity of personal dialogue—both inner and outer—where the feelings and the whole person are engaged, and where the participants enter fully into the perspectives and feelings of the other. It is only when "questions and answers are exchanged in good faith and without malice," said Plato, "that finally, when human capacity is stretched to its limit, a spark of understanding and intelligence flashes out and illuminates the subject at issue."[20] Authentic learning—the learning that engages the whole person, not just the abstract intellect—is a kind of transformative conversation. And to achieve its real aim, this sort of conversation must become a kind of friendship, because the participants are necessarily engaged in a new community, bound together by a "fusion of horizons," by the truth of that for which they are searching. And this new community changes us. It draws us into a new space, a new moral contract—a new "educational" contract—within which we cannot remain what we were.[21] We are transformed by the moral experience of community.

In other words, the threads of creative form in everyday life, of concreteness, particularity, and enjoyment, of friendship and conversation, lead us back, inevitably, to the theme or "idea" of community that has been central to Tom Symons's life and work. Because friendship, as Aristotle remarked, "seems to be the bond that holds communities together."[22]

Tom Symons has led a Canadian life in two senses: both quintessentially and archetypically.

Quintessentially, it would be difficult to imagine someone more deeply rooted or more broadly involved in Canadian life over the last half century. His family gave him deep Canadian roots and identity and taught him to be conscious of and to value the concrete, soil-rooted community into which he was born, with its dense social, cultural, and institutional fabric. But he also chose to devote himself to that community and to develop it further, serving in such a large number of institutional roles that merely reading a listing of them can fill an ordinary mortal with a growing sense of exhaustion. In the course of this exhausting public life, he has not only led innumerable national institutions and initiatives but has also forged ties with institutions and communities in almost all parts of the country. He has served the north as well as the south. He has served French as well as English. He has served Aboriginal as well as non-Aboriginal Canadians. He has served in PEI as well as in Peterborough.

But giving himself so completely to Canadian public life was not enough. He was also conscious, from the beginning, of the need to understand, cherish, and celebrate Canadian life, in all its rich and sometimes contradictory forms. Indeed, if there is a theme, rightly or wrongly, with which Symons's name remains connected in the public mind, it is the theme of Canadian studies. One of Symons's first policy proposals, while still Dean of Devonshire House, was for a U of T summer program in Canadian studies, including "Canadian history, politics, institutions, law, literature, music and art."[23] This was not incidental or accidental. Four years later, at the official opening ceremonies for Trent University, its young President declared,

> It is very much the hope and wish of everyone associated with Trent University that it may become in the fullness of time a useful and significant centre for Canadian studies. By this is meant the study of our Canadian civilization—for such there surely is—in its totality: its history, literature, art and institutions, its people and its sciences. In relation to this programme, Trent University is planning in the near future to give sponsorship and support to a new quarterly, to be named a *Journal of Canadian Studies.*[24]

He was true to his word, and Trent University did all those things, establishing one of the first and most imaginative Canadian studies programs in the country. Then, eight years later, as he was concluding his presidential term, Symons became chair (as David Cameron recounts) of a Commission on Canadian studies established by the Association of Universities and Colleges of Canada (AUCC) to study the "state of teaching and research in various fields of study relating to Canada at Canadian universities." The Commission's historic report, *To Know Ourselves,* was not exactly consistent—it both rejected and affirmed Canadian identity as a rationale—but, on the whole, it put forward a persuasive case for studies related to Canada in Canadian universities, based on the traditional importance attached to self-knowledge within western culture: "the need to know and to understand ourselves: who we are; where we are going; what we possess; what our responsibilities are to ourselves and to others." And it did so within the perspective of community that is a *leitmotif* both in Symons's thought and in his life:

> Self-knowledge of the individual cannot be divorced from knowledge of the society in which one lives. . . . The quest for self-knowledge. . .must embrace the study of culture and community. Hence if a Canadian is to seek the self-knowledge that is essential for both health and wisdom, he must have access to a wider self-knowledge of his historical community and its contemporary circumstances.[25]

So, both by his actions and by his thought, Symons's life has been quintessentially Canadian. But such a life can also be seen as archetypically or paradigmatically Canadian. That is to say, it embodies characteristics we might associate with the "idea" of Canada or with the ideal Canadian, if there were such a thing.

The most obvious theme of Symons's life that offers guidance for the future is his ever-present refrain of community. At a time when the forces of contemporary life—especially now the all-pervading electronic environment of the Internet—are dissolving societies more than ever (even in modernity) into collections of isolated, self-asserting individuals, Symons's emphasis on community is a message and an example of great significance. But it is not just the importance of community that Symons's life helps us to see, but, even more, what community can and should mean today.

The first thing we can learn from it is the need to see the community *whole*, in all its richness and diversity. Symons's life helps us to see what, in philosophical language, might be called the "transcendental necessity of holism."[26] More than forty years ago, he already recognized, for example, that the heritage of a community included much more than buildings. The heritage of a community must also be conceived as including its "natural" and physical environment, its culture, its own myths and symbols, "its legendary and continuingly significant figures," its literary and artistic achievements.[27] This was a theme to which he returned throughout his life. Almost thirty years later, he was still tirelessly promoting the "twin message that the cultural world is part of our environment and that the natural world is part of our cultural heritage."[28] Yet another decade later he took heart—perhaps too optimistically—that "the penny has finally dropped."

> Just as our definition of "heritage" has expanded to include the natural environment, landscapes and myriad cultural components, we now recognize that 'heritage,' 'arts' and 'culture' are not three separate and distinct entities but integral parts of each other.[29]

This same instinct also helps explain his parallel, holistic instinct for culture—his belief that, in the end, "it's all about culture"—and his natural sympathy for multidisciplinary, "studies" perspectives and for interdisciplinarity. No matter what the community—whether Canada or the Commonwealth, or the Valley of the Trent—he has always wanted to see and understand it *whole*, in all of its diverse manifestations and expressions. For Tom Symons, the community is much more than a group of people living together in a geographic space. It is a culture, a culture in its broadest possible sense, as a "civilization"—"in its totality: its history, literature, art and institutions, its people and its sciences." It is the "sum total of how one lives and what one values," the "sum of all we have and are."[30]

One of the obvious corollaries of his bias for holism is Symons's vision of the community as inclusive. Of course inclusion is such a common theme of the modern rights-based state that this aspect of Symons's life might appear almost banal, were it not for three important features of his own holistic inclusiveness. The first is its authenticity and spontaneity, the depth of its genuine human warmth. Symons's inclusiveness is not an abstract, intellectual principle. It proceeds from a real interest in other people—an interest encompassing but going beyond both curiosity and respect to affective rapport—and a natural empathy with their whole situation, culture, or condition. And this first, striking feature of Symons's inclusiveness is the key to the second: its far-sighted boldness. The fact that he was usually ahead of others in seeing where the community needed to go: in making room for everyone, or repairing the wrongs of the past. Whether it was the death penalty, or the Aboriginal peoples, or French-language education and Ontario-Quebec relations, or human rights, Symons was leading the way to justice, not despite his own background and values but because of them.

Which suggests the third and perhaps the most significant feature of Tom Symons's inclusive holism. Symons's life and actions illustrate that respect for others and self-respect go together. That there is no need to reject or be ashamed of what you are, or where you come from, in order to embrace others. It is very common today to assume that being inclusive must involve wiping out the past or abandoning key features of one culture and its attachments in order to accommodate others. Tom Symons shows us this doesn't have to be the case and that indeed this path leads nowhere except to rootlessness, or to an ugly backlash, or to both. He remained completely, uncompromisingly himself, while reaching out to others. And it was because he was so much himself that he could do so.

The horizontal community of today cannot be genuine or strong, Symons reminds us, if it is not also a community of memory, an inclusive community of memory where all the traditions blend and are mutually cherished. Symons's own attachment to Canada's constitutional community of memory—its heritage of parliamentary government, its long traditions of liberty and order going back to the middle ages, its links to Crown and Commonwealth—is a case in point. This community of memory is not at odds with Canada's bilingual and multicultural future, his life suggests. It is more likely the condition for that future. The miracle that is Toronto today, for example, has not come about despite its past but because of it. Because all these cultures came into a pre-existing tradition of civility and order which made (and, for the time being, still makes) their peaceful coexistence possible in a way that is a marvel and a model for the rest of the world.

The "best chance—perhaps the one chance" to create "satisfying and stimulating" communities, Symons has argued, is to build on their distinctive experience and character. And the "main elements of that character are to be found in our history," he suggests. For individual communities, as for Canada as a whole, "the way to the future must lie in a sensitive and dynamic appreciation of our past, and an imaginative and constructive building forward from the past."[31] That is as true for social justice, for cultural policy, for sustainable economic development, and for national unity as it is for architectural heritage and urban planning.

Symons's life also shows us that a sense of community can and should reach out, not just within Canada but beyond it. His leadership of the international board of the United World Colleges reflected a belief in the importance of a truly international perspective—a genuinely "multi-national, multi-racial and multi-cultural approach"—in secondary education, and the contribution such an approach can make to shaping the outlook of tomorrow's world leaders, giving them "better international knowledge and understanding both of human rights and of the conditions making for peace, and of the inter-relationships between the two."[32] His lifelong effort to strengthen the wider community of memory that is the Commonwealth reflects a view that this kind of community is not archaic but post-modern. From this angle, loyalty once again puts Symons ahead of the game, not behind it. His own rootedness allows him to recognize that sovereignty is not a zero-sum proposition, nor an absolute. Communities are not diminished by taking their place within still wider communities.

While he did not invent the expression, Symons would no doubt be very comfortable with the idea that Canada is a "community of communities," which takes its proper place within even wider communities of communities, especially communities of memory and culture such as the Commonwealth and Francophonie, as well as communities of economic interest and self-protection, and global communities such as the United Nations. In a global world, the nation state cannot be the end of the story. It is just the beginning. So our first international community is the cornerstone for others. It reminds us of the traditions of civil governance we have to offer the world, and of those who can do it with us because they share those same traditions. We do not have to renounce old ties and practices in order to be authentically ourselves in a borderless world. In this kind of world, such communities of memory might even be more important than ever.

In the old debate between Underhill and Creighton, Symons was very much on Creighton's side, on the side that held the question to be not whether Canada is an American nation—it obviously is—but rather whether it can afford to be *only* an American nation. "Continentalism," he once said, "can generate a kind of fortress thinking in which the countries of a region become inward-looking while they put up economic, social, cultural and intellectual barriers against the rest of mankind." It is precisely within this kind of world that other communities of memory "take on a new and heightened importance" as a means both to balance power and influence and to "retain a diversity of windows on the world."[33] This diversity is important for many reasons, including a greater potential for freedom and moral leadership in international affairs. Blending his devotion to the parliamentary tradition with his internationalism, Symons once suggested that Canada should be more ready to employ a "loyal but different voice" in the councils of its allies. This would involve, he explained, "fostering in the international sphere the concept of Her Majesty's Loyal Opposition which is the hard-won product of centuries of parliamentary government."[34] Such are the practical, contemporary uses of a community of memory and practice.

Tom Symons's life can also serve to remind us of the limits of abstraction and the virtues of the concrete, including in our concept of Canada itself. His own conservative temperament has always shied away from intellectual or analytic abstraction, preferring the concrete, particularity of the artist and the historian. Even his internationalism builds outward from specific communities and associations, and is rooted in a very concrete sense of place, whether those places are Toronto or Oxford or London or Peel County or Peterborough or the Trent Valley or Brackley Beach.

Similarly, Symons's idea of Canada seems to be carried less by abstract notions of the Canadian identity as by loyalty to specific places, memories, institutions, and practices. His example can thus be emblematic for us because, in more areas of life than we normally recognize in the modern world, it is our practices that actually "carry" our understanding, not the other way around. That is to say, the understanding is deeply embedded in and implicitly justified by the practice.[35] That's part of the meaning of *sittlichkeit.* We can think of institutions and practices as "a kind of language" in which ideas of fundamental importance for human beings are expressed. And because of the difficulty of expressing these ideas in other ways, the practices may well be the best, or maybe even the only way, to express them.[36] So the best way not only to cherish but even to express the deep ideas that are carried in them is to attend with proper care to the institutions and the practices themselves.

For Symons, such institutions begin with the central institutions of the state; the Crown as the symbol of continuity, liberty, and order, and the parliamentary institutions and traditions of self-government that developed from it. For Symons, the state in a parliamentary democracy is not the enemy; it is an expression of the community itself, one of the chief means through which a vulnerable, geographically dispersed, bilingual, dual, multicultural, and regionalized community like Canada can organize, develop, protect, and express itself, and also pursue its own ideals of justice and sharing. While he recognizes that "caution and balance are needed" and that there can be danger in excessive reliance on "the creation of bureaucracies,"[37] the overwhelming bias of his many reports and recommendations for public policy has been in favour of a positive role for public authority, as a means for building community. His policy prescriptions show he believes the public space of the community is every bit as legitimate as the private space of individuals and corporations, perhaps more legitimate, since it establishes the prior conditions for the latter to flourish.[38] In this sense, he again turns out to be a genuine conservative, not one of those unreconstructed liberals, currently disguised as Conservatives, who are more at home with Cobden and Bright than with Johnson or Burke or Disraeli or John A. Macdonald or Leslie Frost or Robert Stanfield. Nor would he approve of those who distort or harm parliamentary institutions by aggressively exploiting their unwritten flexibility—pushing it to the limits for partisan advantage—rather than being governed by self-restraint, by a due respect for the institutions themselves and for all those who participate in them, and by "the high code of personal honour. . .essential in the conduct of our public affairs" in a parliamentary democracy.[39] In this kind of democracy, as in life itself, the only way to nourish the deep ideas carried in our institutions and practices is to act as responsible, discerning stewards. And pass them on unimpaired, or even enriched, "a living tradition, and accumulating inheritance, which can and should be passed forward to succeeding generations as their birthright."[40]

That is what Tom Symons has spent his life doing. And it is one of the things that life shows us, and can mean for us.

On at least one occasion Tom Symons deliberately quoted the same passage from *City of God*, which the Massey-Lévesque Commission chose as the epigraph for its historic report, a passage in which Augustine offered a definition of a "people": "an association of reasonable beings united in a peaceful sharing of the things they cherish; therefore, to determine the quality of the nation, you must consider what those things are."[41] Symons has clearly done more than his share to support and enhance those things Augustine and the Massey Commission referred to—the things Symons himself called "our intangible legacy of customs, values, knowledge and beliefs." He has sought to preserve this legacy, rooted in "the total historical experience of our society to this moment," in the "context into which we have been born and in which we now live," which "provides us with our sense of identity and our bearings for the next journeys into coming generations."[42]

But he has not been content merely to remember and pass on. He has also sought to improve and make more just. Neither he nor the Massey Commission mentioned Augustine's other observation that true community exists only where justice is truly sought: "where this justice does not exist, there is certainly no 'association of men united by a common sense of right and by a community of interest.' Therefore there is no commonwealth; for where there is no 'people,' there is no 'weal of the people.'"[43] But if Symons did not say it here, he said it amply elsewhere, even more by actions than by words. Much of his life was given to making Canadian communities better exemplars of the idea of justice already embedded in their institutions and practices.

It has somewhere been said that a nationalist is someone who hates his or her own country, who is ashamed of it and wants to change it, wants it to be different than it is. A patriot, on the other hand, is someone who loves his or her country, who relishes and enjoys it as it actually is. Michael Oakeshott suggests that patriotism is one of those modes, like friendship and conversation, where a conservative disposition for enjoyment is to the fore. In these modes of being "the condition of enjoyment is a ready acceptance of what is."[44] From this perspective, Symons is clearly a patriot rather than a nationalist. His enjoyment of the Canadian reality, in all its diversity and self-contradiction, is too lively and deep to allow the narrower emotions of the nationalist. He understands the romance of the familiar, the pleasures of repetition and of ritual, the fulfilment of continuity and loyalty, the richness of diversity, the grateful delight in what is. But he is also a progressive who wants the community he loves to change and evolve, in keeping with its own traditions, to become even more worthy of the ideas and potential it embodies.

On that score his tone has become more urgent over the years as he argues that Canadians are now in a "race against time," a race "that we are not currently winning." It is a race against "cultural amnesia" and "rampant me-firstism," against the "mad rush and uncertainty of technological change," the "abandonment of values," and the "atomization of what was once a shared community of beliefs."

"In these circumstances," he observes, "it is difficult to know who we are and to decide what matters." As a result, Canadian society "finds itself engaged in a perilous balancing act" between memory and forgetfulness, between continuity and discontinuity, between preservation and loss, between the past and the future. If Canadians do not "soon rediscover our sense of history and our sense of purpose," they risk falling into "a rootless condition like the tumbleweed."[45]

Symons takes heart from what he calls "the essential conservatism of Canadian society," for he believes that Canadian history displays "a remarkable degree of continuity which is perhaps the most fundamental characteristic of our society." But with the same breath, he also acknowledges that "ours has proven to be, thus far, a remarkably destructive society," as destructive of its past as of its physical environment. To remedy both kinds of destructiveness he advocates the values, goals, and outlook of a "conserver society." Given its "innate conservatism" he thinks Canadian society "should readily understand and relate" to this conserver ethic, but admits, perhaps somewhat quizzically, that "it has not yet quite done so."[46]

Perhaps it has not done so because Canada is not quite as conservative as Symons would like to think. Canada is as modern as any other western country, and the dominant ethic in the modern world is not continuity and conservation but rather "the centrality of freedom as a good."[47] The moral vision underpinning this good is that of individuals associating together freely, to secure certain benefits for themselves. So the idea of freedom is also closely linked to a rational "cost-benefit" calculation or, at best, to a calculation of "mutual benefit."[48] These virtues of self-assertion have brought many precious things to the modern world, but the fall-out from them has been the high level of "destructiveness" Symons deplores.

The interesting question hidden in Symons's challenge, however, is whether this kind of world presupposes certain moral goods that it cannot furnish by itself. Can such a world really exist without support from another kind of human impulse? Symons's implicit answer is that it cannot. That without something else, this kind of world leads only to the destructiveness about which he warns.

What might this something else be? It would have to be something that "goes way beyond any possible mutuality, a self-giving not bounded by some measure of fairness."[49] And here Symons's own life and gifts can again be instructive. Because a traditional name for this kind of human impulse is the word "friendship." Friendship implies something that is not measured by fairness, and perfect friendship would be a self-giving going far beyond mutuality, perhaps even to the point, if necessary, of laying down one's life for one's friends. Thomas Aquinas suggested, in fact, that we find what is most important for human beings "working through friendship."[50]

So the gift for friendship that is a hallmark of Tom Symons's life can be emblematic for us on a much broader canvas. At the level of western civilization or culture, it can point us to virtues that are missing, or no longer as highly developed as we need them to be, or hidden from our view. Within Canada itself it can point us to the spirit we need to adopt toward our natural environment, toward our past, present, and future—which form a whole that "cannot be split up into individual elements"[51]—and, above all, toward each other: men and women, French and English-speaking, Québécois and the rest of Canada, north and south, Aboriginal and non-Aboriginal, westerners and easterners, newcomers and fifth-generation Canadians, and so on.

While we all come from different places and different pasts, we are not limited by them. We can embrace them and build outward from them. Through a genuine spirit of friendship, conversation, and community, we can indeed become an association of reasonable beings united in a peaceful sharing of the things we cherish. We can, as Symons put it (in a specific context), "transcend the differences of language and. . .join together more closely and usefully in a bond of shared experience and common understanding."[52] Of course, the quality of this association will depend, as Augustine suggested, on the quality of what we cherish. But we do not have to look far to find such things. We do not need to look for abstractions or conceptual formulations, or start drawing up lists. They are already here, Tom Symons's life reminds us, in our own institutions and practices. And we can start by genuinely loving and caring for them as our own.

Notes

1 Samuel Taylor Coleridge, *On the Constitution of the Church and State*, ed. John Colmer, *The Collected Works of Samuel Taylor Coleridge* 10 (London and Princeton: Routledge and Kegan Paul and Princeton University Press, 1976), 12. Italics in original.

2 Thomas Aquinas, *Summa Theologica*, 3a. viii. 3, in St. Thomas Aquinas, *Theological Texts*, selected and translated by Thomas Gilby (London: Oxford University Press, 1954), 338.

3 Robert N. Bellah, Richard Madsen, William M. Sullivan, Ann Swidler, and Steven M. Tipton, *Habits of the Heart*, updated edition with a new introduction (Berkeley and Los Angeles: University of California Press, 1985, 1996), 219–49, 275–96.

4 Alasdair MacIntyre, *After Virtue*, 2nd ed. (Notre Dame, Indiana: University of Notre Dame Press, 1984), 223.

5 Gilbert K. Chesterton, *Orthodoxy* (New York: Dodd, Mead and Company, 1924), 85.

6 Samuel Johnson, "From a Review of Soame Jenyns's *A Free Enquiry into the Nature and Origin of Evil*," in '*Rasselas' and Essays*, ed. Charles Peake (London: Routledge and Kegan Paul, 1967), 162.

7 John Rawls, *A Theory of Justice* (Cambridge, Mass.: The Belknap Press of Harvard University Press, 1971), 118–92.

8 Charles Taylor, *Hegel* (Cambridge: Cambridge University Press, 1975), 376.

9 Spinoza, *Ethic*, Third Part, Propositions VI and VII, in John Wild, ed., *Spinoza Selections* (New York: Scribners, 1930), 215–16; G. W. F. Hegel, "The Spirit of Christianity and its Fate,' in *Early Theological Writings*, trans. T. M. Knox and Richard Kroner (Chicago: University of Chicago Press, 1948), 186, cited in Charles Taylor, *Hegel* (Cambridge: Cambridge University Press, 1975), 58; T. H. Green, *Lectures on the Principles of Political Obligation* (London: Longmans, Green, 1927), 10; J. S. Mill, *On Liberty* (Harmondsworth: Penguin Books, 1974), 127; Paul Tillich, *The Courage to Be* (New Haven: Yale University Press, 1952), especially 18–31.

10 Bernard Lonergan, "Variations in Fundamental Theology," a lecture of 1973 at Trinity College, Toronto, 10, cited in Frederick E. Crowe, "Editors' Preface" in Bernard Lonergan, *Verbum: Word and Idea*, eds. Frederick E. Crowe and Robert M. Doran (Toronto: University of Toronto Press, 1997), viii. Emphasis added.

11 Dennis Lee, "Grant's Impasse," in Peter C. Emberley, ed, *By Loving Our Own: George Grant and the Legacy of Lament for a Nation* (Ottawa: Carleton University Press, 1990), 11–13.

12 Laurendeau paid Symons a return visit in Peterborough in May 1964, right in the middle of the hearings of the Royal Commission on Bilingualism and Biculturalism. He described Symons and his ilk as "des conservateurs intelligents—espèce d'homme que les Britanniques réussissent mieux que nous." André Laurendeau, *Journal tenu pendant la Commission royale d'enquête sur le bilinguisme et le biculturalisme* (Outremont: vlb éditeur/le septentrion, 1990), 202–05.

13 D. G. Creighton, *John A. Macdonald: The Young Politician* (Toronto: University of Toronto, 1952), 226–27.

14 André Laurendeau remarked that Symons's Peterborough home (also the former home of Robertson Davies, therefore named *Marchbanks*) was "furnished like a museum." *Journal tenu pendant la Commission royale d'enquête sur le bilinguisme et le biculturalisme* (Outremont: vlb éditeur/ le septentrion, 1990), 203.

15 Thomas H. B. Symons, "Trent University," in Ronald Borg, ed., *Peterborough: Land of Shining Waters* (Peterborough: City and County of Peterborough, 1967), 504–07.

16 Thomas H. B. Symons, "Commemorating Canada's Past: From Old Crow to New Bergthal," in Thomas H. B. Symons, ed., *The Place of History: Commemorating Canada's Past* (Ottawa: Historic Sites and Monuments Board of Canada and The Royal Society of Canada, 1997), 19.

17 Michael Oakeshott, *Rationalism in Politics and other essays* (London: Methuen, 1962), 172, 170, 173.

18 William Perkins Bull, "Autobiographical Notes," *Wm. Perkins Bull Collection*, Peel Heritage Complex, Brampton, Ontario, quoted in Robert J. Burns, "William Perkins Bull, K.C., LL.D., 1870–1948: Historical Background," in Ontario Heritage Trust, *Featured Plaque of the Month, November 2007*, 6.

19 Michael Oakeshott, *Rationalism in Politics and other essays* (London: Methuen, 1962), 175–77.

20 Plato, Seventh Letter 344, in Walter Hamilton, trans., *Plato: Phaedrus and Letters VII and VIII* (London, 1973), quoted in Karen Armstrong, *The Case for God* (New York: Alfred A. Knopf, 2009), 68.

21 Hans-Georg Gadamer, *Truth and Method*, 2nd, revised edition, translation revised by Joel Weinsheimer and Donald G. Marshall (New York: Continuum, 2002), 377–79; Northrop Frye, *Spiritus Mundi: Essays on Literature, Myth, and Society* (Bloomington & London: Indiana University

Press, 1976), 42; Ralph Heintzman, "The Educational Contract," *Journal of Canadian Studies* 14, no. 2 (Summer 1979): 1–2, 142–45.

22 Aristotle, *The Nicomachean Ethics*, Book 8, Chapter 1, 1155a, 20–25, trans J. A. K. Thomson, revised by Hugh Tredennick (London: Penguin Books, 2004), 201.

23 Dean T. H. B. Symons, *The University in Summer*, A Report prepared for the Presidential Committee on Policy and Planning of the University of Toronto, April 1960, 16–18. Symons Papers, Trent University Archives, Box 31, Files 12–17.

24 *Trent University Official Opening Ceremonies*, Saturday 17 October 1964 (Peterborough: Trent University, 1964), 15.

25 T. H. B. Symons, *To Know Ourselves: The Report of the Commission on Canadian Studies*, vol. I and II, (Ottawa: Association of Universities and Colleges of Canada, 1975), 12, 14.

26 Charles Taylor, *A Secular Age* (Cambridge, Mass.: The Belknap Press of Harvard University Press, 2007), 157.

27 Thomas H. B. Symons, "Trent University," in Ronald Borg, ed., *Peterborough: Land of Shining Waters* (Peterborough: City and County of Peterborough, 1967), 505–06.

28 Thomas H. B. Symons, "Commemorating Canada's Past: From Old Crow to New Bergthal," in Thomas H. B. Symons, ed., *The Place of History: Commemorating Canada's Past* (Ottawa: Historic Sites and Monuments Board of Canada and The Royal Society of Canada, 1997), 15.

29 Thomas H. B. Symons, "Notes for Remarks to the Opening Session of the 2009 Ontario Heritage Conference," Trent University, Peterborough, Ontario, 29 May 2009, 5.

30 T. H. B. Symons, "Canadian Postsecondary Education: The Cultural Agenda," in Alexander Gregor, Keith Wilson, eds., *Monographs in Education* (Winnipeg: University of Manitoba, 1986), 2; Thomas H. B. Symons, "Commemorating Canada's Past: From Old Crow to New Bergthal," in Thomas H. B. Symons, ed., *The Place of History: Commemorating Canada's Past* (Ottawa: Historic Sites and Monuments Board of Canada and The Royal Society of Canada, 1997), 19.

31 Thomas H. B. Symons, "Trent University," in Ronald Borg, ed., *Peterborough: Land of Shining Waters* (Peterborough: City and County of Peterborough, 1967), 504–05.

32 Thomas Symons, "Human Rights and Peace—Some Canadian Priorities? An Overview of the Colloquium," in Michael R. Hudson, ed., *Human Rights and Peace—Les droits de l'homme et la paix*, A report on the

Proceedings of a Colloquium which took place in Ottawa, Feb. 10–11, 1984 (Montreal: Canadian Human Rights Foundation, 1985), 93.

33 Thomas H. B. Symons, "Cultural Diplomacy: Some Thoughts on the Current State of Academic and Cultural Relations between Canada and the United Kingdom," in David Dilks, ed., *Britain and Canada: A Colloquium held at Leeds, October 1979*, The Commonwealth Foundation Occasional Paper Number XLIX (London: The Commonwealth Foundation, 1980), 85.

34 Thomas Symons, "Human Rights and Peace—Some Canadian Priorities? An Overview of the Colloquium," in Michael R. Hudson, ed., *Human Rights and Peace—Les droits de l'homme et la paix*, A report on the Proceedings of a Colloquium which took place in Ottawa, Feb. 10–11, 1984 (Montreal: Canadian Human Rights Foundation, 1985), 91.

35 Charles Taylor, *A Secular Age* (Cambridge and London: The Belknap Press of Harvard University Press, 2007), 173.

36 Charles Taylor, *Hegel* (Cambridge: Cambridge University Press, 1975), 382; *Sources of the Self: The Making of the Modern Identity* (Cambridge, Mass.: Harvard University Press, 1989), 91–92; Bernard Williams, *Ethics and the Limits of Philosophy* (Cambridge, Mass.: Harvard University Press, 1985), 114, 146–48, 152–54.

37 Thomas H. B. Symons, "A Race Against Time," in Thomas H. B. Symons, ed., *The Place of History: Commemorating Canada's Past* (Ottawa: Historic Sites and Monuments Board of Canada and The Royal Society of Canada, 1997), 294.

38 Aristotle, *The Nicomachean Ethics*, Book 1, Chapter 2, 1094b, 5–10; Book 6, Chapter 8, 1142a, 5–10, translated by J. A. K. Thomson, revised by Hugh Tredennick (London: Penguin Books, 2004), 4–5, 155.

39 John Farthing, *Freedom Wears a Crown* (Toronto: Kingswood House, 1957), 126.

40 Thomas H. B. Symons, "Trent University," in Ronald Borg, ed., *Peterborough: Land of Shining Waters* (Peterborough: City and County of Peterborough, 1967), 504–07.

41 Thomas H. B. Symons, "A Race Against Time," in Thomas H. B. Symons, ed., *The Place of History: Commemorating Canada's Past* (Ottawa: Historic Sites and Monuments Board of Canada and The Royal Society of Canada, 1997), 293; Canada, Royal Commission on National Development in the Arts, Letters and Sciences, 1949–1951, *Report* (Ottawa: Edmond Cloutier, Printer to the King's Most Excellent Majesty, 1951), xxiii. For some reason, the Massey Commission chose to translate "populus" as "nation."

42 Thomas H. B. Symons, "Commemorating Canada's Past: From Old Crow to New Bergthal," in Thomas H. B. Symons, ed., *The Place of History: Commemorating Canada's Past* (Ottawa: Historic Sites and Monuments Board of Canada and The Royal Society of Canada, 1997), 19.

43 Saint Augustine *City of God*, translated by Henry Bettenson (London: Penguin Books, 2003), 890.

44 Michael Oakeshott, *Rationalism in Politics and Other Essays* (London: Methuen, 1962), 177.

45 Thomas H. B. Symons, "Commemorating Canada's Past: From Old Crow to New Bergthal" and "A Race against Time," in Thomas H. B. Symons, ed., *The Place of History: Commemorating Canada's Past* (Ottawa: Historic Sites and Monuments Board of Canada and The Royal Society of Canada, 1997), 21, 294.

46 Ibid., 294, 14.

47 Charles Taylor, *Sources of the Self: The Making of the Modern Identity* (Cambridge: Harvard University Press, 1989), 395.

48 Robert N. Bellah, Richard Madsen, William M. Sullivan, Ann Swidler, and Steven M. Tipton, *Habits of the Heart*, updated edition with a new introduction (Berkeley and Los Angeles: University of California Press, 1985, 1996), 127; Charles Taylor, *A Secular Age* (Cambridge and London: The Belknap Press of Harvard University Press, 2007), 171.

49 Charles Taylor, *A Secular Age* (Cambridge and London: The Belknap Press of Harvard University Press, 2007), 430.

50 Thomas Aquinas, *Summa Theologica*, 1a-2ae. cviii. 1, in St. Thomas Aquinas, *Theological Texts*, selected and translated by Thomas Gilby (London: Oxford University Press, 1955), 154.

51 Ernst Cassirer, *An Essay on Man* (New York: Bantam Books, 1970), 54–55.

52 T. H. B. Symons, "Some Thoughts on the Nature and Value of National and Regional Atlases," in Barbara J. Gutsell, ed., *Cartographica*, Monograph 23: *The Purpose and Use of National and Regional Atlases*, (Toronto: Department of Geography, York University, 1979), 9.

Remarks on the Occasion of the Retirement of Professor T. H. B. Symons as President and Vice-Chancellor of Trent University at the Seventy-fourth Meeting of the Trent University Senate 24 May 1972

STUART ROBSON

There is a custom in polite society whereby institutions demonstrate the virtue of retiring leaders by offering themselves as the incontrovertible evidence of greatness. "A measure of the man," it is said, "has been his wise choice of colleagues, . . . if you seek his monument, look around—at us!" This sort of harmless self-promotion might be appropriate in polite society, or even in academic society, but it would be a presumptuous way for the Senate of Trent to salute our retiring president. Our excellence is still too putative to serve as an unambiguous testimonial.

In the wider world, we are known as Tom Symons's university. Such a public opinion reflects in part the nature of the office which the president of any university must serve. He must, in some way or other, speak for the whole institution, and never more so than when a university is new and is establishing itself through the process one might call "emergency." The identification of Tom Symons and Trent, however, arises as much from the nature of the man as from the nature of his office. It would be a disservice to him and to his associates to think that he alone created Trent, but it is a matter of record that, without him, Trent would not have been created. In conception, in planning, and in patient administration, his was the mind and character which gave unity to the parts. The coherence ties our name to his.

Each of us could describe a different Tom Symons. That is not because the man is evasive or his qualities difficult to perceive. Rather it follows from our being relatively so small and intimate an institution, with less of the precision which roles in large institutions confer upon those who occupy them. For good or ill, we stand close enough to see each other in the round, and so we must naturally have a distinct personal view of the one man whom we have all met. Some of us know Tom Symons as an academic who acts upon the novel belief that students are interesting adult human beings. Some of us know him as a fellow teacher. And, although I am being arbitrarily selective, the Tom Symons I would salute is the graceful, civil man who has presided over the Senate. Let it be understood that grace and civility are not his only virtues; rather, they merit attention if only because there is a persistent notion in the land that they are not virtues at all. To the cynical, civility is an anachronism obscuring what is thought to be the "real" nature of affairs; to the romantic, it is a cousin to hypocrisy and the enemy of inner truth. To care for exact meaning, to treasure form because it is inseparable from content, to pause until implications are clearer, to worry not only that one be protected against the error of others but that others be protected against one's own truth, to act on the premise of fallibility—in sum, to be civil—means that one must swim to some extent against the current. But that current may not be serving universities, and if civility restrains spontaneous impulse, it may do so in a higher cause. Cathedrals were not built by heaving blocks around until they lodged in a pile, nor should the free play of intellect be confused with group therapy. Whatever else the university may be, it must first be a place where care is taken, care for words, care for implications, care for others. If this Senate has been competent, if it has been at all effective as a parliament of academic change, credit must go above all to its chairman, who has shown us that we must take care. Ideas have competed here, but not men, for the chairman has gently and consistently turned us away from *ad hominem* debate.

The tolerance which has guided the Senate has shaped the university. To build what might be called the House of Second

Thoughts is a painstaking labour, and Tom Symons has not had the chance to forget about Trent for ten years. He might have had an easier time had he crushed dissent or decreed an end to argument. But to proceed that way would be to make nonsense of the journey; only the means of civility nourish trust, and, through trust, freedom of thought.

We must not puff ourselves up by saying that what we are now testifies to the spirit of the president. We have far to go; that is why, in the deepest sense of the word, it is fun to be where we are now. Sir, you have given us ten years of your life, you have given us an idea, and you have given us the civil spirit to pursue the idea. We thank you, for those are gifts indeed.

Curriculum Vitae

THOMAS HENRY BULL SYMONS
Founding President and Vanier Professor Emeritus
Trent University

Education:

Primary and secondary education in Toronto, 1935–47

Undergraduate studies in the honours course in Modern History, University of Toronto, 1947–51

Graduate studies in Modern History, Oriel College, Oxford University, 1951–53

Independent studies, Paris, Leyden, Rome, 1953

Research fellowship, Harvard University, 1956

Degrees and Academic Honours:

BA, with first-class honours, University of Toronto, 1951

BA, Oxford, 1953

MA, Oxford, 1957

LLD (honoris causa), Wilfrid Laurier University, 1971

LLD (honoris causa), University of New Brunswick, 1972

LLD (honoris causa), York University, 1973

DU (honoris causa), Université d'Ottawa, 1974

LLD (honoris causa), Trent University, 1975

LLD (honoris causa), Laurentian University, 1977

FRSC, 1977
LLD (honoris causa), Mount Allison University, 1979
LLD (honoris causa), Concordia University, 1981
LLD (honoris causa), University of Prince Edward Island, 1983
LLD (honoris causa), Dalhousie University, 1983
DLitt (honoris causa), University of Colombo, 1985
LLD (honoris causa), University of Manitoba, 1990
DCnL (honoris causa), St. John's College, Winnipeg, 2001

Academic Awards:

The C. S. MacInnes Scholarship in Political Science, University of Toronto, 1949
The first Maurice Cody Scholarship in Canadian History, University of Toronto, 1950
The Trinity College Prize in History, University of Toronto, 1951
The University Honours Award, University of Toronto, 1951
The Edward Kylie Award for post-graduate studies, 1951–52, renewed 1952–53
The Massey Fellowship for post-graduate studies at Oxford University, 1951–52, renewed 1952–53
Scholarship to study international relations in Germany, awarded by the National Federation of Canadian University Students, 1952
Elected to the Cumming Fellowship by Trinity College, University of Toronto, 1954, renewed 1955
Rockefeller Grant, Harvard University, 1956
University of Toronto Research Grant, 1960
Trent University Research Grant, 1968
Recipient of the first honorary diploma awarded by Sir Sandford Fleming College, 1970
Research grants awarded by:
The Canada Council, 1972
The Science Council of Canada, 1973
The W. M. Messecar Foundation, 1974
The Canada Council, 1975
Visiting Fellow, the Calgary Institute for the Humanities, 1977
Associate, Australian Studies Centre, University of Queensland, Brisbane, Australia, 1980

Research grants awarded, 1980, by:
The McLean Foundation
The W. M. Messecar Foundation
Research grants awarded, 1981, by:
The Leon and Thea Koerner Foundation
The Walter and Duncan Gordon Charitable Foundation
Honorary Diplôme d'Etudes Collégiales, Dawson College, 1981
Scholar in Residence and Ward Lecturer, St. John's College, University of Manitoba, March 1983
Elected a Visiting Fellow by Clare Hall, Cambridge University, 1984
Visiting Scholar, Scott Polar Research Institute, Cambridge, 1984
Award of Merit of the Association for Canadian Studies, 1984
Elected a Distinguished Member by the Canadian Society for the Study of Higher Education, 1985
Elected an Honorary Fellow by Oriel College, Oxford University, 1988
Elected to a Bye Fellowship, Robinson College, Cambridge University, 1992
Visiting Scholar, Scott Polar Research Institute, Cambridge University, 1992–93
Visiting Fellow, Centre of International Studies, Cambridge University, 1992–93
Elected a Senior Member, Robinson College, Cambridge University, 1993
Elected a Fellow of the Royal Geographical Society, 1993
Award of Merit, Canadian Bureau for International Education, 1993
Governor General's International Award for Canadian Studies, 1998
The Keith Matthews Award presented by the Canadian Nautical Research Society for the best Canadian book on a maritime topic, 1999
Elected a Senior Fellow, Massey College in the University of Toronto, 2003

Other Honours and Awards:
Fellow of the Royal Society of Arts, 1964
Canadian Centennial Medal, 1967
Civic Award conferred by the City of Peterborough, 1969

Knight of the Military and Hospitaller Order of Saint Lazarus of Jerusalem, 1971
Officer of the Order of Canada, 1976
Medal of the Ontario Arts Council, 1977
The Queen's Silver Jubilee Medal, 1977
Distinguished Service to Education Award of the Council for the Advancement and Support of Education, Washington, DC, 1982
Commendation of the Toronto Historical Board for the encouragement of heritage preservation, 1990
125th Anniversary of the Confederation of Canada Medal, 1992
Heritage Activities Award of Prince Edward Island, 1997
Companion of the Order of Canada, 1997
The Peter Robinson Award on the Sesquicentennial of the City of Peterborough, 1999
Civic Award for contribution to the community, City of Peterborough, 2001
The Queen's Golden Jubilee Medal, 2002
The Arbor Award of the University of Toronto, 2002
The Order of Ontario, 2002
The Key to the City of Peterborough, 2004
Honorary Citizen of the Yukon, 2005
The Downsview Park Legacy Award, 2006
Presentation from the Canadian Education Standards Institute on the occasion of its 20th Anniversary, 2008

University Appointments:

University of Toronto

Dean of Men and Tutor in History, Trinity College, 1953–55
Dean of Devonshire House, and Instructor in the Department of History, 1955–63

Trent University

President-designate and chairman of the Academic Planning Committee, 1960–62
President and vice-chancellor, 1962–72
Assistant Professor of History, 1963–66
Associate Professor of History, 1966–79

Vanier Professor, 1979–94
Founding President and Vanier Professor Emeritus, 1994–

Other Academic and Professionally-related Experience, current:

Chair, the Ontario Heritage Trust, 2010–; Vice-Chair, 2009–10; Board member, 2005–

Member, External Committee of Experts on Commemorations of the National Capital Commission, 2009–

Member of the Panel on the Future of the Trent-Severn Waterway: A National Historic Site of Canada, 2007–08

Member of the Panel appointed by the Government of Canada to review the programmes and expenditures of Statistics Canada, 2005–06

Member of the Awards Jury, the Heritage Canada Foundation, 2001–08

Member, Advisory Board, Canada's National History Society, 2002–

Member, Board of the Frost Centre for Canadian Studies and Native Studies, Trent University, 1982–

Trustee, the Symons Trust for Canadian Studies, 1995–

Member of Council, the Historica Foundation of Canada, 2002–

Chairman of the Curriculum Advocacy Committee, 2003–

Member of the Board, Parc Downsview Park Inc., 2002–07

Chair of the Park Development Committee of the Board, 2004–07

Member of the Board, Downsview Park Foundation, 2004–

Chairman of the Council of the Canadian Canoe Museum, 2001–06

Founding member of the Trent-Kanawa Canoe Museum Advisory Committee, 1980

Member of Council, Institute of Commonwealth Studies, the University of London, 2002–

Founding Chairman of the Association for Commonwealth Studies, 2001–09

Member of the Board, the Carnegie Institution of Canada, 1995–

Chairman of the National Statistics Council of Canada, 1986–2005

Member of the Task Force on Social Science Research Capacity

Member of the Working Group on Outsourcing Census Communications

Member of the Working Group on Relations between Statistics Canada and the Universities

Member of the Working Group on the Communication of Statistics Canada's Analytic Results to Policy Makers and the Public

National Director of the Fathers of Confederation Buildings Trust and the Confederation Centre of the Arts, Charlottetown, 1985–2010; Governor, 2010–

Trustee, the Bagnani Endowment, 1996–

Chairman of the Commission on Commonwealth Studies, 1995–96

Member of the Board of the *Encyclopedia of Music in Canada*, 1989–2005

Founding member of the Board of the Bata Shoe Museum Foundation, 1985–2008

Companion of the Order of St-Crispin

Chairman, *Meta Incognita* Project Steering Committee: archaeological, historical, archival, sociological, and oral history studies of the Arctic voyages of Martin Frobisher sponsored by the Canadian Museum of Civilization, the Smithsonian Institution of Washington, and the Prince of Wales Northern Heritage Centre, 1990–

Founding Chairman, the Canadian Educational Standards Institute, 1987–

Chairman of the National Advisory Committee on the National Atlas of Canada Programme and its associated Geographical Information Systems, 1980–90

Member of the Advisory Council of the Association for Canadian Studies, 1979–

Consulting editor, *Interchange*, the Ontario Institute for Studies in Education, 1978–

Member, national advisory board, Meewasin Valley Foundation, 1989–

Member, Oriel College Development Trust, Oxford University, 1980–2006; honorary member, 2006–

Other Academic and Professionally-related Experience, previous:

Member, Prizes Adjudication Committee of the Social Sciences and Humanities Research Council, 2006

Member, Minister's Round Table on Parks Canada, 2003

Member of the National Heritage Advisory Board for Founders' Hall at Confederation Landing, Charlottetown, 1999–2001

Chairman, *Meta Incognita* Project International Symposium, Trent University, 1997

Chairman, Symposia on Commonwealth Studies, 1995–96

Chairman of the Historic Sites and Monuments Board of Canada, 1986–96

Member of Board Committees on: historic buildings, inscriptions, systems and thematics, cultural pluralism, including Native and northern affairs, heritage railway stations, chairman of the executive committee

External Assessor, Proposal for a Master's Program in Canadian Studies, Collège universitaire de Saint Boniface, University of Manitoba, 1993–94

External Consultant, Canadian Studies Program Review, York University, 1993

Chairman of the National Heritage Symposium, Ottawa, 1994

Vice-Chairman, National Capital Planning Committee, 1991–93; member, 1987–93

Founding member, Canadiana Fund, Official Residences Council, 1990–95

Member of the Confederation Birthplace Commission, appointed by the Province of Prince Edward Island to advise upon the historical and heritage role of Charlottetown in Canadian Confederation, 1990–91

Member, National Design Competition Committee for the Confederation Birthplace Commemorative Area, Charlottetown, 1993

Member, Robinson College Development Committee, Cambridge University, 1993

Member, Census Analytical Program Working Group, 1991–92

Chairman, the Canadian Polar Research Commission Study, 1988–90

Chairman of the Conference on Northern Science and Northern Society convened by the Science Council of Canada at Yellowknife, NWT, 1990

Chairman of the Northern Science Award Selection Committee, 1986–90

Founding member of the Board of the Northern Studies Trust, Association of Canadian Universities for Northern Studies, 1982–90

Chairman, National Advisory Committee on Education Statistics, 1984–86

Member of the Board of the Arctic Institute of North America, 1981–85

Member of the Board of Directors of the Robert and Mary Stanfield Foundation, 1976–92

Member, Advisory Board, History of the Literary Institution in Canada, University of Alberta, 1987

Special advisor on Human Rights to the Secretary of State for Canada, 1982–92

Chairman, the Jules and Gabrielle Léger Fellowship Award Committee, 1978–91

Chairman of the National Library Advisory Board, 1986–90; member of the Board, 1978–90

Chairman of the Commission on Canadian Studies, 1972–84

Special advisor on higher education to the Secretary of State for Canada, 1976–83

Vice President and founding member, Social Sciences and Humanities Research Council of Canada, 1978–84

Member of the Science and Education Committee of the Science Council of Canada, 1978–83

Consultant to the Science Council of Canada, 1978–84

Founding member of the Board of the Canadian Institute for Historical Microreproduction, 1978–85

Member of the Federal Cultural Policy Review Committee (the Applebaum-Hébert Commission), 1979–82

Member of the Canada Council, 1976–79

Chairman of the Ministerial Commission on French Language Secondary Education in Ontario, 1971–72

Member of the Advisory Committee on Confederation to the Prime Minister of Ontario, 1965–72

President of the Canadian Association in Support of the Native Peoples (formerly the Indian-Eskimo Association of Canada), 1972–73; Vice-President, 1971–72; member of the Board of Directors, 1968–75

Member of the Task Force on the Native Peoples and Employment Opportunities in the Public Service of Canada, 1975–76

Member of the Advisory Committee on Land Claims of the Native Council of Canada, 1972–73

Founding member of the Editorial Board, *Journal of Canadian Studies*, 1965–91

Member of the Board of Trustees of the Canada Studies Foundation, 1979–85

National Advisor, *The Canadian Encyclopedia*, 1980–85

Co-chairman, the First Canadian Conference on Multiculturalism, 1973

Member of the Advisory Committee for Heritage Ontario, 1971–72

Member of the Council of the Champlain Society, 1972–87

Member, Board of Trustees, John Graves Simcoe Memorial Foundation, 1972–76

Historical advisor and honorary president, Peel County Historical Society

Member of the founding Board of the Toronto Historical Foundation, 1955–66

Member of the Council of the Architectural Conservancy of Ontario, 1963–66

Member of the Board of Governors of the Ontario Medical Foundation, 1975–87

Founding member of the Advisory Board of the Jack Chambers Memorial Foundation, 1980–83

Co-chairman, Colloquium on the State of the Official Languages in Canada, convened by the Commissioner of Official Languages, 1982

Chairman of the Ontario Human Rights Commission, 1975–78

Chairman of Commission's task force to review the state of human rights in Ontario, 1976–78

Chairman of the Ontario delegation to the Federal-Provincial Conferences on Human Rights, 1975, 1976, 1977

Chairman of the federal-provincial task force on Canadian ratification of the United Nations Covenants on Human Rights, 1975

Chairman of the federal-provincial committee on education and human rights, 1976–77

International Academic and Professionally-related Experience:

Member, Trent University International Advisory Council, 2004–

Member of the Council of the Institute of Commonwealth Studies, the University of London, 2002–

Trustee, the Caine Prize for African Writing, 2001–

Founding Chairman of the Association for Commonwealth Studies, 2001–

Chair of the Conference on the Health of the Commonwealth, Halifax, 2003

Chair of the Conference on the Literatures of the Commonwealth, Windsor, 2005–

Chair of the Conference on Educating the Commonwealth about the Commonwealth, Windsor, 2007

Founding Chairman, Celanese Canada Internationalist Fellowships Programme, 1997–2001

Chairman of the Commission on Commonwealth Studies, 1995–96

Visiting Fellow, Centre of International Studies, Cambridge University, 1992–93

Visiting Scholar, Scott Polar Research Institute, Cambridge University, 1984; 1992–93

Visiting Fellow, Robinson College, Cambridge University, 1992

Honorary Fellow, Oriel College, Oxford University, 1988–

Trustee, Oriel College Development Trust, 1980–

Fellow of the Royal Geographical Society, 1993–

Member of the Advisory Committee on Academic Relations, the Department of External Affairs, 1978–98

Co-chairman, bilateral conference on Canadian-Soviet Co-operation in the Arctic, 1989

Member of the Commonwealth Standing Committee on Student Mobility, 1982–88

Chairman of the Canadian Commonwealth Scholarship and Fellowship Committee, 1983–87

Visiting Fellow, Clare Hall, Cambridge University, 1984

Founding member, Canadian Bureau for International Education (originally, Friendly Relations with Overseas Students), 1948–

Chairman of the International Relations Committee of the Social Sciences and Humanities Research Council of Canada, 1978–81

Chairman of the International Academic and Cultural Relations Sub-Committee of the Federal Cultural Policy Review, 1981–82

Chairman of the International Board of United World Colleges, 1980–86

Chair, Co-chair, or participant in UWC meetings in Italy, India, Venezuela, Jamaica, India, Hong Kong, Wales, France, Germany, Netherlands, Zambia, Swaziland, South Africa, New Zealand, Malaysia, Singapore, Australia, Malta, Canada, Nigeria, England, the United States, Sri Lanka, Bermuda, Guyana, Switzerland

Vice-President of the International Council of United World Colleges, 1986–

Member of the Board of Governors of Lester B. Pearson College of the Pacific, 1976–94; Special Patron, 1994–

Chairman of the Association of Commonwealth Universities, 1971–72

Honorary Treasurer, the Association of Commonwealth Universities, 1974–88

Delegate to the Commonwealth Universities Conferences: Australia, 1968, 1988; Ghana, Nigeria, and Kenya, 1971; Canada, 1972; Britain, 1973; Hong Kong, Malaysia, and Singapore, 1975; New Zealand, 1976; Malta, 1977; Canada, 1978; India, 1980; Hong Kong, 1981; Jamaica, Trinidad, Guyana, Barbados, 1982; United Kingdom, 1983; Sri Lanka, 1984; Nigeria, 1985; Malaysia, 1986; Mauritius, 1987

Chairman of the Association of Commonwealth Universities Committee on Future Developments, 1983–86

Chairman of the Association of Commonwealth Universities 75th Anniversary Appeal and Special Projects, 1986–89

Participation in the Commonwealth Foundation Seminars: Sussex, 1973; Jamaica, 1975

Participant in the Colloquium on United Kingdom-Canada Relations, Leeds University, 1979

Member of the Canadian delegation to the United Kingdom-Canada Cultural Talks, Ottawa, 1979

Chairman of the Selection Committee for the Canada-United Kingdom Canadian Studies Fellowships, 1974–78

Member of the Board of the Foundation for Canadian Studies in the United Kingdom, 1986–2000

Chairman of the Selection Committee for the Canadian Studies Visiting Professorship in Japan, 1977–85

Associate of the Australian Studies Centre, the University of Queensland, Brisbane, Australia, 1980–

Canadian Co-chairman of the Australia-Canada Colloquium, Canberra, 1981

Canadian Associate member of the Council of the Association for Canadian Studies in the United States, 1973–75

Canadian participant in the Seminar on Higher Education in Federal Countries, sponsored by the International Council for Educational Development at the Aspen Institute for the Humanities, Colorado, 1981

Member of the British-North America Committee, 1983–

Chair, executive committee, 2005–2010

Member of the executive committee, 1985–2010

Chairman, British-North American Committee Working Group on Demographic Issues, 1989–91

Member, Comité au Canada de la Maison des étudiants canadiens à Paris, 1989–

Consultant to the Working Party on Official Statistics of the Royal Statistical Society of the United Kingdom

Member, Advisory Board, Canadian Fund for Czech and Slovak Universities

Member of the following:

Council of the Association of Commonwealth Universities, 1970–88

Board of the Association of Universities and Colleges of Canada, 1969–72

Founding member, Council of Ontario Universities, 1961–72

Board of Trustees of the Oriel College Development Trust, Oxford University, 1975–2006

Board of Trustees, Cambridge Canadian Trust, 1984–95

Advisory Board of Lakefield College School, 1964–96; Trustee, 1996–2002

Board of Governors of Upper Canada College, 1969–73; 1976–82

Chairman, Aims and Objectives Committee of Upper Canada College, 1989–91

Corporation of Trinity College, University of Toronto, 1963–74

Board of Governors of Sir Sandford Fleming College of Applied Arts and Technology, Peterborough, Ontario, 1964–69 (charter member)

Board of Governors of Loyalist College of Applied Arts and Technology, Belleville, Ontario, 1964–67, (charter member)
Policy and Planning Committee of the University of Toronto, 1959–62
Charter member, World University Service of Canada
Founding member, National Committee for Friendly Relations with Overseas Students (now the Canadian Bureau for International Education)
International Council, United World Colleges, 1986–
Board of Directors, London House Association of Canada, 1982

Some Other Activities and Interests:
Chairman, The Peterborough Lakefield Police Services Board, 2005–2010
Chairman of the Board of the Bata Shoe Organization, 1997–2001
Member of the Board of Directors of Celanese Canada, Inc., 1980–98; Chair of the Board's Social Responsibility Committee; member of the Audit Committee
Member of the Board of Directors of the Broadview Press, 1986–; Chair of the Compensation Committee, 2003
Member of the Board of Directors of UDV Canada Inc., 1991–2000
Ontario Business Ambassador, 1997–2000
Patron, Saint George's Restoration, Halifax, 1995–
Chairman, The Perkins Bull Collection Inc., 1995–
Member of the Ontario Arts Council, 1974–76
Chairman of the Canadian Conference on Social Development, 1976
Member, the Citizen's Task Force on Social Security of the Canadian Council on Social Development, 1971–73
Member, the Mayor's Committee on Peterborough's Economic Prospects, 1976–78
Founding member, chairman, the Greater Peterborough Economic Council, 1978–82
Member, Otonabee Region Conservation Authority, 1962–72
Founding member, Otonabee Region Conservation Foundation, 1968–83
Member, Board of Directors, Peterborough Red Cross and Community Fund (United Community Services), 1964–72
Past-President, Canadian Club of Peterborough

Honorary Chairman, Save the Market Hall Appeal, Peterborough, 1999–2001

Past-Chairman, Henry Mulholland Board of Trustees

Founding member, National Council of Amnesty International (Canada), 1973–80

Member, Canadian Civil Liberties Association

Founding member, Canadian Society for the Abolition of the Death Penalty

Mediations:

Appointed by the government of Ontario to mediate the dispute concerning French-language school arrangements in Sturgeon Falls, Ontario, 1971

Appointed by the government of Ontario to mediate the dispute concerning French-language school arrangements in Cornwall, Ontario, 1973

Served as mediator in various other disputes concerning labour and management, government and the Native peoples, and educational issues

Ontario-Quebec Relations:

Report for the Advisory Committee on Confederation to the Prime Minister of Ontario in 1965 which proposed the establishment of an Ontario-Quebec Joint Permanent Commission and an agreement between the two provinces for co-operation and exchange in the fields of education and culture; the recommendations of this report have been implemented.

Chairman, Policy Advisory Committee to the Honourable R. L. Stanfield, 1968–75

Chairman, the Priorities for Canada National Policy Conference of the Progressive Conservative Party, 1969

Chairman, policy programme committee for the 1971 and 1974 Annual Meetings of the Progressive Conservative Party of Canada

Honorary President, Trent University Alumni Association, 1972–

Honorary President, Trent Legacy Society, 1996–

Publications:

A. Reports/books in print

It's All About the Water: Report of the Panel on the Future of the Trent-Severn Waterway, with Douglas Downey et al. Ottawa: Department of the Environment, 2008.

Report of the Panel Appointed by the Government of Canada to Review the Programmes and Expenditures of Statistics Canada, with Ian Green et al. Ottawa: 2006.

Meta Incognita: A Discourse of Discovery; Martin Frobisher's Arctic Expeditions, 1576–1578. Vol. 1 and 2. Ottawa: Canadian Museum of Civilization, 1999.

The Place of History: Commemorating Canada's Past. Ottawa: Royal Society of Canada and Historic Sites and Monuments Board of Canada, 1997 / *Les lieux de la mémoire: la commémoration du passé du Canada.* Ottawa: Société royale du Canada et Commission des lieux et monuments historiques du Canada, 1997.

Learning from Each Other: Commonwealth Studies for the Twenty First Century. Report of the Commission on Commonwealth Studies, with Suma Chitnis et al. London: Commonwealth Secretariat, 1996.

Interim Report of the Commission on Commonwealth Studies, with Suma Chitnis et al. London: Commonwealth Secretariat, 1995.

Canadian Studies Programs Review, York University, with Patricia Smart. (1993).

Powerful Memories Powerful Dreams, Final Report of the Confederation Birthplace Commission, with Wendy McDonald et al. Charlottetown: 1991.

Interim Report of the Confederation Birthplace Commission, with Wendy McDonald et al. Charlottetown: 1991.

The National Atlas Information Service: A Report to the Minister of Energy, Mines and Resources Canada by the National Advisory Committee for the National Atlas of Canada / *Service d'information de l'Atlas national:* Rapport du Comité consultatif de l'Atlas national du Canada au ministère de l'Énergie, des Mines et des Ressources du Canada, with Richard Groot et al. Ottawa: Geographical Services Division, Department of Energy, Mines and Resources, 1990.

The Fifth Edition: The National Atlas of Canada: An Information System, by the National Advisory Committee of the National Atlas of Canada / *La cinquième édition: l'Atlas national du Canada, un système d'information*, Comité consultatif pour l'Atlas national du Canada. Ottawa, Geographical Services Division, Department of Energy, Mines and Resources, 1989.

The Shield of Achilles: The Report of the Canadian Polar Research Commission Study. Ottawa: Circumpolar and Scientific Affairs Directorate, Department of Indian Affairs and Northern Development, 1988 / *Le bouclier d'Achille: Rapport d'étude sur la création d'une Commission canadienne de la recherche polaire*. Ottawa: Direction des Affaires circumpolaire et scientifiques, Ministère des Affaires indiennes et du Nord canadien, 1988.

The National Atlas Information System, A Report to the Minister of State (Forestry and Mines), by the National Advisory Committee for the National Atlas of Canada / *Le Système d'information de l'Atlas national*, Rapport au ministère d'État (Forêts et Mines) du Comité consultatif national pour l'Atlas national du Canada, with Pierre Camu et al. Ottawa: Geographical Services Division, Department of Energy, Mines and Resources, 1988.

Some Questions of Balance: Human Resources, Higher Education, and Canadian Studies / Où trouver l'equilibre? Ressources humaines, enseignement supérieur et études canadiennes, with James E. Page. Ottawa: Association of Universities and Colleges of Canada, 1984.

Towards a Commonwealth Higher Education Program: Strategies for Action, with Sir Roy Marshall et al. London: the Commonwealth Secretariat, bk 1, 1982; bk 2, 1983; bk 3, 1984; bk 4, 1985; bk 5, 1986.

Report of the Federal Cultural Policy Review Committee / Rapport du Comité de la politique culturelle fédérale, with Louis Applebaum, Jacques Hébert, et al. Ottawa: Department of Communications, Government of Canada, 1982.

Companion volumes:

Summary of Briefs and Hearings / Compte rendu des mémoires et des audiences publiques Ottawa: Federal Cultural Policy Review Committee, Department of Communications, 1982.

Speaking of Our Culture: Discussion Guide / Parlons de notre culture: Guide de discussion Ottawa: Federal Cultural Policy Review Committee, 1981.

Life Together: A Report on Human Rights in Ontario / Vivre Ensemble: un Rapport sur les Droits de l'homme en Ontario, with Rosalie Abella et al. Toronto: Queen's Printer / Imprimeur de la Reine, 1977.

To Know Ourselves: the Report of the Commission on Canadian Studies / Se Connaître: le Rapport de la Commission sur les études canadiennes. Vol. 1 and 2. Ottawa: Association of Universities and Colleges of Canada, 1975.

Abridged edition: *The Symons Report.* Abridged by J. Holmes. Toronto: McClelland and Stewart, and the Book and Periodical Development Council of Canada, 1978.

Native People and Employment in the Public Service of Canada / Les autochtones et l'emploi dans la fonction publique du Canada, with A. E. Belcourt et al. Ottawa: 1976.

Report of the Ministerial Commission on French Language Secondary Education / Commission ministérielle sur l'education secondaire en langue francaise. Toronto: Queen's Printer / Imprimeur de la Reine, 1972.

B. Chapters in books

"The Charlottetown Conference in Perspective," Foreword to Catherine G. Hennessey, David Keenlyside, Edward MacDonald, *The Landscapes of Confederation: Charlottetown, 1864.* Charlottetown: Prince Edward Island Museum and Heritage Foundation, 2010. v–xii.

"Two Likely Lads," Foreword to Rae Fleming, ed. *The First World War Correspondence of Leslie and Cecil Frost.* Waterloo: Wilfrid Laurier University Press, 2007.

Foreword to Henry E. Duckworth, *One Version of the Facts.* Winnipeg: University of Manitoba Press, 2000.

"The Significance of the Frobisher Expeditions of 1576–1578," in T. H. B. Symons, ed., *Meta Incognita: A Discourse of Discovery; Martin Frobisher's Arctic Expeditions, 1576–1578.* Ottawa: Canadian Museum of Civilization, 1999.

"The Meta Incognita Project," in Ibid.

"Commemorating Canada's Past: From Old Crow to New Bergthal," in T. H. B. Symons, ed., *The Place of History: Commemorating Canada's*

Past / Les liéux de la mémoire: la commemoration du passé du Canada. Ottawa: Royal Society of Canada and Historic Sites and Monuments Board of Canada / La Societé royale du Canada et la Commission des lieux et monuments historiques du Canada, 1997.

"A Race Against Time," in Ibid.

"Educating the Commonwealth about the Commonwealth," in Oonagh O'Farrell, ed., *The Future of the Commonwealth—A Golden Opportunity.* London: The Royal Commonwealth Society, 1997.

"Canadian Studies and the Canadian University in the Twenty-First Century," in Rodney Clifton, Alexander D. Gregor, and Lance Roberts, eds., *The Canadian University in the Twenty-First Century.* Winnipeg: 1995.

"The Greening of Heritage: Historic Preservation and the Environmental Movement," in John Marsh and Janice Fialkowski, eds., *Linking Cultural and Natural Heritage.* Peterborough: 1995.

"Polar Science: A Canadian Viewpoint," in John Stager, ed., *Canada and Polar Science* Yellowknife: Canadian Polar Commission, 1994.

"A Challenge to the Independent Schools," in N. Thomas Russell, *Strength of Choice: A History of the Canadian Association of Independent Schools.* Toronto: 1993.

"Culture in the Commonwealth: Some Questions about the Definition, Variety, and Diversity of Culture, and the Relationship of Culture to Education," in T. Craig, ed., *What Can We Do for Our Countries? The Contribution of Universities to National Development.* London: Association of Commonwealth Universities, 1988. Reprinted as "Culture in the Commonwealth," in *Policy Options* 10, no. 2 (March 1989).

"The Contribution of Investigatory Commissions to Political Education," in Jon H. Pammett and Jean-Luc Pepin, eds., *Political Education in Canada.* Ottawa: Institute for Research in Public Policy, 1988.

"Canadian Postsecondary Education: The Cultural Agenda," in Alexander Gregor and Keith Wilson, eds., *Postsecondary Education in Canada* 16, in the *Monographs in Education* series. Winnipeg: University of Manitoba, 1986.

"Human Rights and Peace—Some Canadian Priorities? / Les droits de l'homme et la paix—quelques priorités canadiennes?" in Michael R.

Hudson, ed., *Human Rights and Peace / Les droits de l'homme et la paix.* Montreal: Canadian Human Rights Foundation, 1985.

"Ontario Universities in a Broader Context: The Need for a National Strategy in Canadian Higher Education and Research," in David W. Conklin and Thomas J. Courchene, eds., *Ontario Universities: Access, Operations and Funding.* Toronto: Ontario Economic Council, 1985.

"The Cultural Impact of Industrialization and Technological Innovation," in T. Craig, ed., *Technological Innovation: University Roles.* London: Association of Commonwealth Universities, 1984.

"Archives and Canadian Studies," in Terry Cook, ed., *Archives, Libraries, and the Canadian Heritage: Essays in Honour of W. Kaye Lamb, Archivaria,* no. 15 (1983).

"Cultural Diversity, Canadian Identity and Canadian Federalism," in R. L. Matthews, ed., *Public Policies in Two Federal Countries: Canada and Australia.* Canberra: Australian National University Press, 1982.

"The Arctic and Canadian Culture," in Morris Zaslow, ed., *A Century of Canada's Arctic Islands.* Ottawa: Royal Society of Canada, 1981.

"Cultural Diplomacy: Some Thoughts on the Current State of Academic and Cultural Relations between Canada and the United Kingdom," in David Dilks, ed., *Britain and Canada.* London: The Commonwealth Foundation, 1980.

"Nationalism and Higher Education," in A. D. Gregor and K. Wilson, eds., *Issues in Higher Education* 1, in the *Monographs in Education* series. Winnipeg: University of Manitoba, 1979.

"The Canadian National Opportunity: The Preservation of Identity in a Multi-Cultural Setting," in *Canadian Confederation Forum.* Hamilton: McMaster University, 1978.

"Ontario's Quiet Revolution: A Study of Change in the Position of the Franco-Ontarian Community," in R. M. Burns, ed., *One Country or Two.* Montreal and London: McGill-Queens University Press, 1971.

"Proposals for an Ontario Cultural and Educational Exchange Program and an Ontario-Quebec Cultural and Educational Exchange Agreement," in *The Confederation Challenge, Background Papers and Reports of the Ontario Advisory Committee on Confederation* Toronto: Queen's Printer, 1967, 1970.

"Local History and the Canadian Consciousness" in C. V. Charters, ed., *A History of Peel County.* Toronto: 1967.

"Trent University and the Peterborough Community," in R. Borg, ed., *Peterborough Land of Shining Waters.* Toronto: University of Toronto Press, 1967.

Foreword to Leslie M. Frost, *Fighting Men.* Toronto: 1967.

C. Occasional papers and monographs in print

"The Royal Society of Canada, the Conservation Movement, and the Department of Canadian Heritage," in *Profile, Newsletter of the Royal Society of Canada* 4, no. 1 (1995).

"The Confederation Centre of the Arts." Charlottetown: Fathers of Confederation Buildings Trust, 1994.

"The George Back Sketchbooks." Montreal and Ottawa: Celanese Canada Inc., 1994.

"Demography, the Carapace of the Economy," in *Demographic Currents,* Occasional Paper No. 7. Washington: British-North America Committee, 1991.

"The Nature and Importance of Canada's Academic and Cultural Relations with Italy and the Mediterranean World." Ottawa: Canadian Mediterranean Institute and the Samuel and Saidye Bronfman Foundation, 1989.

"A Canadian Perspective on Canadian Studies," in Patricia McLaren-Turner, ed., *Canadian Studies,* British Library Occasional Papers No. 1. London: British Library, 1984.

"Some Thoughts on the Current State of Teaching and Research about Northern Canada," Occasional Paper No. 6. Ottawa: Association of Canadian Universities for Northern Studies, 1980.

"To Redress the Balance," Occasional Paper No. 1. Toronto: Association for Canadian Studies, 1980.

"Some Thoughts on the Nature and Value of National and Regional Atlases," in *The Purpose and Use of National and Regional Atlases,* papers presented at an International Symposium sponsored by the Pan-American Institute of Geography and History, *Cartographica,* Monograph 23. Toronto: University of Toronto Press, 1979. Also published in *Revista Cartografica,* numero 35, Instituto Panamericano de Geografia e Historia, Mexico, Junio, 1979.

"Some Notes on the Evolution of Language Policy in Ontario," *Proceedings of the Twelfth International Symposium on Comparative Law.* Ottawa: University of Ottawa Press, 1976.

"George Ridout," "John Ryerson," "William Ryerson," in the *Dictionary of Canadian Biography* 10. University of Toronto Press and Les Press de l'université Laval, 1972.

"George Ridout," reprinted in Robert L. Fraser, ed., *Provincial Justice: Upper Canadian Legal Portraits.* Toronto: The Osgoode Society, University of Toronto Press, 1992.

D. Articles and reviews in periodicals

Polar Record; CAM; Trent; Queen's Quarterly; Times Educational Supplement; Times Higher Education Supplement; Canadian Forum; Journal of Canadian Studies; University of Toronto Alumni Quarterly; Bulletin of the Indian-Eskimo Association of Canada; Human Relations; University Affairs; Canadian Ethnic Studies; Canadian Independent School Journal; UWC Review; Network Journal of the United World Colleges; Loyalist Gazette; Baker Street Journal; Journal of Education Policy; Bulletin of the Canadian Mediterranean Institute; Newsletter of the Association for Canadian Studies; Language and Society; Museum Quarterly; National Library News; LOG, Oslo; Profile, Newsletter of the Royal Society of Canada.

E. Other

"The State of Canadian Studies at the Year 2000: Some Observations," in *Canadian Studies at the Millenium: The Journey Continues, Journal of Canadian Studies,* 30th Anniversary Issue 35 no. 1 (2000).

"The Meta Incognita Project, 1990—1999," in the Canadian Museum of Civilization website, Ottawa, 1999.

"Commonwealth Studies in the Curriculum," in John May, ed., *Proceedings of the Annual Conference of the Council for Education in the Commonwealth.* London: 1997.

"A Mission Defined: Report of the Aims and Objectives Committee of Upper Canada College," with Vernon T. Mould, et al., *Old Times.* Toronto: Upper Canada College, 1991.

Heritage in the 1990s—Towards a Government of Canada Strategy, Summary Report, Edmonton: 1990.

"The National Statistics Council of Canada," in *Official Statistics: Counting with Confidence, The Report of A Working Party on Official Statistics in the UK*, Appendix 3, London: 1990.

"Canada and Polar Science," in *Proceedings of the Tenth Anniversary Conference of the Association of Canadian Universities for Northern Studies*, 1988.

"Towards a New Concept of Internationality," in *Proceedings of the Tenth International Council of United World Colleges*. London: 1985.

"Language and Culture Retention," *Report of the First Canadian Conference on Multiculturalism*. Ottawa: 1974.

"Education and Language," *Heritage Ontario: the Report of the Heritage Ontario Congress*. Toronto: 1973.

Native Rights in Canada, ed. D. Sanders. Toronto: 1970.

Member of the Research Committee, commissioned to undertake the preparation of this study by the National Indian Brotherhood, the Canadian Métis Society, and the Indian-Eskimo Association of Canada. Rev. ed. Ed. P. A. Cumming and N. H. Mickenberg. Toronto: 1972.

Proceedings of the National Conference of Canadian Universities. Winnipeg: 1971; Ottawa: 1957; Montreal: 1951.

The University in Summer. Toronto: University of Toronto Library, 1960.

Teaching experience:

I. At Trent University, 1964–

Undergraduate Teaching:

1. *History 100*, a first year course in Canadian History
2. *History—Politics 400*, a fourth-year honours interdisciplinary course to examine *Contemporary Canadian Problems*, making an intensive study of some aspects of bilingualism and cultural pluralism, constitutional change, Canadian sovereignty and Canadian-American relations
3. *Canadian Studies 400*, an honours colloquium on culture and communications
4. *Canadian Studies 413—Cultural Studies 413—Administrative and Policy Studies (the Vanier Seminar)*, Cultural Policy in Canada. Studies in the formulation and operation of Canadian public

policy in the fields of culture, education, research, and human rights

5. *Canadian Studies 480,* a reading course
6. *Canadian Studies 495,* honours thesis, double credit
7. *Administrative and Policy Studies 499,* supervision of research projects
8. *Environmental and Resource Studies 499,* supervision of a special topics course
9. Guest lectures for various courses in the Departments or Programmes of: Administrative and Policy Studies, Canadian Studies, Cultural Studies, English, Environmental and Resource Studies, Chemistry, Geography, History, Native Studies, Political Studies, Sociology

Graduate Teaching:

10. Thesis supervisor in the Graduate Studies Programme in Methodologies for the Study of Western History and Culture (M.590)
11. Theses supervisor in the Graduate Studies Programme of the Frost Centre for Canadian Heritage and Development Studies (F.C. 500)
12. Member, MA theses committees, Frost Centre
13. Occasional lectures in the core programme of the Frost Centre

II. At the University of Toronto, 1953–64:

1. *Greek and Roman History*
2. *The Renaissance and Reformation*
3. *Modern Europe*
4. *International Relations*

III. External Examiner:

1. Graduate programme of the School of Architecture, University of Toronto, 1961
2. Department of History, University of Nairobi, 1971
3. Department of Educational Theory of the School of Graduate Studies, University of Toronto, 1974

4. Faculty of Law, Queen's University, 1975
5. Department of Education, the School of Graduate Studies, University of Toronto, 1983
6. Department of Graduate Studies, University of Guelph, 2003

IV. Graduate Supervisor in the Graduate Studies Programme of the Faculty of Environmental Studies, York University, 1982

V. Member of the Distinguished Professors Selection Committee of the University of Manitoba, 1983–86; Chairman, 1986

VI. Member of the Distinguished Research Award Selection Committee, Trent University, 1997

VII. Thesis Supervisor in the Graduate Studies Programme, the University of Guelph, 2002–03

VIII. Visiting academic appointments, guest lectures and seminars, addresses, and papers presented, 1951–2009:

Canada

Memorial University of Newfoundland; Dalhousie University; University College of Cape Breton; St. Francis Xavier University; Mount St. Vincent University; Université de Sainte Anne; University of Prince Edward Island; Mt. Allison University; University of New Brunswick; St. Thomas University; Université de Moncton; Université Laval; McGill University; Université de Montréal; Université de Québec à Montréal; Concordia University; Dawson College; Bishop's University; Université de Sherbrooke; University of Ottawa; Carleton University; Queen's University; Royal Military College of Canada; Sir Sandford Fleming College; York University; Glendon College; Ryerson University; University of Toronto; McMaster University; University of Waterloo; Wilfrid Laurier University; University of Guelph; Laurentian University; University of Manitoba; Collège universitaire de St. Boniface, Manitoba; St. John's College, Manitoba; University of Winnipeg; Brandon University; University of Saskatchewan; University of Regina; University of Calgary; University of Alberta; University of Lethbridge; Athabaska University; University of Victoria; Simon Fraser University; University of British Columbia; Yukon College

The United World Colleges

Pearson College of the Pacific; Atlantic College, Wales; College of the Adriatic; College of Southern Africa, Swaziland; College of the American West, Montezeuma; College of South-East Asia, Singapore; Simon Bolivar College, Venezuela

The United Kingdom

Oxford University: Oriel College; Rhodes House; Nuffield College; University College; Cambridge University: Scott Polar Research Institute; Centre for International Studies; Robinson College; Clare Hall; University of London: Institute of Commonwealth Studies; University College; University of Leicester; University of Manchester; University of Birmingham; University of Sussex; University of Exeter; University of Edinburgh; University of Glasgow; St. Andrew's University; University of Aberdeen

New Zealand

University of Waikato; University of Auckland; Victoria University of Wellington

India

University of Calcutta; University of Burdwan; University of Kerela; University of Delhi; Indian Institute of Technology, Delhi; University of Mumbai; North-Eastern Hill University, Shillong; SNDT Women's University, Mumbai

Australia

University of Sydney; University of New South Wales; University of Western Sydney; Australian National University, Canberra; University of Queensland; University of Western Australia; La Trobe University; University of Melbourne

South Pacific

University of the South Pacific

Hong Kong

University of Hong Kong; Chinese University of Hong Kong

Singapore

University of Singapore

Malaysia

National University of Malaysia; University of Penang

Indian Ocean

University of Mauritius

Sri Lanka

University of Colombo; University of Kelaniya; University of Peradiniya; University of Ruhana

Africa

University of Ghana; University of Ife; University of Ibadan; University of Lagos; University of Sokoto; University of Nairobi; University of Zambia; University of Swaziland; University of Zimbabwe

Malta

University of Malta

Carribean

University of the West Indies: Jamaica; Barbados; Trinidad; University of Guyana

Bermuda

Bermuda College

The United States

University of California, Los Angeles; Harvard University; University of Michigan, Ann Arbor; University of Chicago; Massachusetts Institute of Technology

Europe

University of Paris; La Maison des ètudiants canadiens à Paris; University of Rome, La Sapienza; University of Venice; Canadian School at Rome; University of Zurich; University of Heidelberg; University of Amsterdam; University of Leiden; University of Stockholm; University of Helsinki; University of Copenhagen

Associations and organizations to which guest lectures or papers presented:
Canadian Society for the Study of Higher Education; National Conference of Canadian Universities; National Federation of Canadian University Students; Association for Canadian Studies; Canada Studies Foundation; Historica Foundation; Canadian Mediterranean Institute; Ontario Economic Council; Peel County Historical Society; Peterborough Historical Society; Association of Canadian Archivists; Conference of Architectural Conservation Advisory Committees of Ontario; Science Council of Canada; Canadian Polar Commission; Royal Society of Canada; Association of Universities and Colleges of Canada; Association of Canadian Universities for Northern Studies; Canadian Conference on Social Development; Institute for Research on Public Policy; Canadian Educational Standards Institute; Canadian Human Rights Foundation; Law Society of Upper Canada; Advisory Committee on Academic Relations, Department of External Affairs, Ottawa; Canadian Bureau for International Education; The Aspen Institute, Colorado; Pan-American Institute of Geography and History; British-North American Committee; Association of Commonwealth Universities; United World Colleges; The British Library; Council for Education in the Commonwealth; Royal Commonwealth Society; Association for Commonwealth Studies; The World Economic Forum; La Maison des étudiants canadiens à Paris; The Royal Statistical Society, London.

December 2010

Notes on Authors

Rosalie Silberman Abella has been a justice of the Supreme Court of Canada since 2004. Previously, she served on the Ontario Court of Appeal and on the Ontario Family Court. A member of the Ontario Human Rights Commission from 1975 to 1980, she headed the 1984 federal Royal Commission on Equality in Employment and subsequently served as chair of the Ontario Labour Relations Board and of the Ontario Law Reform Commission. She has written more than eighty articles and written or co-edited four books and is a Fellow of the Royal Society of Canada and of the American Academy of Arts and Sciences.

Marco Adria is professor of communications and director of the graduate program in communications and technology at the University of Alberta. He is the author or co-author of four books in the areas of organizational communication, popular culture, and nationalism, including *Technology and Nationalism.* He has served as president of the Canadian Association of Library Trustees and is a convenor of the Edmonton Citizen Panel.

Stephen Alsford spent most of his career at the Canadian Museum of Civilization, until his retirement in 2008. He is the author of numerous publications on museological and medieval history subjects, as well as editor of the volume *The Meta Incognita Project: Contributions to Field Studies.* He served as secretary to the Meta Incognita Project Steering Committee.

Charles Beer is a partner with Counsel Public Affairs Inc. He is a former minister of Community and Social Services and minister responsible for Francophone Affairs in the Ontario government, and a member of the Ontario Legislature from 1987 to 1995. As an Ontario public servant, he supported the work of the Ontario Advisory Committee on Confederation from 1966 to 1971. In 1971 and in 1973, he was seconded by the Ontario government to serve on the two French-language schools' reviews conducted by Tom Symons in Sturgeon Falls and in Cornwall.

Jamie Benidickson teaches Environmental Law, Water Law, and Legal History at the Faculty of Law, University of Ottawa. His publications include *The Temagami Experience*; *Idleness, Water and a Canoe*; and *The Culture of Flushing: A Social and Legal History of Sewage.*

Christina Cameron is a professor at the School of Architecture at the Université de Montréal, where she holds the Canada Research Chair on Built Heritage. She previously served as Director General of National Historic Sites, Parks Canada, and as secretary to the Historic Sites and Monuments Board of Canada.

David R. Cameron is chair of the Department of Political Science at the University of Toronto, where he previously served as a vice-president. He has also held senior positions at Trent University and in both the Government of Canada and the Government of Ontario. He is the author or co-author of seven books, including *Taking Stock: Canadian Studies in the 90s,* and is a Fellow of the Royal Society of Canada.

Ivan P. Fellegi is Chief Statistician of Canada Emeritus, Statistics Canada, which he headed from 1985 to 2008, during which time it was ranked by *The Economist* as the best statistical office in the world. Past president of the International Statistical Institute, the International Association of Survey Statisticians, and the Statistical Society of Canada, Dr. Fellegi is the recipient of numerous awards and honorary degrees, and has published extensively on statistical methods, on the social and economic applications of statistics, and on the successful management of statistical agencies. He is an Officer of the Order of Canada.

John Fraser is Master of Massey College in the University of Toronto and the former editor of *Saturday Night* magazine. One of Canada's most distinguished journalists, he is the recipient of three National Newspaper Awards and eight National Magazine Awards. He is also the author of several books, including the international best-seller *The Chinese* and *Eminent Canadians*. He has received numerous honours and honorary degrees and is a Member of the Order of Canada.

Ralph Heintzman is adjunct research professor in the Graduate School of Public and International Affairs at the University of Ottawa. A former editor of the *Journal of Canadian Studies*, his career has spanned the university, research, and government worlds. He worked with Tom Symons in his first full-time job and witnessed a model of leadership that was not equalled in the rest of his professional career.

Edward MacDonald is associate professor of History at the University of Prince Edward Island, where he teaches Prince Edward Island, Atlantic, Canadian, and Public History. He has been closely involved with heritage affairs on his native Prince Edward Island for the past twenty-five years as museum curator, editor, author, lecturer, and teacher. His most recent book is *If You're Stronghearted: Prince Edward Island in the Twentieth Century*.

Harvey McCue helped found the Native Studies program at Trent University, where he taught for fourteen years, attaining the rank of associate professor. Service elsewhere includes the director of Education Services for the Cree School Board, in northern Quebec, from 1983 to 1988; the director of Policy and Research, Education Branch, Indian and Northern Affairs Canada, Ottawa, and eventually its director general, in 1991; and the executive director and director of Education of the Mi'kmaq Education Authority, Nova Scotia, from 1993 to 1995.

Tom McMillan is a former cabinet minister in the Government of Canada (1984–88), including as minister of the Environment (1985–88), and was Canada's Consul General to New England, at Boston, from 1989 to 1993. He served as a Member of Parliament (Hillsborough, PEI) from 1979 to 1988. Prior to that, he worked with

Tom Symons for almost a decade in various capacities, including the Progressive Conservative Party of Canada (policy); the Ontario Human Rights Commission (executive officer); and the Commission on Canadian Studies (senior research associate).

Alastair Niven has been Principal of Cumberland Lodge, an educational charity and conference centre in the heart of the Great Park, Windsor, since 2001. Prior to this he served as director of literature at the British Council, director of literature at the Arts Council of Great Britain, and director general of The Africa Centre. He is the author of four books and more than fifty articles on aspects of Commonwealth and post-colonial literature. A judge of the Booker Prize for Fiction in 1994, he was also president of English PEN from 2003 to 2007.

Walter Pitman is a former President of Ryerson Polytechnical Institute (now University), and also a former Director of the Ontario Arts Council and of the Ontario Institute for Studies in Education, and a former Dean of Arts and Science at Trent University. He is also the award-winning author of a series of biographies on Canadian cultural "greats." An Officer of the Order of Canada, and a Member of the Order of Ontario, he has received a number of honorary degrees and fellowships from Canadian universities.

Stuart Robson taught History at Trent University from 1966 to 2001. He won the Symons Award for Teaching Excellence in 1979, which has nothing to do with his address to the Senate honouring Tom Symons when he retired as president and to the banquet for Tom when he retired in 1994.

Denis Smith served on the early planning committees for Trent University and was the university's founding Vice-President, as well as primary author of the Trent University Act and the Brief to the Master Planning Architect. He was Dean of Social Science at the University of Western Ontario from 1982 to 1988, and is the prize-winning author of biographies of Walter Gordon and John Diefenbaker. In 2006, he was awarded the Spanish Orden del Mérito Civil for his book, *The Prisoners of Cabrera: Napoleon's Forgotten Soldiers, 1809–1814.*

John Stevenson, QC, was a founding partner of the law firm Smith Lyons Torrance Stevenson & Mayer, which merged with Gowlings LLP, where he is now partner emeritus. During his career, he acted as legal advisor to corporations, financial institutions, federal and provincial governments, and charitable organizations. He also served as a director of numerous corporations, including Upper Canada College (chairman 1982–87) and CESI.

Sylvia Sutherland is a graduate in journalism from what was then the Ryerson Institute of Technology and was a reporter and feature writer for the *Orillia Daily Packet and Times* and the *Toronto Telegram.* She spent fifteen years as mayor of Peterborough (an amazing five terms!) and is an alumnus and a former member of the Board of Governors of Trent University.

Index

Composed in ITC New Baskerville PS 10 on 14

Québec, Canada
2011